Thomas Mayer

Egypt and the Palestine question

ISLAMKUNDLICHE UNTERSUCHUNGEN · BAND 77

herausgegeben von
Klaus Schwarz

.

KLAUS SCHWARZ VERLAG · BERLIN

ISLAMKUNDLICHE UNTERSUCHUNGEN · BAND 77

Thomas Mayer

Egypt and the Palestine question 1936 - 1945

 KLAUS SCHWARZ VERLAG · BERLIN · 1983

© Dr. K. Schwarz, Berlin 1982
ISBN 3-922968-20-1
Druck: aku-Fotodruck GmbH, Eckbertstr. 19, 8600 Bamberg

ACKNOWLEDGEMENT

I am indebted to Professor Elie Kedourie, who guided me in this work. I would also like to thank my friends, Israel Gershoni, and Mark Lerner, for various services in connection with this work. Needless to say, none of the above is responsible for the views expressed below.

I should like to express my thanks for the assistance afforded to me by the Staff of the Public Record Office, London; the London School of Economics; the School of Oriental and African Studies of the University of London; the Central Zionist and the Israel State Archives at Jerusalem; the Truman's Institute at Jerusalem; the Hagana Archives at Tel-Aviv; the Middle East Centre at St. Antony's College, Oxford; the National Archives at Washington, D.C. and the Library of Congress there.

I should like to thank the Directorate of the Harry S. Truman Institute at Jerusalem; the Anglo-Jewish Association in London and the Central Research Fund of the University of London for providing me financial assistance for research in connection with this study.

ABSTRACT

EGYPT AND THE PALESTINE QUESTION

1936 - 1945

THOMAS MAYER

Egypt's policy makers viewed the Palestine question as an integral part of their Arab policy. A discussion of the national Egyptian outlook on the Arabs in general and the Palestinian conflict in particular between 1911 and 1936 introduces the present study. The introduction also examines the reasons for increased Egyptian interest in this conflict at the beginning of the 1930's, and attempts to answer the question of why this interest failed to lead to political intervention in Arab affairs. I chose the year 1936 as the starting point of this study because it was then that the Arab Revolt broke out in Palestine and the Anglo-Egyptian Treaty was finally signed. The study concludes with the founding of the Arab League in 1945 under the leadership of Egypt.

Through an historical survey, this research traces Egyptian responses to the Arab Revolt in Palestine, and Egyptian reactions to the various pan-Arab projects up to 1940. Further attention is devoted to the various diplomatic and economic contacts between Egypt and the Arab world between 1936-1945. Particular emphasis is placed on the creation of the Arab League (1943-1945), and its immediate implications. The numerous Egyptian statements during this period in favour of Arabism are contrasted with the very slight actual progress made towards Egypto-Arab co-operation. The various conferences held to assist the Palestinian Arabs are examined in light of the limited practical aid to the Palestinians. The ambivalent attitude of Egyptian policy makers towards Arabism is analysed in relation to Anglo-Egyptian relations and the changing British policy in the Middle East.

TABLE OF CONTENTS

ABBREVIATIONS

CID   - Criminal Investigation Department

CO   - Colonial Office

CZA   - Central Zionist Archives

EG   - Egyptian Gazette

FO   - Foreign Office

FRUS   - Foreign Relations of the United States

HMG   - His Majesty's Government

IJMES - International Journal of Middle East Studies

ISA   - Israel State Archives

JA   - al-Jami'a al-'Arabiyya

JIM   - Jaridat al-Ikhwan al-Muslimin

MEC   - Middle East Centre

MEWC   - Middle East War Council

MShM   - Majallat al-Shubban al-Muslimin

PER   - Political and Economic Report

PICME - Political Intelligence Centre, Middle East

RG   - Record Group

RSh   - al-Rabita al-Sharqiyya

WO   - War Office

YMMA   - Young Men's Muslim Association

NA   - National Archives

INTRODUCTION

EGYPT, ARABISM AND THE PALESTINE

QUESTION, 1911 -1936

A. Egypt and the Arab Question

The idea that Egypt is an integral part of the Arab world, and must, therefore, relate both her struggle and destiny to the Arab cause, found few Egyptian adherents in the first three decades of the twentieth century. During this period, most Egyptian nationalists denounced the whole vision of Arab nationalism as anathema. Members of the main Egyptian political parties expressed antipathy towards this idea even before the First World War.

Some nationalists, mainly those from the Nationalist Party (al-Hizb-al-Watani), opposed Arab nationalism because it contradicted their own definitions of their national enemies and allies. The followers of this party pinned their hopes on the assistance of the Ottoman Empire in Egypt's struggle for independence. They believed that pan-Islamic solidarity under the rule of the Ottoman Caliph, was essential to counter the European challenge in the East, and to hasten the British withdrawal from Egypt.[1] Arab nationalism insisting on the separate identity of the Arabs, was viewed by these nationalists as a grave danger to the integrity of the Ottoman Empire and treason against Islamic solidarity. Egyptian nationalists such as 'Abd al-Rahman 'Azzam and Salih Harb Pasha, who later became ardent advocates of Arabism ('Uruba),were still inclined, in these early days, to join the various campaigns of the Ottoman Empire against the

Christian powers.[2] For the same reason, many Egyptian nationalists also condemned the British backed Arab Revolt of Sharif Husayn (1916) as a conspiracy against Islam, and urged all Muslims to defy it.[3]. Even 'Aziz 'Ali al-Misri, "the 'father' of the Arab nationalist movement", withdrew his support for this revolt after a brief, unsuccessful attempt to mediate between the Sharif and the Turks.[4].

Besides the Nationalist Party, the other mainstream of Egyptian nationalism was represnted by the National Party (Hizb al-Umma), and particularly the works of Ahmad Lutfi al-Sayyid, its leading ideologist. In his articles, Lutfi al-Sayyid, the editor of al-Jarida, the party newspaper, elaborated the idea of Egyptianism. As "chief spokesman for the party", Lutfi al-Sayyid publicised his belief that the welfare of the Egyptian nation living within the borders of the Nile Valley, should become the sole interest of the Egyptians.[5]. Consequently pan-Islamism and pan-Arabism were rejected because they added unnecessary and uknwanted responsibilities to the idea of distinctive Egyptian national identity. As early as 1911, Lutfi al-Sayyid himself rejected an Arab nationalist offer to promote the idea of a union between Syria and Egypt. He explained that this idea was "not in Egypt's interest to pursue", since "an Egyptian is one who does not identify himself with any nation but Egypt", and therefore "our nationalism directs our desires towards our nation... and our nation alone".[6] In a famous article in al-Jarida, probably written as a reaction to this Arab nationalist offer, Lutfi al-Sayyid denied the existence of the Arab Question. "There is no Arab Question", he asserted, thereby reducing Arab national aspirations to the local grievance of a few Arabs against the Ottoman administration. He maintained that, "for all those who plead for a party to air the Arabs' complaints in the Ottoman Empire, it would be better to teach the nomadic Arabs (al-A'rab) the meaning of a constitution".[7]

The suggestion that the nomadic Arabs - the Bedouins - should learn the meaning of a constitution was but one expression of the low esteem in which the Arabs were held by Lutfi al-Sayyid and his associates. There were further expressions of contempt after the Anglo-French Declaration of 8th November, 1918, which granted independence to the Arabs. In an interview with a three-man Egyptian delegation (Wafd)held shortly after the declaration, Reginald Wingate, British High Commissioner, was to hear the Egyptian point of view on which countries were deserving of, and entitled to independence. The Egyptian delegates told Wingate that Egypt, by virtue of "its glorious ancient history, its self-contained potential, and its large population consisting of one race possessing a common language", was "far more capable of conducting a well-ordered government than the Arabs, Syrians and Mesopotamians" to whom self-determination had been granted.[8]

Since the people who expressed and subscribed to such views were to lead the Egyptian national movement for the next decade, Arabs could not anticipate any Egyptian support in their struggle for independence. Thus for example, Sa'd Zaghlul, head of the Egyptian Delegation to the Peace Conference in Paris (1919), insisted on a separate representation of Egyptian demands for independence. "Our case", he argued, "is an Egyptian and not an Arab one".[9]

This deliberate insulation from national Arab demands also

continued after the Peace Conference. While in London in 1920, Zaghlul, Egypt's new national leader, refused to comment to a reporter on the situation in Syria and Palestine. He emphasised that the Egyptian delegation had come to discuss only Egyptian demands for complete independence.[10] Arab Unity was regarded as an illusive dream and ridiculed as an "addition of zero to zero".[11]

The Wafd, the party which was formed by Zaghlul and his associates, continued, in the first decade of its existence, to hold the views expressed by its national leaders regarding a distinctive Egyptian identity. The other Egyptian parties, which were formed either by divisions in the original Wafd or as a result of Palace intrigues, did not oppose the Wafd's definition of distinctive Egyptian nationalism.[12] At that time the definition of a distinctive Egyptian identity seemed to be above and beyond the fierce political struggles between the Egyptian parties. Observers who visited Egypt during the 1920s could not discover any differences in the views of Egypt's various political and cultural circles on this question.[13] As late as the end of 1929, Mustafa al-Nahhas, Zaghlul's successor as leader of the Wafd, re-affirmed that Egyptians did not have an Arab problem but an Egyptian one. In an interview, Nahhas added that he did not wish to intervene in external affairs which would impose an additional burden on Egyptian nationalists. Although the aspirations of other for independence were dear to him, his mission was "to promote the well-being of Egypt alone".[14]

B. Egypt and the Palestine Question, 1920-1929

Following this maxim--the promotion of Egypt's well-being alone--

the Egyptian Government encountered no moral difficulties in complying with a British request to recognise the British mandate over Palestine and Iraq. The Government, in approving this request, had but a single reservation concerning the British mandate in Palestine: "the frontier between Palestine and Egypt shall in no way be affected by the delimitation of the Palestine frontiers [as provided under the terms of tne mandate]".[15] This insistence on the definition of the 1906 frontier between Egypt and Palestine appears to have been the only Egyptian interest in Palestine during this period.[16] By and large, Egyptian politicians had no interest in the internal political developments in Palestine. In fact, they were indifferent to, and probably even ill-informed about, the Arab Zionist conflict. The Palestinian journalist, Muhammad 'Ali al-Tahir, then living in Egypt, bitterly described this ignorance in his memoirs. Some Egyptians, he said, asked him who 'Mr. Palestine' was, while others innocently thought that Zionism was the name of a lady with whom he had quarrelled and therefore hated.[17]

Such a description, exaggerated as it may be, sheds some light on the Egyptian Government's lack of interest in the Arab-Zionist conflict. The Government followed a policy of strict neutrality and total non-involvement. As a consequence of this policy, some Palestinaian Arabs were arrested in Cairo after trying to demostrate against Lord Balfour, who passed through the city on his way to the inauguration ceremony for the Hebrew University of Jerusaslem.[18] As a further demonstration of their neutrality, Egyptian consuls in Jerusalem continued to invite representatives of all religious communities in Palestine, as well as Arab and Zionist leaders to receptions in honour of the birthday and anniversary of the coronation of the Egyptian King.[19]

Zionist activity in Palestine aroused neither Egyptian resentment nor Egyptian sympathy for the Palestinian Arabs. Since Egyptianism did not entail any moral or ideological commitment either to Islam or Arabism, Zionists could even gain Egyptian sympathy for their aspirations. Thus, for example, Ziwar Pasha, the Governor of Alexandria, not only permitted but even participated in pro-Zionist celebrations by the local Jewish community after the Balfour Declaration, in 1917.[20] In 1922, Ahmad Zaki, a former secretary of the Egyptian Government, congratulated the Zionist Organisation in Palestine for the recognition of the British mandate by the League of Nations. Zaki, who was to become an ardent sympathiser with the Palestinian Arabs, wrote to Dr. Eder, Secretary General of the Zionist Executive in Palestine, that "the victory of the Zionist idea is the turning point for the fulfillment of an ideal which is so dear to me: the revival of the Orient". The writer further anticipated fruitful Arab-Jewish co-operation and ended his letter by emphasising his hope for the survival of Zionism, whose goal it was "to bare the flame which should illuminate the Orient".[21]

These were not the only expressions of friendship towards the Zionists. In March, 1924, Frederick Kisch, Chairman of the Zionist Executive in Palestine, lunched in Cairo with 'Aziz 'Ali al-Misri. During their conversation, "the 'father' of the Arab nationalist movement" told Kisch that "he wanted the Orient for the Oriental, and further regarded the Jews as such". Two days later, Kişch met 'Aziz 'Ali again, this time accompanied by two associates, Hasan Sabri, an Egyptian dignitary, and Sayyid Kamil Pasha, a son of 'Abd al-Hamid's Grand Vizier. After the meeting, Kisch noted in his diary that "these three men, of such different origins, but all Muslims and true Orientals, were equally emphatic in their pro-Zionist declarations. Their declarations moreover, were sincere; there was no pretence of embracing Zionism pour nos beaux yeux, but each of the three, for a somewhat different reason, recognised that the progress of Zionism might help to secure the development of a new Eastern civilzation".[22] A year later, in 1925, Ziwar Pasha, now Prime Minister, cordially greeted a Zionist delegation which invited him to the dedication ceremony of the Hebrew University of Jerusalem. Ziwar thanked the delegates, praised the contribution made by such a university to mankind, and even sent an official representative to the ceremony.[23]

At that time, Zionism was still regarded as a legitimate concept in Egypt. Activities of Zionist organisations and associations were permitted, pro-Zionist receptions and gatherings were advertised in the local press, and pro-Zionist emissaries were allowed to collect funds from the Jewish community in Egypt for the creation of Jewish settlements in Palestine.[24] That Zionism did not flourish in this period within the Jewish community in Egypt was not the result of local governmental restrictions, but owing to the fact that many Egyptian Jews viewed Zionism sceptically.[25]

The activity of the few Zionist Jews within the various political circles[26] might even have fostered a favourable attitude to Zionism among the major political parties in Egypt. Le Liberté, the newspaper of Leon Castro, a Jewish lawyer and President of the Zionist Federation of Alexandria, was regarded in 1924 as the mouthpiece of the Wafd.[27]

Castro himself was said to have attempted in that year to arrange a meeting between Chaim Weizmann, head of the World Zionist Organisation, and Zaghlul to discuss collaboration between the two national movements.[28] Even as late as 1928, King Fu'ad could hold discussions on the merits of Zionism with Professor David Prato, Chief Rabbi of the Jewish community in Egypt.[29]

During this period Palestinian Arabs and their supporters in Egypt also attempted to attract sympathy and support for their cause. Newspapers and clubs advocating the Palestinian Arab cause were established and Palestinian Arab emissaries visited Egypt in ceaseless attempts to attract official and public support for the Arab cause in Palestine.[30]

The respected religious image of the Mufti of Jerusalem helped him to acquire many friends during visits he made to Egypt in the 1920s. Particularly good relations were cultivated with some of the members of the Eastern Bond Association (Jam'iyat al-Rabita al-Sharqiyya),[31] one of the few associations in Egypt which advocated collaboration between Egypt and the Eastern peoples.[32] However, most of its members were careful not to confuse their sympathy for the Palestinian Arabs with their neutrality towards the Zionists and their respect for Egyptian Jews.[33]

The Mufti's various attempts to use his religious image to attract political support for the Palestinian Arab cause were unsuccessful. In 1928, the Egyptian Government, despite the Mufti's numerous invitations, gave instructions that their Consul in Jerusalem was to be their sole representative in the ceremonies for the renovation of the al-Aqsa Mosque.[34]

The sundry attempts of the Arab and Palestinian emigres in Egypt to promote Egyptian sympathy for the Arab cause were no more successful. During the 1920s these emigres formed several societies, the foremost being the Executive of the Syro-Palestinian Congress (al-Lajna al-tanfidhiyya lil-mu'tamar al-Suri al-Filastini),[35] and the Palestine Committee which was later known as the Association for the Defence of Palestine (Jam'iyat al-Difa' 'an Filastin).[36] They initiated a number of manifestos condemning British policy in Palestine, and protesting against the 'Judaization' of sacred Islamic places there.[37]

However, in spite of the publication of an Arabic translation of the notorious Protocols of the Elders of Zion in Cairo in 1927,[38] Jews retained respected posts in government service. Similarly, influential Egyptian personalities continued to make public declarations of their respect for Jewish tradition. Thus, for example, Prince 'Umar Tusun, Hasan Sabri, the Governor of Alexandria, and the Minister of Education took part in the celebration in Alexandria honouring Maimonides.[39] In 1926, Shaykh Muhammad Abu al-Fadil al-Jizawi, the Shaykh of al-Azhar, rejected appeals to support the Palestinian Arabs, claiming that this was a political issue exceeding his authority.[40]   Furthermore, none of the popular Egyptian newspapers such as Al-Ahram or al-Muqattam, joined the anti-Jewish crusade even though they were owned by Egyptian residents of Syrian and Lebanese extraction. Attempts by the Palestinian Arab journalist Muhammad 'Ali al-Tahir to wage an anti-Jewish campaign in Egypt were short lived. The licence of his newspaper, al-Shura, was revoked and he was forced to make constant appeals to other local newspapers to let him air his views on the Palestine conflict.[41]   Sympathy for the Palestinian Arab grievances was expressed, if at all, only by radical political circles, which were themselves ignored by the great majority of other political parties in Egypt.[42]

Maintaining the neutral Egyptian image in the Arab-Zionist conflict in Palestine was not always an easy task for Egyptian Consuls in Jerusalem. It was only natural for the Palestinian Arabs to look for moral and material assistance from their wealthy Islamic neighbour. Denial of such assistance for the Palestinian Arabs was obviously regarded as political support for the Zionists. Therefore, Egyptian Consuls in Jerusalem found it advisable to distribute money occasionally to local reporters in Palestine to induce a favourable and positive image for Egypt in the local Arab newspapers.[43]

c.   The Wailing Wall distrubances and Egyptian reaction

The Wailing Wall disturbances aroused Muslim feelings not only in Palestine, but also in neighbouring countries including Egypt. In Egypt, feelings towards Muslim Arabs were particularly strong among adherents of the new pan-Islamic Societies which had emerged after the abolition of the Caliphate in Turkey.[44] With the abolition of the

Ottoman Caliphate and the exclusion of the last Caliph from Turkey (1924), the main obstacle to pan-Islamic support for pan-Arab ideas was overcome. The new pan-Islamic societies in Egypt found no conflict between Arab loyalty and Islamic belief. They regarded Arabism as an integral part of Islam, stressing the fact that Islam was born in the Arab East, where it gained its first believers and had its holy shrines.

The obvious, and in fact the only, deduction from this belief for society members was the conclusion that Muslim assistance to Arab co-religionists in Palestine was natural and imperative. Since the Mufti of Jerusalem described the disturbances as a religious struggle aimed at defending one of the most holy of Islamic Shrines, Muslim reaction in Egypt becamse inevitable. Pan-Islamic Societies such as the Young Men's Muslim Association (Jam'iyat al-Shubban al-Muslimin)[45] and the Society of Islamic Guidance (Jam'iyat al-Hidaya al-Islamiyya),[46] initiated special meetings in support of the Palestinian Arab cause. They issued manifestos opposing British pro-Zionist policy in Palestine, collected funds for Arabs injured in the disturbances, and organised medical and material aid for the Palestinian Arabs.[47] It was then that the Eastern Bond Association also began to raise its voice in support of the Arab struggle in Palestine.[48] By this time, Ahmad Zaki, who had previously praised the Zionist ideal, also changed his attitude towards Zionism. He vowed to dedicate himself both spiritually and materially to the liberation and defence of al-Aqsa Mosque.[49]

Numerous appeals for the defence of Islamic sacred places in Palestine were now published in Egypt's most popular newspapers, al-Ahram and al-Muqattam. These appeals contained strong accusations against alleged Zionist and Jewish misdeeds in Palestine. The most common allegation was that the Jews sought to blow up the sacred Mosque of al-Aqsa in order to restore the Temple of Solomon on its ruins. The Jews were further accused of conspiring to revive the Israelite Kingdom in Palestine and to expel the non-Jewish residents. Zionist settlements were defamed as being nests of Bolshevik activists who led a wanton way of life and Prophetic Traditions (Ahadith) were cited as decisive evidence to prove Jewish eternal enmity towards Muslims.[50]

This kind of propaganda no doubt had some effect in Egypt. Although much of the propaganda had been produced by the few traditional supporters of Arab Palestine in Egypt,[51], it seems safe to appreciate that this campaign increased Egyptian public awareness of, and perhaps also sympathy for, the Palestinian Arabs. It was then that the British High Commissioner in Egypt first reported that local public opinion followed the Palestine disturbances "with keen, but by no means impartial, interest". Public opinion, he said was "definitely biased in favour of the Arabs as against the Jews".[52]

Nevertheless, biased as it may be in favour of the Palestinian Arabs, Egyptian opinion still remained very much concentrated on Egyptian affairs. The emotional pleas for help by Palestinian Arabs and the pan-Islamic societies failed to make deep impressions in Egypt. Although a growing number of personalities including Huda Sha'rawi -- President of the Egyptian Women's Association; Fatima Rushdi -- an actress; Ahmad Shawqi -- the poet; Mahmud 'Azmi -- a journalist, and even Prince 'Umar Tusun, raised their voices on behlaf of the

Palestinian Arabs,[53] neither the Palace nor the major political parties deemed it important to intervene in the conflict. While 'Umar Tusun, as President of the Supreme Committee for Aid for the Renovation of al-Aqsa Mosque, may have been concerned by the alleged Jewish threat on the Mosque, the King and his entourage did not respond to the numerous calls for help by the Palestinian Arab supporters in Egypt. In fact, another Prince, Muhammad 'Ali, who by descent was far closer to the throne than 'Umar Tusun, had quite different views on the conflict. In a letter to the British High Commissioner in Palestine, he argued that the Muslims "may be willing to accept a sum of money... and, as the Jews are rich, if this thing [the Wailing Wall] is so much desired by them, there seems no reason why they should not pay for it".[54]

The suggestion to find a financial solution for 'this thing' -- a sacred wall for the Muslims as well -- illustrates the detachment of influential figures in Egypt from developments in Palestine. Reducing the Arab-Zionist conflict to a religious dispute solvable by money indicates how remote certain influential figures in Egypt were from the Palestine conflict.

The main political circles in Egypt hardly showed greater interest in the conflict than the Palace. The only political body which publicly expressed support for the Palestinian Arabs was the Executive of the Nationalist Party.[55] However, the various appeals by the Party to assist the Palestinian Arabs were ignored. By 1929, the Nationalist Party had already been relegated to the margins of the political map in Egypt, and its calls could easily be ignored by the Government. Moreover, the Party's support for the Palestinian Arabs might be attributed largely to the fact that the leaders of the Party were also members of the Young Men's Muslim Association (YMMA).[56]

A few politicians belonging to major political parties were mentioned in connection with aid projects to the Palestinian Arabs. The names of Makram 'Ubayd, General Secretary of the Wafd, and Tawfiq Doss, a fellow Coptic politician, were included in a list of advocates who reportedly volunteered to defend Palestinian Arabs accused of crimes related to the disturbances.[57] Other figures, such as 'Abd al-Rahman Lamlum, a member of the Egyptian Senate (Majlis al-Shuyukh), and 'Abd al-Rahman 'Azzam, a Wafdist member of the Chamber of Deputies (Majlis al-Nuwwab) supported the activities of a Palestinian Arab delegation which had arrived in Egypt in January 1930 to seek official assistance for the Arab cause in Palestine.[58]

However, not even one of the politicians mentioned as having volunteered to defend the Arabs imprisoned during the disturbances ever fulfilled his promise. At least one, Makram 'Ubayd, continued, as shall soon be seen, to oppose any official intervention in the Palestine conflict. Although 'Azzam and Lamlum were probably sincere in their sympathy for the Palestinian Arab cause, they lacked the power to force their views on their parties. Three different governments which ruled Egypt during the short period of August 1929 to June 1930-- the Liberal Constitutionalist Government of Muhammad Mahmud, the 'caretaker' Government of 'Adli Yagan and the Wafdist Government of Nahhas-- avoided commenting on the disturbances in Palestine. In fact, they even took various measures to suppress the propaganda campaign for the Palestinian Arabs.

Muhammad Mahmud's Government, in office when the Wailing Wall disturbances broke out, was particularly active in suppressing support for the Palestinian Arabs. The Ministry of Interior instructed the Press Bureau to censor inciting anti-Zionist and anti-Jewish articles, and special police patrols were sent to protect the Jewish quarters of Cairo and Alexandria against possible rioters.[59] Special measures were taken to suppress religious agitation. Students who were distributing inflammatory tracts in a Cairo Mosque were apprehended, while the Shaykh of al-Azhar, Mustafa al-Maraghi, Muhammad Mahmud's "personal friend",[60] restricted himself to statements that tallied with the neutral policy of the Government. After constant appeals from religious circles, Maraghi sent a private memorandum to the British High Commissioner in Egypt describing the religious colour of the Jewish-Islamic dispute, and urging the British Government "to take steps to remove the causes of dispute in the Holy Places, whether religious or secular, and restore people to a state of peace".[61] British officials reported that Maraghi's memorandum was "a poor production", failing "to inculcate sympathy with the Islamic cause". They further appreciated that the memorandum did not reach the usual high standard of Maraghi's work, and was "no doubt only intended as a sort of platonic gesture in favour of his co-religionists in Palestine".[62]

The Government's impartial attitude towards the conflict was further demonstrated by the reaction of the Egyptian Consul in Jerusalem to the disturbances. The Consul deemed it important to express his condolences for the Jewish casualties when the Palestinian

Chief Rabbi, Yehuda Kuk, visited the Consulate on the anniversary of the King's coronation. The Consul further emphasised that no religious dispute existed between Egypt and the Palestinian Jews. Kuk was greatly impressed by the Consul's statement. "During the whole talk with you", he wrote to him later, "I could not find... but general concern for the welfare of Palestine regardless of race or religion".[63]

When this attitude was criticised by Muhammad 'Ali al-Tahir as 'Pro-Zionist', al-Siyasa, the mouthpiece of Mahmud's Government, sharply warned "our Palestinian Arab guests" that unless they ceased attacking the Consul and defaming "our fellow Jewish civilians" they might find themselves expelled from Egypt.[64]

The fall of Mahmud's Government and the rise of the Wafdist Government of Nahhas (January 1930) did not change the official policy concerning Palestine. Nahhas refused to permit a special Palestinian delegation to Egypt to hold meetings it had intended to convene. Although Wafdist members, such as 'Azzam and Hamad al-Basil supported this delegation, and in spite of the permit given for such meetings by the Director of Public Security and his British adviser, Nahhas still opposed these meetings. He justified this objection by stressing the concern felt by the Jewish community in Egypt about the activities of the Palestinian delegation. Makram 'Ubayd supported Nahhas's refusal, adding that any propaganda for the Palestinian Arabs in Arab countries was wrong. He told the Palestinian Arab delegates that their call for Arab Unity "frightens the West by increasing its fears that the East seeks to create a united independent bloc". This, Makram 'Ubayd maintained, would be "dangerous" for Arabs and Egyptians alike.[65]

Such statements by two of the more powerful politicians in Egypt illustrate the thinking of Egypt's national leaders at that time. The Egyptian Jews' appeals to Nahhas to cancel the meetings of the Palestinian Arab delegation[66] were given greater consideration and support than the Arab cause in Palestine. Arab Unity was taken as a 'dangerous' trend that was bound to damage the East's relations with the West. Having been utterly engaged in the thorny question of the Anglo-Egyptian Treaty, the Wafdist leaders could not agree to the presence of a Palestinian Arab delegation in Egypt at a time when they themselves were contemplating the renewal of Anglo-Egyptian negotiations. The activity of a Palestinian delegation in Egypt at that time could distract public attention from Egypt's national cause. Moreover, the relations between the Wafd and the Palestinian Arab leadership were tense following the Mufti's request to the Wafd to warmly welcome Lord Brentford, who had intended to come to Egypt to examine the prospects of future Anglo-Egyptian negotiations.[67]   In view of all these difficulties it should not be seen as surprising that the Palestinian Arab delegation was forced to leave Egypt soon after its arrival.[68]

The hostile Wafdist attitude towards the Palestinian Arab leadership prevailed during 1930. In April, Makram 'Ubayd, a member of the Wafdist negotiating team in London, rejected a plea for help by Jamal al-Husayni, head of a similar Palestinian Arab delegation there.[69] A few months later, in June, Nahhas was reported to have rejected a fresh plea for help, made this time by Shaykh 'Abd al-Qadir Muzaffar, the Mufti's personal assistant. Nahhas was reported to have

said that he did not trust "any of the Palestinian or Syrian leaders".
A month later the Wafd turned down yet a further appeal by Palestinian
and Syrian students in al-Azhar to sponsor their new society.[70]

D.   Arabism, the Palestinian Question and the Internal Political
      Struggle in Egypt.

The Wailing Wall disturbances broke out during a severe political
crisis in Egypt. This crisis was marked by sharp polemics between the
government and the opposition. Egypt's politics were to feature in most
of these polemics. However, for the first time a Government's attitude
towards the Palestinian Arabs and Arabism was also to appear as a
factor, if only a minor one, in the Egyptian political arena.

After the Wailing Wall disturbances, the editor of the main
Wafdist Opposition newspaper, Misr, allowed Tahir to criticise the
alleged pro-Zionist attitude of the Egyptian Consul in Jerusalem. In
addition, the editor of Misr urged the Government to replace the
Consul, and to clarify its stand towards the Palestine question.[71]

The editor's comments were all but remembered when the Wafd came
to power. Once in power the Wafd followed the old policy of neutrality
and non-intervention in the Palestine conflict. However, the Wafd did
not remain in power for long. In the middle of 1930, King Fu'ad
dismissed Nahhas, and invited Isma'il Sidqi, a former Wafdist leader
(who had left that party), to form the new cabinet. Sidqi's rise to
power was followed by the adjournment of the Parliament, the abrogation
of the 1923 Constitution, and the restriction of political activity by
strict regulations and censorship.

Less than a month after Sidqi's rise to power and the adjournment of Parliament, a prominent opposition member, Muhammad 'Ali 'Alluba, General Secretary of the Liberal-Constitutionalist Party, considered it the proper time to devote his efforts to better the conditions of the Palestinian Arabs. In his memoirs, 'Alluba briefly mentions that he had been persuaded by some figures to advocate the Arab cause before the International Wailing Wall Commission in Jerusalem. 'Alluba mentions only three figures with whom he discussed his trip to Jerusalem: Ahmad Zaki, of the Eastern Bond Association, 'Abd al-Hamid Sa'id, President of the YMMA, and Shaykn Muzaffar, the advisor of the Mufti of Jerusalem.[72] 'Alluba doen not mention any other persons with whom he discussed his trip to Jerusalem. However, it is unlikely that 'Alluba went without consulting, or at least informing, his party colleagues. The split between him and his party occurred only years afterwards.[73]

Accompanied by a few associates, fervent supporters of the Arab and Islamic cause,[74] 'Alluba made his way to Jerusalem, where he advocated Arab sovereignty over the Wailing Wall before the International Commission. He told the Commission that Palestine and Jerusalem belonged to the Arabs and Muslims, and that the Jews had become prominent there only a short while before.[75] In speeches and interviews that he gave soon afterwards in Egypt, Syria, Palestine and Lebanon, 'Alluba extolled the virtues of a pan-Arab orientation. He described Egypt as an Arab country, deriving her spiritual and cultural orientation from the Arabs, and destined to lead the Arab world and help her Palestinian Arab neighbours.[76]

The new vision which 'Alluba attempted to spread throughout Egypt was not accepted at that time by many Egyptians. One Egyptian intellectual went so far as to denounce the idea of an Arab union as "a remnant of decaying Islamic culture which does not suit the advanced qualities of Egypt". In this intellectual's view, the Jews rather than the Arabs were to be regarded as Egypt's potential allies, since they were more enlightended and richer and could therefore enhance Egyptian progress.[77]

'Alluba and his followers in Egypt hurried to respond to this challenge. In Arabism, they claimed lay an ideal remedy to all of Egypt's ills. Egypt's economic weakness would disappear through her connections with her Arab neighbours. United Arab pressure would also ease Egypt's struggle for independence. Zionism was nothing but a foreign body planted by the British in the heart of the Arab nation to prevent the political independence of Egypt and her Arab sisters. Egyptians should therefore fight Zionism, not only because of the religious bonds between themselves and the Palestinian Arabs, but also because of the Zionist threat to Egypt's independence.[78]

The new ideological approach towards Arabism did not seem to affect the Egyptian Government. Having obtained the approval of the Palace to his policy lines, Sidqi could afford to ignore 'Alluba's new crusade. 'Alluba was evidently aware of the King's influence on Government policy. Upon his return to Egypt, 'Alluba had asked for an audience with Fu'ad. But the King turned him down.[79] Even his own Party, the Liberal-Constitutional Party, was reluctant that time to follow a pan-Arab line. In the course of 1930, not many Egyptians were attracted to Arabism. In February, 1931, Percy Loraine, British

High Commissioner in Egypt, felt that "Egypt is so isolated from the Arab World that it is not easily drawn into movements such as pan-Arabism and pan-Islamism". The influence of these movements in Egypt was estimated as "inconsiderable". Arab propaganda against Zionism and the territorial partition of the Arab World seemed unable to make "any direct appeal in Egypt."[80] Sidqi's Government did not find any moral or political difficulty in following the neutral policy towards Palestine which had been practised all along. Dozens of Palestinian Arabs, mainly from the Hebron region in Palestine, who had fled to Egypt after the Wailing Wall disturbances, were expelled and sent back to Palestine. The formal reason for their expulsion was that they were fugitives from the British authorities who had warrants for their arrest.[81] Sidqi could find no reason why he should prevent his son from going with his Cairo University team to play in a Jewish tennis tournament in Jerusalem.[82] In March 1931, an Iraqi mission examining the prospects of an Arab Alliance (Hilf 'Arabi) with the neighbouring regimes,[83] found that Egypt was utterly isolated from Arab affairs.[84] Although Nuri al-Sa'id, Iraq's new Premier and head of the mission, held talks with Fu'ad, Sidqi and also pan-Arab advocates,[85] the most he could get was an Extradition Agreement between the two countries.[86]

It was, however, in 1931 that a wider range of Egyptians became intellectually and politically involved in Arab affairs. The great advocates of Egypt's new Arab identity were the pan-Islamic societies in Egypt, notably the YMMA, and the Society for Islamic Guidance.[87] However, also economists, such as Tal'at Harb, Chairman of Bank

Misr,[88] and intellectuals,[89] sought closer relations with the Arab countries to end Egypt's economic and cultural dependence on the West.

The result of this search was an upsurge in pan-Arab activity, which obviously attracted the attention of British officials in Cairo. In June 1931, Loraine reported "a marked recrudescence of pan-Islamic and pan-Arab feeling in the Middle East, particularly in Palestine and Syria and, to a lesser extent, in Egypt". Loraine attributed this recrudescence to the activity of Shawkat 'Ali, the President of the Caliphate Society in India, in connection with the pan-Islamic Congress in Jerusalem and the "Muslim Federation". Nonetheless, Loraine estimated that "Shawkat's efforts in Egypt did not meet with any very marked response." This was "doubtless" due both to "the local political situation", and to the fact that Egypt had "never shown any great enthusiasm for an Islamic movement".[90]

It was the internal political situation, regarded by the High Commissioner as one of the two obstacles to the growth of pan-Arabism, which inspired the new wave of pan-Arab feeling in Egypt in 1931. The man most responsible for the renewed debate, which intensified the previously 'inconsiderable' impact of pan-Arab idea, was Makram 'Ubayd, the Coptic Secretary General of the Wafd. 'Ubayd attributed his sudden sympathy for the Arab cause to emotional attachment. In 1937, during a reception for a Palestinian Arab delegation, he recalled his visit to Palestine in 1931, and maintained that his support for the Palestinian Arabs was not motivated by religious, linguistic or genea-logical ties, but by deep emotional feelings. "A spiritual bond ties the brethren Arab nations", he said, "a belief that we, Arabs, compose a new union...based on mutual love and respect".[91]

If one takes into account 'Ubayd's adamant rejection of Arab Unity while a Cabinet Minister at the beginning of 1930, it becomes difficult to understand his new stand, less than a year later, as a result of a change in emotional feelings alone. Internal political events in Egypt might have been no less responsible for 'Ubayd's ideological shift. In March 1931, the Wafd and the Liberal-Constitutionalist parties decided to form a united front against Sidqi's regime. The seven points of the joint manifesto publicly announcing this collaboration dealt exclusively with Egypt's internal affairs.[92] However, this does not exclude the possibility that during the discussions held between the representatives of these parties, 'Alluba succeeded in persuading 'Ubayd of the merits of adopting a pan-Arab policy. Since 'Alluba's tours through the Arab countries gained him great prestige there, there was no reason to doubt that a similar tour by 'Ubayd expressing similar views would result in growing popularity for the Wafd. Since Sidqi's strict censorship prohibited any local criticism against the regime, would it not be wiser if such criticism, instigated by Wafdist emissaries, could penetrate Egypt by means of the Arab media outside the country?

The first opportunity to examine the advantages to the Wafd of a pan-Arab platform was presented when the Mufti of Jerusalem made yet a further visit to Egypt in March 1931. The Mufti held talks with both Opposition and Government leaders.[93] While the talks with Government officials evoked no sympathetic response to his appeal for support, the Mufti's encounters with Wafdist representatives were more fruitful. Friendly relations were established between the Wafd and the Palestinian Arab leadership. Following this development a prominent Wafdist member, Baha al-Din Barakat, a former Minister of Education, visited Palestine during April and May. In the course of the visit, Barakat became an ardent advocate of Arab rights in Palestine.[94] It is likely that upon his return to Egypt, Barakat reported his findings and impressions to his fellow Wafdists.

Barakat's account might have contributed to 'Ubayd's decision to follow a pro-Arab line. This line was first disclosed to the public during 'Ubayd's trip to Palestine, Lebanon and Syria, in the summer of 1931. During the trip, which he described as a tour for "rest and convalescence",[95] 'Ubayd took pains to advertise his support for Arab solidarity. He described himself as "a soldier for the Arab countries", and pleaded for the creation of an Arab Economic Union which would include Egypt, Syria, Iraq, Trans-Jordan and Palestine. This union was also to co-operate against the mandate system and encourage future political unity between the member states.[96]

'Ubayd did not restrict his views to general statements in support of Arabism. He also commented on particular Arab affairs such as the Palestine conflict. During his stay in Palestine, he blamed British policy for creating "racial dissension" there, and maintained that Jews and Arabs could live together, though under Arab sovereignty. 'Ubayd praised Jewish talent in the spheres of economics and finance, and welcomed Jewish immigration into Palestine provided that the promised Jewish homeland remained "spiritual". He warned that any attempt to establish a Jewish State under a British mandate or dominion would be met "with the strongest opposition throughout the Near and Middle East and Arabia".[97]

Palestinian Arabs, mainly those of the Husayni faction, responded to 'Ubayd's pro-Arab sentiments with loud applause. Since Arabism meant the end of Egyptian neutrality in Arab affairs, Palestinian Arabs obviously appreciated the way that 'Ubayd separated himself from Egypt's traditional isolationist policy. 'Ubayd, for his part, made sure that his Palestinian Arab hosts would not forget his political identity. Years later, while recalling this tour, 'Ubayd declared proudly that he had succeeded in drawing the sympathy of a great number of Palestinian Arabs for the Wafd.[98] This sympathy was demonstrated in news reports praising Wafdist pro-Arab and democratic thinking, while denouncing Sidqi's dictatorship and isolationist policy.[99]

Zionist officials, whose reactions could be taken as an indicator of the state of Egyptian-Arab relations, were not particularly alarmed at 'Ubayd's ideological turn. While becoming aware of the potential danger to their position from an Egyptian pan-Arab policy, Zionist officials found some comfort in 'Ubayd's moderate attitude towards their desires for a Jewish national home in Palestine. Chaim Arlozorov, Director of the Executive of the Jewish Agency in Jerusalem, was pleasantly "surprised" by 'Ubayd's views. He regarded them as a proof that Egypt was "an open field" for possible Zionist activity as yet unexamined. Referring to 'Ubayd's interviews in Palestine, Arlozorov further assumed that it was "still possible to hold successful discussions with the more moderate and less Arab political leaders of Egypt."[100]

The Zionist definition of 'Ubayd as one of the more moderate and less 'Arab' leaders of Egypt was not shared by Sidqi's Government. The Government was evidently far more concerned by the methods 'Ubayd had used to increase his, and the Wafd's popularity and prestige in the neighbouring Arab countries. 'Ubayd's attempts to incite the Arabic media abroad against Sidqi's regime were deplored. The Government urged the authorities of Syria and Palestine to expel him, labelling him a "conspirator and instigator".[101]   'Ubayd's pro-Arab views were sharply denounced. A Government newspaper accused him of provoking the destruction of Palestine, since he stirred up "hatred, disorder and disputes" there at times when Palestine needed "a reasonable language to promote the mutually peaceful work and life of Arabs and Jews".[102]

The Government campaign against 'Ubayd stimulated a Wafdist reaction. This because 'Ubayd was not a mere party official, but the Secretary General and spokesman of the party, and in fact, its "real manager" after Zaghlul's death. Zaghlul treated him like a son (he was nicknamed Ibn Sa'd), and this helped 'Ubayd to consolidate his control of the party and to significantly influence even Zaghlul's successor, Mustafa al-Nahhas.[103]   In view of 'Ubayd's important status in the Wafd, it is hardly surprising that the whole machinery of the Party went out of its way to defend his new Arab outlook. 'Ubayd's views became the Party's views. Party newspapers praised 'Ubayd's pro-Arab statements; the leaders of the Party expressed their assent to them, and even persuaded the 'Mother of the Egyptians' Safiya Zaghlul, widow of the first leader of the Wafd, to welcome 'Ubayd on his return.[104]

Sidqi, of course, was not to acquiesce in this development. Palestinian newspapers that praised 'Ubayd's views and attacked the official policy were banned, and their import licence into Egypt annulled.[105] Even the project to convene an inter-Eastern conference of students and academics was rejected by the Government.[106]

Both Government and opposition attitudes towards pan-Arabism and the Palestinian Arabs were to be tested when the Supreme Islamic Council (al-Majlis al-Islami al-A'la), the stronghold of the Mufti of Jerusalem, issued invitations to numerous Egyptian personalities to participate in a General Islamic Congress scheduled to take place in Jerusalem in December, 1931. The vague agenda of the Congress gave rise to rumours that it would discuss the nomination of a new Caliph and initiate the construction of a new Islamic University in Jerusalem which would endanger the status of al-Azhar as the cultural and scientific centre of the Muslim world. These suspicions aroused the opposition of all the political circles in Egypt to the Congress.

The Mufti, alarmed at this opposition, went to Egypt and denied these rumours, promising in public that the Congress would in no way deal with "the political or national interests of Egypt". However, since he continued to take part in receptions held for him by the Egyptian Opposition, Prime Minister Sidqi suspected that the Mufti would not honour his promise. Consequently, the Egyptian Government continued to denounce the Congress and even sent agents to torpedo it.[107]

The Egyptian Opposition, for their part, had been deterred by the Mufti's public undertaking to prevent discussion on Egyptian affairs in the Congress. Therefore, only two Opposition representatives, 'Alluba and 'Azzam, showed up for the Congress. Of them only 'Azzam stressed his partisan identity during the Congress. In spite of 'Azzam's and 'Alluba's expressed support for the Palestinian Arab cause, and although Opposition newspapers in Egypt stressed its importance, some significant differences remained between the Palestinian Arab outlook on the struggle and that of their new allies in Egypt. While the Palestinian Arabs condemned the report of the International Wailing Wall Commission, 'Alluba regarded it as "a victory".[108] Even Zionism was not commonly accepted as the main threat to Islam. 'Azzam himself estimated the Italian threat in Libya far more dangerous to the Arabs and the Muslims. In a speech at the Islamic Congress, which brought about his deportation from Palestine, he argued that while the Jews were weak and dependent on a constant flow of funds for their activities, the Italians were powerful and sought to uproot Islam in Libya.[109]

What perhaps illuminates the nature of the new Egyptian involvement in Arab affairs even more is the response to the resolutions of this Congress. Opposition leaders, as well as Prince 'Umar Tusun, promised to endeavour to form an Islamic University in Jerusalem, to protect Muslim rights in Palestine and Jerusalem and defend Islam.[110] Nahhas even made a financial contribution to the project of the Islamic University in Jerusalem. However, this was probably one of the last gestures made by an opposition leader towards the Congress. In Egypt, interest in the goals of the Congress did not outlast the Congress itself. Only six months after it had ended, the Palestinian journalist, Tahir, complained that the Congress and its resolutions were almost completely forgotten in Egypt.[111]

The only Egyptian politician who continued to advocate the resolutions and attempt to realise them was 'Alluba. As treasurer of the Permanent Committee of the Congress, he joined the Mufti of Jerusalem, in 1933, on a long trip through the Arab and Islamic world to raise funds for the building of the Islamic University in Jerusalem.[112] However, by this time 'Alluba was no longer active in the Liberal-Constitutionalist Party. In fact, he had totally disassociated himself from the political scene, to which he returned only some years later. Moreover, 'Alluba's activities failed to induce greater official Egyptian support for the Palestinian Arabs. Following the failure of the mission to raise funds for the projected University in Jerusalem, 'Alluba was reported to have contemplated asking Fu'ad's assistance. But the report went on to say that 'Alluba decided against this plan, fearing that the King would again turn down his appeal for an audience.[113]

The King, indeed, was far more concerned with the activities of one of his cousins, the ex-Khedive 'Abbas Hilmi, in Palestine, than in the Arab-Zionist conflict there. Following suspicions that 'Abbas Hilmi was bidding for the Syro-Palestinian throne, Fu'ad sent his Premier to Palestine and the Levant in February 1932. While endeavouring in private to foil 'Abbas Hilmi's suspected intention to obtain the Syro-Palestinian throne,[114] Sidqi described in public his tour as an attempt "to listen to the demands of the citizens of the sister countries". He expressed support for closer relations between Egypt and Palestine on the basis of "the union of the Arabic language and the Islamic religion".[115] The new emphasis on the ties between Egypt and her Arab neighbours probably led Sidqi to deny that he held talks with Zionist Jews in Palestine.[116] The need to deny the existence of such talks reflected the real change in Egypt's attitude towards the Arab-Zionist conflict in Palestine in this period.

However, aside from paying lip-service to his Arab and Islamic bonds, Sidqi did nothing to put a pro-Arab policy into practice. When the Arab merchants in Palestine and Lebanon asked him to reduce a new tariff on the citrus fruits exported to Egypt, Sidqi firmly rejected their requests. "Egypt", he argued, "by her tariff policy, attempts first and foremost to protect her interests and requirements".[117] Since imports from Palestine amounted to only 1.5% of total Egyptian imports in 1931,[118] such a statement was significant inasmuch as it indicated the degree of importance which the Egyptian Premier attached to promoting the aspirations of his recently recognised Arab brethren. Sidqi eventually made concessions in the tariff rate, but these concessions were not to come into force until after the citrus season,[119] bringing little relief to the Palestinian Arabs. A Palestinian delegation which came to Egypt in 1935 to discuss commercial problems between the countries succeeded in achieving only minor modifications in Egypt's tariff policy regarding Palestine.

Sidqi's cynical appraoch to the requests of his newly recognised Arab brethren also characterised the attitude of Egyptian politicians towards Arab affairs for quite a few years. Thus, for exmaple, 'Azzam and Hamad al-Basil were reportedly included in the Preparatory Com- mittee for an Arab Congress which was to be held in Baghdad sometime in 1933. However, up until December 1932, neither of them had yet attended a meeting of this Committee. In this month, an Iraqi emissary, Yasin al-Hashimi, arrived in Cairo to promote support for the Congress. Yasin met Nahhas and complained to him about Egypt's lukewarm attitude towards Arabism, and asked for Wafdist participation in the Congress. The fact that both 'Azzam and Hamad al-Basil had already been regarded as Wafdist dissidents might have encouraged Nahhas's refusal to permit any Wafdist participation. According to a report from the Criminal Investigation Department (CID) in Palestine, Wafdist members pressed Yasin to postpone the Congress on the ground of existing divisions between "certain sectors of the Arabs."[121] The Congress was to be postponed indefinitely owing to further disputes between Faysal's supporters and Ibn-Sa'ud's adherents, as well as British opposition to the whole scheme.[122]

During September and October 1933, a fresh opportunity to attract public attention to Arab affairs presented itself in Egypt. An "incidental discussion" between Dr. Taha Husayn, the famous Egyptian writer, and 'Azzam was manipulated by the latter into a general debate on Egypt's national identity. "I focused the discussion", 'Azzam reported triumphantly, "on one topic: 'Is Egypt an Arab country'? The Arab Press outside Egypt unanimously took my side and young enthusiasts in Damascus and elsewhere declared a boycott and burnt Dr. Taha's publications. The Egyptian Press was cautious, but clearly pro-Arab. The public feeling was for Egypt [as] an Arab country. While this was going on, the League of Literature called for a debate on the point, and writers, journalists and poets met. The debate was ended by an enormous vote in favour of Egypt [as] an Arab country. Dr. Taha felt defeated and closed the discussion, but the topic is still in the Press and it is quite clear that Egypt on this subject is something very different from what it was ten years ago".[123]

'Azzam might have been right in his assertion that Egyptian verbal sympathy with Arabism in 1933 was greater than it had been ten years earlier. Since 1931, Wafdist politicians, and thereafter, Government circles, were expressing sympathy with their Arab and Islamic relations. Nevertheless, none of these politicians demonstrated at that time that this sentiment committed Egypt to an Arab or pro-Arab policy. This ambivalent attitude towards Arabism was demonstrated once again during the Palestinain disturbances of October 1933, the month in which 'Azzam celebrated his 'victory' over Taha Husayn.

Egyptian reactions to these disturbances may illustrate to what extent the intellectual debate affected the actual attitude towards the Palestinian Arabs. An examination of these reactions shows that the Palestinian disturbances did not arouse a greater Egyptian involvement in the conflict. Although pan-Islamic Societies under the leadership of the YMMA formed a Supreme Committee for the Relief of the Palestine Victims (al-Lajna al-'ulya li-i'anat mankubi Filastin), they could not claim great achievements. The Opposition was once again engaged in accusing the Government of indifference to the conflict rather than in assisting the Palestinian Arabs. The Government, for its part, kept silent on this issue, and took steps to suppress the activity of the Palestinian Arabs in Egypt. As a result of these steps, Egyptian interest in the disturbances soon diminished. A new fund-raising campaign for the Palestinian Arabs was abandoned shortly after it had started.[124]

What was perhaps more illuminating were Egyptian attitudes towards the Palestinian Arabs' national demands. The two outstanding issues that marked the Arab struggle against the Zionists in Palestine -- Jewish immigration and the sale of Arab land there to Jews -- were both ignored by the Government and the Egyptian Opposition. It is striking that during the 1933 disturbances in Palestine, the Egyptian Government permitted 1000 new Jewish immigrants to land in Port-Said on their way to Palestine. No one in Egypt seemed to be touched by the protest of the Arab Youth Organisation of Jaffa which stated that "in times when Arab blood is being shed in Palestine, and Palestine uprises against the Zionist immigration, the neighbouring Muslim Arab Government helped such immigration".[125]

The few proposals advanced by Egyptians to solve the land sale issue in Palestine were ignored. As early as 1930, 'Alluba suggested that rich Arabs, including Egyptians, should be encouraged to buy Arab lands in Palestine.[126] In 1935, a prominent Egyptian journalist, Ibrahim 'Abd al-Qadir al-Mazini, attempted to revive 'Alluba's abortive proposal after a visit he made to Palestine. Mazini proposed the formation of an Arab joint stock company which would raise funds throughout the Arab world to buy up Arab land in Palestine.[127] However, Egyptian capitalists were apparently unwilling to invest their money in a country as politically unstable as Palestine, and Mazini's proposal never got off the ground.

Publicly, opposition leaders, headed by the Wafd, constantly expressed sympathy with the Palestinian Arabs. In the beginning of 1935, a delegation of the Palestinian Arab Youth Organisation was warmly welcomed by Wafdist circles, including Nahhas. Nevertheless, Nahhas and the rest of the Wafdist leadership rejected the Palestinian-Arab requests for Wafdist support for the Arab cause. Nahhas was reported to have criticised the Palestinian Arab strategy and divisions, arguing that this state of affairs prevented any Wafdist aid to them.[128] Despite a pro-Palestinian Arab statement of 'Ubyad at the 1935 Wafd General Conference,[129] the political platform which emanated from the Conference dealt solely with domestic Egyptian problems and failed to mention either Arabism or the Palestinian Arab struggle.[130] The Palestinian Arab leadership was quite aware of the Wafdist double-faced policy. In September, 1935, Yusuf Francis, editor of the Husayni's organ, al-Jami'a al-'Arabyya, told a Zionist official that the Wafd supported the Palestinian Arab cause only when in opposition, exploiting this issue for internal considerations and a desire to improve its stance against Britain.[131]

Francis further asserted that this attitude was not only evinced by the Wafd, the largest Egyptian party, but also by all major political circles in Egypt. His impression was supported by the similar views of numerous observers. The general consensus was that internal disputes and the thorny question of the Anglo-Egyptian Treaty absorbed the whole energy of Egypt's politicians, and Arab affairs, particularly the Palestine conflict, could not therefore attract any attention.[132]

PART ONE

FROM RESPONSES TO CO-OPERATION

CHAPTER ONE

ARABISM WITHOUT ARABS:

EGYPTIAN RESPONSES TO THE ARAB REVOLT

IN PALESTINE, 1936 - 1937

A. Egypt during 'Ali Mahir's caretaker Government
    (January 1936 - May 1936)

When a general Arab strike, marking the beginning of the Arab
Revolt in Palestine, broke out in April 1936, few Egyptians seemed
aware of this development. In Egypt most politicians were probably
attracted to the new round of Anglo-Egyptian negotiations being held in
Cairo during this period. When not discussing Anglo-Egyptian
relations, the various party leaders were no doubt engaged in their
election campaign, which lasted until 2nd May, 1936.

Those politicians not running in the elections, Premier 'Ali Mahir
and his Cabinet Ministers, far from paying attention to the Arab strike
in Palestine, were engaged in other affairs. 'Ali Mahir, for example,
who had been appointed by King Fu'ad to supervise fair Parliamentary
elections, at this period showed none of the characteristics that at a
later date labelled him as one of the main advocates of Egypto-Arab
relations. Although his Government included an ardent advocate of

Arabism --Muhammad 'Ali 'Alluba, the Minister of Education--it is doubtful whether his nomination should be attributed to 'Alluba's pro-Arab outlook. Had 'Alluba still belonged to the Liberal Party, he surely would not have served in Mahir's Government. This was because Mahir, as head of a caretaker Government which promised to be apolitical, was not expected to appoint any party politicians. Moreover, as head of a transitional Government, Mahir was not supposed to deviate from the policies of former Egyptian Governments. Such a privilege was reserved only for the next elected Government. In view of the traditional isolationist policies of the former Governments, Mahir had to follow this isolationist line, even if he did not like it.

By and large Mahir's Government followed this rule. Aside from the nomination of 'Azzam, a former Wafdist, as Envoy Extraordinary and Minister Plenipotentiary in Teheran and Baghdad,[1] it is difficult to point to further speeches or deeds by Mahir which could prove that his Government was inspired or guided by a pan-Arab philosophy.[2] Although an Iraqi Parliamentary delegation, as well as school delegations of Syrian and Palestinian students and journalists, were warmly welcomed in Egypt during Mahir's mandate, there is no evidence that these receptions led to greater official involvement in either Iraqi or Syrian or Palestinian affairs. In fact, these receptions resembled similar ones given in the past to Arab dignitaries who had visited Egypt. A report prepared in March 1936 by the Sudan Agency in Cairo on the pan-Arab movement in the Middle-East, though pointing at the upsurge of pan-Arab activity in the area, could not name any of

Egypt's political leaders as members or advocates of pan-Arabism. The only Egyptian figure mentioned in this report was Prince 'Umar Tusun, who, together with unidentified "partisans of the pan-Arab movement", was said to have been convinced that the only possible reaction to European colonialism was an "Arab Pact".[3] Had Mahir or any of his Ministers been active in the pan-Arab movement in Egypt, it is unlikely that their names would have been omitted from this detailed report.

While avoiding any dramatic moves towards the Arab world, Mahir, as Chief Royal Chamberlain, took great pains to preserve and promote the interests of his direct superior, King Fu'ad. While public opinion in Egypt was attracted to the Anglo-Egyptian negotiations, the Premier, himself excluded from these fateful talks, found ample time to look after the interests of his monarch. Aside from preparing the Royal Cabinet (al-Diwan al-Maliki) to serve as liaison between the King and the elected Government, Mahir also entered into negotiations with Saudi delegates in an attempt to end the religious dispute between the two Muslim monarchs. It was, therefore, the Islamic rather than the Arab appeal of the Egyptian King which Mahir set himself to defend. The treaty of friendship that settled the old religious dispute between Egypt and Saudi-Arabia lacked any reference to Arab ties between the two countries. It was entirely devoted to the new settlement concerning the annual Egyptian pilgrimage to Mecca.[4]

It should not, therefore, be surprising that up unto Fu'ad's death, on 28th April, 1936, Mahir could not be recorded even once to have supported the political demands of the Arab strikers in Palestine. After all, Fu'ad's interests, which Mahir was eager to safeguard, required no involvement in Palestine. Fu'ad's death; the subsequent proclamation of his son, Prince Faruq, as the new King; the formation of a Regency Council; and the Parliamentary elections in Egypt, no doubt further prevented any official Egyptian attention to the Palestinian crisis. Until 10th May, the day when Nahhas, following his overwhelming majority in the elections, formed an all-Wafdist Government, no official comment on the Palestinian disturbances had been made. By this time the Arab strike in Palestine was almost three weeks old.

B.   Egyptian responses to the Arab strike in Palestine

Not only the politicians but also the intellectual and religious circles in Egypt were slow to respond to the Arab strike in Palestine. It was not before the strike entered its second month, and appeals for help from Palestinian Arabs poured into Egypt,[5] that Pan-Islamic Societies and the Arabic Press began to pay some attention to the Palestinian crisis.

Societies, such as the YMMA, the Muslim Brethren (Jam'iyat al-Ikhwan al-Muslimin). The Azharite Union, and the Egyptian Women's Union, issued manifestos and protests against British policy in Palestine. These Societies further initiated a fund raising campaign for the Arab victims in Palestine.[6] The YMMA, adopting a method already practiced during the 1929 and 1933 disturbances in Palestine, called for a special conference at its Cairo club to discuss means to help the Palestinian Arabs. As on previous occasions, this conference also culminated in the formation of a Supreme Committee for the Relief of Palestinian Victims (al-Lajna al-'uliya li-ighathat mankubi

Filastin, alternatively known as al-Lajna al-'uliya li-i'anat mankubi Filastin).'Abd al-Hamid Sa'id, President of the YMMA, was elected president of this Committee, which included several politicians. Among them were traditional supporters of the Arab cause, such as Hamad al-Basil, as well as new sympathisers, such as Mahmud al-Basyuni, the Wafdist President of the Senate, and Dr. Muhammad Husayn Haykal, editor of the Liberal newspaper al-Siyasa.[7]

In spite of the participation of several politicians, the committee preserved its non-political identity. It consisted overwhelmingly of adherents of the various pan-Arab and pan-Islamic associations, who regarded the Palestinian Arab cause as standing above politics and of concern to the Egyptian people as a whole, regardless of religious or political differences. To this end, the pan-Islamic Societies, controlling this Committee, took pains to gain the support of the Coptic community in Egypt for the Palestinian Arabs. Thus, for example, Hasan al-Banna, leader of the Muslim Brethren, in spite of his Islamic bias, asked the Coptic Patriarch to join the contributions campaign.[8] The YMMA even formed a special Coptic Committee, which included Coptic politicians such as Tawfiq Doss, to conduct a fund-raising campaign for the Palestinian Arabs within this community.[9]

The new campaign for the Palestinian Arabs obtained great publicity in the Arabic press in Egypt. This press, in its search for a new source of news after the election campaign in Egypt had ended, found in the Palestinian disturbances an exciting issue to attract readers. Basing themselves largely on Palestinian Arab sources, newspapers such as <u>al-Ahram</u>, <u>Kawkab al-Sharq</u>, <u>al-Jihad</u> and <u>al-Balagh</u>,were now competing with each other in publishing sensational news about desecration of mosques by British soldiers and Jewish fanatics in Palestine. Further stories were published about a British-backed Jewish-Zionist conspiracy to revive the Israelite Kingdom and to restore the Temple of Solomon on the ruins of the Aqsa Mosque.[10]

It is hardly surprising that Muslim opinion in Egypt responded emotionally to these stories. The Shaykh of al-Azhar, Mustafa al-Maraghi, now that his close friend Muhammad Mahmud was no longer in power, found no political reason to restrain his sympathy for the Palestinian Arabs. He communicated with the High Commissioner in Palestine and expressed concern for both the welfare of the Arabs and the conditions of the Islamic shrines in the Holy Land.[11] This communication might have stirred further reaction. Students of al-Azhar, the barometer of public excitement, assembled at a special meeting and drew up an emotional manifesto protesting against the anti-Muslim policy of Britain in Palestine.[12] In various mosques, Muslim believers initiated petitions urging the British authorities to preserve the Islamic character of Palestine.[13] On the radio, the Qur'an commentators, two dignified professors of al-Azhar, made in their weekly commentaries such anti-Jewish remarks as to arouse the concern of the local Chief Rabbi for the safety of the Jewish community in Egypt.[14]

This religious reaction left its marks on the population. In a report to London, High Commissioner, Miles Lampson, could state without doubt that "all educated and uneducated opinion in Egypt" was convinced that Britain was committing "a cruel injustice to a neighbouring Moslem country".[15] Special emissaries who had been commissioned by the Palestinian Arab leadership to seek Egyptian assistance[16] enjoyed growing support. Egyptian dignitaries, such as Princes 'Umar Tusun, Muhammad 'Ali, and Hafiz 'Afifi, a confidant of the new Premier, donated money to the special fund for the Palestinian Arabs, appealed for peace and justice in Palestine and even offered their personal mediation to solve the conflict between Britain and the Palestinian Arabs.[17]

The anti-British agitation by some of the media aroused the concern of David Kelly, Acting High Commissioner in Egypt. He feared that the 'masses', being "easily worked up into artificial excitement" might be influenced by this propaganda and poison the friendly atmosphere of the Anglo-Egyptian negotiations. Nahhas was asked, therefore, to exert his influence to silence the critics.[18]

Nahhas gave Kelly a very pessimistic account of public feeling in Egypt concerning the Palestinian disturbances. The disturbances, he warned, inflamed public feeling in Egypt like an "oven". Only "a miracle", he said, and his own continuous influence, had prevented violent agitation and possible anti-Jewish outbreaks. He told Kelly that his "greatest wish was to found an Anglo-Egyptian alliance reposing on the goodwill of the whole Arab world", adding that Egyptians, after all, were also Arabs.[19]

Nahhas was not to remain the only prominent politician who took pains to disclose his Arab identity. In a conversation with Walter

Smart, Oriental Secretary of the British Residency in Cairo, Muhmmad Mahmud, leader of the Liberal Constitutionalist Party, proudly pointed out his Bedouin extraction,. He was an Arab himself, he said, and therefore, "could not help sympathising with the Arabs in Palestine".[20]

British officials were inclined to dismiss these statements as hypocritical cliches. Muhammad Mahmud's statement was mocked,[21] while Nahhas's definition of himself seemed to be of "doubtful accuracy".[22] Kelly evidently believed that the religious feelings shown by the Egyptians towards co-religionist Palestinian Arabs were neutralised by the traditional Egyptian contempt for Arabs. He appreciated that there was "no genuine solidarity between Egyptians and Palestinian Arabs".[23] Miles Lampson, Kelly's direct superior, quite agreed. "The Egyptian", he believed, "is inclined to look on the Arab as an uncivilised person and the Arab is inclined to despise the Egyptian for lack of moral fibre". This, in turn, led to the 'geographical and psychological' isolation of Egypt from her neighbours. Consequently the pan-Arab movement had "very little real strength in Egypt."[24]

Were these British conclusions correct? If so, why did Nahhas, as well as other Egyptian politicians, deem it necessary to stress time and again their Arab relations?

C. Arabism and Nahhas's mediatory efforts during the Arab
   Strike in Palestine

During the first months of Nahhas's Wafdist Government, Egypt's public attention was concentrated on the Anglo-Egyptian negotiations.

However, alongside growing public interest in these negotiations, several academic and intellectual circles also began paying some attention to Egypt's relations with the Arab world. On 27th May, 1936, Amin Sa'id, a Syrian-born editor of the Eastern Affairs section of al-Muqattam, published the first number of his new magazine al-Rabita al-'Arabiyya(the Arab Bond). In its first edition Sa'id described his periodical as aiming to strengthen the ties between Egypt and the Arab countries by dealing with various Arab affairs and discussing the means with which to defend the Arab cause.[25] The magazine soon became the mouthpiece of Arabism in Egypt, gathering around it those pan-Arab supporters who advocated various kinds of cultural, economic and political co-operation between Egypt and the Arab countries.[26]

The activities of the magazine staff encouraged the emergence of further pro-Arab organisations in Egypt. Not long after al-Rabita al-'Arabiyya had first appeared, a Society bearing the same name (Jam'iyat al-Rabita al-'Arabiyya) was born. It was headed by Mahmud Basyuni, President of the Senate, and stated as one of its goals the need to promote the scientific, social and economic ties between Egypt and the Arab countries.[27] A similar Society, the Society for Arab Unity (Jam'iyat al-Wahda al-'Arabiyya), was created by university students. It proclaimed as its motto the phrase that there was no Arabism without Egypt, and that neither Arab Unity nor independence could be realised without Egyptian assistance.[28]

The number of members of these Societies was rather small. The Societies never became popular like the Islamic Societies. They further suffered from constant splits,[29] which did not improve their image. Nevertheless, they were loud enough to attract the attention of British officials in Cairo. By September 1936, only one month after Lampson had sent his clear-cut opinion that the pan-Arab movement had very little real strength in Egypt, Kelly deemed it necessary to provide his superiors with an up-to-date review of the "changing outlook" of the Egyptians. In several communications, Kelly emphasised that "the point does not lie in what the Egyptians are really by blood, but in what they are being or likely to be talked into imagining they are". Kelly was convinced that a new "Arab state of mind" was emerging in Egypt.[30]

At that time, however, Egyptian politicians by and large did not consider the 'Arab state of mind' as the most prominent feature of their political outlook. The Anglo-Egyptian negotiations were given the utmost attention and there was not much room for sentimental expressions in favour of the Palestinian Arabs. Therefore when Kelly expressed concern that the propaganda for the Palestinian Arabs might damage the friendly atmosphere of the Anglo-Egyptian negotiations, Egyptian policy makers were quick to curb this propaganda. Nahhas summoned the editors of the most critical newspapers, and explained the Government's priorities to them in "very severe" language. Although he agreed that "every Egyptian must necessarily sympathise with the Arab cause in Palestine", Nahhas, nevertheless, emphasised that in times when his Government were trying to come to a friendly settlement with Britain, and wished by all means to preserve a friendly atmosphere, the editors had to censor the various reports on the Palestinian disturbances, "even if the stories were true".[31]

Similarly, when he heard that the YMMA intended to send a special fact-finding commission to Palestine, Nahhas instructed the Ministry of the Interior to frustrate this project.[32] Moreover, although he permitted the Palestinian Arab emissaries to stay in Palestine, and even donated some money to the fund for Palestinian Arabs,[33] Nahhas imposed heavy restrictions on the activity of the Palestinian Arabs in Egypt. The Arab News Agency of Muhammad 'Ali al-Tahir was refused the right to report on the Palestinian disturbances. Tahir's further effort to renew the license of his newspaper, al-Shura, failed, and a propaganda booklet that he had published for the Palestinian Arab cause was confiscated.[34] Special measures were taken to restrain religious propaganda. The Ministry of Education distributed a circular among the mosque preachers warning them not to comment on the Palestine disturbances.[35]

While curbing Palestinian Arab propaganda in Egypt, Nahhas made several approaches to British officials offering to mediate in the Palestine conflict. Pointing at public pressure, his Arab ties, and his own friendship to Britain as reasons for his intervention, Nahhas offered "to publish a manifesto to the Arab world" praising British policy and calling for peace between Jews and Arabs if Britain stopped Jewish immigration into Palestine.[36]

The nature of Nahhas's initiative does not support the reasons he himself gave to justify his intervention in the conflict. Nahhas never turned the Palestine conflict into a national issue. His approaches to British officials were secret and could not possibly be taken as attempts to ease alleged internal pressure. Moreover, aside from his requests to British officials to permit his mediation, Nahhas never took actual steps to meet either Zionist or Palestinian Arab representatives, and discuss with them the prosepcts of a peaceful solution. The evidence about Nahhas's efforts to obtain the mediatory role suggests that the Egyptian Premier, far from being pressed, was quite eager to intervene in the conflict. This evidence also shows that Nahhas, while facing no difficulties in silencing Palestinian Arab propaganda in Egypt, was very sensitive to the involvement of other Arab and Egyptian leaders in the conflict. The information about the involvement of other leaders in the conflict was not kept secret. In fact, these very Arab leaders took pains to publicise their own intervention in the conflict.

Thus, for example, in August, 1936, Nuri al-Sa'id, the Iraqi mediator, arrived in Cairo and discussed his proposal to end Jewish immigration with a number of Egyptians. Nuri succeeded in attracting Prince Muhammad 'Ali's interest in the conflict. The Prince conveyed Nuri's ideas to British officials, and further offered his personal assistance to solve the conflict.[37]

Nahhas clearly was not going to leave either Nuri or Muhammad 'Ali as the only contenders for British favours. He himself had already learnt during private talks with Lampson and Wauchope, that both officials-- the most authoritative exponents of British policy in this area-- supported restrictions on Jewish activity in Palestine.[38]

If the British Government were going to make concessions to the Palestinian Arabs-- as Nahhas may have assumed from private talks with British officials-- why should only the Arab leaders of Iraq, Saudi

Arabia or Trans-Jordan gain prestige for their mediation? Why should Nahhas deny himself a share of the advantages from the expected generosity of Britain? Should he remain idle while the most poweful personality in the Palace, the Prince Regent, attempted to obtain the promising mediatory post which carried significant advantages?

The answers that Nahhas gave to these questions led him to revive his initiative. By late July, 1936, after the main problems of the Anglo-Egyptian Treaty had been settled, Nahhas allowed resumption of criticism against British Palestinian policy. Articles criticising this policy were again published. A ban on the export of Egyptian labour to Palestine was declared and even the two houses of Parliament, where the Wafd enjoyed an overwhelming majority, expressed the desire for the restoration of peace and justice in Palestine.[39]

Backed by this, and aware of the mdeiatory attempts by other Arab and Egyptian figures, Nahhas resumed his own mediatory proposals. On 12th August, 1936, after initialling the Anglo-Egyptian Treaty in Cairo, Nahhas formally revived his initiative. He disclosed to Lampson that now that the Treaty negotiations were over, he was "most anxious" to play a mediatory role in Palestine. He argued that his intervention could be of "signal assistance" and asked for British concessions to the Palestinian Arabs concerning Jewish immigration.[40]

D. British reaction to the Egyptian mediatory efforts

Lampson did not like any Egyptian intervention in Arab affairs. In February, 1936, commenting on a report on the pan-Arab movement in the Middle East, Lampson asked London to bear in mind the importance of detaching Egypt "as far as possible from the anti-European fermentation in neighbouring countries".[41] When he heard that the Saudis attempted to involve Prince Muhammad 'Ali in the efforts to end the Palestinian Arab strike, his belief that the isolation of Egypt from Arab affairs was Britain's best policy remained as strong in July, 1936 as before. Lampson warned London that Egyptian involvement in the Saudi mediation would "increase the weight" of the general Arab attitude, and would bring Egypt directly into Palestinian and Arab affairs, "which we have so far succeeded in avoiding".[42]

Lampson's objection was readily accepted in London. He and the rest of the British representatives in the Middle East were instructed to take steps intended not only to restrain the anti-British agitation in Egypt, but also to insulate Palestine from her neighbouring countries, including Egypt. Following London's instructions, British officials in Cairo made several representations to Nahhas to restrain the press. When they feared that his preventive measures were not succeeding, they intervened directly; Smart requested Party leaders such as Muhammad Mahmud, to avoid criticising British Palestinian policy.[43] In addition, British officials in Egypt and Palestine took censorship measures to prevent any movement of persons and news from Palestine to Egypt and vice versa.[44]

However, although these restrictions remained in force until late October, 1936,[45] the outlook of British officials in Cairo concerning the conflict began changing as early as August, 1936. At that date Lampson first began claiming that Anglo-Egyptian relations were dependent on, and subject to, British Palestinian policy.[46] Part of the reason for this changing outlook was the conviction that a new Arab state of mind was developing in Egypt. The strong emotional reaction in Egypt to the plight of the Palestinian Arabs shattered the belief that a deep emotional and practical gap existed between Egyptians and Arabs. By September, 1936, Kelly, Lampson's second in command of the Embassy, already suggested looking into the possibility of exploiting the new pan-Arab factor to British advantage. "After all", he said, there was "nothing intrinsically fantastic in the vision of a Near Eastern 'Little Entente' headed by Egypt and working in close harmony with HMG"[47]

There were, however, other pragmatic reasons which affected this changing attitude towards the Palestine conflict. Lampson maintained that Britain lacked adequate forces in the area to quell the ensuing troubles; then there were the Italians, who were only waiting to take advantage of Arab hostility to Britain's Palestinian policy; lastly even Anglo-Egyptian freindship was not safe as long as the Arab struggle in palestine continued. Egypt, Lampson explained, proud of her recent independence, and guided by an ambitious leader who sought prominence in the Arab world, could not ignore appeals from neighbouring Muslim countries. There was always the opposition just waiting to take advantage of such appeals. In light of all these dangers, Lampson "earnestly urged" that Britain should initiate a new regional policy which would consider the Palestine issue in connection with the overall British position in the Middle East.[47]

Lampson's pressing request to examine the Palestine issue in connection with the entire Middle Eastern policy was seriously considered in London. His report was distributed to the Cabinet and his views as the highest British representative in Britain's most important strategic stonghold in the Middle East must have carried significant weight. It encouraged the impression built by numerous previous reports that the Palestine conflict rather than British or French presence in the area had become the core of Arab distress in the Middle East. All these reports fostered hopes that a solution meeting Arab demands in Palestine would not only appease the Arab world, but would also preserve Arab friendship with Britain and secure British interests and positions in the Middle East. Following all these reports, British policy makers abandoned the traditional policy which encouraged local nationalism, and set about initiating a new policy which would take into account the wishes of Arab countries, particularly Saudi-Arabia , regarding Palestine.[49]

Nevertheless, while Lampson's reports helped create a new pan-Arab policy, they did not, and were not intended to, persuade the Foreign Office to hand Nahhas the mediatory role he sought. Part of the reason for British reluctance to permit Nahhas's mediation was the unacceptable substance of his proposals. These proposals, which Nahhas first disclosed to British officials in Cairo, tied any Egyptian intervention in the conflict to a halt to Jewish immigration into Palestine. While in Europe, Nahhas reiterated these proposals. He first discussed this issue with the Foreign Secretary, Anthony Eden, and the Colonial Secretary, Ormsby-Gore, and then with other British officials in Europe.[50] He repeated his offers to persuade the Palestinian Arabs to end the strike provided he was given a 'private' promise to stop Jewish immigration. Such a private promise, he maintained, was necessary "to avoid any appearance of a bargain between HMG and the Arab leaders and to save the <u>amour proper</u> of HMG".[51] Moreover, this assurance, he said, was needed because he, as the "Chief Arab leader", was the only person able to persuade the Mufti of Jerusalem to end the strike.[52]

The 'Chief Arab leader' naturally attempted, to persuade his British intermediary that Britain, first and foremost, should heed the Egyptian proposals. Needless to say, the failure or success of any negotiations with the Arabs depended largely, if not entirely, on the approval of the chief Arab leader rather than the ordinary public. In this statement, Nahhas, rather than describing his actual position, revealed his hidden ambitions. The leadership of the Arab world was to be the reward of his successful mediation. This mediation should have placed Nahhas in the position of being the only Arab politician able to negotiate with British officials on an Arab question. To this goal, Nahhas was obviously prepared to approach British officials time and again.

It is quite clear that in making these proposals, Nahhas was expecting to promote his reputation rather than preserve British interests as he had pretended. His opposition to the appearance of a bargain between HMG and the Arab leaders obviously did not deter him from advocating his own bargain to British officials. His proposals, not surprisingly, were dismissed because British officials found other Arab mediators who at that time did not tie their mediation to clear-cut conditions.

Nahhas's proposals and the particular manner in which they were made sheds some interesting light on his Arab approach. Although advertising himself as "the Chief Arab leader", his entire approach remained, in fact, non-Arab, if not anti-Arab. In times when Arab leaders were contemplating a joint stand concerning the conflict, one cannot find even a single Egypto-Arab encounter concerning this issue. Moreover, when British officials asked him about the possibility of the Egyptian King joining the Arab declaration, he rejected the proposed step. Having been perhaps concerned that the King may intervene in a field that he himself had set his eyes on, the Chief Arab leader objected to any Egyptian participation in the joint Arab Kings' letter. Egypt, Nahhas argued, should be left alone as "a card to be played later", in case the Arab letter proved futile.[53]

The mild Egyptian reaction to the Arab Kings' letter might reflect the amount of Egyptian support and sympathy with such a move. Nahhas was still on vacation in Europe and did not find the letter warranted a response. Upon the publication of the Kings' letter, his Acting Prime Minister, Wasif Butrus Ghali, delivered a statement congratulating the goodwill of the British government as well as the wise counsel of the Arab rulers. However, the statement, which expressed hope for an era of peace and prosperity in Palestine,[54] lacked any support for the Palestinian Arabs. Consequently it was bitterly criticised by the Palestinian Arab press.[55]

This criticism did not appear to change Nahhas's pattern of intervention in the conflict. Although he renewed his initiative after the Arab Higher Committee had declared a boycott against the Royal Commission in November, 1936, he still avoided any contact with other

Palestinian Arab or Arab leaders. Rather, he reminded British officials that he had been correct in refusing to sign the ineffective letter of the Arab Kings. Once again he asked for an immediate halt to Jewish immigration as a condition for his proposed call to the Palestinian Arabs to stop their boycott.[56]

Once again this initiative was firmly rejected by British officials who suspected his true intentions. Lampson was instructed not to let Nahhas believe that by helping to persuade Palestinian Arabs to co-operate with the Royal Commission, he would be placing HMG under any obligation to him.[57]

E.   Egypt and the Arab movement, 1936-1937

The ambivalent nature of Egypt's Arab approach at that period was also demonstrated in the actual policy towards Arab countries.   In public and in conversations with British officials, Egyptian leaders stated both their sympathy for, and ties with, the Arabs. Nonetheless, they showed a marked reluctance to translate this sympathy into action. Few practical steps were taken towards closer relations with Arab countries.   In August, 1936, 'Azzam's duties as Minister pleni-potentiary and Consul-General were extended to Saudi Arabia.[58] The fact that one person only was to represent Egyptian interest in Iran, Iraq and Saudi Arabia, may illustrate the small amount of interest that the Wafdist Government really had in these countries.   It was as late as December, 1936, that the formation of an Oriental (not an Arab) Department in the Ministry of Foreign Affairs for organisation of propaganda in the East was first contemplated.[59]   Although the need for closer relations with the "sister" Arab countries was stressed on numerous occasions and even reiterated in the Speech from the Throne,[60] the Wafdist leaders not only showed little entusiasm for discussing Arab affairs with Arab leaders, but also obstructed various attempts to hold pan-Arab congresses in Cairo.

The first attempt to hold a pan-Arab Congress in Cairo apparently began as a result of an initiative of the Higher Arab Committee in Palestine. The Committee, having been concerned by the possibility of an unfavourable Report by the Royal Commission, thought to unite Arab opinion behind the Palestinian Arab stand by holding an all Arab Congress in Cairo at the end of 1936. The project, however, never materialised because of rejection by Wafdist politicians, intimating that "the moment was not suitable to hold the meeting in Egypt.[61] The calmness with which Wafdist representatives could reject this proposal indicates, perhaps, the small amount of support that the regime was in fact prepared to grant to the Palestinian Arabs, as well as the limited attraction of Arab issues in Egypt. Had the Palestinian Arab cause really been a popular issue in Egypt, it is doubtful whether Wafdist politicians could or would have ignored such a project so easily without facing the negative reactions of public opinion.

The second attempt to hold a pan-Arab Congress in Cairo was also made in December, 1936. During a reception that Basyuni's Arab Bond Association held for the members of the Ninth Near Eastern Medical Congress, the possibility was raised of convening an all-Arab Congress in Cairo at some unspecified time in the near future. The aims of this Congress differed considerably from that initiated by the Palestinian Arabs. This one lacked any politicial intentions and was expected to concentrate only on the promotion of cultural links among the Arab countries.[62] Nevertheless, in spite of rumours that Nahhas himself was in favour of the cultural aims of this Congress,[63] he did little to encourage the project. In fact, his reluctance to assist the Congress may also have influenced Basyuni to remove his own support for the project. Basyuni was reported to have rejected the idea on the ground that his position as President of the Senate prevented him from being "associated with activities likely to acquire a political complexion."[64] His lukewarm attitude to the project led to a split in the Society, which in turn brought about its paralysis.[65]

None of the pan-Arab cultural projects discussed during this period in Egypt ever materialised. In spite of various projects to unite the programme of studies in the Arab medical schools, to hold annual student Congresses, and to form a Society for the Unification of Arab Culture (Jam'iya li-tawhid al-thaqafa al-'arabiyya) which would publish magazines and hold cultural conferences,[66] the first Arab cultural conference was not convened until 1947.[67]

Perhaps even more striking than these futile attempts to hold Congresses in Cairo was the Egyptian reaction to an official Iraqi proposal for a joint treaty. If the version of 'Abd al-Rahman 'Azzam, Egyptian Minister for Baghdad at the time, is to be trusted, the bearer of the new plan was Nuri al-Sa'id of Iraq. According to 'Azzam, Nuri had first approached him with the idea of an Egypto-Iraqi treaty during the summer of 1936. At the beginning of 1937, Nuri and Dr. Naji al-Asil made a further attempt to attract 'Azzam's support for this project. 'Azzam was by no means delighted by this plan. He believed that Egypt, even after the Anglo-Egyptian treaty, was too busy with her internal problems to take on further commitments. He also felt that there was "nothing much" in the plan, and Egypt could gain "nothing" by joining it.[68]

The reaction of 'Azzam to this idea raises some doubts as to the veracity of his description at the time as "a fanatical enthusiast for Arab Unity".[69] His own evidence certainly shattered Kelly's previous speculation, supported by the British Ambassador to Iraq, that 'Azzam was the one who planted in Nuri's mind the idea of a pan-Arab Entente.[70] Beneath his pan-Arab guise, 'Azzam revealed a keen zeal for Egyptian interests, and showed little passion for sacrificing Egyptian interest solely for a pan-Arab cause. It may also be that the passionate pan-Arab ambitions of the Iraqis deterred 'Azzam and encouraged his suspicions concerning their true intentions.

British officials in Cairo, having created an impression of 'Azzam as a fanatical pan-Arabist, doubted the sincerity of his evidence and preferred to rely on the very optimistic report of the Iraqi Charge d'affaires in Cairo, who drew a rather different picture of Egyptian reception to the project. Nahhas, the Iraqi Charge d'affaires reported, "seemed to welcome the idea" of the treaty and even asked him to talk the proposal over with the Minister for Foreign Affairs, Wasif Butrus Ghali. Ghali, the Iraqi representative continued, also "had given the proposal a favourable reception and had spoken of a treaty in the nature of the Pact d'Entente Balkanique".[71]

British officials in Cairo and London were alarmed at these reports. The Egyptian Premier seemed to be preparing to negotiate an important treaty without consulting his British ally, thus breaching paragraph five of the Anglo-Egyptian Treaty. Moreover, the new treaty Nahhas seemed to have discussed might lead to increased Egypto-Arab co-operation with the Palestinian Arabs against both the Zionists and the British.[72] Some reaction was necessary, but which kind? Lampson beleived that public British opposition to Egypto-Arab co-operation was "dangerous" since such a project was popular and "inevitable". He thought it better to convince Nahhas that a separate treaty with Iraq was preferable to a Balkanic style Entente. In urgent discussions in London, Lampson's advice was accepted,[79] and Walter Smart, Oriental Secretary of the Residency, was sent to discuss the matter with Nahhas.

Smart must have been very surprised to discover that Nahhas was not quite so enthusiastic about the whole project as the Iraqi Charge d'affaires in Cairo had believed. Nahhas stated that he "wished first to consolidate Egypt's own position", and that he had informed both Ghali and 'Azzam that "he was too busy with other things for the moment and that, before starting on such an affair, he must consult the British".[74]

This ambivalent diplomacy -- expressing in public and in private meetings with Arab delegates his devotion to pan-Arab issues, while at the same time declaring his reservations about these issues before his confidants and British representatives-- characterised Nahhas's Government until its fall at the end of 1937. Thus, on his way to the Montreux Conference Nahhas promised that upon his return he would encourage the creation of political, economic and cultural ties between

Egypt and the Arab countries, including treaties between the Eastern and Islamic countries and Egypt's entry into the Arab Alliance (al-Hilf al-'Arabi).[75] In the light of such statements, which drew attention to the Iraqi programme, it is hardly surprising that public debates continued to take place over the method of establishing Arab solidarity.[76] What did in fact result from the grandiose pan-Arab Entente evnisaged by Nuri was a modest draft of an unremarkable commerial agreement between Egypt and Iraq, which dealt with certain specific and restricted products.[77]

F. Egypt's Arab approach and the Palestine conflict

The Palestine conflict, being an Arab issue and representing a pan-Arab interest, elicited a similar ambivalent attitude in Egyptian politicians. In public, Egyptian politicians were very receptive towards the Arab cause on the various occasions during which this cause was raised. Thus, for example, during a reception held for a Palestinian Arab delegation in Cairo, one of the leading figures of the Wafd, Makram 'Ubayd, forecast the amalgamation of the local nationalities, Egyptian as well as Palestinian, into one powerful Eastern-Arab nationality. To emphasise this point 'Ubayd did not hesitate to describe Safiya Zaghlul, "the Mother of the Egyptians", as "the Mother of the Easterners".[77] The new Egyptian Consul to Jerusalem, Ahmad Ramzi, developed this image even further. Upon his arrival in Jerusalem, he anticipated relations between Egypt and Palestine to improve significantly because his Governement had decided to strengthen cultural and economic relations with Palestine.[79]

As long as such statements needed no practical proof, their

reliability and sincerity could not be tested. The inclination of numerous Egyptian visitors to Palestine to express their unconditional support for the Palestinian struggle on behalf of their country might have only provided further assurance for Palestinian Arabs that Egypt was entirely committed to their cause. Thus, during one of these tours, a professor in an Egyptian academic group vowed that the Egyptians would not rest until the Palestinian Arabs achieved their independence. He promised that Egypt and the Egyptian people would sacrifice everything "to defend your honour which is ours, and your country which is also ours".[80]

The difficulties arose when the Egyptian Government were asked to translate these emotional undertakings into practical aid to the Palestinian Arabs. The appointment in March, 1937, of an economic attache to the Egyptian Consulate in Jerusalem,[81] did not encourage significant commerce between the two nations. An Egyptian commercial delegation which came to Palestine in the second half of 1937 -- later than expected -- gave prominence to Egyptian national interests rather than to sentiments of pan-Arab solidarity. The delegates were mainly concerned with reducing the Palestinian tariff on Egyptian exports of vegetables, and showed a marked reluctance to reduce the high Egyptian tariff that had been imposed on Palestinian exports to Egypt.[82]

Egyptian reluctance to increase economic and political co-operation with Arabs was not only noticed by Arab nationalists such as Yusuf Haykal,[83] and Sati' al-Husri.[84] The Zionists also did not seem unduly alarmed by Egyptian support for the Palestinian Arabs. The reports sent at that time by Nahum Vilenski, the representative of the Political Department of the Jewish Agency in Egypt, were, in fact, rather optimistic. Upon his arrival in Cairo as head of the "Eastern Agency", Vilenski began cultivating close relations with local politicians as well as Arab nationalists. He discussed with 'Alluba the possibility of direct negotiations between the Palestinian Arab leaders and Zionist representatives[85] and was further involved in attempts to bring Zionist and Arab leaders together to settle the Palestine conflict.[86]

Egyptian and Arab responses to these attempts was very positive. 'Alluba, for example, was most receptive towards his new Zionist friend's proposal to initiate an Arab-Jewish accord. 'Alluba disclosed to Vilenski that he considered the prospect of an Arab-Jewish entente as "un titre de gloire, et le courounement de mon activite politique".[87] Loyal to this statement, 'Alluba took part in subsequent attempts to persuade Palestinian Arab leaders to discuss a solution to the conflict with Zionist leaders in Cairo.[88] When these attempts failed, because of the refusal of the Palestinian Arab leaders to negotiate a settlement with the Zionists without preconditions, 'Alluba expressed his disenchantment with the Palestinian Arab leaders.[89]

'Alluba was not the only Egyptian advocate of Arabism whose pragmatic attitude towards the Zionists varied substantially from both the Palestinian Arab stand and his own previous statements. A similar ambiguity also characterised the journalist, Mahmud 'Azmi. He negotiated with Zionist activists the possibility of promoting the

Zionist cause throughout the Arab world,[90] while criticising in public this very cause.

This ambivalent attitude towards the Palestine conflict also prevailed in the Arabic press in Egypt. Popular Arabic newspapers, such as al-Ahram and al-Misri, did not think it immoral to advertise the Zionist achievements in their pages. This publicity, which was assisted consistently by Vilenski's propaganda machinery in Egypt,[91] helped to neutralise the opposite campaign in the press for the Palestinian Arabs.

The state of tranquility in Palestine during the inquiry of the Royal Commission further diminished public interest in the conflict. Domestic problems again occupied the Arabic press in Egypt, and "little attention was paid to the future of Palestine".[92] As far as interest in the Peel Commission was concerned, the press expressed all shades of opinion. One of the more influential dignitaries who took the opportunity to put forward his own views about the solution of the conflict was Prince Muhammad 'Ali. In May 1937, the Prince presented High Commissioner, Wauchope with a scheme to solve the conflict. The Prince suggested that the time was ripe to fulfil the First World War promise to create the Arab Empire. "Syria, Palestine and Trans-Jordan should constitute this Arab Empire. The British Government would remain in Jerusalem and Haifa as efficient police and observers to safeguard their interests and to keep their word towards the Jews... France should remain in Beirouth and Tripoli for the same purpose... The whole Empire would be divided into 'Cantons' or 'States' on the model of Switzerland or the U.S.A., each of which would be governed by its own people... The Mohamedan Arabic element would thus get the satisfaction that is due to it and at the same time the Jews would have a zone on the coast under British jurisdiction".[93]

The Prince did not elaborate on who the Emperor of this Empire should be; how England should persuade France to give up her hold on Syria; or how the Palestinian Arabs could be persuaded to give up some of their land to foreign elements. One cannot be sure what the Prince's views on these issues were, but it is quite certain that the Prince was eager to advertise his scheme. His "private and confidential" communication to Wauchope soon became known to the public through the Prince's good friend, Dr. Nimr, the editor of al-Muqat-tam.[94] Upon publication of the Prince's proposal, the Egyptian magazine al-Dunya asked pan-Arab advocates such as 'Alluba, Shahaban-dar, and 'Abd al-Hamid Sa'id, for their opinion. By and large all of them expressed satisfaction with the project.[95] The Prince's plan was reported to have been the subject of further "impromptu conferences" held in Damascus between Syrian, Iraqi and Palestinian Arab nationalists. The discussions, in which the Mufti of Jerusalem also participated, ranged inconclusively over the selection of a ruler for the projected Empire. 'Azmi, the Egyptian participant in these conversations, did not think that the Prince's project indicated any Egyptian interest in Arab affairs. In fact, even he, one of the keenest advocates of Arabism in Egypt, believed that Egypt was not deeply concerned with the Palestine problem, and that she would "always" remain outside pan-Arab or pan-islamic confederations.[96]

G. Egyptian reaction to Peel's recommendation of partition

The initial reaction of the Egyptian press to Peel's report justified 'Azmi's claim that Egypt was not deeply committed to the Arab cause. The publication of the Peel Report by the Egyptian Press was a result of British pressure rather than an independent or spontaneous Egyptian reaction. High Commissioner Wauchope had asked all the British Ambassadors in neighbouring countries to ensure an "impartial response" by the Arabic Press to the Report; Lampson reluctantly agreed to this request, although he pointed out that this publicity might give the Report an "importance that might not automatically be attracted to it".[97] Following the publication of the Peel Report, the full text in Arabic and English of the summary of the Report (with map) and the Statement of HMG were made available to the local press. Representatives of the leading daily newspapers were invited to collect copies, while further copies were sent to the principal weekly papers.[98] Consequently, the Arabic press was fully occupied with the reproduction of the texts, and "there was scarcely physical room for editorial comment" on the Report.[99] When such room was available, the reaction was cautious. Mahmud Abu al-Fath, editor of al-Misri, strongly recommended that Muslims, Christians and Jews give the project their careful consideration before expressing any opinion. Amin Sa'id of al-Muqattam remained equally non-committal.[100]

Rumours that the Nashashibi faction in Palestine had accepted the partition in principle and that St. John Philby, representing King Ibn-Sa'ud's views, had advised the Arabs to accept the Report, appeared to deter criticism against the Report.[101] Al-Ahram printed a proposal by Wolfenson (Ben-Ze'ev), a Jewish professor at the Egyptian

University, to convene a Round Table Conference between Jews and Arabs in order to discuss Peel's recommendations. The editor of al Ahram even expressed, albeit in private, his approval for such a proposal.[102] The official circles, aside from expressing their admiration for "the impartiality of the Report", were so involved in internal affairs that they showed "little interest" in it.[103] Some politicians even went as far as to approve the Report. During a reception, Dr. Ahmad Mahir, one of the Wafd's leading figures, expressed the opinion that Peel's partition plan "was the only workable solution". He could see no other solution to the problem, and added that he had said as much to many of his colleagues.[104]

Attacks against the Report emanated at that time mainly from two opposite sides, namely the supporters of the Revisionist faction of the Zionist movement,[105] and the Palestinian Arab advocates in Egypt.[106] The great majority of the Arabic press in Egypt appeared to be still waiting for "a lead [how to treat the Report] from countries other than Palestine."[107]

The press reaction to the Report convinced Lampson that the Muslim section, namely the vast majority of public opinion was "not wildly interested in Palestine". It was, he reported, the criticism of the Iraqi Premier, Hikmat Sulayman, rather than internal Egyptian agitation, that turned the balance against partition. Lampson estimated that Hikmat Sulayman's criticism affected Egypt's Arabic Press as a "bombshell". It provided this press with the lead it had been looking for. The leading Arabic newspapers quickly altered their non-committal stand and hurried to attack the Report. The subsequent news that neither the Nashashibis nor the Saudis supported partition, promoted expectations for a similar Egyptian reaction. "The eyes of the Arab world", wrote al-Ahram, "are turned towards Egypt".[108]

The Egyptian Opposition was the first to respond favourably to Arab expectations. Muhammad Mahmud, leader of the Liberal Constitutionalists, hurried to assure the Mufti of Jerusalem that "all Egyptians who believed in the Arab and Islamic cause" supported Palestinian Arab rights. Mahmud further promised, though still in opposition, Egypt's assistance for the fulfilment of these rights. Nahhas's silence was denounced by the Opposition as a further demonstration of his dependence on Britain, and Husayn Haykal, of the Opposition, put down a question to Nahhas in the Senate enquiring about Egypt's policy regarding the Palestine question and Arab countries in general.[109]

Nahhas was furious. Haykal's question was not a sincere expression of solidarity with the Arab cause, but merely "a plot to embarrass him". Similarly, he saw the Iraqi reaction as consisting of "irresponsible indiscretions". "How came it", he asked Lampson, "that the leader of a friendly and allied government could do such a thing"?[110] Expressing his own true friendship to Great Britain, he invited Lampson to advise him "as to the line to adopt in reply" to Haykal's question.[111]

As a result of Lampson's advice, Nahhas's reply was far more moderate than the Iraqi attack on the Report, though not less passionate regarding Arab solidarity. Nahhas opened his reply with a statement that his Government was "most anxious to strengthen the cordial and brotherly bonds between Egypt and the Arab Nations", but before taking any definite action in a particular matter, the Government would not consider it in Egypt's interest to express beforehand their aims or intentions. He disclosed that his Government had been holding discussions on the Palestine question with British representatives since the summer of 1936. He assured the Senate of the pains he had taken to safegurd the rights and interests of the Arabs "in that country which includes the holy places to which Egypt was bound by glorious religious and historical memories". However, his Government did not consider it in the interest of Egypt or of Palestine to discuss the matter in public. He requested that Haykal's question be withdrawn. The Senate accepted the Premier's request.[112]

Nahhas's reply was received with "acclamation" by all the parties involved in the Palestine conflict. British officials involved in the drafting of that part of the statement which referred to Palestine, regarded the whole statement as "harmless".[113] Zionist officials, pleased by the fact that the Statement avoided rejection of partition, saw it as an indication of Nahhas's moderate attitude towards their movement.[114] The Palestinian Arab press also expressed satisfaction with Nahhas's statement, emphasising the commitment that Nahhas took towards the safeguarding of Arab rights in Palestine.[115] Nahhas encouraged this last impression. He sent the Mufti of Jerusalem a copy of his Parliamentary reply as a proof intended to show the extent of his interest in the Palestinian Arab cause.[116]

While Nahhas was defending his secretive policy on Palestine in the Egyptian Parliament, the Peel Report was exposed to a far more devastating attack in the British Parliament in July 1937. The climax of this criticism was the impressive speech made by Sir Herbert Samuel, which rejected partition and cast doubts about the wisdom of creating an indeplendent Jewish state in Palestine.[117] This criticism obviously did not help in either restraining criticism or encouraging a favourable reception of the Peel Report in Arab countries, including Egypt.Indeed, if highly respected politicians in Britain raised their voices against partition, why should Egyptian politicians as well as other Arab leaders remain silent over this issue?

It should not, therefore, be surprising that the Report aroused considerable criticism in Arab countries. Once again Arab leaders attempted to consolidate a common Arab stand concerning this issue. Subsequently, Nahhas was approached by various Arab representatives with offers to participate in a joint Arab statement against the partition of Palestine. In July, 1937, he was asked by the Saudi Minister in Cairo-- apparently on instructions from Ibn-Sa'ud-- to join Iraq, Syria, Yemen and Saudi Arabia in working out some joint scheme of protest against partition. Nahhas rejected the proposal on the grounds that it was "far wiser to keep his hands entirely free, and thus not cramp his potential utility as ally of Great Britain to help either with his own initiative or as an intermediary between Britain and other Arab States".[118] Nahhas further rejected a Palestinian Arab appeal to bring about his participation in the Arab Conference of Bludan (Syria), and even dismissed a proposal to induce all other Arab Governments to delegate him as their spokesman against partition. "The time has not yet come", he argued.[119]

The time indeed had not yet come because during this period Nahhas was taking pains to persuade British officials that he alone could convince the other Arab countries to accept his own proposal to end the conflict. While using common Arab feeling as a reason for this intervention in the Palestine conflict, Nahhas refused to take part in a joint Arab initiative to exert pressure on Britain to give up partition. If Britain was going to abandon Peel's scheme of partition anyhow, as the mounting opposition to the project in London might have indicated, why should all the Arab countries share the credit as defenders of Arab interests? Why should Nahhas and Egypt alone not gain the prestige of an expected British concession for the Palestinian Arabs?

Once again the Egyptian initiative started with a rejection of Arab co-operation. Nahhas told Lampson that his non-co-operation with Arab countries was a proof of his loyalty to the British ally. However, he warned that Egypt could not acquiesce in the creation of an independent Jewish State on her borders. "Apart from questions of defence etc." he argued, "who could say that the voracious Jews would not claim Sinai next? Or provoke trouble with the Jewish community in Egypt itself"?[120]

The use of such an anti-Semitic expression as "voracious Jews" by Nahhas indicates, perhaps, the growing impact of anti-Jewish propaganda of Nazi Germany in Egypt. Nahhas who held talks with Hitler and his Minister of Propaganda, Dr. Joseph Goebbels, during his visit to Berlin in 1936,[121] might have been affected by their anti-Semitism. Pan-Islamic Societies, such as the YMMA, the Muslim Brethren and Young Egypt (<u>Misr al-Fatat</u>), also fostered this anti-Jewish outlook by warning the public against the mighty economic power of the Jews.[122] The fears expressed even by educated Egyptians against the creation of a Jewish State on the Egyptian borders[123] may indicate that this propaganda had gained some ground in Egypt.

However, the Jewish threat to Egypt's security was not the sole argument with which Nahhas attempted to persuade Lampson that he was the ideal mediator for the conflict. When Lampson reminded him of Britain's pledge to establish a Jewish national home, Nahhas dismissed it as "madness". "Why should HMG deliberately estrange the whole Arab world as they seemed set on doing"? , he asked. "Italy was only waiting to profit by it." The "only" solution that he "as genuine friend, supporter and ally of Great Britain" urged Lampson to consider was the creation of "an independent Arab State allied with Great Britain and with fullest guarantees of religious and racial toleration for the Jews, Arabs and Moslems alike. There should be Jewish immigration, but limited strictly to the normal absorptive capacity of the land". If Britain found this solution unacceptable, he concluded, then he should be allowed at least "to go on trying to devise ways out of the impasse".[124]

Nahhas's appeal was, this time, seriously considered in London. In the summer of 1937 the risk of letting Nahhas play the role he was seeking did not seem as dangerous to British interests in Egypt as it had a year before. "It is all a question of atmosphere", wrote a staff member of the British Embassy in Cairo to a colleague in London, explaining why they would not be able to succeed in persuading the Egyptian media to adopt a favourable attitude towards the Peel Report. Indeed, the whole atmosphere had changed. While Egypt's Arab identification became more pronounced, British policy in Palestine was losing its precise direction. There was no use in trying to persuade the Egyptian press to favour the idea of partition as long as that idea was questioned in London itself. It was equally useless to deny Egypt the right to protest against partition as long as such protests were freely expressed in other Arab countries. In view of growing Arab feeling in Egypt, any intervention to silence protest against partition might have led to strong anti-british feelings. Moreover, the relatively moderate reaction of the leading Arabic newspapers in Egypt to the Peel Report could have been used to influence Arab public opinion. Why not use the powerful affect of this press to moderate the attitude of other Arab public opinion? It was, therefore, better to create a current of opinion in Egypt which, while not "the exact opposite of the declared aspirations of the Arab world", attempted "to break the powerful stream of destructive criticism into small currents of constructive ideas".[125] Furthermore, Nahhas's response to the Peel Report showed him to be a loyal British ally. While the Iraqi Premier surprised British officials with his unexpected criticism, Nahhas was consulting consistently with British officials. While Arab leaders were looking for an all-Arab approach, Nahhas refused co-operation, and insisted on approaching the British alone. Such a friendly attitude could not simply be ignored. Nahhas was, therefore, thanked for both his refusal to be drawn into collective action and his discouragement of local agitation. He was further told that while Britain viewed Peel's recommendation as "the best hope" of a future solution, "an opportunity would be afforded after the League of Nations' expression of opinion, for a full examination of the situation with representatives of both Arabs and Jews".[126]

The British reply appeared to encourage Nahhas's desire to play a more active role in the conflict. If the Palestine question was going to be raised in Geneva, Nahhas declared, then despite difficulties at home, he would leave for Geneva entirely on account of Palestine. "Otherwise", he maintained, "Arabs would reproach him with lack of interest". He regarded his expected trip as a "duty" owing to his dual role as friend and ally of HMG, and his deep interest in the Arab cause.

To demonstrate, perhaps, his high regard for this issue, Nahhas presented Lampson with a paper prepared, he said, by the Egyptian Government as a guideline for the official stand regarding the Palestine conflict. The five pages of this document, described as instructions to the Egyptian delegation to Geneva,[128] were an impressive collation of the up-to-date views on the conflict in Egypt. Egyptian interest in Palestine was attributed to geographical proximity, Arab and Islamic ties, and the Anglo-Egyptian alliance. Egypt's rejection of the partitioning of Palestine was based on nine points. Among them were Britain's First World War promises for Arab independence; the 'Natural Law' which protected Palestinians from being driven out of their country by foreign immigrants; a rejection of a religious style state which would "bring back the hateful spirit of the Crusades"; and the fear of a Jewish State which might become a centre of propaganda of socialist doctrines "already professed by many Palestinian Jews". The proposed solution to the problem was in the spirit of Nahhas's previous proposals, with the additional suggestion that the League should ask Britain to find a solution which would be acceptable to both parties and in which "they could count upon the help of Egypt".[129]

Although the instructions demonstrated an impressive manifestation of Egyptian feelings and interests concerning the conflict, it is doubtful whether Nahhas felt entirely committed to them. Presenting the directive to Kelly, Nahhas explained that those instructions were subject to "modifications", should the British have any reservations, and invited British comments.[130].

This kind of attitude towards his own official stand sheds further light on Nahhas's ambiguity towards the conflict. While attempting to establish his pan-Arab image by passionate statements like the ones in the directive, Nahhas at the same time sought to appease British officials by refusing to carry the burden of any practical commitment implied by his pan-Arab position. It is noteworthy that the official Egyptian attitude towards the crucial issue of Jewish immigration was not exactly a reflection of the Palestinian Arab stance and demands. While the Palestinian Arabs persisted with calls for an immediate halt to further Jewish immigration into Palestine, Nahhas condoned it, though only on a limited basis.

Moreover, in spite of his promise to fulfil his 'duty' by going to

Geneva, Nahhas remained in Cairo during the annual meeting of the League of Nations. The increasing threat to his regime by the new coalition of the Opposition and the Palace was evidently deemed more important than representing the Arab cause abroad. Instead, Nahhas sent his Minister for Foreign Affairs, Wassif Butrus Ghali, to represent Egypt's position regarding the Palestine question. During the League session in September, 1937, Ghali delivered two speeches presenting his Government's stand regarding the Palestine conflict. By and large, Ghali followed the instructions that had been prepared by the Government. He ignored, however, the alleged socialist threat of the Jews, apparently being concerned at the adverse affects that this accusation could have on the socialist members of the League. Ghali also included in his speeches, several phrases praising the Jews which, in light of the zealous anti-Zionist speech of the Iraqi delegate, furthered the image of Egypt as having a moderate attitude towards the conflict.[131]

It should not be surprising that following these speeches, both Zionists and Palestinian Arabs believed that Egypt supported their side.[132] It was, of course, the Palestinian Arabs rather than the Zionists whom the Egyptian leader took pains to placate. Although he refused to take part in the Congress of Bludan, Nahhas sent his personal confidant, Amin 'Uthman, to discuss the situation in Palestine with the Mufti of Jerusalem, under a pledge not to inform the British authorities of the trip.[133]

British officials in Cairo, who at first had been "shocked" at what appeared to be a secretive and treacherous move against them, were

quickly assuaged when they learnt that not only was 'Uthman restricted
to convey Egypt's Palestinian stand at the League of Nations, but also
his tour was soon published in all the Arabic newspapers.[134]   By
and large, British officials in Cairo remained unimpressed by the
response of the various Egyptian stratas to the Palestine conflict. In
October, 1937, more than a year after he had first begun to warn London
of the emergence of an Arab state of mind in Egypt, Kelly deemed it
necessary to inform his superiors what the real scope of this changing
outlook was. Kelly assumed that Nahhas would have gladly played the
role of a "leader of Arab opinion" had not his time been completely
taken up with his anxieties as Premier. The views of opposition
leaders such as Muhammad Mahmud and Sidqi seemed to Kelly to be
"largely coloured by their desire of making local political capital out
of the question". Kelly was doubtful whether either of them had
"personally any strong feelings for the Arab cause". The educated
middle classes also expressed, according to Kelly, "little interest" in
the problem because they had "hardly any instinctive sympathy with the
Arabs as such", and were busy with their "own professional affairs".
The educated Egyptian women were also influenced by Europe rather than
by the Arabs, "whose outlook they regard as benighted and retrograde".
Even 'the masses' showed "little interest in the matter" because they
were kept busy "earning their daily bread". The main supporters of the
Palestinian Arabs were to be found among the al-Azhar circles and
within the Palestinian Arab emigres in Egypt and the pan-Arab and
Islamic associations there. Kelly maintained, however, that their
"agitation" could not affect the general Egyptian "apathy" towards the

conflict.[135]

Kelly's views are very interesting not only because they provide additional weight to similar evidence from Egyptian, American, German, Arab and Zionist sources.[136] It was Kelly, who, by calling attention to the emergence of an Arab state of mind in Egypt, attempted to persuade his superiors to adopt an 'Arab policy' which would favour the Arab rather than the Zionist stand in the conflict. The narrow perspectives of this Arab state of mind a year after Kelly had first alerted London may illustrate how small and unimpressive was the ground gained by Arabism during this period.

Kelly, indeed, warned London again not to take too sanguine an attitude to the current Egyptian indifference to the conflict. Egypt's Islamic ties, the Opposition's temptation to attack the Government, and the ambitions of the present leadership, particularly the Palace, to play a greater role in the area, were factors which could provoke "an articicial and inconvenient interest in the Arab cause in Palestine."[137]

However, until Nahhas's dismissal at the end of 1937, none of these factors really provoked any interest in the Palestine conflict. By and large, the public's and politicians' eyes remained focused on domestic affairs, and shifted only marginally and sporadically to events in Palestine. These sporadic shifts were dictated by developments in Palestine rather than by internal Egyptian initiatives.

One such upsurge of sympathy erupted following the proclamation of Martial Law in Palestine, and the dissolution of the Higher Arab Committee. Palestinian Arab leaders such as 'Awni 'Abd al-Hadi and

Munif al-Husayni, who fled to Cairo, revitalised the propaganda campaign for the Arab cause in Palestine. 'Awni became the leading figure in the Syro-Palestinian Executive which intended to replace the Higher Arab Committee.[138] The new campaign was supported by the pan-Arab and Islamic associations in Egypt[139] and by traditional supporters of the Palestinian Arab cause, such as 'Umar Tusun, and several newspapers, particularly al-Jihad.[140]

Nevertheless, this campaign never turned into a national issue involving all political, social and intellectual circles. Although the Government only reluctantly complied with a British request not to grant the Mufti asylum,[141] they never turned it into a bargaining issue. By this time Nahhas was already far too involved in internal politics to pay attention to the Palestinian Arab cause. Divisions within his Party, and the campaign of the Palace and the opposition against the Government's alleged corruption did not leave Nahhas, the opposition, or the media great time for the Arab cause.

An appeal signed by a group of 59 Deputies and Senators calling for recognition of the unquestionable rights of the Palestinian Arabs was given hardly any publicity.[142] The fact that 'Abd al-Hamid Sa'id, the author of this appeal, could achieve the support of only 59 members of Parliament to his initiative may illustrate the amount of support that the Palestinian Arab cause gained in Egypt. Perhaps the most illuminating example of the state of affairs in Egypt concerning the Palestinian Arabs at this period was a desperate call made by the proprietor of al-Jihad, Tawfiq Diyyab, who asked the public not to let internal affairs obscure the Palestine issue.[143]

CHAPTER TWO

MUHAMMAD MAHMUD'S GOVERNMENT AND THE

PALESTINE QUESTION, 1938-1939

A. Islam, politics and the Palestinian conflict, 1938

With the relegation of the Wafd into oppostion, all the factors
which Kelly had pointed out-- Egypt's Islamic ties; the Opposition's
reaction and the ever-growing ambitions of the Palace-- began playing a
role in provoking increasing Egyptian interest in the Palestinian Arab
cause. It was Muhammad Mahmud, Egypt's new Premier, who decided to
re-introduce Islam as a weapon in the internal political campaign in
Egypt. Upon his nomination at the end of 1937, Mahumud, leader of the
Liberal-Constitutionalists, began stirring Islamic feelings in Egypt.
Islam was not only portrayed as the remedy for the Wafd's alleged
corruption, but was also presented as the true national way of life
which had been blurred by the Coptic politicians of the Wafd. This
campaign, during which the Shaykh of al-Azhar, Mustafa al-Maraghi, was
allowed to preach on the radio for the adoption of the Qur'anic principles in the Egyptian Penal Code, aroused considerable religious tension. This tension sometimes took the form of Islamic demonstrations,
during which anti-Coptic banners bearing slogans such as "Copts go to
Palestine" were raised.[1]

This development, which may illustrate the ignorance of some of
the demonstrators of the sanctity of Palestine to Islam, encouraged
Muslim support for the Palestinian Arab cause. The combination of

news of the violence in Palestine with the excessive official freedom granted to Islamic propaganda, further encouraged the campaign for the Palestinian Arabs by pan-Islamic Societies. Old accusations describing Jewish intentions to take over the Haram and destroy the 'Umar and al-Aqsa Mosques were once again revived.[2] Pan-Islamic Societies, notably the YMMA, and the Ikhwan, held joint meetings with pro-Palestinian Arab groups, such as the Syro-Palestinian Committee, in which manifestos against partition and Britain's alleged atrocities in Palestine were drawn up and distributed.[3] By the end of April 1938, shortly after Mahmud had won the elections, this propaganda bore its first unpleasant fruits. Al-Azhar students, agitated by inciting speeches concerning alleged British brutalities in Palestine, rushed from their institute and marched to the Ministry of the Interior shouting anti-Jewish slogans. When they reached the Ministry, which was under the responsibility of the Premier, a delegation of the demonstrators met Mahmud and handed him a petition protesting against both partition and the Jews' alleged designs on al-Aqsa Mosque. Mahmud expressed sympathy with the cause of the demonstration, but warned the students not to interfere in politics and urged them to disperse. His call was ignored. After leaving him, the students met several Deputies and Senators and pleaded with them to raise the voice of Islam in Parliament. The following day more demonstrations broke out in Cairo and Alexandria.[4]

Mahmud was faced with a delicate situation; not only did the religious fervour with which he attempted to suppress the Wafd erupt beyond the Government's control, but it was also being used by rival political forces. The Wafd, the initial target of the Government's Islamic campaign, was exploiting the demonstrations to wage a new anti-British campaign with a view to reviving its own popularity.[5] Also, the Palace watched the demonstrations with keen interest. According to one report, 'Ali Mahir, Chief of the Royal Cabinet, was behind the Azhar agitation. His intention was to embarrass both Maraghi and Mahmud so that they would seek Palace intervention. The Palace was reported to have aspired to issue, as a peace-making step, a plan to link Palestine to Egypt as a part of its pan-Islamic aspirations.[6]

This news stirred Mahmud into action. He asked Lampson "most earnestly" for some British action "to remove this cause of Muslim discontent". He excused this request not by the need to assist the Palestinian Arabs, but rather to deny Nahhas any political capital out of the issue and save the country from following "an Islam lead on this question".[7]

Alongside this appeal, Mahmud also took other precautions to neutralise the adverse effect of Muslim discontent. While police dispersed the demonstrations and arrested a number of Palestinian Arab students. Mahmud approached his close friend Maraghi, and arranged for Maraghi to submit a petition to him regarding this issue. The Shaykh of al-Azhar's petition, the content of which was apparently also approved beforehand, reiterated the fears of alleged Jewish aspirations to control the Aqsa Mosque, and asked Mahmud to intervene in order to solve the Palestine conflict. Mahmud's greatly advertised reply helped secure his Islamic reputation. However, this was only

temporary, because the religious propaganda which provoked the demonstrations continued. Numerous articles, circulars, and manifestos
labelling the Jews as enemies of Islam continued to be published. They
in turn, contributed to a further demonstration during the festivities
of the Prophet's Birthday (<u>Mawlid al-Nabi</u>).Hundreds of al-Azhar students again burst out from the institution towards the Jewish quarter
of Cairo, beating and abusing Jewish merchants.[9]

The leaders of the Jewish community in Egypt became increasingly
concerned by this anti-Jewish atmosphere. They appealed to Mahmud to
protect them.[10] Mahmud promised his aid. He urged Lampson to ask
for an official British declaration denying any Jewish intentions on
the Haram.[11] In addition, the police made further arrests and
warned the leaders of the Palestinian Arab student community that they
would be expelled if they continued to meddle in politics.[12]

Maraghi, once again, was recruited to help to control the
agitation. He summoned the leaders of the Palestinian Arab students in
al-Azhar and warned them that on no account would the agitation against
Egyptian Jews be permitted. "If you want to demonstrate about your
country", he told the students, "that is your affair".[13]

Had the pan-Arab, pan-Islamic and political circles in Egypt
adopted Maraghi's views, namely that the developments in Palestine were
the affair of the Palestinians alone, Mahmud might not have encountered
substantial difficulties in suppressing the agitation. But this was
not to be the case. Maraghi's disbelief in the likelihood of Arab
unity[14] was overshadowed by the sympathy towards Arabism expressed
by religious fundamentalist circles in Egypt and by all major political

circles in Egypt.[15] Mahmud's coalition Government, for example, included figures such as Baha al-Din Barakat, Muhammad 'Isa, Husayn Haykal, and Ahmad Khashaba, who had more than once publicly expressed their support for Arabism and for the Palestinian Arab cause. British officials in London even suspected that "at least" two ministers in this Cabinet were, prior to their taking office, "active propagandists for, and may be even furnishing financial assistance to the Palestinian Arabs".[16] Husayn Haykal, Minister of Education in this Government, gave 'Awni 'Abd al-Hadi the impression that he was aware of "the danger that the Zionist dream posed regarding Egypt". Even Lutfi al-Sayyid, a Minister without Portfolio, who had totally rejected Egyptian involvement in Arab affairs two decades before, expressed sympathy with the Palestinian Arabs. He told 'Awni that the conflict, which had been caused by the British military power and the Jewish financial ability, had reached a stage where it could be solved only by the annihilation (fana)of either the Arabs or the Jews. In these circumstances, Lutfi believed that the power of right (the Arabs) would overcome might.[17]

Similar sympathy for the Palestinian Arabs was also manifested in Parliament. Several Deputies, such as 'Alluba, 'Abd al-Hamid Sa'id, and Tawfiq Doss, contemplated sending a Parliamentary delegation to testify before the Woodhead Commission in Palestine on the dangers of partition.[18] Although they decided not to go, they continued their independent activity over this issue in Egypt. On 28th May, 1938, 'Alluba, induced by appeals for help from the Mufti of Jerusalem, invited some 25 persons to his house to discuss assistance for the

Palestinian Arabs. The discussion culminated in a decision to form a Permanent Parliamentary Committee. This was intended to co-ordinate action with Parliamentarians of other Arab and Islamic countries concerning Palestine.[19]

The formation of this Committee, which marked the inception of the Inter-Parliamentary Congress, took place during the Parliamentary debate on Palestine. In the Senate, Shaykh 'Abd al-Sattar al-Basil, a member of the Arab Unity Association, delivered an emotional speech asking that Egypt, being "an Arab and Islamic Kingdom", should intervene to stop the slaughter of innocent Arabs and Muslims in Palestine.[20] In the Chamber of Deputies, 'Abd al-Hamid Sa'id, Shaykh 'Abd al-Latif Draz, a member of the YMMA, and Inspector of Religious Studies in al-Azhar, and Muhammad Abu Rahab put down questions concerning Jewish intentions on both the Haram and Palestine. They maintained that Egypt, as "the leader of the present Arab revival and the protector of the holy places", should act firmly against these intentions. Mahmud promised, as Nahhas had done before, to provide through diplomatic channels a solution which would "ensure Palestinian Arab rights" and would "satisfy the Arab world". However, in contrast to Nahhas's reply, Mahmud's statement was met with shouts that this was not enough.[21] Shortly after this debate, 'Alluba was able to present the British Embassy in Cairo with a petition backed by the signatures of more than 160 Deputies and Senators, almost three times as many as the previous Parliamentary petition. 'Alluba's petition called for both a halt to Jewishimmigration and the formation of a constitutional Government in Palestine.[22]

It is doubtful whether this Parliamentary petition supporting the Palestinian Arabs could have been put together without Mahmud's approval. The Parliament, particularly after the elections which resulted in a major victory for the coalition parties, was not much more than a rubber stamp for the Government's policy. Although the questions by the pan-Islamic deputies were probably genuine, they were not highly considered. Mahmud's Director General of Public Security regarded the pan-Islamic Societies as a kind of "safety valve", which could "do little, if any harm". These societies, he said, were "trivial" lacking any "background"; their members were "of no importance" and consequently their opinion carried "no weight with influential Egyptians".[23]

Neither the religious nor the social activity of these societies aroused Mahmud's concern. He was, however, concerned about the inclination of both the Wafd and the Palace to advance their partisan aims through the religious appeal of the pan-Islamic societies in the street. The Wafd was attempting to incite the street against the Government through the Ikhwan. The Wafd was reported to have provided the Ikhwan with funds to stir up public unrest. Both the Wafd and the Ikhwan were further reported to have co-operated in initiating joint demonstrations in various Egyptian towns.[24]

In addition, Wafdist newspapers, in spite of official refutations, reiterated allegations concerning Jewish intentions on the Haram. Maraghi's silence was criticised and even the Premier himself was attacked. Wafdist newspapers attributed to him a view that Zaghlul was known to have expressed before. According to a Wafdist report, Mahmud announced in England that he was the Prime Minister of Egypt, not of

Palestine, thus hinting that he intended to discuss Anglo-Egyptian relations alone.[25] That such a statement could not pass without criticism was an indication of the changing atmosphere in Egypt regarding the conflict.

Nevertheless, aside from growing verbal support for Arab Palestine, this changing atmosphere failed to produce greater material aid for the Palestinian Arabs. Wafdist leaders assured Palestinian Arabs of their support for the Arab cause. They even initiated a fund-raising campaign for the Palestinian Arabs.[26] But the funds collected for this cause were reported to have been transferred to the Party's own account.[27]

Lampson, who was aware of the small practical aid given to the Palestinian Arabs, was nevertheless irritated by the anti-British activities of the Wafd. He requested Mahmud to suppress the religious agitation.[28] Mahmud was not keen to comply with this request. Although he suppressed the activities of the Palestinian Arab community in Egypt,[29] Mahmud allowed the Government media to advocate the Palestinian Arab cause. Thus, pro-Government newspapers ridiculed the Wafd for its sudden hypocritical interest in Palestine; Maraghi's endeavours for the Palestinian Arab cause were acclaimed, and he was permitted to summon the Body of the 'Ulama for a special meeting which rejected partition and called for co-operation between the Islamic countries for the protection of Palestine.[30] Mahmud himself, to demostrate the Government's sympathy with the Palestinian cause, contemplated an official financial contribution to the Mufti of Jerusalem, whom he considered "a personal friend of his". Only under

British pressure, did Mahmud agree to turn the official contribution into a personal one.[31] But he soon pressed for further British concessions for the Palestinian Arabs in which he expected to play a major mediatory role.

B. Mounting expectations: the Inter-Parliamentary Congress in Cairo

Mahmud did not hide from British officials his intention to play a more important role in the conflict. In July, 1938, while in England, he once again emphasised his influence on the Mufti and offered to mediate in the conflict.[32]

In contrast to Nahhas, who never agreed to participate in a joint Arab move, Mahmud suggested an Arab-Jewish Conference to solve the conflict. He told Malcolm MacDonald, Colonial Secretary, that the Conference should discuss a settlement on the lines of Lord Samuel's formula, which had been personally presented to him by Samuel a few days earlier. Mahmud, however, thought that Samuel's formula had to be modified to meet Arab demands. "The Arabs", he assumed, "would not agree to the Jewish population being as much as 40%, but they might agree to 33% or something a little less". He insisted on a complete halt to Jewish immigration during the conference and maintained this to be an "essential preliminary" of the negotiations.[33]

MacDonald's disagreement with this idea might have encouraged Mahmud to look for potential supporters for such a project among other circles. When he met two Zionist activists, who had been sent by Weizmann, he reiterated that "the way to an understanding with the Palestinian Arabs lies through negotiations with their leaders, ...more especially the Mufti". While emphasising the "quite natural and legitimate" interest of all the Arabs in the conflict, Mahmud maintained that Egyptian interest was that of "a good neighbour". He claimed neutrality in the conflict and offered his personal assistance to solve it.[34]

The real nature of this neutrality soon became known in public when Egyptian delegates expressed Egypt's views on the conflict during various international conferences that year; Mahmud Riad, the Egyptian delegate to the annual Inter-Parliamentary Conference that was held in the Hague, requested in the name of the Egyptian people, the restoration of the legitimate rights of the Palestinian Arabs.[35] 'Abd al-Fattah Yahya, Minister for Foreign Affairs, made similar appeals during the annual meeting of the League of Nationos. In a speech similar in nature to Ghali's speeches a year earlier, Yahya expressed sympathy with the Jewish plight in Europe. Nevertheless, like Ghali; Yahya argued that Arab-Jewish co-operation should be based on an Arab majority and be approved by "the whole Arab and Islamic world".[36]

Yahya did not elaborate how this solution should be achieved, but in Cairo Mahmud offered his capital as the future site for an Arab-Jewish Conference in which he would exercise the great "financial hold" he had on the Mufti to force him to come to terms with Weizmann.[37]

The Foreign Office was rather pleased with this initiative. In contrast to the cold shoulder given to Nahhas's initiative, both Cadogan, Under-Secretary of State for Foreign Affairs, and Halifax, his Minister, suggested bringing about "a direct agreement between Arabs and Jews, perhaps with Egyptian mediation", but without direct British involvement, in order to prevent the appearance of British recognition of the Mufti.[38]

This deviation from previous decisions to isolate Egypt from the Arab world was not due to the change of Egyptian Premiers. Rather, to the belief that Egypt could not be isolated from Arab affairs, and that the potential threat of the Nazi-Fascist Axis necessitated a new strategic position in the area.

The Colonial Office strongly opposed the Foriegn Office stand. MacDonald, who had already decided to hold an Arab-Jewish Conference in London, could not permit an Arab-Jewish encounter--a "hopeless possibility" in itself-- before his conference.[39]

MacDonald's objection to Mahmud's initiative prompted officials in the Foreign Office to re-examine this initiative. They agreed that the arrival of the Mufti in Cairo would have adverse affects on the Inter-Parliamentary Congress.[40]   This, and MacDonald's objection, tipped the balance against both Mahmud's initiative and the Inter-Parliamentary Congress in Cairo. Mahmud was asked to postpone the Cairo Congress because of "the coming war in Europe".

Mahmud was not placated. Indeed, he said, only in case of war in Europe would he cancel the Congress. He promised to deny official recognition to the Congress, and further promised to talk with the Congress organisers, especially with 'Alluba and 'Azzam, and ask them "to influence Congress in the sense of moderation"[42]

Since Lampson suspected that 'Alluba was "not a partisan of the Prime Minister", and that consequently influences "not well disposed to the Prime Minister" would be at work in Congress, he also asked other influential figures to induce "restraint and discretion" in the

Congress. He met Prince Muhammad 'Ali, 'Alluba's personal friend, and 'Ali Mahir, and asked them to impress upon 'Alluba the importance of moderation.[43] He further welcomed Mahmud's suggestion to allow Maraghi to participate in the Congress provided that he would be "duly primed and warned to exercise a moderating influence".[44]

In addition, British representatives took steps to limit Arab participation in the Congress. The French authorities were asked to secure the confinement of the Mufti of Jerusalem in Lebanon during the Congress.[45] The local rulers of Trans-Jordan and Saudi-Arabia were further requested to boycott the Congress.[46]

Britain was not the only enemy of the Congress. Zionist officials such as Elias Sasson, of the Political Department of the Jewish Agency, discouraged Lebanese and Syrian delegates from joining the Congress.[47] However, the most formidable enemy of the Congress was the Wafd. Wafdist leaders viewed the Inter-Parliamentary Congress with considerable suspicion and contempt. Although the Government declined to support the Congress, Parliament was commonly taken to be under the Government's control. The Wafd, which had only twelve representatives in that Parliament, could not have any influence in the Congress. For this obvious reason, the Party attempted to distract public attention from the Inter-Parliamentary Congress. In July, 1938, while 'Alluba's Parlimentary Committee was sending out invitations to the forthcoming Congress, the Wafd called for a special popular conference-- a term which was supposed to stand in contrast to the alleged unrepresentativeness of the Parliament-- in support of the Palestine cause. According to the Palestinian Arab press, this people's conference was a massive demonstration in favour of the Palestinian Arabs. About 20,000 invitations were sent, and an estimated 60,000 people from all over Egypt attended the meeting. The climax of this mass gathering was a speech by Nahhas, who accused the Government of using the Palestinian Arab cause in internal politics and demanded active Egyptian involvement in the conflict.[48] Wafdist activists further ridiculed the future inter-Parliamentary Congress as 'not serious', and announced plans for another inter-Arab People's Congress. The new Congress was due to convene in Cairo in November, 1938, shortly after the Inter-Parliamentary Congress. and 100,000 people were expected to attend, far more than the rival Congress.[49]

The measures taken in and outside Egypt against the Congress bore some results. 'Alluba's Paliamentary Committee claimed to have sent 25,000 invitations to the Congress. However, its opening ceremony was attended by around 2,000 people only, while the number of foreign delegates was not estimated at more than 50. No Arab or Islamic country officially authorised, or endorsed, any delegate's visit to the Congress, while Saudi-Arabia and Trans-Jordan even boycotted it.[50] Initial attempts by several delegates to attract official Egyptian recognition for the Congress failed. Syrian delegates who sought to meet Faruq in order to gain his personal support for the Congress were refused permission to meet the King on the grounds that his Government had not recognised the Congress.[51]

However, even before the beginning of the Congress both the Palace and the Governmnet revised their cold attitude. For Mahmud the Congress was an ideal opportunity, especially in light of the Wafdist boycott of it, to enhance his reputation as a defender of the Palestinian Arabs. He requested of Lampson that in the event of a British Statement on Palestine, his name should be included as helping both Palestinians and British officials. This, he maintained, would greatly help him politically.[52] He further asked British permission to go back on his previous promise to Halifax not to meet any delegates. He told Lampson of his intention to receive delegates of the Congress at a tea--party in order to modify their expected extremism.[53]

Shortly afterwards, the idea of a private tea-party to delegates of the Congress-- an idea only reluctantly approved by London-- was expanded into a general official reception for all delegates. The driving force behind the move this time was Faruq. The King, apparently acting upon the advice of 'Ali Mahir, planned to invite the delegates to the Palace. Faruq told Mahmud that he intended to invite the delegates for tea, and suggested that Mahmud invite them for dinner. Mahmud agreed. He justified his move as both a manifestation of the traditional hospitality of the East and a salve to Egyptian pride. This pride, he said, was "snubbed" by MacDonald, who had given priority to the views of the Iraqi Minister "on a matter [Palestine] where Egypt feels she should have more to say than any other Muslim country".[54]

Lampson did not feel himself betrayed. He himself did not like MacDonald's rejection of Mahmud's offer. He was further confident that feelings with regard to Palestine were running high again and that consequently, there was not "a soul" friendly to Britain in Egypt. With this thought in mind, he preferred to persuade London to change her Palestinian policy, rather than urge Mahmud and the Palace to keep their previous promise. While asking both Mahmud and the Palace not to deliver any statement that might hint at an imminent change in Britain's Palestinian Policy, he warned his superiors that "this wretched Palestinian business" risked alienating "the whole Arab and much of the Moslem world" from Britain. He estimated that although the Arabs might have "no positive value", they nevertheless might have "great nuisance value in the event of trouble".[55]

The Inter-Parliamentary Congress was one of the events which carried with it "a great nuisance value". In spite of internal controversies between Palestinian Arab and Egyptian and other Arab delegates over anti-British, anti-Saudi, and pan-Arab resolutions,[56] the Palestinian Arab cause obtained immense publicity. Once this cause had been discussed, the delegates could unite behind a joint rejection of both partition and the idea of an independent Jewish State. 'Alluba's opening speech was indicative of this trend. He warned against Jewish intentions in Palestine and neighbouring countries and appealed to Chamberlain "to give the Arabs the same justice as the Sudeten".[57]

This last appeal indicated the other main feature of the Congress: all the delegates were united behind opposition to Britain's Palestinian Policy. The resolutions of the Congress, described by Mahmud as "an appeal of equity... designed to restore justice",[58] were in harmony with the previous resolutions of the Bludan Conference. As in the Bludan Conference, the Mufti of Jerusalem had approved the final resolutions in advance. The Congress called for the nullification of the Balfour Declaration; a halt to Jewish immigration, and an amnesty for the Palestinian Arab political exiles. Britain's partition proposal was unequivocally rejected in favour of a demand to end the mandate through the establishment of a constitutional Government with a proportional Arab and Jewish representation. This Government was supposed to conclude an alliance with Britain on the lines of the Anglo--Iraqi treaty. The Congress also resolved to submit a warning to both England and the Zionists to accept these resolutions lest the Arab and Islamic world should alter their political, economic and social relations with them. Finally, the Congress urged all Arab Governments to adopt these resolutions and elected a Permanent Executive to convey the resolutions to the British Government and the League of Nations.[59]

The Congress obtained favourable publicity in the Arab press. Numerous interviews with the various Arab delegates were published in Egyptian newspapers, and Arab leaders such as Imam Yahya, Amir 'Abdullah and the rulers of the Persian Gulf sent telegrams praising the Congress and its aims.[60] Faruq's invitation to the delegates was well received by them. They rewarded his interest by cheering him as a Commander of the Faithful, a title pertaining to the Caliph alone.[61]

Mahmud also took personal interest in the Congress. During the luncheon he gave to the delegates, he congratulated them on carrying out "this great human duty". In his speech, which had been approved by Lampson as "harmless",[62] Mahmud stressed the importance of Egypt's co-operation with other Arab countries, and promised to give his "personal attention" to the Arab cause.[63]

The favourable reception of the Congress by the media influenced the Wafdist opposition towards changing its attitude. Nahhas, himself, took pains to meet the delegates, and explained to them that the absence of the Wafd did not signify any coolness towards the Palestinian Arab cause which his party had "powerfully befriended". Other Wafdist leaders also met the delegates, and endorsed the Congress resolutions.[64]

Backed by this support, a deputation of the Permanent Executive of the Congress presented Lampson with a copy of the resolutions.[65] The delegates, whose views were taken by Lampson to be "moderate",[66] asked permission to present their resolutions to British officials in London.

Their request was opposed by London, which was already preparing the Arab-Jewish Conference there. British representatives in the Middle East were therefore instructed to obstruct the intention of Arab delegates to come to London.[67] However, in spite of various preventive measures, 'Alluba, President of the Congress, arrived in London and asked to meet MacDonald. Had MacDonald arranged an official meeting with 'Alluba, he might have aroused the anger of Britain's Arab allies, who followed British advice and boycotted the Congress. MacDonald decided to see 'Alluba unofficially as an Egyptian Senator rather than as the President of the Inter-Parliamentary Congress. During the meeting, in which British Palestinian policy was discussed, MacDonald expressed his hope that the future Arab-Jewish Conference would reach a compromise solution that would satisfy the Arabs.[68] As a further gesture, MacDonald invited 'Alluba to listen to his Parliamentary speech on the Palestine question, of which 'Alluba rather disapproved.[69]

The publicity given to the Inter-Parliamentary Congress, and the immediate and enthusiastic support it obtained from Arab and Egyptian leaders, encouraged a new spate of activities on behalf of the Palestinian Arabs in Egypt. At the end of the Congress, Madam Huda Sha'rawi, President of the Egyptian Women's Association, with the assistance of Palestinian Arab activists, particularly 'Awni 'Abd al-Hadi and Akram Zu'aytar,[70] convened the Eastern Women's Congress. This congress, which also drew semi-official recognition,[71] reached decisions similar to those made by the inter-Parliamentary Congress.[72]

The Women's Congress was followed by a student Congress. The University Youth for the Defence of Palestine convened a Congress which passed resolutions resembling those determined by the previous Congresses.[73] Other Societies and organisations also held meetings in which manifestos were drawn up in support of the Palestinian Arabs.[74]

Backed by these numerous resolutions, Egyptian leaders renewed their attempts to obtain British concessions for the Palestinian Arabs. Views that were expressed during these Congresses found their way to British ears through official Egyptian appeals. Following 'Alluba's appeal to Britain to adopt a solution similar to that of the Sudeten, Mahmud sent a private letter to Chamberlain, asking him "to lend his personal authority and prestige to a solution doing justice to the Arab cause".[75]

Nahhas also delivered speeches in which he called for an

independent Palestine allied to Britain in a treaty. He declared that an immediate halt to Jewish immigration and the prohibition of land sales were the only conditions under which Arab countries would accept a solution of the Palestinian conflict. He added that the best way to reach this solution was to form a "united front" of the Eastern Peoples against Imperialist designs.[76]

The various manifestations of support for the Arab cause greatly impressed British officials in Cairo and London. Lampson reported that by dealing with an issue that was "increasingly becoming the nerve centre of the Muslim World", the Congress aroused "the sense of unity existing between the Arab countries, both in the particular aspect of opposition to the policy of HMG in Palestine and in the more general aspect of Muslim co-operation against Western encroachment". An impetus had been given, he said, to a "sentimental solidarity" which would have its practical effects in "an Eastern world governed by sentiment more than by reason".[77]

Lampson's report was highly regarded by both the Colonial and Foreign Offices. In their joint appreciation of his report, officials of both Ministries agreed that the pan-Arab movement was a force to be reckoned with in the Near and Middle East. Britain, it was further agreed, gave this movement cohesion by her Palestine policy. Since Britain was supposed to lose more than gain by "openly opposing pan-Arab aspirations", British officials recommended that London should move with the pan-Arab current by showing it sympathy, "for it will only be by doing so that we may be able to shape its course a little".[78]

This statement of policy, which laid down the foundations of what was later known as Britain's 'Arab policy' reduced Britain, the Imperial power, to a mere observer of 'movements' and 'currents', the real power and direction of which British officials could not control. Kelly, now Head of Eastern Department in the Foreign Office, supported this belief. Commenting on Lampson's report, kelly emphasised the importance of Egypt to this sense of unity. The great and growing influence of the Egyptian press throughout the Near East; the relatively large population and wealth of Egypt; the attraction of the Egyptian Universities, and particularly al-Azhar, affected, to Kelly's mind, Egyptian predominance over the Arab countries. It might be true, he concluded, that the majority of Egyptians were "not predominantly Arab in race", but as Muslims and speakers of Arabic, and because of political vanity, they were "rapidly coming to regard themselves as such and to aspire to moral leadership".[79]

Egypt's political forces were quickly adjusting themselves to their new role. Anti-British and anti-Jewish propaganda increased. The Palace was spreading rumours that the Mufti of Jerusalem would soon be given asylum in Egypt.[80] Lampson's representations to stop the anti-British camaign[81] were met with growing reluctance. In spite of Muhammad Mahmud's claims that he had instructed the police to re-press all agitation,[82] Lampson gained the impression that Egyptian police officers could no longer be relied upon in the event of anti--Jewish riots. Lampson further thought that the authorities·declined to use the Courts to suppress inflamatory pamphlets. Mahmud asserted that it would be useless to involve the courts because of "the long proce-

dure which would merely be publicity for those prosecuted".[83] This
was a remarkable comment by a man who used to close newspapers that
criticised the Government's corruption. Mahmud, however, agrgued that
agitation could not be stopped by the use of force or by judicial
measures. He maintained that agitation would subside only if the
British agreed to his making a public statement that "Egyptian people
could rest assured that the Egyptian Government were very much concerned over Palestine". He hoped that Chamberlain might provide him with a
sort of assurance which he would be able to present to the Egyptians.[84]

Lampson could see no wrong in such an appeal. He believed that
the growth of anti-British agitation in Egypt and the deterioration in
public security there, were all a direct result of British Palestinian
policy. An immediate halt to Jewish immigration was, therefore, the
only policy that he could recommend as "a right middle policy".[85]

In spite of their growing respect for the power of the pan-Arab
movement, British officials in London opposed both Mahmud's and
Lampson's proposals. Lampson's advice was rejected because British
officials preferred to reach a decision on immigration only during
the London Conference. Also Mahmud's proposal aroused difficulties.
Chamberlain doubted the wisdom of adopting in Palestine the same
"spectacular procedure" that had been adopted in Munich. The
circumstances, he argued, in connection with Palestine, were "very
different" from those with which he had dealt in Munich.[86]

Mahmud's plea was not, however, entirely rejected. Lampson was
instructed to permit the release of a 'neutral' statement which would

assure the Egyptian people of their Government's concern regarding Palestine, and would mention the efforts of this Government "to put fully before HMG the views of the Egyptian people on this question".[87]

Mahmud was not satisfied with publication of this statement alone. To emphasise the importance of this issue in Egyptian politics, he also included in the Speech from the Throne, at the opening of Parliament, a paragraph reviewing his activities for the Palestinian Arabs and affirming his Government's confidence in an equitable solution to the conflict.[88]

C. Intrigues and politics: the composition of the Egyptian delegation to the London Conference

By the time that the Speech from the Throne was delivered in Parliament, Mahmud had already been informed by Lampson of the British intention to hold an Arab-Jewish Conference in London. Drafts on the formal invitations to the Conference reached Cairo by about the middle of November, 1938. Before submitting the formal invitation, Lampson was instructed to ensure that the chosen representatives possess "sufficient prestige and goodwill to exercise a moderating influence". The instructions even went so far as to allow the participation of Arab rulers of the highest rank, such as Imam Yahya and King Ibn-Sa'ud, in the Conference.[89]

The Embassy conveyed the content of these instructions to Mahmud. The latter, quite naturally, believed that the invitations referred to him, but refused to commit himself. He mentioned his poor health as an obstacle.[90]   However, privately, Mahmud's confidant, Amin 'Uthman, intimated that Mahmud would head the Egyptian delegation if Chamberlain presided over the Conference.

This was not to be the only condition put forward by Mahmud or Yahya. Mahmud expressed regret that such an important Conference was not to be held in Cairo, where he "could and would exercise more effective restraint than in London". Both he and Yahya asked for the Mufti's participation in the talks. Yahya further requested an immediate halt to the punitive policy of blowing up Arab houses in Palestine in order to create a friendly atmosphere in the forthcoming Conference.[91] In addition, both Yahya and Mahmud asked to be informed beforehand as to the limits of British concessions at the Conference.[92]

British officials in London were not prepared to reveal their concessions before the Conference,[93] and Mahmud, in turn, declined to accept the invitation. 'Uthman informed Lampson that as a result of the abortive 1921 and 1929 negotiations, it was now Mahmud's concern "to frame a geographic Arab front" which would guarantee the Conference's success. A failure of such a Conference, in which Mahmud's own prestige was involved, would be devastating to him. If Mahmud was not given the range of British concessions in the projected Conference, a subordinate figure, such as Nash'at Pasha, Egyptian Ambassador to London, would head the Egyptian Delegation.[94]

Shortly afterwards, Mahmud told Lampson that his "original intention" had been to go to the Conference accompanied by 'Ali Mahir and Amin 'Uthman. However, British refusal to discuss with him in confidence something which "he knew he could ensure in advance with other Arab countries", prevented him from carrying out his original intention. Mahmud firmly rejected Lampson's suggestion to delegate 'Azzam to the Conference, if he (Mahmud) could not go to it. 'Azzam was disqualified because he had intrigued with 'Ali Mahir, and might "let us all down". The only alternative, in view of British intransigence, lay in the nomination of the Egyptian Ambassador to London to head the Egyptian delegation to the Conference.[95]

Lampson viewed Mahmud's arguments with sympathy. He believed that Mahmud's participation in the Conference was essential for the success of the Congress. This success was crucial for securing British interests in the area. Friendship with "this Arab-Muslim movement of co--operation" became an essential British priority, if Britain did not,or could not afford to, keep a large military force in the area. The London Conference offered a unique opportunity to achieve Arab friendship and co-operation. A halt to Jewish immigration to Palestine should make sure that "in case of a European war the Arab East will remain silent". An immediate halt to Jewish immigration to Palestine would surely create a friendly atmosphere in the Conference.[96]

MacDonald, who had already been occupied with the arrangements for the London Conference, was shattered by Lampson's proposal to suspend Jewish immigration. Had the British Government followed this proposal, the Conference would have been cancelled, since the Jews would surely have boycotted it. Halifax's wish to circulate Lampson's views to the Cabinet further disturbed MacDonald. He sent Halifax a private letter expressing deep disappointment with Lampson's activities. While perceiving it to be of vital importance that Arab demands be met,

MacDonald refused to go "to the extent of completely breaking our promises to the Jews and completely surrendering to the Arab demands". Lampson, MacDonald maintained, was giving rein to "his own preconceived ideas" during his private conversations with various people including Arab sympathisers. The result of this attitude was that Lampson was "out-Arabing the Arabs", encouraging views that "happened to be very different" from British views.[97]

Halifax maintained, of course, his "complete faith" in Lampson's loyalty to carry out "any instructions". He reminded MacDonald that they were all agreed on "the main anxiety entertained by Lampson about the imperative need of going as far as possible to meet the Arabs' views".[98] However, in spite of this defence, Foreign Office officials also doubted whether Lampson's efforts to obtain Mahmud's personal participation in the Conference were wise. They feared that the Conference might continue for a long time, and that Mahmud might not have the patience to stay in London because of internal unrest in Egypt. Lampson's superiors allowed him to make his own personal choice, but suggested 'Uthman, or a man of that calibre, "as the preferable appointment".[99]

However, by the time these instructions reached Cairo, both Mahmud and Yahya had reversed their attitude towards the projected Conference. Both began expressing a desire to go to London. It appears that the release of six exiled Palestinian Arab leaders from the Seychelles, their arrival in Cairo and the consequent consultations between them and other Arab and Egyptian politicians[100] stimulated the political appetite of Egyptian politicians. Mahmud not only had dropped all his pre-conditions, but he and his foreign Minister also insisted on their participation in the Conference. Yahya was the first to agree that "someone of outstanding calibre" should be appointed to lead the Egyptian Delegation in order to emphasise Egypt's interest in this issue. He disclosed that he contemplated "the possibility of going himself". Soon afterwards, Mahmud expressed a personal desire to preside over the Egyptian Delegation.[100] He informed Lampson that he had persuaded the Mufti to withdraw his demand to send the whole Higher Arab Committee to the Conference. The Mufti, Mahmud asserted, had empowered him to compose the Palestinian Arab delegation. With this role established, Mahmud asked Lampson to provide him with names of Palestinian Arabs who were unacceptable to Britain, so that he could select the Palestinian Arab Delegation.[102]

Confronted by similar initiatives by other Arab leaders, and notably Ibn-Sa'ud, London advised Mahmud to consult other Arab leaders concerning this matter. Lampson was further instructed to inform Mahmud of HMG's "hope" that the Egyptian, Iraqi and Saudi-Arabian Governments would put forward "jointly" a list of Palestinian Arab delegates to the Conference. Apart form its objection to the Mufti's participation in the Palestinian delegation, London gave the Arab countries a free hand to nominate the Palestinian Arab delegates.[103]

Informal consultations between Egyptian and Arab representatives concerning the Conference had already taken place. In Jedda, 'Azzam and Fu'ad Hamza, Ibn-Sa'ud's adviser, held talks on this subject which resulted in a recommendation to convene an all-Arab meeting in

Cairo.[104]   Similar consultation were held in Cairo between Mahmud
and   Nuri   al-Sa'id,   and,   also   perhaps,   other   Arab   personalities.[105]   London's   permission   for,   and   encouragement   of,   such
talks paved the way for Mahmud's new initiative to call for a joint
Arab meeting in Cairo to discuss future policy at the London
Conference.   Consequently, Mahmud asked for a postponement of the
Conference until the Arabs had consolidated their position.[106]

Mahmud's first thought was to obtain, during these meetings, a
common Arab "formula" which would be presented in London by the Arab
side.   However, after consulting Lampson, Mahmud agreed to drop this
idea, and to attempt instead, to achieve a united front which would act
with an "open mind" at the Conference.[107]

Satisfied with this attitude, Lampson did not mind supporting
Mahmud's efforts to distinguish himself as the champion of the Palestinian Arabs.   He recommended the acceptance of Mahmud's pleas for com-
muting death sentences on an Egyptian subject and several Palestinian
Arabs who had been condemned by Palestinian Courts for terrorist activities.[108]   Lampson also supported Mahmud's expressed wish to
send the Egyptian Red Crescent to Palestine.   Only the firm rejection
by the High Commissioner of Palestine, who feared this might involve
Egyptians in direct contact with the rebels,[109] prevented the
visit.

Lampson justified his support for Mahmud's proposals by the need
to help Mahmud overcome internal criticism of his Palestinian policy.
Mahmud, however, considered these gestures insufficient.   He requested
that the British forces stop their military operations in Palestine as

a gesture facilitating a friendly atmosphere during the Conference.[110]   He further suggested inviting the Mufti, "the Sa'd
Zaghlul of the Palestinian Arabs", to Cairo for consultations over the
composition of the Palestinian Arab delegation. He argued that this
would be the best solution since the French authorities were forbidding
entry into Lebanon of Palestinian Arab representatives who wished to
consult with the Mufti.[111]

Lampson began suspecting that Mahmud's proposals were nothing but
"a deep laid scheme to bring the Mufti here". Alarmed by the new surge
of anti-British agitation, Lampson rejected Mahmud's proposals and
demanded that agitaion stop.[112]

Doubts concerning Mahmud's true intentions were also raised in
London. The talks that Egyptian representatives held with other Arab
delegates-- one result of which might have been the new suggestion made
by Mahmud to bring the Mufti to Cairo-- raised fears in London that the
Arabs were adopting a rigid position. The Foreign Office instructed
Lampson to remind Mahmud that the inter-Arab talks should not result in
a binding "cut and dried scheme", but in a flexible one.[113]

British concern for the direction of the talks was shared by the
Palace, though for entirely different reasons. Premier Mahmud's
intention to head the Egyptian Delegation did not please the Palace,
notably 'Ali Mahir. Mahir was "anxious to prevent Mahmud from going to
London where he might gain glory, and would be secure from eviction at
any rate until his return".[114]   Mahir, therefore, persuaded the
young King to reject Mahmud's nomination.[115]   Neither Mahmud's
protest,[116] nor appeals by other Arab leaders, such as Nuri and

Faysal, helped to reverse the King's mind. The King told Nuri and Faysal that he had already instructed Amir 'Abd al-Mun'im, the son of the deposed Khedive, 'Abbas Hilmi, to head the Egyptian Delegation. He argued that in view of the presence of other Arab Princes at the head of both the Saudi and Yemeni delegations, Egypt should be represented in the Conference by a Prince.[117]

The Arab delegates, Mahmud, and Lampson were all dissatisfied with this nomination. Nuri al-Sa'id speculated that Munim's nomination was a plot devised by 'Ali Mahir with a view to a dynastic claim upon the throne of Syria and Palestine.[118] Also, Mahmud viewed Mahir's activities against him with increasing concern. By the end of 1938 and the beginning of 1939, Mahmud's coalition Government was shaken by a series of scandals, intrigues and defections. Two out of the twelve Ministers-- the Minister of Agriculture and the Minister of War--resigned, while a third one, Ahmad Khashaba, Minister of Justice, had come under Palace influence and started to act according to Mahir's dictates. Moreover, Mahir's activities against Mahmud encouraged an increasing number of Deputies and Senators to desert the coalition parties, and to become, "in fact, if not in name", independent. With a sliding economy, hindered by growing financial debts, strikes and unemployment, and with a new anti-Government campaign conducted by the Wafd and assisted by student demonstrators, Mahmud's chances of survival looked slim. In fact, changes of Cabinets were already "in the air".[119]

This situation must have affected Mahmud's decision to preside over the Egyptian Delegation in order to prevent his dismissal. Mahir, who played an important role in initiating and escalating this crisis with a view to replacing Mahmud, used his influence with the King to prevent Mahmud from going to London. Mahir succeeded in preventing Mahmud from going to London, but the latter devised a new plan which would foil Mahir's intention to dismiss him.

Mahmud's initial intention was to send his Minister for Foreign Affairs in case he himself could not go. Yahya was chosen despite defects of "extreme touchiness, lack of intelligence and ignorance of English", because Mahmud maintained that "he could send no other Cabinet Minister"[120] Indeed, in view of the internal crisis, Mahmud could not allow the absence of any of his other Ministers from Egypt.

Since Mahir had aspired to ensure Mahmud's presence in Egypt. where he could be easily deposed, Mahmud, in turn, attempted to rid himself of Mahir's presence in Egypt. The best way to do this was to send Mahir with the Egyptian Delegation to London. 'Abd al-Mun'im, it was patently clear, could not really represent Egypt in this "matter of national and world importance". He was a man who "neither knew much about the Arab question, nor took part in Egyptian politics", but was "principally interested in wirelesses,motor cars, etc."[121] Mahmud insisted that "someone of political weight and experience should accompany the Prince on this vitally important business". If the King's wish was that his Premier stay in Egypt, "the only public spirited thing" was to send Mahir.[122]

Lampson thought it "most unlikely" that the King would agree to this. Indeed, neither Faruq nor Mahir was delighted with Mahmud's proposal.[123] Mahir's final decision to take up this assignment was, perhaps, not so much owing to his devotion to the Palestinian Arab cause as to his concern for his public prestige if he refused. Other Arab delegates, and even Lampson, thought that Mahir was the only possible alternative to Mahmud.[124] Mahir had therefore to postpone his bid for the Premiership, and to go instead to London, where he could, at least, hope to promote his own prestige.

Mahmud was not content with ridding himself of Mahir's presence. While expressing "a great relief to get 'Ali out of the country,"[125] Mahmud also made a "most anxious" appeal to Lampson, asking that shortly after the beginning of the Conference he should receive a message from HMG "urging him to come owing to the complexity of issues at stake". Thus, Mahmud explained, he would "snap his fingers at the Palace and fly to London".[126] Mahmud repeated this plea several times through various channels and hinted that he would be "extremely hurt" if he was not invited to attend the Conference before its conclusion.[127]

One significant result of the ill feeling between the Egyptian delegates and Mahmud was that the delegates did not have a say during the preliminary meetings of the Arab delegations in Cairo. 'Azzam was the only Egyptian delegate who took part in these consultations, but, as we shall soon see, Mahmud did not intend to include him in the Egyptian Delegation to London.

The official meetings, which sometimes have been referred to as the "Cairo Conference",[128] started on the 17th January, 1939, under the presidency of Mahmud and with the participation of delegates from Iraq, Palestine, Saudi-Arabia, Yemen, Trans-Jordan and Egypt.

Aside from 'Azzam, representatives of the Inter-Parliamentary Executive, 'Alluba, 'Abd al-Hamid Sa'id and Hamad al-Basil, were also present. The delegates were expected "to discuss the attitude to be adopted at the London Conference".[129]

However, a prominent part of the three sessions that the delegates held was devoted to the composition of the Palestinian Arab delegation; British insistence on the inclusion of representatives of the Nashashibi's Defence Party in the Palestinian Arab Delegation,[130] and the Mufti's refusal, prevented agreement on the composition of this delegation. A mission of several Arab delegates to Beirut failed to solve all the difficulties; the Mufti insisted that his representatives should be considered as the sole Palestinian Arab representatives. He further insisted that his programme be adopted in its entirety by the other Arab delegates whose role he restricted to following and supporting his platform.

The Arab delegates accepted his formula which demanded a complete and immediate cessation of Jewish immigration; nullification of the Balfour Declaration and Palestinian independence under a treaty with Britian.[131] The Mufti, in turn, agreed to include two members of the Opposition in the Palestinian Arab Delegation. But the Mufti's nominees were rejected by both Raghib Nashashibi, head of the Opposition, and British officials.[132] While the final composition of the delegation was to be settled only in London, the rest of the Arab delegates agreed broadly with the Mufti's insistence that political Zionism must cease. They further agreed that the Palestinian Arabs should have priority in approving whatever solution might be proposed.

Mahmud, who presided over the Arab talks, did not seem to mind this binding undertaking to the Palestinian Arabs. Ignoring the complications which had arisen during the meetings concerning the Palestinian Arab representation, he praised the "cordiality, frankness, sincerity and perfect harmony [which] reigned among the delegates".[134] While such feelings were rare even between himself and the Egyptian delegates, Mahmud did not miss this opportunity to propagate the idea of Egypt's leadership over the Arab people. At a banquet given for the delegates, he stressed the significance of the reunion of Arab representatives in Cairo. "Could they forget", he asked, "the events luminously written in the pages of history during the past Arab period when Cairo was their focal point?". Stressing the historical, linguistic, and social ties between Egypt and Palestine, and the other Arab countries, Mahmud assured his audience that Egypt had never forgotten its Arab past.[135]

Faruq also took steps aimed at reminding the Arab delegates of his claim to Arab and Muslim leadership. In the presence of other Arab delegates Faruq himself, led the congregation in the Friday prayer, a prerogative of a Caliph. On leaving the Mosque, the Arab delegates could further hear Faruq being hailed as the future Caliph.[136]

It may well be that 'Ali Mahir, whom Lampson persistently labelled as an "intriguer",[137] stood behind Faruq's activities. As Chief of the Royal Cabinet, Mahir did not meet great difficulties in reversing the initial Arab resentment against him. Shortly after arriving in London, Mahir invited 'Azzam to join the Egyptian Delegation.[138]

'Azzam's nomination aroused the wrath of Mahmud, while pleasing the other Arab delegates. Mahmud permitted 'Azzam, who was still Minister to Iraq, Iran and Saudi-Arabia, to serve only as Prince Mun'im's Secretary. This 'Azzam refused and threatened to resign. Arab delegates intervened and appointed him as a counsellor of all the delegations.[139] 'Azzam's nomination established Mahir's predominance over the Egyptian Delegation, and he was soon to use this position to become one of the key figures in the Conference. Even before the Conference, Mahir succeeded in creating cordial relations with Nuri al-Sa'id, who had previously opposed him. They both sent a joint appeal to the Palestinian Arab parties asking them to settle their differences and to send a united delegation to the Conference.[140]

D.   The London onference, 1939

The London Conference was opened on 7th February, 1939. As the Arabs refused to confer with the Jews, the Arab and Jewish delegations held separate talks with the British representatives. The Arab-British Conference began with a general statement by the Palestinian Arab delegation. The spokesman of the delegation, Jamal al-Husayni, pleaded for the creation of an independent Palestinian Arab State which would conclude a treaty with Britain. He further asked for an immediate halt to Jewish immigration, the prohibition of land sales to Jews, and an end to the Jewish National Home Experiment.[141] These demands, which were in line with the Cairo understanding, were supported by all the Arab delegates.

However, the tactics which the Egyptian Delegation, and notably Mahir, practised during the Conference succeeded in confusing British,

Zionist and other Arab delegates. Mahir, who did not take part in the 'Cairo Conference', lacked the doctrinal commitment which characterised the Palestinian Arab delegates. This created the impression that Mahir was a moderate politician and earned him, in turn, the admiration not only of British officials, but also of Zionist leaders.

MacDonald, who presided over the British side, was particularly pleased with him. Their personal relations were described as "excellent",[142] and, consequently, Mahir's image changed. While before the Conference he was regarded as an intriguer who should be watched carefully,[143] he was acclaimed towards the end of the Conference as "a very experienced politician", who "was working night and day to promote the success of the Conference".[144]

Mahir's positive approach to both British and Zionist positions in the Conference led both sides to believe that his stand differed from the joint Arab stand. This impression was created as early as the beginning of the Conference in a private meeting with Chamberlain during which the Arab delegates were given a precis of the Cabinet's Palestine Committe Report. While the other Arab delegates, Nuri and Fu'ad Hamza, expressed shock and disappointment with the Report, and demanded an immediate halt to Jewish immigration, Mahir disclosed an attitude that was regarded even by MacDonald as "over-optimistic". Mahir agreed to see the British proposals, "with slight modifications", as the basis for an agreement.[145]

It was only when he presented these modifications-- British recognition of an independent Palestinian State, a complete halt to immigration, and a prohibition of land sales to Jews -- that British offi-

cials realised that they amounted to "a quite different set of proposals".[146] Nevertheless, Mahir's reputation as a moderate survived, because by then British officials got the impression that he was
not insisting on Britain's immediate evacuation of Palestine and was
more concerned with the form rather than with the substance of Palestinian independence.

Mahir's expressions of sympathy with the initial British proposals
succeeded in deceiving even the Palestinian Arab delegates. When,
during the seventh session of the Conference, Mahir welcomed
MacDonald's consent to establish a Palestinian State, the Palestinian
Arab delegates were quick to protest. They reminded the Conference that
the Arabs had already agreed in Cairo to the demand for an Independent
Arab State.[147] Their insistence on this terminology led Mahir in
the next session to propose a "joint Arab statement" which would
clarify the Arab position concerning the British definition for the
Independent Palestinian State.[148]

The 'joint Arab Statement' was read during the ninth session by
Mahir. It was, in fact, an Egyptian statement, prepared by an Egyptian,
maybe Mahir himself, and devoted, by and large, to the Egyptian view of
the conflict. The statement lacked the passionate criticism of
Britain's Palestinian policy which had characterised other previous
Arab statements. Mahir suggested that the solution of the conflict be
based on the internationally accepted principle of equal rights for
minorities as well as for vital British interests. He, however,
maintained that Jewish immigration damaged the Arab character of
Palestine and was carried out against "the will of the country's

people". The most generous, far-sighted, and tolerant solution, he said, would be to secure "for all those Jews equal rights with the original inhabitants". Therefore, he urged the British Government to establish an independent Palestinian State. "The Arab states", he promised, were prepared, at the same time, to urge the Palestinian Arabs to accept "all reasonable guarantees and safeguards that might be required".[149]

This statement did not, and probably was not intended to, solve the differences between the Palestinian Arab delegates, who persisted in demanding an immediate halt to immigration, and the British repre-sentatives, who supported future immigration, even though limited to the absorbtion capacities of Palestine. To bridge this gap, Mahir proposed the formation of a special Committee on immigration.[150] British officials did not like the proposal. They were reluctant to allow a sub-Committee to decide on one of the main issues of the Conference. Instead, MacDonald announced a short break in the Conference, during which he initiated informal meetings between Arab and Jewish delegates in an attempt to reach a compromise.

During these informal meetings with the Jewish delegates, Mahir established both his reputation as a moderate politician and as a speaker, thus also the informal 'leader', of the other Arab delegates. During the first informal meeting with the Jewish delegates, Mahir called for Arab-Jewish co-operation, though only on a basis of a change of the immigration policy. In these talks he did not reject off-hand any Jewish immigration, but he did emphasise that this immigration would not be allowed on a basis of a principle or a treaty, but would be tolerated only if the whole Palestinian community benefitted from it. He preached "a peaceful solution" in which an independent Palestinian State, based on the current proportions of the populations, would be created after a transitional period under British guidance.

Mahir's insistense on British guidance for the proposed state, must have pleased British officials. A day after this meeting, MacDonald presented the Arab camp with British proposals regarding the constitutional aspect of Palestinian independence. The porposals included the establishement, after a transitional period, of an independent Palestinian State in treaty relations with Britain. During this transitional period, a constitution was expected to be drawn out by a projected Round Table Conference between Arab and Jewish representatives. No definite formulation regarding immigration was suggested, but a proposal for a round figure of immigration to be absorbed over a five-year period was advanced. The future of immigration after these five years was to be decided in the Round Table Conference or formally established under the new constitution.[152]

Both Jewish and Palestinian Arab delegations rejected the proposals. The Jewish delegates refused to be condemned to permanent minority status (as the proposals indicated), while the Palestinian Arab delegates demanded an immediate advance towards a Palestinian State under Arab domination.[153]

In an attempt to break the deadlock with the Arabs, British officials set up a Committee of Policy which had to consider all these questions. During the various sessions of this Committee, the Arab delegates expressed their complete support for the Palestinian Arab stance. The Egyptian delegates, Mahir and 'Azzam, were, this time, among the vociferous advocates of a pro-Arab settlement. Both 'Azzam and Mahir complained that too much was being done to preserve the minority rights while not much was being done for the majority. Both also insisted on substantial British concessions to apease the Arabs.[154]

Realising that these meetings were getting nowhere, MacDonald decided to summon another informal meeting between the Jewish and Arab delegates in an attempt to reach some basis for a Jewish-Arab understanding. During this informal meeting, Mahir, once again, adopted a moderate tone. The Jews, he said, deserved a state of their own, and had Palestine been empty, they would have been welcome to it, but there was the reality of an existing Arab population who felt that their rights were being violated by the Zionists. The time had come for the Jews to slow down their advance and consolidate the position that they had already occupied. If they were to make any further advance, it would be necessary for them to do so in agreement with the Arabs. Such an agreement, he maintained, could be achieved if the Jews accepted Palestine as a spiritual rather than a national centre for world Jewry.

Mahir's emotional appeal to slow down Jewish immigration to Palestine, met different Zionist reactions. Shertok, who regarded Mahir as a "typical Egyptian [with] small tricky eyes and a sweet smile",[155] and Ben-Gurion-- two of the Zionist representatives of Palestinian Jewry-- were not too impressed by Mahir's conception of a compromise. They argued that the Jews could never give up their right to Palestine. Weizmann, who regarded Mahir as "personally friendly" in contrast to

the "intransigent" Nuri al-Sa'id,[156] was rather impressed by
Mahir's manners. Such a friendly attitude from a Muslim reminded him of
the spirit of his talks with Faysal in 1918. Consequently, Weizmann, in
spite of declining to be held to any specific figures on immigration,
expressed general agreement to negotiation with the Arabs on the basis
of give and take. Had not Ben-Gurion decided to correct the impression
that the Zionists were ready to accept a slow-down of immigration,
Mahir might have been left with the difficult task of persuading the
Palestinian Arabs to accept the principle of Jewish immigration to
Palestine. But Ben-Gurion evidently did not believe that such a
possibility could exist. He intervened and re-emphasised the Zionists'
firm objection to a slowing down of immigration, and even took the line
that it should continue at an ever-increasing rate.[157]

The failure to achieve a basis for an Arab-Jewish accord did not
frustrate MacDonald. Aware of the reluctance of the Jewish side to
accept the British proposals, he concentrated his efforts on reaching
an understanding with the Arabs. In an apparent attempt to find out how
far the Arabs were ready to press the Palestinian Arabs for a
compromise, MacDonald invited Mahir, Fu'ad Hamza, and Tawfiq
al-Suwaydi, to see him on the day he was presenting his proposals to
the Cabinet. Without disclosing the content of his proposals, MacDonald
asked the delegates to persuade the Palestinian Arabs to moderate their
demands and convince them to drop their veto to immigration after the
five-year transitional period. While the Saudi and Iraqi delegates
doubted their ability to persuade the Palestinian Arabs unless they
were given a definite date for independence, Mahir displayed, as usual,

a positive view. He asserted that this scheme was worth trying, provided that a three-party agreement could be achieved.[158]

MacDonald's proposals went a long way to appease the Arabs. He conceded to the Arabs the right to approve immigration after the five-year period. In turn, he hoped that the Arabs would agree that no definite date for independence would be specified. During the five years of limited immigration, MacDonald assumed that the Arabs would agree to the entrance of between 80,000 and 100,000 immigrants into Palestine. The Cabinet did not raise any substantial objection to these proposals,[159] leaving MacDonald free to present them to the Jewish and Arab delegations.

The Jewish delegation rejected the proposals in toto, and MacDonald sensed that the Palestinian Arabs were likely to reject them as well.[160] The attitude of the representatives of the other Arab states became, therefore, a matter of great importance, since it was their appeasement which London first and foremost sought. MacDonald once again summoned the delegates of Egypt, Saudi-Arabia and Iraq to a further set of informal meetings. He soon found out that the delegates were reluctant to consent to further Jewish immigration after five years, and that they found the figure of 100,000 Jewish immigrants within this period too high. All the delegates, including Mahir, pressed for a decrease. Mahir, for example, suggested that the period during which limited immigration would be permitted into Palestine be extended to ten years instead of the proposed five. This, to minimise as far as possible the effects of the immigration on the Arab population of Palestine.[161]

MacDonald presented the Arab delegates with two proposals. He first suggested reaching a written agreement between Britain and the Arab side. This proposal was dropped after the Arab delegates had rejected any sort of agreement which would not include the Palestinian Arabs. Both sides then agreed on a second proposal of a British unilateral statement concerning Palestine's future. The nieghbouring states, in turn, were expected to issue another statement appealing to the Palestinian Arabs to stop the violence on the grounds that the British Statement, though not accepting all the Arab demands, went a long way towards meeting them.[162]

As a result of his talks with the Arab delegates, MacDonald presented the Conference with British proposals that were once again modified in favour of the Arabs. The number of Jewish immigrants permitted into Palestine during the transitional period was reduced to 75,000. However, even these modifications did not satisfy the Palestinian Arab delegates. Their objection was supported by all other Arab delegates.[163] Acting in accordance with the Cairo understanding they allowed the Palestinian Arabs to determine their own fate and followed the Palestinian Arab rejectionist stand. From the British point of view, only the Egyptian delegate had "behaved really well" on this occasion.[164] Mahir thanked the British and Arab sides for their efforts, praised Arab co-operation which had helped to moderate the attitudes of both sides, and argued that the main difference between the Palestinian Arabs and the British side remained the controversy over the transitional period.[165]

This statement was grossly inaccurate. Arab co-operation did not succeed in inducing moderation in the Palestinian Arabs. Moreover, as we shall soon see, the issue of the transitional period was not the only obstacle preventing a British-Arab agreement over the Palestine question. However, at that time MacDonald was still optimistic concerning the prospect of reaching an Arab-British understanding. He informed the Cabinet that although the representatives of the neighbouring Arab States had publicly rejected the British proposals, they regarded them, "behind the scenes", as "wise and reasonable". This attitude must have encouraged MacDonald to revive the informal talks with Arab delegates. During these discussions, considered to be of "utmost importance" to British interests, MacDonald hoped "to find a formula, which without committing us to a given period of years for the transition period, would not enable the Jews to hold up consitutional progress by a refusal to co-operate with the Arabs".[166]

E. Cairo, and the Arab-British Discussion

While Mahir was engaged in London in promoting both his and Egypt's reputation, his rivals in Cairo were taking steps intended to diminish his influence. Premier Mahmud, having been denied the expeted invitation to join the Conference, sent his confidant, Amin 'Uthman, to Beirut where he was reported to have held talks with the Mufti.[167]

While both Mahmud and 'Uthman denied this report, both were evidently concerned by Mahir's activities in London. The possibility that Mahir might increase his prestige and improve his relations with British officials during the Conference, must have been a source of constant concern for Mahmud. It should not, therefore, be surprising that upon the breakdown of the Conference, Mahmud renewed his attempts to damage Mahir's reputation. He approached Lampson expressing the "gravest concern" that with Mahir now back in Egypt, the breakdown of the Conference would be exploited "for the purpose of anti-British propaganda especially by the Palace".[168]

Mahmud's warning was not based on correct information. During Mahir's absence from Egypt the King found a new favourite, Bindari Pasha. When Mahir returned to Cairo, he was so upset by Bindari's great influence at the Palace that he even presented his resignation as Chief of the Royal Cabinet. Mahir did eventually withdraw his resignation but his influence at the Palace was greatly reduced[169]. As a result, he tried to get on good terms with both Mahmud and British officials.

The potential risk of public uproar in Egypt on behalf of the Palestinian Arabs was also slim; Cairo remained calm at the news of the collapse of the Conference. The news was accepted "relatively ordinarily". Sutdents of some faculties in al-Azhar went on strike and anti-British speeches were delivered, but no demonstrations broke out.[170]

This atmosphere did not prevent Mahmud from asking "to try his hand at getting Palestinians to accept a solution". As Nahhas had done before, Mahmud also maintained that his initiative was motivated by a desire to assist his British ally. If no solution to the problem proved practicable, he said, he would like to be acquainted with the proposed policy of HMG "in order that he might endeavour to secure Arab acquiescence to it and the cessation of the campaign of lawlessness" in Palestine.[171]

Mahmud's initiative was accepted with satisfaction. He was invited to send "immediate instructions to the Egyptian Ambassador in London to do his utmost to promote such an agreement". The Foreign Office, apart from reiterating its objection to negotiating with the Mufti, did not stipulate any other conditions for Egyptian mediation. Rather, the Ministry stressed the hope that the restoration of peace would be established if the Egyptian Government were willing "whole-heartedly to co-operate in urging the Palestinian Arabs to settle down and help to work out the future constitutional developments foreshadowed in the British proposals".[172]

Following the Foreign Office invitation, an Egyptian memorandum setting out Egyptian proposals for settlement of the Palestine conflict was presented to the British side.[173] This encouraged a series of negotiations that started soon after the collapse of the London Conference. The Arab side consisted of Nash'at, Egyptian Minister in London, and Iraqi and Saudi delegates. The discussions centred on the formation of the projected Palestinian Government rather than on the question of immigration and land sale.[174]

The reason for the particular content of these talks was MacDonald's confidence that the Arab side accepted the British stand on the immigration quota.[175] For their part, the Arab participants in these talks did not refute categorically this impression. Thus, for example, the Egyptian memorandum dealt exclusively with the future composition of the Palestine Government. Nash'at further promised British officials that once London approved the Egyptian proposals concerning the Palestine Government, Mahmud would support the British scheme, and the Mufti of Jerusalem "could do nothing" if the Prime Minister of Egypt were to back it.[176]

The optimistic mood that prevailed as a result of British beliefs and Egyptian promises contributed to British-Arab understanding in London. By April, 1939, the Cabinet Committee on Palestine accepted by and large the conclusions of the Anglo-Arab team in London.[177] Nash'at regarded the British reply as a great achievement and decided to present it personally in Cairo.

He found that Mahmud had asked for further British concessions, as well as requesting London to permit the arrival of the Mufti to Cairo "for a day or two" to make him "toe the line".[178] Affected perhaps by the activities in Egypt of Palestinian Arab delegates, who were "priming" his ministers with stories about British brutalities in Palestine,[179] and loyal to his previous promise to give priority to the Palestinian Arabs in determining their future, Mahmud began pressing for the participation of Palestinian Arab representatives in these talks.

British officials in London, who were sure that the Palestinian Arabs would not be content with the settlement of the issue of the Palestine Government alone, rejected Mahmud's request. Lampson, however, thought that this refusal referred only to the British objection to the Mufti's presence in Cairo. Consequently, he conceded Mahmud's request to allow four Palestinian Arab leaders, 'Izzat Darwaza, Mu'in al-Madi, Musa al-'Alami, and Jamal al-Husayni, to come to Cairo to approve the British proposals.[180]

Lampson's generous concession, which was eventually to ensure the

breakdown of the Anglo-Arab understanding, annoyed his superiors.
Lampson was told that his gesture might "seriously affect" the success
of the policy that HMG had in mind. While he should have had an idea
of that policy from reading London's previous instructions,[181]
only at that late stage was Lampson first personally informed that
Britain did not contemplate achieving a written agreement with either
the Arabs or the Palestinian Arabs prior to their consent to the
British proposals.[182]

Lampson was infuriated by this directive. He thought that British
officials in London had made a grave mistake by omitting the
Palestinian Arabs from the Anglo-Arab understanding.[183]   As it
turned out, London's apprehensions rather than Lampson expectations
came true.   Mahmud, in spite of previous promises to obtain the
Palestinian Arab approval to the Britrish proposals,[184] could not
change the negative attitude of the Palestinian Arabs to the British
proposals. The Palestinian Arab delegates rejected both Mahmud's and
'Ali Mahir's request to accept the proposals. They refused to
compromise with proposals that offered less than complete
independence-- a stand that had been common among Egyptian nationalists
during their 1919 Revolt in Egypt. "When the Revolution started", they
maintained, "we had aims in view to attain. We cannot now tell our
people, stop the revolution because we got [sic.] some high
posts."[185]

Mahmud, who had accepted at the beginning of his conversation with
the Palestinian Arab leaders that they had the final say on this
matter, conceded their demand for further modifications of the British

scheme. New demands were formulated and Mahmud was to present them to British officials.

Approaching Lampson, Mahmud asked for "some assurance" that well before the end of the period during which immigration on a reduced scale was to continue, an exact census should be made of the total population of the country. "If the census showed that Jews had already reached one third of the population, immigration should be, at once, discontinued; if the census showed that already one third of the figure had been passed, excess Jews should be compelled to leave the country".[186]

This private view was to be included, though somewhat more vaguely, in a new Egyptian memorandum which was presented for British approval. The memorandum promised Arab support for the White Paper if three unconditional demands were fulfilled; a Palestinian Ministry with British advisers should be formed "immediately after the restoration of peace and security" in Palestine; Jewish immigration was not to exceed 75,000 during the five-year period, while the proportion of the Jewish population was to be restricted to one third of the total population; the question of land sales was to be settled by mutual consent between the High Commissioner and the Palestinian Ministers. Besides these threee demands, a forth one was added which stressed the "hope" that three years after the restoration of peace and order, a constituent assembly would be formed with the purpose of drawing up a constitution.[187]

Submitting this memorandum, which presented specific Palestinian Arab demands, Mahmud expressed, once more, his desire to see the

Palestinian question settled in order to get British troops back from Palestine to Egypt.[188]Lampson was very pleased with this expressed desire, which coincided with his own hopes. He regarded the memorandum as "not too bad". In his opinion, the differences between the British stand and the memorandum were "much more in the nature of shadow than of substance".[189]

In London the memorandum was viewed quite differently. "This is just what we expected and feared" commented a Foreign Office official on the memorandum. Mahmud's "most unfortunate move" of inviting the Mufti's people to Cairo raised new obstacles "which were bound to prejudice understanding with Arab countries".[190]

The previous Anglo-Arab understanding included consent to the British proposal that a Palestinian Ministry was to be established "in due course" and not "immediately" after the restoration of peace and order. Moreover, the new idea for a population census was not a practical reality, since "complete accuracy in such a case could never be proved". London also could not accept the demand that the question of land sales should be resolved by mutual consent between the Arabs and the High Commissioner. The ultimate authority regarding this problem had to be the High Commissioner. Finally, London maintained that the British proposal to operate the timing and the procedure of the new constitution within a timetable of five years rather than three, had already been accepted by the Arabs.[191]

Lampson was instructed to ask Mahmud to adhere to the previous Anglo-Arab understanding. Mahmud promised to do his best, but changed his mind after learning that London had decided to exclude the Mufti indefinitely from Palestine. He maintained that under the new circumstances he would not be able to press for Arab approval of the White Paper Policy.[192] It appears that this decision had been encouraged by the intention of the Iraqis to oppose the new British policy. 'Abd al-Qadir al-Gaylani, the Iraqi Charge d'affaires in Cairo, reported that Mahmud would not have condemned the White Paper, had not Nuri al-Sa'id told the press that Iraq opposed the British policy in Palestine.[193]

The Egyptian-Iraqi rivalry probably contributed to the leakage of detalis of the British policy to the Higher Arab Committee before the official publication of the White Paper.[194] This, in turn, finally determined Arab rejection of it. Mahmud, having been assured of both the Palestinian Arab and the Iraqi opposition to the British policy, hurried to make a statement to the press denouncing the White Paper. On behalf of the other Arab States-- a position he had claimed without the official consent of any of the other Arab States-- Mahmud announced that the Arab Governments could not "recommend the inhabitants of Palestine to collaborate with the British authorities on the basis of the project of the British Government".[195]

Mahmud's statement to the press was followed by numerous articles and reports from other political and public bodies which hurried to denounce the White Paper.[196] This criticism probably encouraged Societies, such as Young Egypt (Misr al-Fatat), to initiate a new anti-Jewish campaign calling for a boycott of Jewish businesses in Egypt.[197] Mahmud's Government was reluctant to take steps to control this activity. Mahmud preferred instead to rest on the prestige he had gained in the Arabic press by his statement. He was now giving interviews to Arab papers criticising the Colonial Office's attitude to the conflict, and blaming this Ministry (as Lampson was doing) for the bad treatment of the Mufti.[198] Arabs were praising his devotion to the Arab cause, and even the Mufti expressed his personal gratitude for this stand.[199]

No one seemed to be aware of the fact that this ostensible devotion to the Arab cause did not lead to greater Arab co-operation or to growing material assistance for the Palestinian Arabs. The sentimental feelings that were expressed to the Palestinian Arabs failed to produce financial or economic assistance for this people. Moreover, the public and Arab and Egyptian leaders soon lost interest in the issue. The growing international tension, and the expectation of Mahmud's resignation, distracted attention from the conflict. Sporadic moves to revive the Anglo-Arab dialogue over Palestine continued. In June, 1939, 'Ali Mahir, regaining his influence with the Palace, contacted the British Embassy, and informed officials there that the Palestinian Arab leaders, 'Awni 'Abd al-Hadi, Ya'qub Ghusayn, and Hilmi Pasha, had told him that they would like to discuss the White Paper policy with HMG.[200] Lampson conveyed this report to Mahmud, attempting to revive his interest in the conflict. He asked Mahmud not to let the initiative "slip into other hands".[201]

Mahmud showed little enthusiasm for engaging in a new round of negotiations. He promised to do his best. As an indication of this promise, Mahmud asked Basil Newton, the new British Ambassador to Baghdad, to convey a message to Nuri suggesting that "the Arabs might take their cue from the Jews and consider whether a settlement which was so unacceptable to the latter was not likely to be favourable to themselves".[202]

The fact that he preferred to convey such a message through a British diplomat, rather than through his own representatives, may indicate that Mahmud intended to impress British officials more than he expected to persuade his Arab colleagues. It should not be surprising that his message to Nuri failed to renew the Anglo-Arab talks on the Palestine conflict. By July, 1939, Mahmud was already a sick man, whose influence was once again eroded by the ambitious 'Ali Mahir. He soon resigned on medical grounds and left the Premiership to 'Ali Mahir.

Mahmud's period of rule had been characterised by Egypt's increasing involvement in the Palestine conflict. In January, 1939, Lampson attributed Egypt's increasing intervention in this conflict to "religious fanaticism"; a sympathy with the Arabs motivated by fear "perhaps not without reason" that a powerful and neighbouring Jewish State would seriously affect Egypt's economic primacy in the Near East, and the growing influence of the Palestinian colony in Egypt.[203]

Through other numerous reports, Lampson, with other officials, also displayed the affects of the internal political rivalries on the Government's involvement in the conflict. The involvement of the Wafd, the Palace, the use of the pan-Islamic associations by the various political forces, all helped to encourage Egypt's political engagement in the conflict. To these reasons, one may also add the changing attitude of the British Government, which fostered, if not motivated,

Egyptian intervention in Palestinian politics. By 1938, British officials, with Lampson's persistent insistence, first allowed and then even encouraged, Mahmud's involvement in the inter-Arab talks in the hope of moderating the Palestinian Arab stand.

As a result of British permission, Cairo became the centre of Arab activity regarding the conflict. The inter-Arab Congresses were followed by official Arab discussions in Cairo. They established Egypt's prominent position in the Arab world. The other Arab leaders, though entertaining their own dreams for leadership of the Arab world, did not express opposition to Egypt's centrality. According to Daghir, it was Faysal, Ibn-Sa'ud's son, who asked MacDonald to continue the Anglo-Arab talks in Cairo rather than in Paris, after the breakdown of the London Conference.[204] This was largely owing to reasons of convenience. The Arab delegates, had, in any event, to pass through Egypt on their way home - so why not confer there?

Once Cairo became the centre of the Arab talks, Egypt's leaders attempted to establish their prominent position in this region. Both Mahmud and Mahir tried to impress every party involved in the conflict that they were the leaders most able to mediate in the conflict. Both promised British officials that they would be able to moderate the stand of the Palestinian Arabs. At the same time, both attempted to impress the other Arab parties that they alone could modify British policy towards Palestine. While flirting with Palestinian Arab leaders, both also assured Zionist officials that they still remained neutral in the conflict.

Both Mahmud and 'Ali Mahir held very friendly talks with Weizmann.

During the London Conference Mahir invited his Zionist friend to come to Cairo for talks on the conflict. In Cairo, Weizmann discussed "co-operation between Egypt and the Jews of Palestine in the industrial and cultural field" with both Mahir and Mahmud. The Egyptian leaders suggested various means to bridge the gulf between the Zionists and the Palestinian Arabs. They assured Weizmann that the White Paper would be adopted by England, "but its effects might be mitigated, perhaps even nullified, if the Jews of Palestine showed themselves ready to co-operate with Egypt.[205]

The Egyptian Consul in Jerusalem, presumably upon directives from his Government, expressed similar views to Zionist officials. He expressed sympathy with any action that could bring the Arabs and the Jews closer together and offered Egypt's mediation.[206]

Although Weizmann was aware of the need to discount "both the usual Oreiental politeness and the fact that private utterances are somewhat less cautious than official ones", he was still impressed by this attitude. He felt that if the British Government had "really" applied themselves "with energy and goodwill to the establishment of good relations between the Jews and the Arabs", much could have been avoided. But, he complained, "whenever we discussed the problem with the British, they found its difficulties to be insuperable".[207]

Had Weizmann known the intense pressure that the same Egyptian leaders exerted upon the British Government to prevent the establishment of the Jewish National Home in Palestine, he would have probably been less enthusiastic about promised Egyptian co-operation and far more understanding towards Britain's "insuperable" difficulties in creating good relations between Jews and Arabs.

The ambivalent Egyptian attitude towards the zionist leaders evidently had one clear objective. This attitude was intended to induce zionist support for the Egyptian bid to lead the mediation effort to solve the conflict. A similar attitude was shown towards the Palestinian Arabs. Egyptian leaders hailed the Mufti of Jerusalem as the "loyal friend" and the "dedicated fighter",[208] but their actual assistance in this fight was rather limited. In camera, Egyptian leaders promised Zionist and British officials to impress moderation on the Palestinian Arabs, but in public they endorsed the 'right' and 'noble' resolutions of the Inter-Parliamentary Congress.

Ironically, British officials helped to consolidate the Arab camp against Britain's Palestinian policy. British officials had encouraged a joint Arab involvement in the conflict in the hope of moderating the Palestinian Arab stand. Owing to British acquiescence, Cairo became the centre of the Arab talks. In these talks, Egypt's leaders, anxious to lead future negotiations, agreed to support the Palestinian Arab demands. The united Arab stand had first been revealed during the London Conference, and demonstrated once again during the Cairo talks. British officials, who opened these talks optimistically, ended up facing united Arab pressure to give in to the Palestinian Arab demands.

PART TWO

FROM ISOLATION TO THE ARAB LEAGUE

CHAPTER ONE

THE RETREAT TO ISOLATIONIST POLICY

A.   Egyptianism and Arabism during 'Ali Mahir's regime-- 1939-1940

Shortly before the World War, the British Consul-General in Alexandria reported that the Egyptian Government and people were "far too engrossed in facing problems of mutual defence to pay much attention to Palestine".[1] By and large, this report proved correct. The increasing concern about the effects of the War on Egypt's economy, defence and even independence, and the formation of the greatly publicised "Territorial Army" by 'Azzam, at first Minister of the Endowments (Awqaf) and then Minister of Social Affairs in 'Ali Mahir's Government, distracted the attention of even ardent advocates of Arabism, such as 'Azzam, from the Palestine conflict.

Mahir did make some appeals on behalf of the Palestinian Arabs. Soon after assuming the Premiership, Mahir instructed Nash'at, his Ambassador to London, to express "great alarm" at the idea of raising a Jewish army from volunteers in Palestine and elsewhere.[2] Mahir was further reported to have intended bringing up the Palestinian issue in the coming session of the League of Nations.[3] When this plan failed because of the War, Mahir, during various encounters with Lampson and General Wavell, stressed the need for an amnesty for the Palestinian Arab exiles.[4] He asked for mitigation of court penalties imposed upon Palestinian Arab convicts, urged clemency for them,[5] and even offered to initiate a joint Arab appeal for Arab-Jewish co-operation in Palestine.[6]

In addition, Mahir promised the journalist Muhammad 'Ali al-Tahir to do his best for the Palestinian Arab cause. This, he said, was in accordance with the neighbourly and racial ties which connected him with the Arabs.[7] Loyal to this promise, Mahir ordered Hamdi Mahbub, his Director-General of Public Security, to stop the process of deportation of Palestinian Arab exiles. He further supported a newly created Arab Committee, initiated by Tahir, which pleaded for the release of the Palestinian Arab prisoners.[8]

Backed by Ministers such as 'Alluba, 'Azzam and Muhammad Salih Harb, all known for their support of Arabism,[9] Mahir could instruct his diplomats in Arab countries, and particularly Palestine, to emphasise Egypt's national, racial and cultural ties with the Arabs.[10]

However, these activities were overshadowed by the great engagement of Mahir, as well as his Ministers, with Egyptian affairs. Only once during Mahir's mandate was the Government policy towards the "Eastern [and not only Arab] nations" discussed in the Chamber of Deputies. Even then no Deputy contested Mahir's brief and rather mild declaration on the Government's position regarding the situation in Palestine and Syria.[11]

Moreover, in spite of Mahir's expressed support for the Arab cause, it was still subjected to certain reservations. Committed to Arabism as he may have been, Mahir never allowed the Palestine conflict to interfere with his relations with Britain. After all, his own position, as well as Egypt's economy and independence, were still dependent on British support. Although, as we shall soon see, Lampson, by and large, supported Mahir's initiative concerning Palestine, he was less pleased with the continuous anti-British agitation by "local malcontents" such as Ahmad Husayn, leader of the Young Egypt Society, and Muhammad 'Ali al-Tahir. Consequently, Mahir had to control the anti-British and anti-Jewish propaganda of these advocates of Arabism. Although he refrained from apprehending these persons, as British officials suggested, Mahir did check their political activities.[12] Bowing to another British request, Mahir also authorised his Director-General of public Security to prevent the fugitive Jerusalem Mufti from entering Egypt.[13]

Furthermore, the ideological commitment to the Palestinian Arabs had not only to take account of Britain's goodwill, but also to yield to Mahir's political aspirations. Although, as early as September, 1939, Mahir promised to send the Palestinian Arabs food and clothes worth altogether EP 25,000,[14] he postponed this aid for quite some time. In November, 1939, Mahir decided to change the nature of the promised aid, and to devote the whole contribution to something of "a permanent form". He thought to spend the entire donation on an orphanage in Palestine which would be named after King Faruq.[15]

Even this new project did not hasten the arrival of the Egyptian donation. The Arab community in Palestine flooded the Egyptian authorities with many other suggestions of how to spend the money. The Mufti, now exiled in Baghdad, also sought a share.[16] The many suggestions helped, perhaps, to bury the whole project under a mountain of bureaucracy, as no decision concerning the donation was taken. By March, 1940, the Palestinian Arab Press started to wonder what had happened to the promised aid, and by April, this developed into criticism.[17] By this time, however, the project had already undergone another futile change. A suggestion that Egypt, Iraq and Saudi-Arabia should establish a common fund for the relief of the destitute Palestinian Arabs was immediately rejected by Ibn-Sa'ud, and consequently abandoned.[18]

Only as late as May, 1940, more than eight months after the initial offer, did the Egyptian aid arrived in Palestine. Significantly, it had experienced yet another change. Only EP 5,000 of the original donation were delivered to the local Arab Committee for Orphans. The rest was spent on buying Egyptian goods and food which were distributed by the Egyptian Consulate.[19]

The constant changes and delays in Egyptian aid to the Palestinian Arabs did not prevent Mahir from continually calling for further British concessions to the Palestinian Arabs. Shortly after receiving a British reply to his plea for amnesty to the Palestinian Arabs, Mahir delivered a statement to the Press, asserting the existence of "negotiations" with Britain on this issue.[20] A British protest against this inaccuracy, was "lamely" rebutted. Mahir told Lampson that all he wanted was to distract the attention of the Press from the White Paper.[21]

As it turned out, Mahir himself attempted to attract press attention to this issue by advertising his talks with Nuri al-Sa'id concerning the Palestine conflict.[22]   In addition, Mahir also allowed his representatives to discuss the conflict with Zionist officials.   The contacts with the Zionists took place mainly through the Consul-General in Jerusalem, or his deputies.[23]   One of these Consul-Generals, Bahjat, developed particularly good relations with the Zionists.   Before leaving for his new post in Jedda, Bahjat met a Zionist official and praised the value of the Zionist contribution to the moral and material growth of the neighbouring countries.[24]   He further promised to do his utmost to enhance "rapproachement" between the Jews and the Arabs and attempted to arrange a meeting between Shertok, of the Jewish Agency, and Mahir.[25]

One may wonder whether Bahjat's initiative was merely a personal move.   However, be that as it may, Mahir did not reject it.   The 'promotion' of Bahjat to the prestigious post in Jedda may indicate Mahir's satisfaction with his services.   Moreover, although the arranged meeting with Shertok did not come off, Mahir kept his contacts with the Zionists through his Ambassador in London.   Nash'at met Weizmann, and told him that the Egyptians had a common interest with the Jews. He even went so far as to agree with Weizmann that the White Paper was "dead", and that a new policy was needed.   He suggested holding further talks with Weizmann, and added that he might invite other Arabs, "Iraqis and so on" to these meetings.[26]

Nash'at's efforts to become the centre of an Arab-Zionist dialogue indicated the nature of the Egyptian talks with the Zionists.   Since Nuri al-Sa'id held conversations with Zionists, Egyptian officials had to step in to prevent the possibility that Nuri might be left as the sole Arab link with the Zionists.

However, these contacts remained of minor importance compared to the diplomatic contacts that Mahir held with British and Arab delegates. The personal participation of Mahir in these talks indicated their importance. After all, in order to establish himself as the chief negotiator with the Palestinian Arabs, Mahir needed neither Zionist goodwill nor solely Palestinian Arab public approval; he also needed the agreement of Britain and the rest of the Arab countries to his intervention.

Britain had to be persuaded that Mahir, more than any other Arab leader, was the ideal mediator in the conflict. In his various encounters with British officials, Mahir did not miss an opportunity to discredit Nuri. Thus, for example, he let it be known to British officials that he disapproved of Nuri's loud rejection of the White Paper.[27] Mahir took pains to portray himself as a moderate and rational leader, a man unlike any other Arab leader, who was only "raising" the issue of amnesty to the Palestinian Arabs, not "pressing" it.[28] He further told Lampson that he "absolutely" refused Nuri's proposal to make the return of the Mufti a first condition for a joint appeal by the Arab Kingdoms.[29]

His own proposed Joint Arab appeal was far more moderate. It involved an all-Arab appeal to the Palestinian Arabs "to co-operate with the Jewish population in a spirit of loyalty towards Great Britain". Such an appeal, he added, would be far more effective if it followed, or was to be followed by, a British announcement of a general amnesty to the Palestinian Arab exiles and prisoners.[30]

Nevertheless, since the other Arab parties from Iraq and Saudi Arabia did not approve this scheme, Mahir did not cling long to it. Nuri, for example, stipulated that the joint Arab appeal be subjected to a British undertaking of a total amnesty.[31] Consequently, Mahir amended his own scheme. He adopted Nuri's suggestion and communicated in this spirit with Iraq and Saudi Arabia, asking their co-operation.[32] While the Saudis remained non-committal, Nuri arrived in Cairo, where further talks concerning the joint Arab appeal took place.

In front of Lampson, both leaders displayed perfect unity concerning the Arab demand for amnesty.[33] However, this harmony disappeared when the two leaders started to consider ways and means of pressing Britain to modify her Palestinian policy. Not only did Nuri insist on the Mufti's inclusion in the proposed amnesty, but he also envisaged a joint Arab appeal whereby Britain was to be asked to state that peace in Palestine would be rewarded by "complete independence of Arab states at the end of the war".[34] Moreover, in an apparent attempt to emphasise the growing importance of the Arabs, Nuri reintroduced his proposal for a treaty of alliance between Egypt and Iraq.

These schemes did not suit Mahir. Nuri's proposals endangered Mahir's evident desire to lead the mediation between Britain and the Palestinian Arabs, whilst also appearing to exceed the scope of his pan-Arab aspirations. Expressing sympathy with Arabism as a manoeuver intended to obtain Arab prestige and a better political stand vis-a-vis Britain was a well-proved policy. But to try and fulfill the idea of pan-Arab unity by concluding a treaty of alliance with Iraq was a far-reaching aim even for a pro-Arab leader such as Mahir.

Mahir was not only reported to have discouraged Nuri's idea to press for the Mufti's return to Palestine. He was also reported to have rejected Nuri's proposal for a mutual treaty on the grounds that "no sufficiently important Egyptian interest would be served by the conclusion of such a pact at the present time."[35]

Nuri, having opened the discussions optimistically, probably dazzled by Mahir's open pro-Arab outcries, returned to Baghdad frustrated and disappointed. He blamed Mahir for failing to reach an agreement and asserted that consequently, the whole idea of a joint Arab declaration was shelved.[36]

Nuri's determination to shelve the idea of a joint Arab statement on the Palestine conflict did not appear to discourage Mahir. In spite of his refusal to join an Egypto-Iraqi alliance, he was sill reported to have advocated Arab co-operation. In Egypt, Arab co-operation was advocated by the small but loud Misr al-Fatat. This society acclaimed Arab Unity as a major political principle intended to thwart the colonial powers. In March, 1940, Ahmad Husayn turned his organisation into the National Islamic Party. The five-year Party programme published and circulated secretly by Ahmad Husayn, leader of the Party, advocated unity between all Arab countries in matters of foreign policy, defence and culture, and the eventual abolition of customs barriers between them (Article I). The Party further announced its intentions to gain power in Egypt in order to attain this Arab Unity (Article II).[37]

The role that both the Palace and Mahir had played in the publication of this programme is not entirely clear. It is known that both the Palace and the Government gave funds to the Party and its newspaper. Mahir was further reported to have had advance knowledge of Husayn's circular, which took the form of a petition to the King. Nevertheless, it is unlikely that this manifesto was a Government publication because, as the pamphlet clearly shows, Husayn had proclaimed his own intention to play the leading role in Egyptian politics. Moreover, after publication of this platform, all official contributions to Husayn stopped, and Mahir further agreed with Lampson that Husayn "must be crushed". As a result of this development, Husayn switched his loyalty to the Wafd, and began supporting the Wafd's national demands, which had been published at the beginning of April, 1940, and which, incidentally, lacked any trace of Arabism.[38]

Although Mahir stopped official support for Husayn, he continued to express sympathy with the various calls for Arab co-operation. A new opportunity to demonstrate this sympathy presented itself in April, 1940, when Hafiz Wahba, the Saudi Minister for Foreign Affairs, came to Cairo. Wahba suggested that Iraq, Saudi-Arabia and Egypt should hold talks with Britain concerning the need to grant a general amnesty to the Palestinian Arabs. Mahir praised Wahba's idea and expressed his concurrence with the idea of a joint communication to London. Wahba's protest that he did not agree with Mahir's interpretation of his proposal made little impression.[39] Also, the Iraqi disapproval of Mahir's interpretation[40] did not deter Mahir. In spite of this disagreement, he instructed Nash'at to present a "common" Arab appeal, made "on behalf of three Governments", which requested a total amnesty for the Palestinian Arabs and the re-introduction of the Civil Courts in Palestine.[41]

British officials in Cairo and London were aware of the Arab leaders' desire to obtain all the credit for any British concession in Palestine for themselves, and the rivalry between them over this objective.[42] However, the possibility that Britain might exploit this rivalry was not even discussed in London. Instead, British officials were inclined to discuss the various Arab proposals and to make further concessions for the Palestinian Arabs.

The reason for this phenomenon should be attributed neither to British lack of imagination nor to Mahir's short period of rule. Nor should it be attributed only to the human instinct to accept appeals, such as the Arab appeals for amnesty in Palestine, which raised moral or humanitarian arguments. Aside from the sympathy of officials in London with the Palestinian Arabs, there was also a strong self-induced certainty that a quick implementation of the White Paper would maintain Arab friendship. The military defeats in Europe further encouraged an atmosphere in London in which the preservation of this friendship was believed to be an essential British interest. Loss of this friendship, so it was believed, could endanger the military position of Britain in the Middle East because of the gloomy prospect of internal uprisings in the Arab countries.[43] The numerous reports by British agents and officials in Arab countries gave additional impetus to the belief that Arab friendship, and consequently, the British position in the Middle East, depended on Britain's Palestinian policy.

Most prominent and consistent among British officials in the
Middle East who preached such an idea was Lampson. Lampson's support
for a pro-Arab policy may be attributed neither to his allegedly
anti-Zionist stance[44] nor to his admiration for the Arabs. In
numerous reports to London, Lampson did not leave much doubt about his
concern for the British strategic position in the Middle East. This
patriotic concern encouraged him to go "beyond his own beat",[45] and
to urge time and again a pro-Palestinian Arab solution, the adoption of
which would ensure Britain against the grave risk of losing Arab
friendship.

The constant approaches to the Embassy by Palestinian Arab,[46]
Saudi,[47] Iraqi,[48] and Egyptian delegates -- all expressing
similar requests for the implementation of the White Paper policy in
Palestine, and the need for complete amnesty there -- may have led
Lampson to over-estimate Arab co-operation. Although he still
maintained that the Arabs had nothing more than a "nuisance
value",[49] he, nevertheless, began citing reports about "a strong
movement" for "some sort of confederation of independent States in the
Northern Arabic World".[50] By citing such reports, Lampson hoped
perhaps to convince his superiors to heed his advice. Although Egypt,
Britain's main strategic stronghold in the Middle East, was not
included in the proposed confederacy, Lampson still insisted that a
failure to meet the Arab demands in Palestine might alienate the Arabs,
including Egypt, and consequently weaken the British position in this
area.[51]

Lampson's warnings were carefully examined in London. Aside from the Colonial Office, whose dislike of Lampson emanated from his previous row with MacDonald, he now also faced further criticism from his superiors in the Foreign Office. Baggallay, Head of the Eastern Department, doubted the accuracy of Lampson's assumption of a strong Arab movement of co-operation. Not only were the Arab rulers far from united, he noted, but Ibn-Sa'ud even rejected the whole idea.[52] Baggallay was also aware of the fact that the only thing that might ease Arab suspicion and distrust of Britain's intentions was the prospect of Britain's "clearing out altogether" from the area, rather than a pro-Arab solution of the Palestine conflict.[53] He suspected that in the light of the British defeats in Europe, the Arabs might even interpret a British concession in Palestine as a sign of weakness and insecurity, and would consequently press for further far-reaching concessions.

Nevertheless, the rationality of this critic did not result in a total rejection of Lampson's advice. The cumulative weight of military defeats and Lampson's persistent warnings appeared to erode much of the critic's confidence. Although Lampson's main advice calling for immediate implementation of the White Paper was not heeded,[54] some concessions in the spirit of Lampson's advice were made to the Arabs. Significantly, it was Baggallay - who destroyed Lampson's pan-Arab theory -- who also recommended the consideration of further concessions for the Palestinian Arabs. His main argument was that Britain should not "needlessly provoke a conflagration".[55] Hence, although R.A. Butler, Under-Secretary of State for Foreign Affairs, regarded the "common" Arab demands that were presented by Egypt as being of "a somewhat far-reaching character",[56] he, nevertheless, participated in inter-Departmental talks in London intended to appease these "common" demands. The talks between the Foreign Office and the Colonial Office not surprisingly resulted in a decision to grant partial clemency to Arab exiles, and to re-introduce the Civil Courts in Palestine.[57]

The impact of Lampson's views in Egypt may have been of no less importance. Lampson's relations with Mahir lacked, indeed, the somewhat intimate character of his relations with Mahir's predecessor, Muhamad Mahmud, Lampson treated Mahir suspiciously, regarding him as the "outstanding example" of an intriguer.[58] Following suspicions that Mahir was double-crossing him and Britain, Lampson pressed for, and achieved his replacement.[59] It is, therefore, likely that the private discussion which Lampson used to have with Mahmud over the Palestine conflict did not continue during Mahir's regime. However, since Lampson did not take the trouble to conceal his private views on the Palestine conflict from his Egyptian hosts, Mahir, the 'outstanding examle' of an intriguer, may have attempted to exploit these views to his advantage. Aware of Lampson's views, Mahir may have been encouraged to persist in his initiative, hoping perhaps that Lampson, unconsciously, would help him obtain influence and prestige in the Arab world.

B.   The retreat to an isolationist policy: Egypt and the
     Palestine Question, 1940-1942

The fall of 'Ali Mahir's Government in June, 1940, put an end to Government involvement in Arab affairs. Relegated to Opposition, Mahir, in an apparent reaction to his dismissal, attempted to organise a joint Arab approach to Germany. Soon after his fall, he, together with 'Azzam and 'Alluba, went to the Iraqi Charge d'affaires in Cairo, and proposed to proceed on a mission to concert an Arab overture to Germany.[60]

Nuri, however, was not prepared to risk his relations with Britian. He preferred rather to secure the future of the Arab States by the formation of a federation in the event of a British defeat in the Middle East. In August, 1940, Nuri attempted to promote this idea by proposing to convene in Baghdad a pan-Arab Conference. He visited Arab countries, approaching leaders such a 'Abdullah, Ibn-Sa'ud, and Hasan Sabri, the new Egyptian Premier, with this idea.[61]

Egypt, like other Arab countries, was no warmer to him this time than during his previous attempt, and Nuri returned to Iraq "a good deal abashed".[62] While 'Ali Mahir and his pro-Arab circle now supported Nuri's move, Hasan Sabri remained unreceptive. In his talks with Nuri, Sabri did not go beyond the limited co-operation that his predecessor had offered. He had "definitely inclined to pooh-pooh the idea of any direct Egyptian interest as an 'Arab State'", and restricted the scope of help to gestures such as lending technical experts for the development of Iraq and so on.[63]

This visible apathy concerning Arab solidarity seemed to result from renewed concentration on domestic problems. The severe economic crisis which erupted in Egypt following falling trade with Europe, particularly Britain, during the War,[64] led to considerable social and economic problems. These problems were intensified by growing internal tension between the pro-British and pro-German camps in Egypt.

The pro-German camp, comprised of 'Ali Mahir's circle and ultra-
-nationalistic organisations, such as Ahmad Husayn's National Islamic
Party, viewed Britain's activities in Egypt with growing contempt. The
appointment of a British Minister of State in Cairo and the
ever-growing flow of allied troops into Egypt, increased nationalistic
fears that Egypt was being subjected to a new Protectorate.

However, the Allied defeats in Europe during 1940, and the new
Axis offensive in North Africa and the Balkans (March-May 1941),
encouraged the impression that Britain, this time, was weak, and
therefore unable to hold Egypt for much longer. In April, 1941, Lampson
felt that Egyptian public opinion had become "fundamentally
pessimistic" regarding the outcome of the War. Defining this pessimism,
which no doubt touched the ruling pro-British elements, Lampson
reported that the average Egyptian believed that Turkey would allow the
German troops through to Syria and Palestine in order to encircle the
British position in Egypt.[65] Shortly afterwards, Lampson got the
impression that the fall of Crete (May 1941) was taken in Egypt as a
further indication of Nazi intentions to invade Syria.[66]

These beliefs led to different appreciations of the Syrian and
Iraqi roles. The pro-German and ultra-nationalistic circles in Egypt
viewed the Iraqi Coup with affection. Rashid 'Ali's revolt against the
British forces may have even encouraged similar plans in Egypt.[67]

The attitude of the Egyptian Government towards Rashid 'Ali's
regime was rather different. During Rashid 'Ali's first period of rule
(January 1941), the new Egyptian Premier, Husayn Sirri, firmly rejected
an Iraqi attempt to include him in a joint Arab protest against

Britain's Palestinian policy. In the name of the common bonds of Islam-- bonds which were used by Rashid 'Ali in his attempt to concert Egyptian and Saudi support with his anti-British stance -- Sirri urged him not to betray the Allies but to remain loyal to the Anglo-Iraqi treaty.[68]

In April, 1941, when Rashid 'Ali retook power in Iraq, this time by force, Sirri attempted to minimise repercussions in Egypt. He told Lampson that since the average Egyptian disliked the Iraqis as "a very poor lot", no particular reaction to the Iraqi Coup was to be expected in Egypt.[69] Sirri readily assented to British requests to withhold official recognition of the new Iraqi regime and instructed his representatives in Iraq in this spirit.[70] In spite of the damage that this policy caused to Eypgt's prestige in Iraq,[71] the Government persisted in its execution. The Egyptian Cabinet decided to recognise the new regime de facto only after similar British recognition.[72]

The loud support given in Iraq to pro-German politicians such as 'Ali Mahir, the Egyptian Government's most vociferous opponent, could not improve relations between the two Government. In May 1941, following the growing anti-British campaign in Egypt, the Government began a massive crackdown on the opposition. 'Ali Mahir was temporarily silenced by being dismissed to the country. In the beginning of June, 1941, the police arrested 'Aziz 'Ali al-Misri following his futile attempt to desert to the German camp. Warrants for arrest were also issued against Ahmad Husayn and Muhammad 'Ali al-Tahir, who were caught and jailed after being on the run for a short while.[73]

The fact that many of the pro-German and ultra-nationalistic activists in Egypt were also keen advocates of Arabism could not increase the popularity of this issue among the Government supporters. It is, therefore, likely that the Government's reported relief at the Allied invasion of Syria[74] expressed the joy felt at the Axis threat being removed from Egypt, rather than from satisfaction at the emancipation of Egypt's fellow-Arabs from the Vichy regime.

The Government's pursuit of these subversive circles affected, perhaps, the rather cold reception in Egypt of Eden's Mansion House Speech. Lampson was anxious to show evidence of public suport for a speech of which he himself was one of the main advocates. He gladly reported that "even" the fugitive Ahmad Husayn supported Eden's statement.[75] However, he was unable to cite a favourable reception of the speech by any other Government or opposition politican. This failure may indicate the scope of Egyptian interest in Eden's pro-Arab statement. Also, Alexander Kirk, the American Minister in Cairo, in his endeavour to learn of "representative opinion" in Egypt on the speech, could not find great support for it among "Egyptians consulted". The only sector in Egypt which showed professed satisfaction with the speech was the British Embassy in Cairo. Those 'Egyptians consulted', whose number, names and importance remain obscure, invariably qualified their approbation of Eden's speech with strong reservations.[76]

Kirk's further reports shattered the impression that behind these critics stood a genuine interest common to many. Shortly after Eden's speech, rumours circulated in London that discussions were to be held in Cairo on the future of Palestine and the formation of an Arab Federation.[77] Had these issues attracted great interest in Egypt at that time, one might expect to find, as on previous occasions, a general debate on these rumours in the Egyptian Press. However, even Kirk admitted that these issues were dealt with "very inconspicuously" by the Cairo Press, and only one local newspaper, al-Misri, mentioned a possible discussion of the matter in Cairo.[78]

Egypt's deteriorating relations with Vichy Syria and Gaylani's Iraq were also manifested in a decrease of trade with these countries. Palestine, Egypt's main importer in the Arab East even before the War, became Egypt's main trading partner during 1940-1941. During this period, trade with Palestine almost doubled, while Egyptian exports to the unfriendly regimes in Syria and Iraq sharply declined.[79]

Egypt's trade relations with Palestine were maintained and developed with both the Jewish and Arab communities. During the first years of the War, various Egyptian officials visited Palestine in an ever-increasing effort to promote mutual trade between the two countries.[80] Not surprisingly, Zionist activists could enjoy now a warmer reception for their achievements. Various Egyptian admini- strators visited Jewish settlements in Palestine, praising their economic achievements.[81] During these visits the Zionists could also listen to further statements rejecting Egyptian involvement in Arab affairs. Thus, for example, Hafiz 'Afifi, the new Director-General of Bank Misr, told Vilenski, in September, 1941, that all the political circles in Egypt opposed the possiblity of an extended Arab Federation which would include Egypt, Palestine, Trans-Jordan, Lebanon, Syria and

Iraq. 'Afifi declared that aside from the numerous problems and complications that such a project would arouse, the "decisive majority" of Egyptian intellectuals also rejected that scheme on the grounds that Egyptians neither belonged to, nor originated from, the Arab race.[82]

'Afifi was probably aware that such views might please the Zionists and facilitate the creation of a convenient atmosphere for business. During these talks, 'Afifi was careful to limit Egypt's relations with the Arabs only to economic interests. Although it is doubtful whether 'Afifi, in view of his support for the Palestinian Arabs in previous years, sincerely believed in his statement, it is clear that he did not regard Arabism as a rigid doctirne that committed him to anti-Zionism.

This pragmatic attitude might not have been held only by 'Afifi. The temporary increase in Egypt's trade with Syria and Iraq after the fall of Vichy Syria and Gaylani's Iraq[83] may have increased the number of pro-Arab calls in Egypt. Nevertheless, such calls should not be taken as more important or more significant than 'Afifi's talk with Zionist officials. In fact, there was no direct correlation between Egypt's economic and political activity in the Arab East. By the time Egypt signed the Pact of the Arab League, her trade with Europe and the United States recaptured the prominent position it had reached before the War. In spite of growing pan-Arab acitvity in Egypt during this period, Egypt's trade with Arab countries decreased in comparison with her trade with Europe and the United States.[84]

Also, the debate in Arab countries over the possibility of revived

Arab Unity -- a debate inspired by the Allied invasion of Syria (June 1941), the subsequent Allied declaration of Syria independence, and the invitation to Arab countries to acknowledge this independence -- did not leave a marked impression in Egypt. 'Abdullah's campagin in July, 1941, for a Greater Syria did not lead to any particular reactions by Egypt's politicans. Rather, it was the a-political inelligentsia which began to deal with schemes for Arab Unity. In the beginning of August 1945, Ahmad Amin, a Cairo-born writer who edited the literary magazine al-Thaqafa,[85] called for the formation of an Arab Alliance (al-Hilf al-'Arabi). In an article published in apparent response to 'Abdullah's political programme, Amin supported the creation of an Arab League of Nations ('Usbat al-Umam). This League was to be comprised of Egypt, Iraq, Saudi-Arabia, and a union of Syria, Lebanon, Palestine, and Trans-Jordan.[86]

The small number of people who responded favourably to Amin's call -- the historian Muhammad Farid Abu-Hadid, the writer 'Abd al-Wahhab 'Azzam, Muhi al-Din Rida, Rashid Rida's brother, and unidentified contributors from Syria and Libya[87] -- may have supported Kirk's report on the very inconspicuous reaction in Egypt to this issue. It is interesting that a similar call for Arab Unity by Fu'ad Abaza gave the union of the Nile Valley predominance over Arab Unity. Abaza, a descendent of a landlord family and the director of the Egyptian Agircultural Association, clearly preferred at that time the hydrological rather than the ethnic ties.[88]

Although Nuri al-Sa'id was at that time in Cairo serving as Iraqi Minister, no upsurge of Arabism occurred in Egypt. Lampson's fears that

Nuri's nomination would lead to "premature raising of pan-Arab issues in Egypt",[89] never materialised. Until his departure to Iraq for the Premiership (October 1941), Nuri, whose activities were carefully watched by British agents, never gave the Embassy a reason to complain against his activity.

It was rather in Baghdad, where pan-Arab feelings were dominant, that Egyptian officials reacted enthusiastically to the propspects of using pan-Arab propaganda to boost Egypt's prestige. In September, 1941, Mustafa 'Abd al-Mun'im, the Egyptian Charge d'Affaires in Baghdad, contacted the British Embassy there, saying he had been instructed by his Government to seek British advice for the restoration of Egyptian prestige in Iraq. 'Abd al-Mun'im added that "recent events" had produced a change in the isolationist thinking of his Government towards the Arab World and he wished to formulate a long-term joint policy concerning this change.[90]

One cannot know to what extent 'Abd al-Mun'im, a junior official in the Egyptian Ministry of Foreign Affairs, was acquainted with the changing policy of his Governemnt. It is also unlikely that 'Abd al-Mun'im, Charge d'affaries in Baghdad, had been commissioned to review, moreover to formulate, Egypt's long-term regional policy. Surely, Egypt's regional policy was neither dependent on, nor affected by, 'Abd al-Mun'im's views.

Furthermore, in his long report on Egypt's future Foreign Policy,[91] 'Abd al-Mun'im left little doubt that it was the present Egyptian policy of "inaction" that he wished to see changed. He expected Britain to support Egypt's claim for regional domination and thought that this domination should become "the primary and principal object" of Egypt's policy. This was because Egypt seemed to 'Abd al-Mun'im to have been "destined by God to be the palpitating heart of the Arabic speaking world" and because it was "a thousand times better" to be head in the Orient than a tail among other nations.

Developing his scheme, 'Abd al-Mun'im divided the Oriental countries into two groups. The first group comprised Turkey, Iran, and Afghanistan, with which Egypt was bound by "relations of religion and certain common traditions". The second group included countries with which the Egyptians were bound "by ties of religion, language, and race": Syria, Lebanon, Palestine, Trans-Jordan, Iraq, Saudi-Arabia, Yemen, the various Arab principalities in the Arabian peninsula, and all Arab countries where Egyptian "aspirations and future glory" were expected to be accomplished.

Examining Egypt's "aspirations and future glory" in each individual country mentioned in both groups, 'Abd al-Mun'im called for the reserving of the "closest attention" to Palestine, Egypt had repeatedly found it necessary to seek the annexation of Palestine because of the defenceless character of her Eastern frontiers. "Accordingly [he continued], to safeguard the integrity of our homeland, we should adopt as object of our policy in Palestine infiltration into that country with the ultimate object of bringing it up under the protection of the Egyptian State". Should this object prove unattainable, Egypt should at least ensure that a friendly power exercise control over Palestine. However, the unstable conditions in Palestine inspired 'Abd al-Mun'im to call for abandonment of the present Egyptian "attitude of inaction". Egypt had to seek either the primary object of annexing Palestine or the secondary object of consolidating British rule there.

'Abd al-Mun'im obviously preferred the first alternative. He regarded the annexation of Palestine as a "right", "natural", and "noble" object. He believed that the Palestinian Arabs "whose customs and character are similar to the Egyptians" and the Jewish immigrants would welcome Egyptian rule. He suggested that Britain be "frankly" approached by Egypt, and promised the same military concessions as in Egypt if she agreed to Egyptian annexation of Palestine.

In order to fulfil this aim, 'Abd al-Mun'im proposed initiating a propaganda campaign intended to portray Egypt as "a strong and respected power", and "the undisputed leader of the Arab East and Muslim powers". Among other means, he also suggested that Egyptians be encouraged to seek and find work in Palestine, and acquire a position of influence there "second only to that of Britain".

'Abd al-Mun'im's desire for Egyptian leadership of the Arab and the Near East was not unique to him. It had been shared already by many other Egyptians. Lampson himself acknowledged this desire in a report to London in October, 1941, in which he confirmed once more that Egypt regarded herslef as the natural leader of the Arab world.[92]

Nevertheless, in view of the remarkably unimpressive realisation of this desire since 1936 -- when it had first been reported by Lampson, Kelly and other British officials -- one is inclined to conclude that this desire was not given prominence in the considerations of Egypt's policy makers. It appears that even 'Abd al-Munim's views were not highly valued by his Egyptian superiors. Egypt's leaders never made any territorial claim on Palestine. Moreover, the development of 'Abd al-Mun'im's career[93] suggests that his influence was of a rather limited nature.

At that time, the political advice of various advocates of Arabism, such as 'Abd al-Mun'im, was ignored not only by the Government. Political opinion in Egypt also questioned both the ability and desirability of political Arab Unity. Karim Thabit of al-Muqattam, known for his sympathy with the Arab cause, was calling in September-November, 1941, to concentrate on less ambitious inter-Arab cultural and economic projects rather than on grandiose political unions.[94]

The Egyptian Government evidently had similar views. While Sirri avoided any political move towards the Arab world until his resignation (February 1942), his Government did contemplate in October, 1941, convening an Arab Cultural Conference in Cairo. The author of this proposal was Husayn Haykal, Minister of Education, whose idea received some public applause by Egyptian supporters of Arabism.[95]

While there was yet no sign that the Government, aside from approval of the project in principle, was making any other preparations to convene the Conference, changes in the internal political atmosphere took place which were to encourage the future spread of pan-Arab and anti-Jewish propaganda in Egypt. One change was the re-introduction of 'mass organisations' especially the Society of the Muslim Brethren, into domestic politics. The reason for this appeared to be political. Towards the end of 1941, the Government's ability to check the

opposition's activities weakened significantly. The new Allied defeats
in the Western Desert led to a revival of the anti-British propaganda.
The campaign that the Government conducted against pro-German circles
in Egypt suffered a further setback by the dragging on of the trial of
'Aziz 'Ali al-Misri, who had been charged with treason. His advocates
were exploiting the international situation by portraying Misri as a
symbol of Egyptian nationalism.[96] 'Ali Mahir, with Palace support,
renewed his attacks against the Government. The Wafd also increased
its activity, blaming Sirri for being a British tool. Sirri's
Government, far from being united behind him, was riven by internal
intrigues.[97]

In these circumstances, Sirri was desperately looking for new
allies to improve his public image. In November, 1941, he decided to
release Shaykh Hasan al-Banna, and Ahmad al-Sukkari-- the leaders of
the Ikhwan al-Muslimin-- and Fathi Radwan-- a leading figure in the
National Islamic Party-- from their internment. Justifying their
release, Sirri told a bewildered Lampson that had he kept these leaders
interned, he would have faced a "religious revolultion". However, in
light of the current Martial Law, and the presence of so many Allied
troops in Egypt-- facts which seemed to deter any potential revolt--
Lampson could not but conclude that Sirri made his move not for fear of
revolution, but to ease tension in the streets and to secure the
non-co-operation of the Ikhwan with the Wafd.[98]

The manoeuvre succeeded and the Ikhwan and National Islamic
followers avoided any attack on the Government. Sirri, however, had to
pay for this loyalty by letting the Ikhwan conduct their pan-Islamic

teaching and allowing them to re-organise and open new branches throughout the country. The growth of pan-Islamic propaganda came alongside with an increase in anti-Jewish feelings in Egypt. These feelings, exploited by the pan-Islamic organisations, emanated to some extent from sympathy with the Palestinian Arabs, but also from the belief that the Jews were responsible for the shortage of food and high prices of essential products.

Although one may doubt the veracity of Lampson's report in the beginning of 1942, that anti-Semitism had become a permanent factor in Egypt,[99] it seems safe to conclude that the pro-Nazi and pro-Fascist propaganda, then at its height in Egypt, contributed to ill feelings against Jews. The combination of the pan-Islamic propaganda of the Ikhwan and anti-Jewish feelings was to cultivate, and indeed dictate, popular support for the Palestinian policy of future Egyptian Governments.

CHAPTER TWO

THE MAKING OF THE ARAB LEAGUE,
EGYPT AND THE ARAB WORLD, 1942-1944

A.   Egyptianism, Arabism and Easternism, 1942-1943

The nomination of Mustafa Nahhas, leader of Egypt's biggest party,
the Wafd, as Husayn Sirri's successor, followed an incident
unprecedented in Egypt's political history.   On the eve of 4th
February, 1942, British armoured units surrounded the Abdin Palace in
Cairo, and Lampson walked in and presented King Faruq with an
ultimatum: his immediate abdication or his consent to Nahhas's
nomination. Faruq capitulated, and invited the leader of the Wafd to
form the new Government.[1]

Although the King's intervention in Egyptian politics had been
diminished as a result of this dramatic event, Nahhas still could not
afford to play great attention to Egypt's external affairs.   The
advance of Rommel's Afrika Korps which ended in al-Alamain (July 1942),
created a very tense situation in Egypt.   Nahhas had to repay the
British authorities for his nomination by waging a massive campaign to
suppress any anti-British activities.[2]   Additional time and effort
were devoted to various schemes to evacuate the King and his Government
in case of German occupation.

When not dealing with these national issues, Nahhas had to pay
attention to the consolidation of his own Party, the Wafd, following
the sensational resignation of his Coptic Lieutenant, Makram 'Ubayd,

from his office as Minister of Finance (May 1942). The bitter dispute with 'Ubayd was to dominate domestic politics during a great part of Nahhas's mandate.

From all this, it is quite clear that the attitude towards the Arab world could not acquire high priority during Nahhas's first year in power. During the first months of his mandate, Nahhas did make several statements on regional affairs. A few weeks after his nomination, Nahhas held a press conference during which he mentioned the need for closer cultural relations with Arab and Eastern countries.[3] This very issue was further adumbrated in the Speech from the Throne delivered at the end of March, 1942.[4]

However, this promise for closer co-operation with the "sister-nations of the East" was not new. It dated back to 1936, and even Sirri had used it.[5] Moreover, the Government's approach towards Arab affairs during the first year of Nahhas's mandate appeared to be casual and inspired by incidental events rather than by a carefully planned policy. Thus, for example, Nahhas granted asylum to the Palestinian Arab journalist, Muhammad 'Ali al-Tahir, who earlier had escaped from an Egyptian jail.[6] Nonetheless, Nahhas still suppressed other advocates of Arabism and the Palestinian Arabs such as 'Ali Mahir and Ahmad Husayn. In April, 1942, Nahhas met Tawfiq Abu al-Huda, 'Abdullah's Premier, who had come to convey the Amir's congratulations on Nahhas's nomination. The two leaders were reported to have raised the question of Arab Unification.[7] However, as no further contacts were made until sixteen months later, one is inclined to suspect that the reported conversation consisted of no more than polite exchanges of greetings.

Perhaps the best example of Nahhas's casual approach towards Arab affairs during this year is the story of his intervention in the Levant crisis.   In March, 1942, Lampson reported that several days after composing his new Government, Nahhas enquired why Britain did not recognise the independence of Lebanon.[8]   Lampson, probably, would not have mentioned this episode, had it not demonstrated the amount of Nahhas's ignorance of the Levant, and had not Lampson himself revealed an interest in obtaining Nahhas's recognition of Lebanese independence. In this event, although Lampson briefed Nahhas regarding the real situation and requested Egyptian recognition of the independence of the Lebanon, Nahhas refused recognition.

Nahhas renewed his intervention in the Levant crisis in May, 1942 -- the month during which he also developed great differences with 'Ubayd. This intervention, the cause of which should be attributed, as we shall soon see, to British officials in Cairo, involved French difficulties in the Levant.   Nahhas first discussed the need for representative constitutional Governments in Syria and Lebanon with General Catroux, de Gaulle's representative in the Levant.   After this conversation Nahhas proposed a deal to the Allies: he would call on Arab countries to make a declaration "in favour of the democracies" if "some   more   nationalistically   representative   Governments   were established in Syria and Lebanon".[9]   In June, 1942-- a month during which 'Ubayd made some of his more vehement accusations against him-- Nahhas invited to Cairo two opposition leaders from the Levant: Bishara al-Khuri,   leader   of   the   Lebanese   Constitutional   Party,   and   Jamil

Mardam, of the Nationalist Party in Syria.[10]   After listening to their views, Nahhas adopted their demand for 'free elections'-- the fulfilment of which would have resulted in the replacement of the current Governments.   Nahhas also proposed the creation of "a Syro-Lebanese organ" which had to run "the services of common interests" in both countries.   This organ was to be subject to the arbitration of "a commission composed of a delegate of the Free French, the British Minister in Beirut, and the Prime Minister of Egypt as President".[11]

As had become usual in such cases, Nahhas's activities inspired a spate of rumours alleging that he was involved in a grandiose project concerning the Arab World.[12]   Habib   Jamati, Head of the Orient Arabe news agency in Cairo, gleaned from conversations with Jamil Mardam and Bishara al-Khuri that Nahhas had "a definite plan of consulting with leaders of Syria, the Lebanon, Iraq and Saudi-Arabia with a view to an agreement on a project of Arab Federation in which Egypt would play the dominant part".   Jamati further maintained that Nahhas had already requested Ibn-Sa'ud and Nuri al-Sa'id to send delegates to these talks.[13]

Jamati's speculations could not be verified by British agents in either Baghdad or Riad. Moreover, they were strongly denied by those Arab parties whom Jamati had claimed to have concluded the agreement. Khuri, for example, was reported to have denounced as "false from A to Z" the alleged agreement reached between him, Mardam, Nahhas, and Nuri for an economic union between Egypt, the Lebanon, Syria, Trans-Jordan and Iraq.[14]   Furthermore, the selection of the Levant as the target for Nahhas's initiative did not necessarily imply that he or his team of advisers had special sympathy for this zone or a particularly good knowledge of local politics there. The ignorance that Nahhas demonstrated in regard to the Levant affairs during his first meeting with Lampson prevailed also during his new mediation effort. Amin 'Uthman, Nahhas's Auditor General and main link with the British Embassy, explained that Nahhas intended to approach only Iraq, Syria, and Lebanon with his initiative, omitting countries such as Trans-Jordan, Saudi Arabia and Yemen. While the exact content of the proposed call in favour of the democracies has never been fully revealed, Amin, an admitted ignoramus in Arab affairs,[15] emphasised that Nahhas had no intention of raising the issue of Arab Federation, and seemed to comply with the British request not to involve the Palestinian question in this declaration.[16]

The choice of the Levant for Nahhas's initiative appeared, therefore, to be rather the selection of an issue which was in the news and attracted British, Free French, and local Arab attention at that time. The internal split in the Wafd might determine the timing of the visit. It is possible that Nahhas attempted through this visit to distract domestic attention from 'Ubayd's allegation of corruption and nepotism.[17] The obvious support, and perhaps even encouragement, of Ahmad Ramzi, Egypt's Consul in Beirut, for such a scheme, may have determined its execution. Ramzi, an ex-Conusl in Jerusalem and a keen advocate of greater Egyptian intervention in Arab affairs,[18] organised the visit to Egypt of the opposition leaders of the Levant.[19]

The only field in which some advance had been made was cultural co-operation between Arab countries. The Government decided to carry out the decision of the previous Government to convene an Arab Cultulral Congress in Cairo. In June, 1942, the Consul in Jerusalem affirmed that his Government intended to convene this Congress, and further asked British permission to promote cultural relations with Palestine through visits of Egyptian lecturers.[20] Soon afterwards, in July, 1942, the Egyptian Cabinet asked Ahmad Najib al-Hilali, Minister of Education, to determine the form of cultural relations between Egypt and Iraq.

Hilali held talks with the Iraqi legation in Cairo and probably also consulted his technical adviser, the writer Taha Husayn. The latter had served also under the former Minister of Education, Husayn Haykal, and was therefore acquainted with, if not responsible for, Haykal's plan to convene the Congress. In August, 1942, Hilali's consultations resulted in a decision to establish a bureau for cultural co-operation between Egypt and Iraq. Its task was to work out the basis of a cultural agreement between Egypt and Iraq to which other Arab countries could adhere, and to organise cultural conferences at which all Arab countries would be represented.[21]

Nahhas did not fail to advertise this achievement. In a broadcast address in November, 1942, he stated that Egypt would spare no effort to labour for the Independence of the Arab countries. "All Arab and Eastern countries", he said, "desire the triumph of democracy and eagerly await the day when the right of the young nations for self determination would be affirmed". "On that day", he added, "with Egypt at their head, the Arab and Eastern countries will form a powerful and cohesive bloc (kutla qawiyya mutamasika), capable of assuming its international responsibilities and its moral obligations, and of taking its worthy place among the Free States (al-Duwal al-Hurra)". To demonstrate how far Egypt had gone to realise this dream of an Arab and Eastern bloc-- a vision which he himself had already raised during the 1930s-- Nahhas pointed at the new cultural bureau as "the most important manifestation" of Egypt's friendly and fraternal relations with Arab and Eastern States.[22]

A few days later, Egypt's cultural contribution to the Arab and Eastern countries was further mentioned in the Speech from the Throne.[23] The fact that the cultural bureau rather than the futile attempts to intervene in the politics of the Levant were emphasised as the most important manifestation of Arab and Eastern co-operation indicates, perhaps, the scope of Nahhas's regional plans at that time. The fact that his projected bloc included also Eastern, non-Arab countries indicates that Egypt's policy makers, in spite of a strong ambition to play a leading role in the region, had not determined a definite policy. It is quite clear that Nahhas's 'Easternism'-- if one is allowed to give a title to such views-- was quite different from the limited notion of Arab Unity which Nahhas himself advocated as his new political goal during the founding of the Arab League a year later.

B.   Nuri, Nahhas, and the Palestinian Arab cause

In December, 1942, there was an upsurge of pan-Arab activity in Egypt. It started with the Middle Eastern Medical Congress in Cairo, continued with visits of Syrian and Lebanese journalists, and culminated with the visits of the Iraqi Prince Regent and Nuri al-Sa'id.[24] Of all these visits, the one by Nuri al-Sa'id probably affected Nahhas's future intervention in Arab affairs most. Nuri, himself, did not see his meeting with Nahhas as his most important business in Cairo. His main consideration was a discussion on the future of the Arab countries with Richard Casey, British Minister of State. Upon Casey's request, Nuri prepared a "Note on the Arab cause", which was distributed to any interested party. The Note, which was the gist of what was later known as "the Blue Book", called for the union of Syria, Lebanon, Palestine and Trans-Jorsan. The Palestinian Jews were to be given semi-autonomy in the united Syrian State. This was to include self-administration in local Jewish municipalities, in education, health institutes, and in police matters. The semi-autonomy was to rest on International Guarantees, but to remain subject to supervision by the Syrian State.[25]

Because neither Nahhas nor Egypt played any particular role in the proposed confederation of the Fertile Crescent, Nuri may have preferred to omit this issue from his discussions with Nahhas. However, as Nahhas's potential support seemed vital to overcome both 'Abdullah's aspirations for leadership of Greater Syria, and Ibn-Sa'ud's staunch opposition to any Iraqi scheme, Nuri attempted to lure Nahhas into co-operation over an Arab issue. Once involved in a mutual Arab project, Nahhas might have extended his co-operation and agreement with Nuri concerning other Arab issues as well. The one Arab issue which must have generated similar reaction and mutual understanding was the Palestinian Arab cause. Nuri notified Nahhas of his concern about the increasing pro-Zionist propaganda in America and suggested sending representatives to Washington on this issue.[26]   Other Arab countries, particularly Saudi-Arabia, were also to be asked to join the protests.[27]

At that time, Lampson was not certain how much importance Nahhas attached to this idea.[28]   However, during January, 1943, several events occurred which apparently hastened Nahhas's decision to intervene in the Palestine conflict.   On 16th January, the Iraqi Government declared war on the Axis. Nahhas was reported to have been "infuriated" by this decision. He interpreted the Iraqi move as tempting the Allies to approve Nuri's pan-Arab plans, thus spiking his own aspirations in this respect.[29]

Moreover, around this time, Nahhas probably also discovered Nuri's precise territorial ambitions in the Levant. Nuri conveyed a copy of his Note to Casey to the Saudis through his Legation in Cairo,[30] and it is only logical to assume that a copy was also delivered to the Egyptian Government.

Having learnt about the Iraqi aspirations in the Levant, Nahhas may have decided to demonstrate that he also intended to have a say in Arab affairs. While reviving his communications with General Catroux concerning the need for constitutional regimes in the Levant,[31] Nahhas also found it necessary to despatch a representation to the United States Government to remonstrate against the growing pro-Zionist propaganda in America. The formulation of this representation may have been encouraged by the visit of a delegation of Palestinian Arab journalists. The visit, which was organised by Mahmud Abu al-Fath, the editor of the Wafdist al-Misri,[32] was used mainly to promote Nahhas's image as a regional leader. During the visit, Government newspapers hailed Nahhas as "the leader of the East and the Arabs" after he and several of his Ministers had entertained the Palestinian Arab delegates.[33]

A few days after, Nahhas instructed his Minister in Washington to submit an Aide Memoire concerning the Palestine question to the Secretary of State. The Memorandum for which Nahhas later took credit[34] opened with a statement that the realisation of the aspirations of Palestine had "always" been "one of the objectives of the Egyptian policy". Butrus Ghali's speech at the Assembly of the League of Nations (Spetember 1937) and the Cairo "convention" of 1939 before the London Conference were mentioned as examples of Egypt's interest in this problem. The Memorandum went on to explain the White Paper, and Egypt's opposition to the transformation of Palestine into "a powerful Jewish nation". It further asked the U.S. Goverment not to make any pro-Zionist promises or declarations and concluded with a promise that Egypt would be "only too glad to collaborate in due time in the solution of this thorny problem."[35]

The Aide Memoire did not lack in errors of detail. It stated that the White Paper promised independence to Palestine after twenty years, when in fact Britain undertook to establish an independent Palestinian State after ten years only, but subject to the co-operation of both Jewish and Arab communities. It also created the mistaken impression that Egypt concurred with the policy of the White Paper.

These errors may perhaps indicate that Egypt's leaders, in spite of their desire to have their say, had no great knowledge about the Palestine conflict. Not surprisingly, the memorandum succeeded in confusing even the Egyptian Minister in Washington. Aside from presenting the Memorandum, the Minister was unable to convey further official views on the solution to the conflict. Stressing that he spoke for himself only, the Minister thought that the ratio of those Jews who were to be allowed to remain in Palestine should not exceed one third of the population. He believed that "a feasible remedy" would be for the twenty-nine United Nations to agree to take their proportional share of Jews from all over the world, and assure them "safety and opportunity for a living".[36]

The Egyptian Memorandum was followed by other Arab representations against the U.S. policy in Palestine. The memorandum encouraged the impression created by numerous previous reports by American agents in Egypt and Arab countries, that neither Egypt nor the other Arab countries would acquiesce to a Jewish State in Palestine.[37] Since the State Department valued Egyptian and Arab friendship as important in the efforts to defeat the Axis, it sent an appeasing response to the Egyptian memorandum expressing understanding of the Egyptian stand.

This response did not help appease Nahhas and might even have encouraged him in insisting on a firm stand concerning the conflict. Two months after presenting his first Memorandum on Palestine, the Egyptian Minister in Washington delivered yet a further representation. The new Memorandum, which Nahhas was also to claim as a product of his pen,[38] protested against an alleged Allied plan to organise entry into Palestine of a large number of Jewish refugees from the Balkans.[39] Presented in March, 1943, the Aide Memoire adopted a hard line opposing any Jewish Immigration to Palestine. This opposition was justified on the grounds that there was an acute food shortage in "overpopulated" Palestine, and that there would be adverse consequences of such immigration upon "the indigenous inhabitants of Palestine". Fresh migration of Jews was proposed to be diverted "to land other than Palestine, better equipped with natural resources and possibilities of production".

The Minister further attempted to minimize the actual Zionist attachment to Palestine. During a private conversation with American officials, the Minister doubted whether Zionism still attracted many Jews. He was inclined to believe that after the War, many of the Jewish immigrants into Palestine would prefer to return to Europe.[40]

The Minister's doubts about the Jews' will to remain in Palestine-- a remarkable opinion in light of the Zionist 'Biltmore Resolutions' which suggested the existence of quite the opposite mood among Palestinian Jews[41]-- might perhaps be a reflection of views and thoughts that were expressed within the Egyptian Foreign Ministry. Such mistaken views obviously could not encourage an Egyptian dialogue with Palestinian Jews. Indeed, why should Egypians hold talks with residents who were believed to dislike their land?

For their part, American officials, either through ignorance or deliberate calculation, preferred to confirm and even support such views.[42] Consequently, the Egyptian Minister in Washington expressed his satisfaction with American denial of helping Jewish refugees. The State Department position that the conflict would be solved after the War through "the negotiation of a friendly agreement on the part of the people directly concerned",[43] must have further pleased Nahhas. After all, as a self-proclaimed leader of the Arabs, he was a party directly concerned in the solution of the conflict. He might have, therefore, derived further confidence from such statements to intervene in the conflict.

C. <u>Eden's Parliamentary reply (February 1943), Nuri's</u>
<u>initiative, and Egyptian reaction</u>

On 24th February 1943, Anthony Eden, Secretary of State for Foreign Affairs, in reply to a question in the Commons, stated that Britain sympathised with the idea of an Arab Federation, but any initiative towards this goal would have to come from the Arabs themselves.[44]

Egyptian politicians, as well as other Arab leaders, were inclined to interpret this reply as a challenge, if not an invitation, to formulate an accepted pan-Arab scheme. The small pan-Arab circle in Egypt must have been particularly pleased with Eden's statement. Since the middle of 1942, this circle had been attempting to attract official support for Arab Union. In May, 1942, "a number of persons of Syrian and Lebanese origin and some few Egyptians", formed in Cairo the Arab Union Club (<u>Nadi al-Ittihad al-'Arabi</u>). Fu'ad Abaza, director of the Agricultural Association in Cairo, was elected President. The aims of the Club were rather pretentious: it aspired to strengthen inter-Arab relations through the formation of similar Clubs in Arabic-speaking countries. These Clubs were expected to provide the independent Arab Governments with the popular support which they presumably needed as a talking point in their negotiations to obtain pan-Arab solidarity.[45]

The bombastic manner in which the Club and its President offered to serve Arab Governments failed to impress British officials in Cairo. The fact that until March, 1943, no Arab Government took the trouble to invite the services of the Club, encouraged the impression that it was "a rather ineffective body", the members of which were of no great importance. Abaza was similarly depreciated as "a well-known self-seeking intriguer", and "a pompous advertiser".[46] Moreover, the inter-Arab character of the members of the Club may have aroused suspicions that Fu'ad Abaza's cousin, 'Abd al-Hamid Abaza, "the dispreputable agent of the Amir 'Abdullah in Cairo", was the driving force behind the Club, and that consequently the Club was "to some extent" under the Amir's influence.[47]

While the true nature of the activities of this Club was debatable, no one doubted the sincerity of another advocate of Arabism in Egypt, Muhammad 'Ali 'Alluba. 'Alluba, whose genuine support for the Arab cause dated back to the beginning of the 1930s, published in July, 1942, a highly acclaimed book entitled: Principles of Egyptian Policy (Mabadi fi al-siyasa al-Misriyya).Two of the Chapters of the book "the defence of the homeland", and "Egypt and the Arab countries", referred to the need to defend Egypt from the Zionists' economic threat, and the necessity for cultural and economic unity between Egypt and its fellow-Arab countries.[48] 'Alluba was not content with the publicity and respect that he acquired through this contribution, but continued to call for greater cultural and economic co-operation with the Arab countries in various interviews given to the local Press.[49]

'Alluba's efforts had produced some results even before Eden made his Parliamentary reply. In the middle of February, 1943, "a well-informed quarter" in Egypt reported on the formation of "Arab Committees" in Cairo, and the attempts of one of Nahhas's Ministers to mediate between 'Alluba and Nahhas with a view to convening an Arab Conference.[50]

The Minister's failure to obtain 'Alluba's co-operation might only have added to the Government's suspicion when 'Alluba, and his ideological partisans expressed their sympathy with Eden's statement. Upon Eden's Parliamentary reply both 'Azzam and 'Alluba hurried to call for an Arab Conference to discuss Unity. 'Azzam, claiming to be writing "at the request of many who sacrificed themselves for Arab Unity", called for a Conference at which all Arab countries, independent or not would be represented. The Zionist danger was to be a major issue at this Conference.[51] 'Alluba also agreed that a Conference "with complete freedom of speech" should be called as an immediate response to Eden's statement.[52]

'Azzam's and 'Alluba's affiliation with the Palace and their demand for a popular Conference, where freedom of speech would be exercised, must have rung alarm bells in Government circles. The Government not only rejected any popular Conference which was not initiated by the Wafd, but also suspected a sinister conspiracy behind the project of an Arab Conference; all the political circles in Egypt were convinced at that time that Britain had an interest in an Arab union. Otherwise, why should Eden take the trouble to express this support from the respected rostrum of Parliament?

Egyptian politicans, having defined the idea of Arab Unity as a British interest, suspected that they, as the wealthiest and most advanced people in the area, would have to pay the dearest price and to make the greatest sacrifice for the fulfilment of this unfication.[53] This was not to their liking because of the commitment implied by the projected unity. Moreover, contemporary observers gained the impression that Arabs were not greatly admired in Egypt. In June, 1942, an Overseas Planning Committee in the British Ministry of Information estimated that Egyptians looked down on the Arabs as having "lower standards of culture and prosperity".[54] During the next two years, in which Egypt's Arab relations developed greatly, various officials and scholars found it necessary to affirm this estimation. Albert Hourani, who had spent six months in the Middle East at the request of the Foreign Office, wrote in Cairo in March, 1943, that relations between Arab-Asia and Egypt rested mainly on "mutual contempt". Egyptians regarded Arab-Asia as a field for commercial and cultural expansion and regarded its inhabitants as "troublesome poor relations".[55]

While cultural and economic projects which could benefit Egypt were welcomed, political unity with Arabs was resented because of the risk of uniting with "poor relations". It is, therefore, not surprising that soon after it had begun, the Government forbade any discussion on an Arab Conference in the Press. Nahhas justified this censorship on the grounds that "irresponsible people were entering the controversy".[56]

Had not Nuri proceeded with his initiative, it might well have been that Nahhas would not have entered history as the founder of the Arab League. But Nuri al-Sa'id had found in Eden's Parliamentary reply the opportunity he was seeking for for the advancement of his plans for the territorial unification of the Fertile Crescent. Shortly after Eden's statement, Nuri sent Jamil Madfa'i, a former Premier, on a special mission to Arab countries to underscore the need for Arab Unity.[57] Nuri paid special attention to obtaining Nahhas's support for this idea. Without waiting for Madfa'i's arrival in Egypt, Nuri sent a personal communication to Nahhas, suggesting the convocation of an Arab Conference under Egyptian leadership, and asking Nahhas's opinion on the form, the place, and a convenient date for such a Conference.[58]

By granting Nahhas the leadership of such a Conference, Nuri obviously expected to obtain both a political ally and a legitimate cover for his territorial ambitions in the Levant. Egypt, so it seemed, was neutral in the rivalry between Nuri, 'Abdullah, and Ibn-Sa'ud. Egyptian support for Nuri's rather than 'Abdullah's claims, or Ibn-Sa'ud's opposition, might have added considerable weight to Nuri's proposals.

Aware of Arab opposition to his ambitions, Nuri, although leaving the decision to Nahhas, made little effort to conceal his support for a semi-official rather than an official Conference. While an official

Conference was bound to confront him with the rival ambitions of Amir 'Abdullah and the profound opposition of Ibn-Sa'ud, an un-official Conference, representing 'pouplar' feelings, might have been more harmonious with Nuri's political vision.

Nuri did not let 'popular' forces alone dictate the structure of the future Conference. Suddenly he showed great interest in the activities of pan-Arab organisations such as the Arab Union Club. He gave his personal blessing to the creation of a Baghdad branch of the Club, and three of his Cabinet Ministers found it appropriate to join the Administrative Committee of the Branch.[59]

Moreover, aside from formulating political objects for the Baghdad branch -- objects which contradicted the "rules" of the parent institution in Egypt[60] -- Iraqi influence may have been behind the moves to create another branch in Palestine; Nuri told Sir Kinahan Cornwallis, British Ambassador in Iraq, that Rashid al-Hajj Ibrahim, President of the Commercial Committe of Haifa,[61] along with other Palestinian Arab activists, had sent him a message suggesting the calling in the near future of a "representative Arab Conference" which would discuss Arab Unity.[62]

Rashid al-Hajj Ibrahim at that time challenged the domination of Arab politics by the Husaynis' Palestinian Party,[63] and through such appeals he obviously attempted to obtain Arab recognition of his bid for leadership of the Palestinian Arabs. Even though this practical reason may have been known to Nuri, Rashid al-Hajj Ibrahim's appeal must have, nevertheless, pleased him. After all, the Palestinian Arab call resembled the Iraqi plan; indeed, it was presented to British officials as the decisive reason dictating the need for an Arab Conference.

Nuri did not tell Cornwallis what he had advised Rashid al-Hajj Ibrahim, but not long afterwards, towards the end of March 1943, the latter informed his Iraqi friends of the formation of a branch of the Arab Union Club in Haifa.[64]

With branches of this Club established in Palestine, Iraq, and Egypt, Nuri may have been more confident that the projected Conference would support his political scheme for the Union of the Syrian countries. He, therefore, sent another special envoy to Nahhas to obtain his approval for a semi-official Confereence on Arab Unity. The envoy, Tahsin al-'Askari, the Minister of the Interior and a member of the Baghdad branch of the Arab Union Club, received a friendly welcome. The Palace, the Arab Union Club, and other pan-Arab activists, such as 'Alluba, 'Azzam, and 'Abd al-Sattar al-Basil, all expressed profound support for the Iraqi proposal of a semi-official Conference.[65]

Having learnt of the Iraqi support for a popular Conference, both 'Azzam and 'Alluba took part in the creation of some new 'popular' Arab Committees.[66] Neither of them took the trouble to join Abaza's Club. Abaza belived that this was because these personalities, being professed opponents of the Wafd, did not wish to arouse the Government's wrath against the Club by their participation.[67] British officials, however, suspected that their true motive emanated from their resentment of Abaza's attempt to form the central group in support of pan-Arabism. This suspicion grew when both personalities, while ignoring Abaza's Club, participated in the resumed activities of the Arab Unity Society. The latter re-emerged chiefly because of the dissatisfaction of pan-Arab activists with Abaza's activities.[68]

The rivalry between these organisations did not prevent the Palace from lending its emphatic support to the Iraqi proposals. The King, being at odds with Nahhas, whose nomination he had never supported, may have found in a popular Conference an opportunity to deprive Nahhas of a glory on which he himself had set his eyes. Adopting, therefore, 'Askari's proposals, Palace circles approached Nahhas with the suggestion of a conference of organisations (such as that of Fu'ad Abaza) from the various Arab countries to discuss Arab Union.[69]

The strong support of the Palace and of the opposition for a popular Conference, contribued, no doubt, to the Government's rejection of this proposal. It was not long before that Nahhas, through a British ultimatum, had succeeded in ridding himself of Palace intrigues in internal politics. Nahhas certainly was not going to allow the Palace to regain influence through such a Conference. Consequently, Fu'ad Abaza was advised not to proceed to the inauguration ceremony of the Baghdadi branch of the Club.[70] Furthermore, Government newspapers and spokesmen discredited the idea of an immediate Conference, and gave instead prominence to the idea of preliminary consultation between the Arab leaders.[71]

When the Iraqi delegates ('Askari met Madfa'i in Cairo, where they formed a deputation) met Nahhas, he was therefore in no mood to compromise on his stand. The Iraqi proposal to hold an unofficial conference was boldly rejected in a manner that upset the delegates.

Nahhas, whom they found knew "nothing" about the Arab world, "monopolised" the conversation "almost entirely", and did not leave any doubts about his intentions to run the show by himself through consultations with Arab leaders on an official basis.[72]

That Nuri's initiative was not rejected altogether was not, therefore, because of the sympathy with the idea of an Arab Conference, but rather for Egyptian hopes to take advantage of an ostensibly British backed project of Arab co-operation. Nuri's initiative presented Nahhas with an offer which he might have found hard to reject; the coveted role as leader of the Arab World. Moreover, Nuri's initiative, carried out soon after Eden's Parliamentary Statement, might have been further interpreted as additional proof of British interest in this project. After all, had Britain rejected such a project, could Nuri have proceeded with his pan-Arab overture?

That Britain took the trouble to support Arab Unity -- and Eden's Parliamentary reply appeared to Egyptians to prove this support -- was reliable evidence substantiating Egyptian belief that the future international system was going to be comprised of unions and blocs. This view was developed during the War, especially after the Allies' great victories in al-Alamain and Stalingrad (October - November 1942), in the course of public debate about the shape of the new international order after the War. The annexation of mass territories by either the Soviet Union or the Axis, the amalgamation of the armies of the various fighting nations into big fighting camps, and the numerous public declarations by the leaders of the fighting blocs to unite against aggression, encouraged the impression that the new international order was to be formed by political alliances, unions, or blocs. The establishment by Britain of the Middle East Supply Centre (April 1941) with headquarters in Cairo, and the various international Conferences or meetings held in Cairo during the War, might have provided additional proof that the big powers had abandoned traditional separatist thinking in favour of co-operative regional arrangmenets.

How then could Egypt secure a respected place, particularly at the Peace Conference, among the great nations? Should she remain neutral, enjoying friendly relations with the various big Blocs? Should she not develop her diplomatic relations with future Great Powers such as Russia, China, perhaps Brazil?[73] Would it not be better if Egypt were to be represented in the Peace Conference as a great local power?

It was within this debate, which involved politicans, journalists, and writers,[74] that Egypt's advocates of an Arab policy appeared to make their greatest contribution by emphasising time and again the strategic importance to Egypt of an Arab Union. Although they belonged to the Opposition, the pro-Arab views of personalities such as 'Azzam, 'Alluba, Mahmud 'Azmi, and Karim Thabit -- all of whom were regular contributors to the most popular magazines in Egypt -- might have been read with interest also in Government circles. The ministerial attempt to recruit 'Alluba to the Government must have been a clear indication of the importance attached to his views.

Alliance (Hilf); Bloc (Kutla); League ('Usba or Jami'a); Union (Ittihad); Unity (Wahda) -- some of the terms which were used during this debate -- became therefore, a necessity not so much because of irresistible feelings of solidarity and fraternity with Arabs, as because of the political need to create a "powerful and cohesive bloc" which would occupy a "worthy place" within the new international system.

In this respect, Nuri's letter to Nahhas did not merely offer Egypt an opportunity to form such a local union; it also signalled that an Egyptian rejection of such a project might be exploited by another Arab country to create the expected Union, under British auspices, leaving Egypt isolated and insecure in a world comprised of alliances, blocs, and super-powers.

Evaluating such alternatives, it was, no doubt, "a thousand times better" to be the head of the Arabs, even though they were regarded as "troublesome poor relations" than remain as an eternal tail of Britain.

The fact that numerous terms were used during this debate suggests that, in spite of the common desire to play a prominent role in the region, no precise project with definite objectives had yet been determined. That the Government did not advertise their reaction to Nuri's initiative, but rather announced it during a Parliamentary reply, is a further indication of the uncertainty of Egypt's policy-makers concerning the precise nature of future Arab co-operation. The policy was first revealed only as a result of a question set down in the Senate by Husayn Haykal, leader of the Liberal Constitutionalists, who enquired about Egypt's reaction to Eden's statement.

Representing Nahhas, Sabri Abu 'Alam, the Minsiter of Justice, read a carefully drafted statement. The Egyptian Government, the

Statement said, believed that the whole question should be examined by the Arab Governments. Accordingly, Nahhas intended to make official approaches to ascertain separately the opinions of the various Arab Governemnets with regard to their aspirations. If an understanding could be reached, or was in sight, it would be necessary to call a Congress in Egypt with representatives of the Arab States under the Presidency of the Head of the Egyptian Government to complete the examination of the question, and take decisions which might attain the objectives of the Arab nations. An oficial invitation to Nuri had already been sent and the Government was awaiting his reply to proceed with their programme.[75]

The opposition leaders, who appeared to be surprised at this detailed programme, could not produce any sound criticism of this project. The only remark on the Government's Statement was made by Hafiz Ramadan, leader of the small Watanist Party, who expressed his hope that the situation of the Palestinian Arabs would be examined sympathetically.[76] However, Opposition leaders preferred by and large to drop, for the time being, their interest in Nahhas's Arab policy, and to amplify instead the allegations against the Government which Makram 'Ubayd had collated in a "Black Book".[77]

D. The popularisation of Arab Policy

Written in the form of a petition to the King, the "Black Book", published at the end of March, 1943, offered Faruq an ideal excuse to dismiss Nahhas. Faruq would have exercised this prerogative had not Lampson warned against such a move.[78] However, although Nahhas survived a confidence vote in the pro-Wafdist Parliament, his prestige and popularity eroded.[79] In their attempts to restore Government prestige, and to detract from 'Ubayd's allegations, Wafdist leaders introduced two new themes into public debate; Islam and Nahhas's Arab leadership.

It is perhaps significant that the Government's proclamation of their Arab policy coincided with the publication of the "Black Book". During April, while the Opposition was particularly active in discrediting the regime, pro-Wafdist newspapers published material intended to demonstrate that neighbouring countries regarded Nahhas as "the leader of Arab Unity".[80]

Had Nuri decided to respond quickly to Nahhas's invitation, he might have obtained, because of Nahhas's domestic difficulties, a favourable reception to his political plan of the Union of the Syrian countries. However, the disappointment of his envoys over Nahhas's reaction, combined with doubts about the stability of the Wafdist Government and domestic problems at home,[81] led Nuri to postpone his visit to Cairo. This delay also seemed necessary to try to appease the rising opposition of both Ibn-Sa'ud and 'Abdullah to the idea of an Arab Conference in Cairo. 'Abdullah regarded this idea as an Egypto-Iraqi conspiracy planned behind his back to settle the future of the Syrian States. Consequently, he issued a new manifesto calling for an Arab Conference in Amman, which was to discuss the Union of the Syrian countries.[82] Ibn-Sa'ud also took offence at not being consulted in advance about this idea, thus being placed in the same category as "the inferior Nahhas or the President of the Lebaness Government".[83]

While, therefore Nuri, (and as we shall soon see, British

officials) took steps to appease Arab opposition to future consultations with Nahhas,[84] the latter was publicising Egypt's new Arab image. In June, 1943, amid other numerous publications in the Press concerning Egypto-Arab relations, the publishing house of the Ministry of Education, Dar al-Ma'arif, published a new contribution by Dr. Yusuf Haykal, a former Mayor of Jaffa, entitled: Towards Arab Unity (Nahwa al-Wahda al-'Arabiyya). A major part of the book, which was introduced by the pro-Arab writer, 'Abd al-Wahhab 'Azzam, was devoted to the vital improtance of Egypt in any Arab Unity.[85]

The Government's pro-Arab campain coincided with the great upsurge of Islamic fundamentalism in Egypt. During the Second World War, a growing number of devout Muslims, frustrated by the influx of pleasure-seeking Allied troops to the big cities, British assistance to a corrupt and inefficient regime, an impotent party system, and a widening social gap, joined fundamentalist Islamic Societies.[86] So popular were these Societies, that a contemporary observer could count "no less" than one-hundred-and-twenty Islamic Societies in Egypt.[87] The biggest and most organised of them all was the Society of the Muslim Brethren.

Nahhas, like his predecessor, Husayn sirri, preferred to co-operate rather than clash with the Society. By "a mixture of bribery and threats", he secured for the Wafd the professed adherence of the Society.[88] This arrangement, which proved very valuable to Nahhas when the Society unequivocally rejected 'Ubayd's allegations, also benefitted the Ikhwan. Safe from Government prosecution, the Soceity grew fast. Although the exact number of its members had never been established,[89] even British officials agreed that it became a significant politcial force in Egypt.[90].

The regime appeared to respect this growing influence and attempted to maintain its good relations with the Society. British officials regarded Muhammad Sabri Abu Alam, the Minister of Justice, as the striking example of the influence the Ikhwan exercised within The Government.[91] Abu 'Alam, devout Muslim who replaced 'Ubayd as the Wafd's Secretary General, enjoyed growing prestige in and outside Egypt. In December, 1943, he headed the annual Egyptian pilgrimage to Mecca. There Ibn-Sa'ud claimed to have become his "close friend", and to exercise a great influence on Nahhas through him.[92] Although these various impression might be specious, they nevertheless illustrate the religious islamic zeal with which Abu 'Alam preferred to be associated. He might have used this image as a means to foster close relations between the regime and Ibn-Sa'ud or the Ikhwan.

Sabri Abu 'Alam was not the only Minister who had contacts with the Ikhwan. Other Ministers also took part in social activities of the Society.[93] It may even be that the formulation of laws abolishing the brothel system and the sale of alchohol on holy days, was envisaged as a gesture to, if not an inspiration of, Ikhwan teaching.[94]

Arab Unity as a separate goal was not included in the tenets of the Society. The Ikhwan saw Arab Unity only as a part of Islamic Unity. Moreover, in the light of its contempt for the Coptic community in Egypt[95] and the secular nature of Nahhas's inter-Arab talks, the Ikhwan may even have had certain reservations concerning Nahhas's consultations, especially with Christian Lebanon. Nevertheless, bound by its commitment to Nahhas's policy and by the belief that Arab Unity was a positive step towards the final goal of Islamic Unity, the Society declared its support for Nahhas's inter-Arab talks.[96] Moreover, this support may have been encouraged by the belief that the Palestinian Arab cause would be discussed in these talks. Although the support of the Ikhwan for a secular Arab League may have been somewhat reserved, the support, indeed pressure, for a precise policy favouring the Palestinian Arabs was unconditional. Proclaiming itself as the defender of Islam, the Society believed that Jewish immigration into Palestine -- a land sacred to all Muslims -- posed the most formidable danger to the integrity of the Muslim countries. Palestine, the Ikhwan believed, was an Arab country by the will of God. Her history, the Society maintained, began with the history of Islam. The Jews, therefore, had no share in Palestine and were advised to remain in other countries, where they could "pile up their capital and accept citizenship".[97] In a lecture given in September, 1944, the head of the Ikhwan branch in Tanta described the Jews as "the parasites of the universe", and "an impudent people who used Muslim and Christian blood for their holy services in Passover". The speaker further called his audience to hate the Jews, "to destroy them like sick dogs", and to unite in a Holy War (<u>Jihad</u>) against them.[98].

Pamphlets and lectures in this spirit, which were published with no real official control, could not leave the people (many of whom were devout Muslims) indifferent. A Zionist delegate found in October, 1944, that respected professors in al-Azhar were citing Ikhwan propaganda alleging that the Zionists aspired to the destruction of Islam by the

takeover of al-Aqsa Mosque. Public theatres presented plays in which
the Jew was protrayed as a thief, and a "Zionist" became a label to
give to the upper class, British officials, and any corrupt or
dishonest person.[99]

It is difficult to ascertain to what extent Ikhwan ideology was
undertstood and accepted. The peculiar turn that the term 'Zionist'
had taken in Egypt suggests that there were still a substantial number
of people who paid little attnetion to the Palestine conflict. Also,
the reputation of Arabs in Egypt was not affected greatly by the pan--
Islamic propaganda in Egypt. In May, 1943, Walter Smart, the Embassy
Oriental Counsellor, was to note that Egyptians took little real
interest in the Arab world. They regarded the Arabs as "uncivilised",
while the arabs regarded them in turn as "degenerate",[100] Later
that year, the British Minister in Baghdad reported that the efforts of
Egypt's Minister in Baghdad to foster Egypto-Iraqi relations were being
hampered by the behaviour of many of the Egyptian teachers in Iraq who
made "no effort to conceal their contempt for this country, its
climate, its institutions, and its inhabitants".[101]

Government circles were also disinclined to follow the attitude of
the Society towards the Jews. The tone of Government officials who
discussed the Palestine problem with British and American officials was
far more moderate. Due respect was shown to the misery of the European
Jews, and a differentiation between the Jews and the Zionists was
carefully drawn.

However, the official attitude to Zionism appeared to harden.
Opposition to further Jewish immigration to Palestine and a persistent

refusal to hold talks with any Zionist delegate,[102] characterised Nahhas's attitude towards the Zionists.

Nahhas's anti-Zionist stand was publicised during a tour he made to Palestine in June, 1943. During the tour, which Nahhas insisted was "purely private",[103] Nahhas, and his team of advisers, devoted some time advertising Egyptian sympathy for the Palestinian Arabs. The organiser of Nahhas's Palestinian trip, Abu al-Fath, editor of the Wafdist al-Misri, maintained good relations with Palestinian Arab journalists, whose previous visit to Egypt he had initiated.[104] With the help of these journalists, Abu al-Fath arranged the presentation of a laudatory address, signed by Palestinian Arab notables, invoking Nahhas's leadership. When Nahhas went to pray in al-Aqsa Mosque, a gathering estimated to number several thousands was quickly organised. A similar demonstration was organised to welcome Nahhas's arrival in Jaffa. Nahhas's donations for the repair of al-Aqsa Mosque and other local charities were greatly advertised, as well as the speeches he made supporting Arab co-operation and Union. During his tour, which lasted several days, Nahhas was repeatedly proclaimed as "the leader of the East and of Arab Unity" by local and Wafdist newspapers.[105]

The tour, in spite of its enthusiastic welcome by the local Press, did not lack unpleasant moments. The manners of Nahhas towards his Palestinian Arab hosts did not seem to demonstrate great respect.[106] The repeated Palestinian Arab calls for precise Egyptian economic and political help apeared to annoy Nahhas rather than to induce a favourable response.[107]

These unpleasant incidents did not prevent Nahhas and his team from seeking similar opportunities to promote his image in other Arab countries. Although reported to have declined Amir 'Adbullah's invitation to visit Trans-Jordan, owing to "pressure of work" in Egypt,[108] Nahhas, nevertheless, was said to have instructed 'Abd al-Fattah al-Tawil, his Minister of Communciation, to tour the Levant, learn local views there on Arab Unity, and prepare the ground for his own future visit to these countries.[109] As a further indication of such intentions, Wafdist and pro-Wafdist newspapers in Egypt began to pay special attention to the political situation in the Levant.[110]

The numerous reports advertising Nahhas as the Arabs' greatest leader did not fail to arouse the Oppoistion. Failing to overthrow Nahhas by the "Black Book", Opposition leaders decided in the beginning of June, 1943, to initiate a new campaign against the Premier.[111] As part of this campain, Opposition politicians began to take an active part in the activities of pan-Arab societies, notably the Arab Unity Society.[112] While the Government newspapers attempted to minimise the contribution of other Arab leaders to the Arab cause, Oppoisition leaders preferred to amplify this role. Thus, for example, 'Azzam, one of the leading figures in the Arab Unity Society, warmly congratulated Ibn-Sa'ud for an interview he gave to an American magazine, in contrast to the Government media which emphasised that Nahhas rather than Ibn-Sa'ud was the pioneer of Arab Unity.[113] 'Azzam, together with other Opposition leaders such as Dr. Ahmad Mahir, 'Alluba, and Hafiz Ramadan, also took part in discussions on Arab affairs with activists from various Arab countries. During these discussions Opposition leaders drew up a manifesto which called on the Arab countries to give priority to the solution of the Palestine conflict. The manifesto emphasised the need to free Palestine from the domination of the Jews, "a foreign race" whose religion was "inalienably opposed" to the Arabs. It further called for the convocation of a free and representative Arab Conference to discuss this conflict.[114]

The Oppoisiton leaders felt that the manifesto alone was not sufficient. At further meetings it was decided to send Mahmud Khalid, editor of al-Dustur, the Sa'dist organ, on a special propaganda mission to Syria, Lebanon, and Palestine.[115] By advocating the convocation of a national and representative Conference which would give predominance to the Palestine problem, the Opposition obviously hoped to break Nahhas's absolute control of a prospective Arab Conference. Nevertheless, by adopting this view the Opposition, wittingly or unwittingly, contributed to the publicity and popularisation of Arab issues, notably the Arab cause in Palestine. Attention to such issues reached new peaks with the beginning of inter-Arab consultations.

E.   The inter-Arab consultations and the Palestine problem

Given more time, the Opposition might have garnered enough support in Palestine and the Levant for a 'popular' and 'liberal' Conference. However, such apparent expectations were jeopardised with the arrival in Cairo on 22nd July, 1943, of Nuri al-Sa'id for consultations with Nahhas on the future of Arab Unity. Nuri arrived in Cairo after passing through Damascus, Beirut, and Amman, where he discussed with local leaders the necessity of inter-Arab talks, and promised to secure the interests of these countries in his discussions with Nahhas. In Cairo he held further talks with British officials.[116]

From the accounts of these talks it appears that Nuri's initial intention was to obtain Nahhas's support for the political solution envisaged in the Blue Book, with which Nahhas and other Egyptian leaders had already become familiar.[117] For Nuri, Arab Union meant a political Union of Greater Syria with which other Arab countries, starting with Iraq, would join in forming a Federation or Confederation. Therefore, in order to prepare a suitable atmosphere for a swift Egyptian adoption of the Iraqi plan, Nuri spared no effort to flatter Nahhas. Playing on Nahhas's vanity, Nuri took every opportunity to praise him as the leader of Arab Unity during his week-long rest in Cairo before the beginning of the official consultations in Alexandria.[118]

Flattered as he may have been by these accolades, Nahhas was reluctant to adopt Nuri's scheme. Free of any pressing internal problem which might have interfered with his judgement, Nahhas was surely aware of the great resentment in the Arab world over Nuri's plan. Nahhas himself was to learn of this opposition even before the beginning of the consultations with Nuri. In an apparent attempt to obtain Ibn-Sa'ud's approval of the consultations, Nahhas informed the King that the consultations with Nuri had taken place first simply because Nuri had raised the subject. This, however, did not mean that Iraq was being given priority over other Arab states.[119] In reply, the King warned Nahhas that Nuri was using him (Nahhas) to annex Syria and

Palestine, and was only interested in engineering a dispute between Egypt and Saudi-Arabia. The King stressed his opposition to any discussion of Arab Unity during the War, and emphasised his rejection of any envisaged Hashemite plan at the expense of the Syrian and Palestinian Arab people.[120]

When therefore, Nahhas began his talks with Nuri on 31st July, he was already acquainted with Ibn-Sa'ud's staunch opposition to the Greater Syrian plan. Moreover, during consultations with Nuri, Nahhas even went so far as to inform Ibn-Sa'ud that he agreed with the Saudi view.[121]

Consequently, the talks between the Egyptian and Iraqi delegations did not result in any substantial achievements.[122] The Egyptian delegation, in accordance with Nahhas's proclaimed promise to learn different Arab views on Arab Unity, presented a detailed questionnaire covering issues related to this subject. The talks, which were held in "an atmosphere of perfect cordiality",[123] took the form of an enquiry rather than a fruitful dialogue between different opinions. Nuri, who was anxious to obtain Nahhas's approval of his Greater Syria scheme, was rather flexible regrading the basic question of Arab Unity. Although he preferred a political Federation with an elected or nominated President and an Executive Council, in which the memeber states would be represented proportionally according to their population and revenues, Nuri did not stick to this scheme. He also suggested a second alternative where the Council had no executive powers and representation was on an equal basis. He left it to Nahhas to decide, after consulting the other Arab parties, which alternative to adopt and even asked him to decide which Arab parties to consult.

These generous concessions not only reflected Nuri's apparent indifference to the broader issue of Arab Union, but also his inclination to play on Nahhas's vanity. By leaving Nahhas to deal with Arab Unity, he hoped, perhaps, to obtain his support for the Union of the Syrian countries. Nuri even went so far as to attempt to involve Egypt in the execution of his political scheme. Explaining his Greater Syria scheme to Nahhas, Nuri substituted Egyptian guarantees for International Guarantees for the Maronite and Jewish minorities. Nuri did not define the scope of these Guarantees but let Nahhas ascertain the views of the Lebanese and the Palestinian Arabs on his scheme. He emphasised, however, that with the entry of Palestine into Greater Syria, the Palestinian problem would be solved: the Palestinian Arab hopes for an Arab State would be satisfied. The Jews, protected by Egyptian Guarantees, would also be satisfied with a quasi-autonomy which would secure them local administration in areas where they formed a majority. Nuri added that this arrangement, which was not to include Jerusalem, was the best way to preserve the status quo of the White Paper. This was because the number of Jews would not exceed the figure fixed by the White Paper, and so the Jews would remain a minority within Palestine and an even smaller minority in Greater Syria.

Nuri was rather satisfied with the discussions. Contrary to the disappointing impression Nahhas had made on the Iraqi envoys, Nuri found him co-operative and helpful, though quite ignorant of Arab affairs. Also the Egyptian team, particularly Najib al-Hilali, impressed him.[124] Hilali was to chair the cultural negotiations between the two countries, which followed the Nahhas-Nuri consultations, and were to be concluded with the only achievement in these talks: a proposed draft of a cultural treaty betwen the two countries.[125]

Nahhas also might have been pleased with the talks. While enjoying the great publicity given to the consultations, he still succeeded in maintaining the initiative by avoiding any commitment to Nuri's political scheme. He ended the talks with growing confidence that he would be able to obtain a common formula acceptable by all Arab parties. The internal situation in Egypt did not arouse his concern. He told Lampson that he was going to inform the King only "in very general terms" about his talks.[126] The King appeared to acknowledge that this was Nahhas's show. Though receiving Nuri, Faruq evinced hardly any interest in the subject and purposely kept aloof from these talks.[127]

The Opposition, disturbed by the growing Egypto-Iraqi co-operation and Nahhas's intentions to invite other Arab leaders, contemplated ways to defeat Nahhas's plans. Opposition personalities held talks with Nuri on Arab Unity, demonstrating that Nahhas was not the only Egyptian leader concerned with Arab Unity.[128] At the same time, Mahmud Khalid, the Opposition envoy, left Egypt to incite Arab objection to an official Conference.[129]

However, Opposition leaders could not determine the best strategy to undermine the talks; Muhammad Husayn Haykal, leader of the Liberal-Constitutionalists, thought that the Oppoisition should press for the solution of the Palestine conflict. Isma'il Sidqi believed that the

best way to block Nahhas was to oppose any inter-Arab negotiations
during the War -- an atittude which was (by accident or on purpose)
similar to Ibn-Sa'ud's views. Makram 'Ubayd suggested a new campaign
against Nahhas, exposing him as a British tool working for a British
interest,[130] while 'Azzam and other opposition newspapers urged
the participation of all parties and non-party political opinion in
these talks.[131]

Such a diversity of opinions, which may illustrate once more the
amount of support for Arab Unity, failed to deter Nahhas. The rumour
that the Oppoistion was preparing to draft a call to Arab leaders to
ignore his invitations was exploited and prompted raids on the houses
of such Oppoistion leaders as 'Ubayd.[132] The contemptuous silence
of the pan-Arab Societies in Egypt for these talks was answered by the
publication of Hasan al-Banna's personal congratulations on the success
of the talks.[133]

Backed by the professed support of the Ikhwan, Nahhas could
proceed with consultations with other Arab leaders without any fear of
domestic difficulties over this issue. Amir 'Abdullah, Ibn-Sa'ud, and
the Imam of Yemen were now invited to send representatives to Cairo for
similar talks.[134]

While Ibn-Sa'ud responded to this invitation by inviting an
Egyptian envoy to Riad,[135] Tawfiq Abu al-Huda, 'Abdullah's
Premier, arrived in Cairo at the end of August to discuss with Nahhas
the future of the Arab countries. The rapid response of 'Abdullah to
Nahhas's invitation was probably motivated by the fear of Nuri
succeeding in drawing Nahhas to his camp. Abu al-Huda was evidently

sent to emphasise the Amir's firm intention to have a say in the Union of the Syrian countries.

As 'Abdullah's amibitions resembled Nuri's, the talks with the Trans-Jordanian delegates followed similar lines. Like Nuri, Abu al-Huda did not seem to pay great attneiton to the final form of Arab Unity, and agreed quite readily with Nahhas's preference for an organisation in the form of a loose bond of co-operation between independent Arab countries. Like Nuri, Abu al-Huda also gave priority to the union of the four Syrian countries: Syria, Lebanon, Palestine, and Trans-Jordan. Similarly, he was not greatly impressed by Nahhas's knowledge of Arab affairs,[136] but attempted to play on Nahhas's vanity by requesting Egyptian assistance for the Greater Syria project.

However, in contrast with Nuri, Abu al-Huda maintained that if the Maronites and the Jews refused to join Greater Syria, the Maronites could be given the privileges which Lebanon had enjoyed under the Ottoman Empire, and the Jews administrative autonomy, provided the four conturies agreed. No mention was made during the talks concerning the possibility of Palestinian Arab participation in future consultations, although Abu al-Huda was to allude to such a possibility in a statement to the Press made on his departure from Cairo.[137]

The somewhat hasty arrival of the Trans-Jordanian delegation appeared to boost Nahhas's confidence in the success of the consultations. Already at that stage of the inter-Arab talks, he hinted at the form of Unity he expected. So confident was he, that he decided not to respond to Ibn-Sa'ud's invitation to send an envoy to discuss the issue. He told Abu al-Huda that both Ibn-Sa'ud and the Imam Yahya

could "fall into line" at a later date if they desired.[138]
Accordingly he sent Ibn-Sa'ud a short letter stating that circumstances
did not permit him to send an envoy, and that he would proceed with
ascertaining the views of other Arab nations.[139]

Nahhas's confidence in his ability to conclude an arrangement
without consulting a Saudi representative eroded quickly. The talks
with the Trans-Jordanian delegate attracted much less journalistic
attention. More interest was shown towards the elections in the Levant.
Faruq, having ignored Nahhas's inter-Arab initiative, took the trouble
to send his chief Aide de Camp, 'Umar Fathi, to convey his personal
congratulations to the newly-elected Syrian President, Shukri al-
Quwatli.[140] Nahhas, jealous of the publicity given in Syria to
the Royal Egyptian delegation, rushed to invite the Syrian Premier to
the inter-Arab consultations, and further announced a Cabinet decision
to open an Egyptian Legation in Damascus.[141]

These moves might have still been regarded as insuficient to
convince the Syrian President to send a delegation to Damascus. This
was because Quwatli was known as Ibn-Sa'ud's protege.[142] The
King's boycott of the consultations might, therefore, have had adverse
effects on Syrian participation in the talks. Indeed, Ibn-Sa'ud already
appeared to work against the continuation of the talks. His envoy in
Egypt advertised the King's denial of his participation in the
discussions. Riad was further reported to have contemplated a Syro-
Saudi-Yemenite Axis against Nahhas's inter-Arab talks.[143]

Moreover, with Egypt left as the only participant in the talks
with the Hashemites, the Greater Syria plan might have been realised.

This, the British Minister in Egypt reported, Nahhas did not like, because it would have endangered Egypt's predominant position in the Arab East.[144] Ibn-Sa'ud's opposition to Nuri, and his close relations with the new Syrian leadership, necessitated the new thrust to involve the Saudis in the inter-Arab consultations. The apparent expectation that Saudi participation in such talks would boost Nahhas's prestige and would improve his position against Faruq, could only encourage a fresh approach to Ibn-Sa'ud. Since Ibn-Sa'ud stipulated that any Saudi participation in the talks must be preceded by prior arrival of an Egyptian envoy to Riad, a special envoy had to be sent. The envoy, Kamal Hubaysha, the Government's Secretary, was provided with a message and a personal letter from Nahhas. In the letter, Nahhas begged the King to send a delegate to Cairo in order to solve the various questions involving the creation of Arab Unity. Flattering the King, Nahhas stated that Ibn-Sa'ud was the best of those working to unite the Arabs and that his help would therefore be crucial. In the message, Nahhas further emphasised that Saudi participation was vital to counter the role played in these consultations by "certain quarters" -- an obvious reference to the Hashemite desires.

Perhaps more effective than these communications were the talks Hubaysha held with Jordan, British Minister in Jedda, and Shaykh Yusuf Yasin, Ibn-Sa'ud's Acting Foreign Minister. Either by Nahhas's instructions or because of his own understanding, Hubaysha protrayed Nahhas's scheme in a manner consonant with Ibn-Sa'ud's inclination. Nahhas, Hubaysha stated, opposed a political Arab Federation, because he could not see Egypt or any other Arab country surrendering any of its prerogatives in favour of such a Federation. The question could never pass beyond the bounds of cultural, social and perhaps economic collaboration. Nor had Nahhas any intention of wider collaboration.[145] Such views may have convinced Jordan to persuade Ibn-Sa'ud to send a delegate, Yasin, to Egypt.

Upon his arrival in Cairo, Yasin discovered that Nahhas's views were not quite the same as the views expressed by Hubaysha. Indeed, by September, 1943, Nahhas could already conclude, in light of his previous talks, that no political union likely to damage Egyptian interests would be realised. With this assurance established, Nahhas could seek ways and means to promote the international importance of the projected Arab body. Nahhas insisted on including political issues, such as the Palestine and Syrian problems, in the discussions on Arab Unity. Moreover, although he accepted Ibn-Sa'ud's idea to form a preparatory Committee that would discuss the preliminaries of future Arab Unity, Nahhas opposed the idea that the Committee would meet in Mecca. The Egyptian Premier insisted on keeping future meetings in Egypt.[146]

The talks were, not surprisingly, suspended in order to let Yasin present the King with Nahhas's real views. During the interval Nahhas was busy in entertaining the Syrian delegation, which had arrived in response to his invitation. The delegation, headed by the Syrian Premier, Sa'd alla Jabri, received a showy welcome. Faruq, whose envoy had been so enthusiastically welcomed by the Syrians, insisted on a Royal banquet for the delegates. Nahhas responded by a big reception of his own,[147] perhaps to impress both Faruq and Ibn-Sa'ud.

This welcome helped to win the delegates to the Egyptian side. The delegates supported Nahhas's stand favouring inclusion of political issues in the future agenda of the Conferene. Moreover, in spite of expressions of support for the union of Greater Syria, the delegates did not appear to be too anxious to realise it. They supported such a Union, provided it was of a Republican nature, and they further tied any Syro-Palestinian Union to a prior settlement of the Jewish problem.[148]

Nahhas, pleased with a stand which parallelled his, hurried to convey it to Shaykh Yasin. The latter, in view of Ibn-Sa'ud's special relations with the Syrians, formulated a draft which would not run contrary to the Syrian attitude. While maintaining his opposition to any discussion on political questions, Yasin approved the idea of a Committee which would discuss cultural and economic co-operation. Moreover, Yasin insisted that the question of the Syro-Palestinian Union must be postponed until after the removal of "the Jewish danger" from Palestine. Yasin was impressed that Nahhas happily accepted his statement.[149]

F.   The Palestinian factor in the inter-Arab consultations

The emphasis that the Syrian and the Saudi delegates laid on the primary need to solve the Palestine conflict was imediately exploited by Nahhas. After the end of his talks with these delegates, Nahhas began pressing for british permission to include Palestinian Arab representatives in the inter-Arab talks. In November, 1943, Nahhas met Eden in Cairo and told him that all the Arab delegates shared "a general feeling" that some consultation with the Palestinian Arabs was necessary. If the Palestinian Arabs were left out of the consultations, he claimed, it would cause ill-feeling. If they were admitted, he promised, he would direct them "in the right way". Accordingly, he asked British permission to invite the Palestinian Arabs who had taken part in the London Conference, including those who were interned, to come to Egypt for consultations.[150]

It is worth noting that the records of the talks between the Arab leaders do not affirm Nahhas's claim that all the Arab delegates pressed for the inclusion of the Palestinian issue in the consultations on Arab Unity. Nuri agreed to the participation of Palestinian Arab representatives, but he also announced that their participation could be allowed only within the scheme of a Greater Syria.[151] Apparently for a similar reason, Abu al-Huda, the Trans-Jordanian delegate in these talks, did not even mention the possiblity of separate representation of a Palestinian Arab delegation in the talks. Both Nuri and Abu al-Huda attempted to play down the Palestinian conflict, maintaining that it would be automatically solved with the unification of the Syrian countries.

Precisely because of their opposition to this Hashemite scheme, the Saudis, the Syrians, and later the Lebanese and Yemenite delegates, attempted to play up the Palestinian factor. Ibn-Sa'ud used the Palestine conflict as an excuse to postpone any inter-Arab Conference until after the War. He claimed that while the Palestine question should be a major issue in any Arab conference, an Arab Conference in the middle of the War might embarrass the Allies and frustrate the united War effort.[152] Similar views were expressed by Ibn-Sa'ud's

client, Imam Yahya of Yemen.[153] The Syrian delegates, because of
their opposition to the Hashemite scheme, also required the solution of
the Palestine conflict prior to any Syro-Palestinian Union. Moreover,
while the Lebanese delegates preferred to concentrate on the potential
threat of the Greater Syria plan to their independence,[154]
Palestinian Arabs themselves were not united in the necessity to
represent Palestine. Thus, for example, 'Awni 'Abd al-Hadi, leader of
the Independence (Istiqlal) Party in Palestine, was reported to have
sent a Memorandum to Nahhas refuting the existence of a Palestine
problem since such a country did not exist. 'Abd al-Hadi was reported
to have claimed that the only existing problem was that of Southern
Syria, the Istiqlalist definition of Palestine.[155] Moreover, so
bitter was the rivalry between the various Palestinian Arab factions
that even Nuri al-Sa'id failed to rally the local Arab politicans round
an accepted leadership during a further visit to Palestine in October,
1943.[156]   .

The domestic Palestinian Arab controversy concerning the question
of representation did not remain a secret. Even pan-Arab activists in
Egypt were impreseed, at that time, that Palestinian Arab opinion
preferred a merger with Syria. 'Azzam, for example, an ardent supporter
of the Palestinian Arabs, avoided any reference to Palestine as a
separate entity. It was now al-Sham, the ancient name of Ottoman Syria
which included most of Palestine, which needed to be liberated from the
French and the Zionist influence.[157]

This great divergence of opinion did not prevent Nahhas from
urging in the name of the Arabs' "general feeling", British approval of

Palestinian Arab representation. While publicising his support for the
Arab cause on various occasions such as the Lebanese crisis (November
1943),[158] the Annual Wafdist Congress,[159], the Speech from
the Throne[160], the Medical inter-Arab Congress (December
1943)[161] and visits of various members of the Royal Saudi family
in Egypt,[162] Nahhas also took pains to remind British officials
that the turn of the Palestinian Arabs was coming.

When a British ultimatum, motivated greatly by fierce Arab
reactions, forced the Free French to reinstate the imprisoned Lebanese
leadership, Nahhas delivered a triumphant statement to the Press
thanking Britain. Nahhas praised the capital role played by the Arab
Bloc in the solution of the crisis and expressed his expectation to see
other Arab countries, notably Palestine, join the Arab Unity
talks.[163] He did not wait for a British resopnse to this call,
but took care personally to present his views to British officials on
the issue of Palestinian Arab representation. From the end of December,
1943, till the convocation of the Preparatory Arab Conference in
Alexandira in October, 1944, the issue of representation of the
Palestinian Arabs in the inter-Arab consultations was to recur time and
again in the Anglo-Egyptian discussions. Nahhas repeatedly asked
British officials to release the Palestinian Arab leaders, Jamal
al-Husayni and Amin al-Tamimi, from their internment in Rhodesia. He
attached considerable importance to their arrival in Egypt for the
talks on arab Unity and reiterated his personal guarantee that these
two would not constitute any danger.[164]

These efforts not only stood in contrast to his policy statement in March, 1943, to consult only delegates of independent Arab Governments, but also contradicted the impression of the Lebanese Premier, who found his Egyptian colleague to be uninterested in the Palestine problem.[165] The great attention devoted by Egyptian governmental and oppositional media to the representation of non-independent countries following the conclusion of the talks with the Lebanese and the Yemenite delegates,[166] could only indicate the change in the direction of Government policy.

Palestine, rather than the non-independent Arab countries in North Africa, attracted Nahhas's greatest attention. Although he and his officials paid some attnetion to the issue of the independence of North Africa,[167] Nahhas's approaches to British officials on behalf of the Palestinian Arabs were of a more consistent nature. In his attempts to persuade British officials to release the internal Palestinian leaders, Nahhas even went so far as to hint that he would also be prepared to invite a Jewish Zionist delegate to his pan-Arab talks.[168] Every opportunity was taken to publicise the Government's sympathy with the Palestinian Arabs. In February, 1944, a Governmental delegation, headed by Amin 'Uthman, by then the Finance Minister, arrived in Palestine for economic talks with Palestinian officials. Although the Egyptian delegates did not show great enthusiasm for making radical consecssions regarding Palestinian exports to Egypt, they nevertheless delivered speeches supporting the Palestinian Arab and the Arab cause.[169]

Pro-Zionist declarations of American Congressmen were not allowed to pass without reaction. In February, 1944, Nahhas instructed his

Minister in Washington to present yet a further demarche to the Secretary of State protesting against "the bombastic utterances and writings of certain Congressmen, whose language was aggressive, intolerant and unfair towards the Arabs". The Aide Memoire was this time far more specific in endorsing the Policy of the White Paper and opposing any intention to turn Palestine into a Jewish homeland. Invoking the Atlantic Charter and "the rising tide of American interestes in the Middle East", Nahhas concluded that no settlement of the Palestine problem could be arrived at without "the concurrence and approval of the party most directly interested", namely the people of Palestine.[170]

In his attempts to obtain British permission for the participation of the Palestinian Arab internees in the talks, Nahhas was not content with expected American support alone. He also warned that no Conference could be held before hearing the views of the people of Palestine regarding their participation in the plan for Arab Unity.[171]

The recurring emphasis on the need to consult the people of Palestine, and the growing engagement with the Palestine conflict, could not be accidental. Part of this growing activity should be attributed, no doubt, to the increasing concern that the situation in Palestine and public opinion in the West were tilting in favour of the Jews. The pro-Zionist declaration of the American Congressmen in February, 1944, was followed in March by a sympathetic promise made by President Roosevelt to American Rabbis supporting Jewish immigration and national aspirations in Palestine. Similar promises were reiterated later that year in the election programmes of both the Republican and

Democratic parties in the United States. Parliamentary questions in Britain and a public announcement by the British Labour Party in support of Jewish National aspirations in Palestine encouraged Arab apprehensions that Britain was going to desert the policy of the White Paper. The numerous talks held between the Egyptian Consul General in Jerusalem and Zionist activists confirmed previous suspicions (based, perhaps, on the Zionist Biltmore Resolutions), that the Zionists were striving for a separate Jewish entity in, if not consisting of, Palestine.[172]

Egyptians were rather suspicious concerning Zionist aspirations in Palestine. The ideological resentment of Zionism was based on the Arab-Islamic character of Palestine. As a foreign race believed to be brought by imperialistic powers to sow the seeds of division among the united Arab nation, Jews were not welcome to the region. The foreign religion of the new colonizers raised Muslim fears that Islam's third holy place was about to fall to Jewish conquerors. The rapid growth of the Ikhwan in Egypt not only helped to spread such fears, but also provided the advocates of Arab Palestine with formidable support. Economic fears that Jewish money might endanger the independence of Egypt's economy and hinder her developing commerce with Arab and Eastern countries also encouraged opposition to the Zionists. The fact that many of the Jewish immigrants came from Russia further helped to feed suspicions that a Jewish state would be a base for dangerous Communist ideas, which might shatter the stability of the neighbouring Arab regimes. The spate of protests against pro-Zionist activity in the U.S., Britain, and Palestine,[173] indicated, therefore, a growing apprehension that the Zionists might succeed in their attempts to create an independent Jewish State.

However, the great emphasis given by Nahhas to the Palestinian factor in the inter-Arab talks could not be wholly attributed to these genuine Egyptian feelings. In view of the evidence of the Lebanese Premier about Nahhas's indifference to the Palestine problem, it might even be that this revived interest in Palestine was artificially encouraged to serve a purely political end. After all, had the regime considered the creation of a Jewish state as a mortal danger to Egypt's independence and sovereignty, would it be content with verbal support only for the Palestinian Arabs?

Nahhas had a very good reason to demand consultation with Palestinian Arab delegates prior to the convocation of a pan-Arab Conference: by the beginning of 1944, Nuri al-Sa'id renewed his efforts to obtain a rapid convocation of an Arab Conference. Exploiting feelings of insecurity in the Levant caused by the presence of the Free French and growing fears of Palestinian Arab leaders of Zionist domination, Nuri attempted to obtain political support in these countries for the unification of the Syrian countries through an immediate convocation of a Conference, even without Palestinian Arab representation.[174] Nuri claimed that even Nahhas did not find it essential to consult with Palestinian Arab delegates.[175]

Nuri's pleas for a rapid convocation of an Arab Conference were rejected not only by British officials but also by Nahhas and other Arab leaders. Nuri's eagerness to convene the Conference must have triggered Nahhas's suspicions. Could it be that during Nuri's last visit to Palestine and the Levant he had succeeded in rallying the local leadership to his political scheme? Surely there must have been Palestinian Arab leaders who were not affected by Nuri's political ideas. The best, in fact the only, choice was to invite those Palestinian Arab leaders who were interned in Rhodesia and could not possibly have been infected by the propaganda for a Greater Syria. Hence, the recurring Egyptian demand to free Husayni and Tamimi, the only "true", "real" leaders of Arab Palestine, who were "suitable" to represent Palestine.[176]

Moreover, Palestinian Arab representation was needed because Nahhas, determined both to boost his prestige and to add a political flavour to the inter-Arab talks, sought a political issue around which all Arab States could unite. At that time the Palestinian Arab issue was the only subject on which all Arab States expressed similar feelings. The representatives of the independent Arab States, far from being united, differed and disagreed over all other political issues raised in the discussions. There was not one common view concerning the form, the place, the content, and even the necessity of an Arab Conference. Personal rivalries further helped widen the differences surrounding the principal problem. Nuri and 'Abdullah, who shared a similar political dream, were fighting each other over the future Kingdom of Greater Syria. The Syrian delegates, who disliked the idea of being part of the Hashemite Kingdom, advocated Republican Greater Syria with a centre in Damascus. Nahhas, who disliked any Arab Union which might endanger Egypt's supremacy in the Arab East, supported the Lebanese stance which rejected any political Union. The Saudis and the

Yemenites opposed any political discussions in an Arab Conference, which they wanted to devote to cultural and economic problems alone.

Nuri's initiative in the beginning of 1944 only underscored Nahhas's inability to control the irredentist aspirations of the Hashemites. The initiative was to reveal how wide the divisions were among the future components of the Arab League. Nuri's talks with Syrian leaders not only alienated him from Nahhas, but also alienated Ibn-Sa'ud from part of the Syrian camp. The talks further encouraged Ibn-Sa'ud to reject and thwart any future Arab Conference.

Nahhas might have, therefore, gambled on the hope that the appearance of a Palestinian Arab delegation would cement diverse Arab opinion and guarantee the successful conclusion of the discussions. Although Saudi Arabia and subsequently Yemen firmly opposed discussions on Palestine during the War to avoid frustrating the Allied efforts to win the War, they might have been persuaded to join the talks had the two Palestinian Arab leaders arrived in Cairo and had Britain permitted a discussion on this issue.

Thus, when Nahhas told British officials that without consultations with the Palestinian Arab delegates, no Conference could be held, he was, in fact, describing the only factor which he believed could unite the rival Arab parties. By emphasising the vital importance of the participation of the exiled Palestinian Arab leadership in future inter-Arab consultations, Nahhas acknowledged the important role that the Palestinian factor began to play in inter-Arab politics. It was also an admission of the important role that he expected Britain to play in such a Conference. Britain was now being saddled with the responsibility for a Conference, which British officials persistently insisted must remain a purely Àrab creation.

CHAPTER THREE

BRITAIN AND THE MAKING OF THE

ARAB LEAGUE

A.   The makers of Britain's 'Arab Policy

It is commonly accepted that Anthony Eden, Secretary of State for Foreign Affairs (1940-1945) was the architect of Britain's 'Arab Policy' during the Second World War. After all, Eden was not only responsible for Foreign Affairs but also issued the two main Statements which were believed to have reflected Britain's Arab policy: the Mansion House Speech (May 1941), and his Parliamentary Reply (Ferbruary 1943).

However, these Statements, which expressed British sympathy with Arab aspirations for unity, were neither clear nor correct reflections of the real views of the Foreign Office on Arab Unity.   Moreover, although Eden's name is frequently associated with Britain's 'Arab Policy', he played no part either in its inception or the direction it was to take. It was the Eastern Department of the Foreign Office which initiated, and formulated, the policy which Eden was to follow.

The basic guideline of this Department concerning Arab affairs during the Second World War was a general memorandum on Arab Federation which was prepared as early as September, 1939. The memorandum, which was in fact a collation of previous views of the Department on Arab Unity, used an incorrect translation for the Arabic term al-Wahda al-'Arabiya.   The memorandum translated this term as Arab Federation rather than Arab Unity.

It is likely that the Oriental experts of the Department chose to give this Arabic term such a clear political connotation as a result of the numerous plans for political union between Arab countries made by Nuri al-Sa'id during the late 1930's. Although none of these plans had impressed the Department, it considered pan-Arabism a popular phenomenon in the Middle East. Thus, although the memorandum dismissed as "a distant dream" the prospect that all Arab countries could be merged into "a single Empire or Federation", it regarded as "unwise" the idea of publicly opposing pan-Arabism. Instead, Britain was advised to guide this movement along "favourable" lines "if the point arose".[1]

However, the Department was reluctant to guide the pan-Arab movement towards unity. Both the escalation of the War and the great difficulties in realising this "distant dream"-- due to constant Arab rivalries-- discouraged any British inclination to foster Arab Unity. Nuri's futile attempts during late 1939 and 1940 to further Unity through discussions with Arab leaders did not succeed in involving London. Nuri's intention to convene an Arab Congress in Baghdad met with British disapproval. In August, 1940, the Foreign Office informed Basil Newton, British Ambassador to Baghdad, that in spite of sympathy for any Arab collaboration receiving unanimous Arab approval, Britain did not think that the time had come for any such initiative.[2]

In October, 1940, George Antonius, the Palestinian Arab activist, delivered to Harold MacMichael, High Commissioner of Palestine, a new Memorandum on Arab Unity calling for British assistance for this

.

project. Summing up Arab desires for Unity, Antonius said: "When Arabs speak of al-Wahda al-Arabiya, they have in mind a somewhat looser association of separate states than is conveyed by the term Federation; an association which is to be achieved, first by the attainment of independence and the removal of artificial (sic. imposed) frontiers and divisions, then by the strengthening of cultural and economic ties, and lastly, in some more or less immediate future, by the conclusion of such political conventions between the separate independent Arab states as time and trial may show to be in the best interests of the collective family of the Arabic-speaking people". Antonius further regarded the treaties between Iraq, Saudi-Arabia, and Yemen, as "a substantial realisation of al-Wahda al-'Arabiya".[3]

Antonius's Memorandum failed to rectify the incorrect terminology used by the Foreign Office in translating al-Wahda al-'Arabiyya. Similarly, it also failed to change the negative British attitude towards this goal. In October, 1940, shortly after Antonius had sent his Memorandum, Geoffrey Mander, M.P., asked the Secretary of State for Foreign Affairs in Parliament whether Britain had made any promise to form "a free pan-Arab Union" after the War.[4] Preparing the negative reply of the Foreign Office, the Eastern Department branded Arab Union as a "hornet's nest" that Britain should not stir up unless compelled to. Nevertheless, since this idea was still assumed to be popular in the Arab World, the Department advised yet again not to be "openly discouraging or critical" towards this project.[5]

The growing Axis propaganda concerning Arab affairs and subsequent Arab discontent, especially in Iraq, over Britain's policy in Arab countries, particularly in Palestine, compelled the Department to review its attitude towards Arab questions. In March, 1941, the Department formulated for the new Ambassador in Iraq, Sir Kinahan Cornwallis, the first official directive which presented new British responses to the major Arab issues. The directive was signed by Winston Churchill (Eden was at that time abroad) but had been prepared by Charles Baxter of the Eastern Department.[6] It included specific instructions concerning three particular Arab issues that were found to be of intense interest to the "politically-minded section" of Iraqis: the Palestine question, the future of Syria, and the possibility of Arab Federation.

Explaining the British attitude towards Arab Federation, the directive equipped Cornwallis with a strategy that was later publicly proclaimed by Eden. Britain, Cornwallis was told, still regarded the 1939 Memorandum on Arab Federation as relevant, and was not willing, therefore, to take the initiative in drawing up any scheme for Arab Union. Nevertheless, to counter Axis propaganda, Cornwallis was instructed not to oppose any federative scheme which was raised in "a practical form". Moreover, he was allowed "to make it clear" that Britain viewed Arab inspirations for Federation with sympathy, and would support "practical proposals to increase [Arab] co-operation".

It took some time until the policy Cornwallis had been advised to follow became a formal British policy. When Lampson, in April, 1941, made specific suggestions calling for British expression of sympathy with the idea of Arab Federation,[7] no official took the trouble to point out that Cornwallis had already been asked to express such sympathy. Instead, officials in London were once again inclined to reiterate the risks of playing with pan-Arab schemes and advised to leave the Arabs "to work out for themselves their schemes for Arab Federation".[8]

Less than a month had elapsed before the same officials found themselves compelled to review their attitude towards Arab aspirations.The clashes in Iraq during May, 1941, between British and Iraqi forces-- activities which also hastened the Allied invasion of Syria-- engendered the sudden necessity to lure the Arabs to the Allied camp. During this month, Churchill, in contradiction of, and perhaps even in ignorance of, the directive he himself had signed two months before, took the initiative of drawing up a scheme for Arab Union. Churchill's scheme, far from being raised "in a practical form"-- a condition regarded as essential in the directive which he had rubber-stamped--called for a radical revision in the political arrangements of the Middle East. An independent Arab State in Syria in permanent alliance with Turkey on the one side, and Great Britain on the other, was to be proclaimed. The possibility of restoring some of the Syrian territory to Turkey was also mentioned. Ibn-Sa'ud was to be crowned as the new Arab Caliph and be given the "general overlordship of Iraq and Trans-Jordan", while "the Jewish State of Western Palestine" was to be formed as "an independent federal unit in the Arab Caliphate".[9]

The Foreign Office experts rapidly dismissed the fantastic scheme which had been suggested by their Prime Minister as impractical. Consequently, only one of Churchill's minor proposals, that regarding the declaration of Syrian independence, was adopted by these experts and was incorporated in the Memorandum on Britain's Arab Policy, submitted by Eden to the Cabinet in May, 1941.

Eden's Memorandum was prepared by the same team that had prepared the Foreign Office directive to Cornwallis, and notably Baxter. The Memorandum, not surprisingly, repeated previous official advice. It doubted the practicability of a policy which would create an Arab Federation, but advised the Cabinet to refrain from opposing the Arab "vague aspirations" for unity, and even to take every opportunity of expressing support for them.[10]

The policy, in short, was an exercise in propaganda; a pragmatic political use of "a distant dream" to promote allied prestige. The risks taken were not believed to be high, since the Arabs, as the Memorandum reiterated, were not able to transform this dream into reality. Being sure of the inevitable success of this propaganda Eden did not wait too long before implementing the suggestions made in his Memorandum. Only two days after presenting the Memorandum to the Cabinet, Eden delivered his famous Mansion House Speech, which expressed sympathy with Arab aspirations for a Federation.[11]

Eden did not intend to commit Britain to more than this verbal expression of sympathy for Arab Unity. In fact, although Eden intended through this Speech to rally Syrian support behind the future Allied invasion of Syria, he did not rely entirely on this propaganda. Like Churchill, Eden also favoured Turkish co-operation in the invasion of Syria even "at the expense of temporarily estranging the Arabs".[12] Had Turkey participated in the invasion of Syria, British sympathy with

Arab aspirations for a Federation, if mentioned at all, might have been forgotten.

Turkey's refusal to take part in the military operations against the Vichy forces in Syria did not leave Britain free to deal with the Arab population of the Levant. Although the Allies fought the Vichy forces in the Levant, there were other Frenchmen, the Free French, who insisted on the preservation of French interests in the Levant. In his memoirs, Eden argued that at no time had Britain any intention of robbing France of its possessions in the Levant. "On the most egoistic grounds", he said, "it was to our interest that France should be strong and that the French Empire should survive, if possible, intact".[13]

Had this egoistic interest been so clear at that time, British officials would not have clashed with de Gaule, head of the Free French forces, over the politics of the Levant. It seems, however, that the occupation of Syria and Lebanon by an Allied army, the commanders of which were British, aroused old desires to bring the Levant under British control. Eden excused British intervention in the Levant with a moral argument: "the Prime Minister [Churchill] and I were insisting that the Arab population should not be made to feel that they had merely exchanged one set of French masters for another".[14]

The scope of British intervention in the administration and the politics of the Levant,[15] suggests, however, that the Free French were never given a fair chance to prove that they were indeed different from Vichy. In his War Memoirs, de Gaulle cited Richard Casey, Minister of State in Cairo, as maintaining that British intervention in the Levant was justified because Britain had "higher responsibility in the East".[16]

Aside from constant involvement in the internal affairs of the Levant, this "higher responsibility" was further manifested by a new spate of pan-Arab schemes envisaged by British officials who ignored the French presence in the Levant. Cabinet Ministers and their respective Departments appeared to be fascinated by the new political option which seemed to be opened by the Allied occupation of the Levant. Suddenly the old dream of enforcing a Pax Britannica in the Middle East appeared to have been given a fresh chance. Should not Britain seize on the new opportunity? Left alone, Britain surely would be able to preserve both Arab friendship and her interests in the Middle East. The Palestine problem could certainly be solved within an Arab Federation to the satisfaction al all parties involved. The immediate egoistic interest of solving Britain's problems in the Middle East triumphed over the egoistic interest of preserving the friendship of the Free French. Cabinet Ministers, led by Churchill, began to formulate various schemes of Arab Federation which greatly ignored the current political reality in the Middle East.

Following such proposals, a meeting of the War Cabinet, with Eden in the Chair, decided in September, 1941, to refer the whole question to the examination of the Middle East Official Committee. The Committee was invited "to examine the various forms which a scheme of Arab Federation might take and to report on their advantages and disadvantages". The Cabinet further instructed the Committee to pay special regard to a federative scheme which might offer a solution to the Palestine problem.[18]

In order to help the Committee determine the practicability and advisability of such a federation, Britain's representatives in the Middle East were asked to send their opinions on Arab Federation. Since all these representatives were convinced that any federative scheme was bound to fail because of Arab rivalries, none of them encouraged any British involvement in this issue.[19]

The negative views of Britain's representatives in the Middle East governed the negative attitude towards Arab Federation of the Middle East Official Committee. Discussing the numerous problems facing any party which aspired to fulfill this goal, the Committee reaffirmed the old advice: aside from verbal sympathy with Arab Unity, Britain should not endeavour to carry out any federative project.[20]

The Committee's consultations had immediate affects on British officials in the Middle East. In November, 1941, while the Committee was discussing the issue of Arab Federation, the Colonial Office, which was represented in the Committee's discussions, informed the High Commissioner of Palestine that although the "official" British attitude towards Arab Federation was that of the Mansion House Speech, "no undue weight" should be attached to any reports regarding immediate foundation of such a federation. The path was very likely to be "long and thorny", and no quick results were expected. MacMichael was further informed that Syria, Lebanon, Palestine and Trans-Jordan would probably be "the most favourable area for any nucleus scheme, especially one of an economic character".[21]

The directive made no mention of a possibility that Egypt might also join such a federation. The reason for Egypt's absence might be

attributed to her exclusion from the considerations of the Middle East
Official Committee. The Committee decided to ignore Egypt because
neither 'Abdullah nor Nuri included her in their federative schemes.
Nor had the British experts seen any signs of active Egyptian interest
in Arab affairs. They estimated that Egypt would not be willing to
limit her own political independence by joining a confederation of Arab
States.[22]

Lampson's report about Egypt's aspirations for leadership[23]
was taken lightly, because Lampson himself did not suspect that these
aspirations, which were not new, could lead to active Egyptian
involvement in inter-Arab politics. Although Egypt's leaders, contrary
to all expectations, began to intervene in Arab affairs, and although
the general Arab concept of al-Wahda al-'Arabiyya departed more and
more from strict federative schemes, no British official in London
proposed to re-examine the advisability and desirability of the new
developments. Once the Middle East Official Committee advised against
British initiative in any federative schemes between Arab countries,
the whole issue dropped out of the agenda of the discussions in
London.

B. The General Headquarters in Cairo and Britain's 'Arab Policy'

While London was shelving any initiative concerning Arab
Federation, other people, whose interpretation of the egoistic
interests of Britain differed from Eden's and even contradicted the
recommendations of the Middle East Official Committee, became involved
in Middle Eastern politics. These were the officers of the General
Headquarters in Cairo who commanded the military operation in the

Levant and controlled the defence of the whole Middle East.

Since no official took the trouble to explain Britain's policies and interests in the Middle East to the military commanders, they remained free to interpret these interests according to their own beliefs and understanding of the situation. The result of this interpretation was immediately felt in the Levant. In his Memoirs, de Gaulle describes with great anger the anti-French activities of General Wilson, Commander in Chief of the Allied forces in the Levant, and his British team of "arabophiles". In the Jezirah, Palmyra, the Hauran, Aleppo, Jabel-Druz, and the "tribal State of the Alawis", British officers were calling for the expulsion of the French from the Levant and advocating Syrian Union with Trans-Jordan under Amir 'Abdullah.[24] In their patriotic desire to safeguard Britain's interests in the Middle East, these officers were inclined to forget that the Free French, Britain's allies, were also entitled to a say, in fact the absolute say, in the Levant. Since even London was not certain to what extent the Free French claims for the Levant should be accepted, relations between the two allies deteriorated during 1942 from bad to worse.[25]

The activities of the British officers in Cairo were not only intended to terminate the French influence in the Levant, but also to rally Arab Opinion behind the Allied war effort. Contrary to the negative recommendations of the Middle East Official Committee, and perhaps in ignorance of them, British officers in Cairo thought to promote the Allied cause through the encouragement, in fact organisation, of pan-Arab projects. In April, 1942, Wing Commander Pat

Domvile, of the General Headquarters in Cairo, circulated among his colleagues a proposal to convene an Arab Congress of leaders from Iraq, Syria, Palestine, Trans-Jordan, and Saudi-Arabia. The Congress had to define the Arab "War aims and the course they should adopt in their long term national interests". Since such a Congress had to be "as representative and as strong as possible", Domvile thought that Egypt might be the best place for its convocation, and Nahhas the best leader to organise it.[26]

Domvile's proposal was not approved by all his colleagues, but was favourably received by Brigadier Iltyd Clayton, Political Adviser in the Minister of State's Office and General Headquarters in Cairo. Clayton thought that it might be a good idea to organise an Arab Congress which would come out "with a declaration in favour of the democracies". Clayton suggested encouraging Nahhas's move in this direction and further proposed to involve George Antonious and 'Abd al-Rahman 'Azzam in this project.[27]

Clayton did not conceal from his Arab friends his approval of an Arab Congress, with the result that they were rather confident that Britain supported such a project. Thus, for example, following their talks with Clayton, Tahsin al-'Askari and 'Ali Jawdat, Iraqi Ministers in Cairo and Washington, got the impression that all British officials welcomed the movement of an Arab Congress to be organised by the Arabs themselves "so that it should not be said that it was a British or a Government movement".[28]

Having been advertised in Arab diplomatic circles in Cairo, the idea of an Arab Congress soon reached Egyptian ears. Not long after the idea was first circulated in Cairo, Nahhas sent Amin 'Uthman to the Embassy suggesting an approach to Arab States in order to organise "some general declaration in favour of the democracies."[29]

Nahhas's proposal was favourably received by local British representatives. Both Lampson and MacMichael advised acceptance of Nahhas's offer.[30] The fact that Nahhas offered a joint Arab declaration in exchange for French concessions in the Levant was, not surprisingly, ignored. Even Eden, who disliked the idea for fear of prolonged Arab discussions which might result in further Arab demands in return for the declarations,[31] did not imagine that the Free French may have reservations concerning their role in the joint Arab declaration.

But General Catroux, the Free French representative, did have strong reservations about Nahhas's involvement in the Levant. Although Lampson advised him not to take Nahhas's activities "too seriously", since "it was more than possible" that Nahhas's interest in Arab affairs would flag,[32] Catroux was not placated. After all, both Nahhas and his Levantine guests -- Bishara al-Khuri and Jamil Mardam -- claimed to have British support for an initiative in the Levant.[33] It is not surprising that Catroux suspected a British hand behind Nahhas's initiative, which he might interpret as a further British attempt to check the French influence in the Levant. Consequently, Catroux became greatly annoyed by this intervention, complained that Nahhas's proposals "complicated matters and caused embarrassment", and urged the Minister of State in Cairo "to damp Nahhas down".[34]

The collapse of Nahhas's initiative, following Catroux's

remonstrances, saved London from a further necessity suggested by
Lampson and supported by the Minister of State in Cairo, to consider
whether Nahhas's initiative suited Britain's post-War policy in the
Arab World. Lampson justified this advice, given in June, 1942 (four
months before al-Alamain, when no one knew how long the War would
last), by asserting that Nahhas might extend his interest in Arab
affairs to the Palestine question.[35] This pessimistic
appreciation, which stood in sharp contrast to the one given to
Catroux, was to be repeated by Lampson during 1943.

At the end of January, 1943, after Nahhas had renewed his
communication to Catroux and further conveyed a representation to
Washington protesting against pro-Zionist propaganda in the United
States, Lampson reiterated his advice to London to formulate an
all-Arab policy. He maintained that "politically minded Egyptians were
full of ideas regarding Treaty revision, Egypt's role in the settlement
of Arab problems and even Egypt's claim for territories outside Egypt
and the Sudan". Lampson warned that Nahhas might exploit the American
factor to lessen the European hold on the countries of the Near and
Middle East. Therefore, before such a development could happen,
Lampson suggested determining "how far the Imperial requirements,
strategic and economic, would permit to satisfy the aspirations of the
Egypto-Arab world".36

A few days later Lampson developed his suggestion further. He
could now count three essential problems facing Britain in the Middle
East: the Treaty revision in Egypt, the French in Syria, and the
Zionists in Palestine. He appreciated that Nahhas's intervention in

the last two might embarrass London if Britain was not prepared to pursue the White Paper Policy in Palestine and to remove the French tutelage from Syria and Lebanon.[37]

Far from concluding, therefore, that for the time being at least, Nahhas must be isolated from Arab politics, the common British belief in Cairo was that Britain should rather expel the French from the Levant and implement the White Paper Policy in Palestine. This was because isolating Egypt from the Arab World was no more considered a practical possibility. Walter Smart believed that though the Egyptians disliked the Arabs, Egypt, because of her claim for Arab leadership, would always intervene in Arab affairs supporting any Arab cause against Britain. He thought, therefore, that Anglo-Egyptian relations would improve if Britain solved other Arab problems, particularly the Palestine conflict.[38]

Lampsons's numerous despatches to London urging a quick implementation of the White Paper Policy in Palestine[39] may only demonstrate the degree of influence that Smart's analyses had on him. In view of this evidence, one may suspect that an illusory belief prevailed among British officials in Cairo that once the White Paper Policy was implemented in Palestine, and the French expelled from the Levant, the Egyptians would find it very difficult to reject or resist the British stand over the revision of the Anglo-Egyptian Treaty.

The irony was that while British officers and officials in Cairo were, out of patriotism, allowing if not encouraging Arabs and Egyptians to believe that Britain supported an Arab Congress and a joint Arab initiative, London, in fact, wanted the very opposite.

Precisely because no post-War policy had been devised, British officials in London were reluctant to deviate from the recommendations of the Middle East Official Committee. In April, 1942, a joint Committee of officials from the Foreign and Colonial Ministries decided to shelve MacMichael's proposal for a Federation of Syria, Trans-Jordan, Lebanon and Palestine under a combined French, British, and American supervision. In August, 1942, Viscount Cranborne, Secretary of State for the Colonies, after consulting the Foreign Office, informed MacMichael that a study of his project at that stage of the War was "not necessary or desirable". This was because there seemed "little point in examining details until decisions have been reached on various questions in principle". The Minister proposed to wait until the Government decided on the lines on which a solution should be sought. Meanwhile, the wisest course was to adopt the policy advised by the Middle East Official Committee. Any immediate departure from this "policy of caution" would be "fraught with danger". Following MacMichael's further queries, Cranborne repeated his stand as late as October, 1942.[40]

Not only Cranborne, but also other Ministers involved in Arab affairs appeared to follow this "policy of caution". Thus, although Richard Casey, Minister of State in Cairo, comtemplated as early as November 1942, beginning examination of the possibilities of an Arab Federation, his proposed study was nevertheless restricted to a field that the Middle East Official Committee had thought it advisable to research, namely: "the desirability of forming large economic units in the Middle East".[41]

By and large the Eastern Department in the Foreign Office also had no desire to change, or to recommend a change in, the current political arrangements in the Middle East. In January, 1943, the Department sharply rejected Nuri's proposal to circulate his private Note to Casey on Arab Federation among around 300 British and Arab personalities in London and the Middle East. The Department had no wish to publicise an issue concerning which there was no Cabinet resolution, and consequently urged Nuri to keep his communication to Casey confidential.[42]

Neither Eden nor the Cabinet was prepared, even at that time, to contemplate a post-War policy for the Arab World. In February, 1943, when Eden was once again asked in Parliament whether Britain had any intention to promote greater co-operation between the Arab States, he could not present any new initiative. His reply in the Commons to Morgan Price's question reiterated the propagandistic policy of the Mansion House Speech. While repeating his sympathy for an Arab Federation, Eden was careful not to commit Britain to any particular initiative concerning the fulfilment of this idea. "Clearly", he maintained, "such an initiative would have to come from the Arabs themselves, and so far as I am aware no such scheme which would command general approval has yet been worked out".[43]

C. Britain and the Arab Conference

Eden's mistake was, of course, that the atmosphere that prevailed in the Arab world in February, 1943, was rather different from that in May, 1941. Propaganda used in May, 1941, to rally Arab support to Britain was interpreted by Arabs in February, 1943, as further proof substantiating views that they had already heard from British officials in Cairo: that Britain aspired to an Arab Union as part of the post-War settlement. With Egypt and Iraq having new leaders who were anxious to play a prominent role in the Arab East, every British statement was interpreted as a signal of future British policy. In this respect Nuri's initiative for an Arab Conference was a logical response to views which he might have honestly believed represented formal British support for such an initiative. While Clayton's 'signals' to the Iraqi Minister in Cairo to organise an Arab Conference may have been neutralised by the Foreign Office's blunt refusal to allow Nuri to advertise his private Note to Casey, Eden's Statement seemed to cancel this last restriction. After all, was not Eden's 'search' for a federative scheme which would command a general Arab approval a clear sign of approval, if not an invitation, to Nuri to publicise his own federative scheme among Arab leaders?

Eden's Parliamentary reply encouraged Nuri to advocate an Arab Conference and no doubt also induced him to publicise his private and confidential Note to Casey, in complete defiance of the British ban.[44] Eden's careless reply stirred up the "hornet's nest".

British reaction to Nuri's initiative may illustrate how incautious Eden's Parliamentary reply had been. Cornwallis, British Ambassador in Baghdad, was "most anxious to avoid anything that might disturb the present peaceful conditions" in Iraq and strongly objected to such a Conference in Baghdad.[45] Both Lampson and Casey shared the view that it was premature to convene a Conference when Britain's post-War policy had not yet been devised.[46] Nuri's determination

to include Palestinian and Syrian representatives in his proposed
Conference.[47] might have fostered further opposition to this
project. No British official was prepared to permit inter-Arab
discussions on these problems at that stage of the War.

How should British officials frustrate an unexpected Arab
initiative which had started as a result of an incautious British
statement? Since Eden's Statement in Parliament prevented the
possibility of open opposition to the proposed Arab Conference, the
Eastern Department now advised the British representatives in the
Middle East to discourage the proposal by objecting to the immediate
convocation of a Conference, demanding prior consultations between Arab
leaders and insisting on confidential discussions between the Arab
parties.[48]

This policy was considered the best because it intended to
prevent the immediate convocation of an Arab Conference without
disclosing British objection. Inter-Arab relations seemed so impaired
that the prospect that such consultations might culminate in a
Conference was evidently dismissed. The Arab reactions to Nuri's
initiative could only have encouraged British impressions that the Arab
world was widely divided: Nuri did not wish to include Saudi-Arabia in
this Conference.[49] Nahhas suspected that Nuri was acting out of
selfish and other dubious motives.[50] Amir 'Abdullah objected
"emphatically" to any Iraqi scheme for fear it would jeopardise his own
claim for the leadership of Greater Syria,[51] while Ibn-Sa'ud was
"seriously annoyed" at being excluded from the picture, and refused to
co-operate with either Nuri or Nahhas.[52]

In the light of such differences of opinion among the Arab leaders, it is quite obvious that by practicing a policy which called for continuous Arab talks, British officials unwittingly kept alive the idea of the Conference. The reason for British encouragement of Arab talks should not be attributed to a tendency to follow blindly Foreign Office directives. Rather, to a belief, which prevailed particularly in the Office of the Minister of State in Cairo, that the Arab talks were bound to lead to greater economic co-operation between the Middle Eastern countries. Future economic co-operation between these countries became one of the main concerns of Richard Casey, Minister of State in Cairo. In May, 1942, Casey presented the Middle East War Council a study prepared by his office, which discussed the prospects of co-operation between the Middle Eastern countries. The study, which the Middle East Official Committee had permitted in January, 1943, examined the prospects of political and economic co-operation between the States of the Middle East. Influenced perhaps by the pessimistic observations of the Middle East Official Committee and perhaps also by Nahhas's cautious reaction to Nuri's initiative, Casey reiterated the view that a political confederation of Arab countries "on a wide scale" was "impracticable" owing to "the conflicting aspirations of the various countries, and the peculiar status of Palestine and Syria". While the initiative concerning such a federation had to be left to the Arabs, the most practical course recommended by Casey's team was "to encourage efforts towards economic and cultural unity, out of which some form of political confederation, at least in 'Greater Syria' might ultimately emerge".[53]

By and large the Middle East War Council approved the proposed scheme, and Casey flew to London to discuss the issue with the War Cabinet. He succeeded in convincing the War Cabinet to agree to transform the Middle East Supply Centre into a Middle East Economic Council which would include representatives from Britain, the United States, and the local governments in the region.[54] Since the United States and the local governments were to be involved in the proposed scheme, it was clear to Casey and the rest of the Cabinet that the whole issue was conditional on both American co-operation and the settlement of the Palestine and Syrian problem.[55]

Neither condition was fulfilled. Following the Cabinet decision and growing pressure from Middle East representatives to contemplate a post-War policy in light of the American and Russian penetration to the Area,[56] the Foreign Office began discussing the possibility of Anglo-American consultations over future policy in the Middle East. These discussions, which also involved the War Cabinet, culminated at the end of October, 1943, in an invitation to the American Government to send representatives to London for an "informal exchange of views" on future policy in Middle Eastern countries, excluding Egypt.[57] However, the State Department was reluctant to send delegates to London as long as British proposals remained vague and incoherent. Only as late as April, 1944, Edward Stettinius, Under-Secretary of State, led a mission to London, where it was agreed in general terms that Anglo-American relations in the area should be conducted "on a basis of co-operation and of mutual frankness".[58] Nevertheless, no practical decisions were taken as to how to reach such a mutual understanding, and as a result no particular action was taken to implement the agreement.

The Palestine problem was also a matter for discussion by a Cabinet Committee, the Committee on Palestine, during 1943. Upon the Committee's recommendations, the Cabinet resumed discussions on the solution of the Palestine problem during 1944. However, in spite of several recommendations for the abandonment of the White Papler policy, the creation of a small Jewish State and the inclusion of Arab Palestine into Greater Syria, no conclusive decision was taken.[59]

Far from having definite ideas about the future face of the Middle East, British officials, who were expected to determine an attitude towards the inter-Arab consultations, remained in the dark. While re-affirming time and again that Britain, as well as the United States, had vital interests in the region and that these interests should be safeguarded, no definite steps or plans were taken to preserve these interests.

It was in this atmosphere of hesitation and ambiguity over the political and economic future of the Middle East that the Arab talks on Unity took place. While there was general agreement among British officials that these talks should not be allowed to be concluded before Britain had decided on her future policy in the area, there was also hope that these talks would encourage Arab co-operation in the cultural and economic fields.

The problem was that there was not much resemblance between the British projects of Arab co-operation and the Arab discussions on Unity. When Nahhas was almost at the end of his first round of talks with Arab leaders, London was still contemplating how "to bring the local Governments gradually into consultations by means of Conference on subjects of interest to them such as transport, food production, and rationing statistics".[60]   Following such considerations, British policy-makers in London succeeded in persuading the Americans to agree as late as April, 1944, that the Middle East Governments, including Egypt, should, if possible, be drawn gradually into closer association with the Middle East Supply Centre, "so that they may be aided to co-operate with each other and provided with general and technical guidance for dealing with their common social and economic problems and for raising the standards of living and health throughout the Middle East".[61]

No one in London appeared to pay attention to the long accounts of the inter-Arab consultations, which proved that aside from joint economic or cultural projects, the local Governments also devoted a considerable part of their talks to inter-Arab politics. No one in the Foreign Office considered whether there was not an immanent contradiction between the deliberate exclusion of Egypt from any joint Middle East project-- preserving her under absolute British influence-- and British acquiescence in Nahhas's Arab initiative.

A generally accepted belief prevailed in British circles in London and Cairo that the Arabs were incapable of concluding any project without British assistance. Casey was to note in his memoirs that "there was little Unity amongst the Arab States, except in hostility to the Jews. There were sporadic moves in 1943 and 1944 in the direction of Arab Unity, but they came to very little by reason of rivalry between the Arab leaders".[62]   Only five months before the general meeting of the Arab leaders in Alexandria, Casey's successor, Lord Moyne, could conclude in relief that the prospect of Arab Union talks seemed "to be for the moment averted".[63]

This over-confidence in Arab inability to agree on joint co-operation might have led British officials to underestimate the consultations and their adverse effects on Britain's position.   In spite of common consent that a convocation of an Arab Conference before Britain had devised her Middle East Policy might hamper British interests, British officials were quite satisfied with the Foreign Office directive of March, 1943, that insisted on Arab consultations as the best means to discourage the Conference.   For those officials who were involved in economic and cultural projects of co-operation in the Middle East, the inter-Arab disccussions might have even seemed a positive move towards this co-operation.   In fact, the numerous conversations that British officials held with Arab and Egyptian leaders fostered an impression that both economic and cultural projects might emerge from the inter-Arab discussions.[64]

It was not surprising, therefore, that British representatives in the Middle East, with such possible hopes in mind, took great pains to persuade the various Arab parties to forgive and forget their rivalries, and enter into consultations with each other.   In April, 1943, when 'Abdullah, in reaction to Nuri's initiative, advertised his own plan for an Arab Conference of the Syrian People in Amman, the high Commissioner of Palestine found it the right opportunity to reprimand him for not discussing this issue in advance with British

officials.[65]   In July, 1943, Smart impressed on Nuri, who had
arrived in Cairo for talks with Nahhas, not to ignore Ibn-Sa'ud and to
involve him in the discussions concerning Arab Unity.[66] Similarly,
the British Minister in Jedda pressed Ibn-Sa'ud not to reject Nahhas's
invitations for talks.   The minister told Ibn-Sa'ud that it was
important that the Arabs present "at least the semblance of a united
front", and therefore recommend acceptance of the invitation.[67]
When Nahhas sent Hubaysha to Jedda to persuade Ibn-Sa'ud to join in the
Arab talks, it was the British Minister there who, believing that the
talks could result in economic and cultural agreements, pressed
Ibn-Sa'ud to send his representative, Shaykh Yusuf Yasin, to
Cairo.[68]

British insistence on Arab consultations was viewed by the Arabs
and the Egyptians as further proof that Britain aspired to establish an
Arab Federation.[69]   Indeed, what should 'Abdullah have concluded
after being reprimanded by the High Commissioner because of his call
for an all-Syrian Conference, while his main rival, Nuri al-Sa'id, was
being permitted full freedom to campaign for an Arab Conference? The
consultations, not surprisingly, encouraged rather than discouraged the
idea of an Arab Conference.   A wide gap had been opened between the
original instructions of the Foreign Office and their practical
implementation in the Middle East.

From time to time the Foreign Office found it necessary to remind
the Middle East representatives of their primary duty.   In October,
1943, the Foreign Office sent a further directive to the Middle East
representatives informing them about the beginning of discussions on

future policy in the Middle East. Because of these discussions, the exact content of which was never fully revealed to the representatives,[70] Britain's representatives in the area were re-instructed to do their best "to discourage any idea of a general [Arab] Conference". If there were any "imminent danger" of such a Conference, they were directed to intimate Britain's opposition to the respective Arab Governments.[71]

The new directive was not well accepted by British officials in Cairo. The Oriental experts of the British Embassy were uncertain about the mysterious discussions in London of which they had no knowledge. They also failed to understand what they were expected to do. Smart pointed out that since Nahhas adopted a procedure which was "in accordance with British advice", it would not be easy to discourage such a Conference.[72] He thought, however, that because of Ibn-Sa'ud's objection to the Conference, it would not be convened. Nevertheless, instead of encouraging Ibn-Sa'ud's opposition to the Conference, he proposed leaving the Arabs to thrash out the matter among themselves, because he feared that if Britain intervened in favour of one of the Arab parties "other Arab countries might be angry".[73]

Both Shone, Lampson's Minister, and Casey approved of Smart's advice,[74] which as a matter of fact did resemble the old directives from London to let the Arabs work out for themselves their schemes of federation. Consequently, although Smart informed Ibn-Sa'ud's representative that any general Arab Conference at that stage was premature, he refused to lend Yasin any British assistance on the

grounds that Britain was not a party in the consultations.[75] In
spite of Yasin's pleas for British support for Saudi opposition to any
political discussions in the Conference, and although Smart himself
realised that the inter-Arab consultations had reached a stage where
the Palestine question might arise, Smart did not alter his stand,
which received, as usual, both Clayton's and Casey's support.[76]

From Cairo, the British view on the future policy in the Middle
East seemed far less complicated than in London. The Embassy, for
example, could see nothing wrong in the participation of the
Palestinian Arabs in the future Arab Conference. In November, 1943,
when Nahhas began to press British officials for the inclusion of
Palestinian Arabs in the inter-Arab consultations, the Embassy was
prepared to accept this demand. Following Smart's apparent advice,
Shone pointed out the difficulty in rejecting this demand in view of
Eden's Parliamentary statement, and advised that the arrival of a
representative delegation from Palestine be allowed.[77]

From Cairo, the ability of Great Britain to prevent the Conference
also appeared rather limited. In February, 1944, the Foreign Office
told Lampson that if Nahhas was going to convene the Conference, he
should be advised first to consult the British Government, as certain
matters, particularly the Palestine question, would require careful
handling. Lampson replied that he could see no objection to talks of
which Nahhas kept him fully informed, and warned that it would be
unwise to try to prevent the Conference for which Nahhas was
pressing.[78]

Lampson's warning was brought to Eden's attention. "Why do we want to prevent it"?, he enquired. Eden's innocent question led Hankey, Baxter's Deputy in the Eastern Department, which was responsible for the formulation of the directives concerning the Arab Conference, to make some clarification. Hankey asserted that Lampson had mistaken the directive. The Office had, in fact, no intention of opposing the Arab Conference and receiving the blame for the failure of Arab Unity. However, London was concerned lest such a Conference should develop into an attack on British policy in Palestine. From the reports it was clear that Nahhas might use the Palestinian Arabs as a means to unite divergent Arab opinion. Lampson was, therefore, instructed to request Nahhas to prepare a concrete agenda for the Conference, which would steer clear of the stickier problems likely to increase tension in the Middle East and avoid harming the Allied War effort.[79]

Lampson was now given the awkward task of preparing the ground for an Arab Conference which British officials did not like, but believed they could not afford to oppose because of Eden's Statement. However, Lampson did not press Nahhas about the agenda, because the latter was no longer certain whether the Conference would be convened. When he was given the content of the Foreign Office directive, Nahhas insisted that Arab Unity must necessarily touch on the Palestine question, and that Palestine must be represented. He also insisted on the release of Amin al-Tamimi and Jamal al-Husayni for the Conference, and 'threatened' not to convene this Conference until a Palestinian Arab delegation was consulted.[80] Nahhas's reaction clearly shows that he was still under the impression that the Conference reflected a British interest, and as such he still hoped to extort British concessions in return for the convocation of the Conference.

The Foreign Office advised Lampson to tell Nahhas that it was "a remarkably poor advertisement" for the Arab Unity movement if its success really depended upon the participation of these two men.[81] Lampson did not like the proposed reply. At that time he was taking part in a special conference on Palestine, which had been summoned by Lord Moyne, the new Minister of State. The participants in this Conference agreed that every effort should be made to delay the holding of the Arab Conference. The participants also agreed that if the Conference could not be postponed, "a warning regarding Palestine should be given to those concerned" before it met.[82] To Lampson, therefore, it was clear that the Foreign Office's proposed reply to Nahhas might cause further damage to the British stand concerning Palestine. He argued that Nahhas might ask Britain to propose Palestinian Arab representatives for the Arab Conference or might request an exposition of Britain's views concerning Palestine. Lampson thought, therefore, that it would be better to ignore Nahhas's demands for the Palestinian Arab participation in the inter-Arab consultations. He further suggested instructing British representatives in Iraq and the Levant to put the brake on the movement for the Conference.[83] The Foreign Office accepted Lampson's advice.

Following Foreign Office approval, Lampson ignored the various communications Nahhas sent during May concerning the release of the Palestinian Arab leaders and Palestinian representation at the Conference.[84] However, the continuing spate of communications and the apparent failure of Britain's representatives in Iraq and the

Levant to slow down the movement for a Conference,[85] forced Lampson to share his growing concern with London. Lampson now thought that the situation was becoming delicate because Nahhas might use the matter to bolster his own internal political prestige, either by strengthening the Government or providing himself with propaganda if forced to retire from office. A categorical refusal of Nahhas's demand might, therefore, have the unwelcome effect of drawing attention to the matter. He requested instructions.[86] No instructions arrived.

In their absence, Lampson followed the line suggested by the Cairo Conference on Palestine and approved by London. He approached Nahhas through Amin 'Uthman at the beginning of June, 1944, and asked both to delay the Conference, and the exclusion from it of the question of Palestine.[87]

Nahhas reacted by sending Amin to the Embassy with a draft of a letter of invitation to the Governments of Iraq, Trans-Jordan, Saudi Arabia, Syria, Lebanon, and Yemen. In the letter, Nahhas laid emphasis on the efforts to release the interned Palestinian Arab leaders, but nevertheless proposed assembling a Preparatory Committee in July or August in spite of the absence of the Palestinian Arabs. The Arab States were accordingly asked to send delegates. Lampson, through Smart, urged 'Uthman to tell Nahhas not to do anything without consulting him, and asked for urgent instructions from London.[88] He himself thought that Nahhas should be told that it was obvious that the convocation of a Conference was inopportune at that stage of the War, and that a discussion on the Palestine question could only do harm.

Lampson was not put on the alert by Nahhas's move. Although he asked for urgent instructions from London, he obviously did not think that this development necessitated his personal intervention. Instead of speaking to Nahhas himself, he allowed Smart to handle the situation through Amin. Also, London did not seem to be particularly alarmed at Lampson's report. Five days elapsed before the Foreign Office approved the Ambassador's line.[89] Although these days were probably spent on consultations, the Foreign Office sent no interim instructions to Lampson, intending to ensure that Nahhas would not make any independent move.

The Foreign Office's slow response to Lampson's urgent request might have further persuded Lampson that the issue was not after all crucial. He waited three more days after receiving the instructions before communicating the reply to Nahhas.[90]

He found out that he was too late. His earlier fear that Nahhas might act without British approval had materialised. Amin 'Uthman took the blame on himself. He said that he had not told Nahhas about Lampson's request for delay, and imagined that once the British refused to release the interned Palestinian Arab leaders, Nahhas could go ahead without them. In any case, Amin added, Nahhas could not have held things up, as "he was being pressed to get a move on".[91] It was obvious that Nahhas, having realised that the British were not prepared to release the Palestinian Arab internees and were exerting pressure to postpone the Conference, attempted to convene the Conference.

It took almost two weeks before London reacted to the report that Nahhas did not heed Amin's undertaking. The Foreign Office took

Nahhas's move philosophically. While a year earlier, an independent move by 'Abdullah over the Arab Conference had been reprimanded by MacMichael, the Foreign Office response was far more moderate. No representations were to be made, but Nahhas was to be advised to abandon political issues and to concentrate instead on economic and cultural topics. In case Nahhas should find it impossible not to include political issues in the Conference, Lampson was instructed to remind him not to exceed "the proper limits" while discussing Palestine or the future of the French in the Levant. The rest of Britain's Middle East representatives were yet again directed to encourage any reluctance to attend the Conference, though they were reminded not to attempt actively to obstruct its holding.[92] Special instructions were given to the British Minister in Jedda. He was advised that if Ibn-Sa'ud seemed reluctant, this reluctance should be encouraged.[93]

Even before, but especially after, this directive, which did not leave many doubts about London's feelings towards the Conference, Britain's representatives in the Middle East pressed Arab leaders not to raise sensitive political issues, particularly the Palestine problem, at the Conference. Both Lampson and Cornwallis requested various Iraqi leaders not to raise the Palestine question.[94] Ibn-Sa'ud promised not to do anything that might embarrass Britain, and even refused to respond to Nahhas's invitation.[95] Spears reported that the Syrian delegates would not raise the Palestine question and would do their utmost to prevent it being raised at the

Conference.[96]   Even Nahhas promised Lampson that if "for War reasons Palestine could not be represented, the problem could be shelved by mutual agreement".[97]

The numerous Arab promises not to raise the Palestine problem at the Conference did not abate the fears of British officials in Cairo that the Conference might be used to attack Britain's Palestinian Policy. These fears, however, did not arouse any prompt action against the convocation of the Arab Conference. This was because by July, 1944, British opinion in Cairo was already convinced that such a Conference was inevitable. Relying on the advice of his Oriental experts, Lord Moyne believed that the Arab Governments would not be able to reject Nahhas's invitation to discuss Arab Unity because of the great popularity of this issue. Since the idea of open opposition to the Conference was rejected, Moyne saw in the participation in the Conference of Saudi-Arabia the best way to secure British interests. Ibn-Sa'ud-- Britain's most loyal ally-- commanded, so it was believed, great influence on Syrian leaders, and was expected, therefore, to exercise this influence at the Conference, securing its moderate nature. Moyne asked the Foreign Office to press for the participation of Saudi-Arabia at the Conference.[98]   The Foreign Office complied with his request without hesitation.[99]

It was perhaps this decision, based on exaggerated, incorrect and unrealistic observations and assumptions, that determined the successful convocation of the Arab Conference. No official suggested that if Syria followed Ibn-Sa'ud's lead, she might as well follow his boycott of the Conference. No official enquired what had happened between May-- the month when Moyne reported that the danger of the early convocation of the Conference had been averted-- and July, when Moyne began to press for Saudi participlation in the Conference. How did Arab frictions so suddenly disappear? Could the great popularity of this issue deter the Arab regimes from turning down Nahhas's invitation? Were these regimes really so dependent on the support of the Arab 'street'? Were Nahhas's or Nuri's initiatives really so popular? Had Arabism really become the force majeure in Egyptian politics? If so, were not all the previous reports from Cairo denying this a terrible negligence that should result in the immediate recall of the Embassy's staff?

No official in London took the trouble to suggest that the danger posed to British interests by the Conference may be greater than the temporary loss of prestige occasioned by direct action against the convocation of the Conference. No official ever enquired whether or not the option of indirect action had been completely exhausted. With Amir 'Abdullah's dependence on Britain, British officials could always have used the Amir's services. In light of the expected boycott of the Conference by Ibn-Sa'ud, and the probability that Yemen, and perhaps also Syria, would follow the Saudi lead, British officials could not have faced great difficulties to persuade the Amir to join the boycott.

In their blind reliance on Smart and Clayton, British officials never questioned the accuracy of reports that affirmed the existence of strong 'currents' and 'movements' supported by a formidable 'public opinion' which aspired to Arab Unity. Suddenly, all those Arab leaders, who came to power by arbitrary means, began playing the unfamiliar role of popular tribunes. Not surprisingly, those British officials who had previously crowned Arab Kings and deposed Arab Governments at will, now found themselves in the position of impotent observers of popular trends and movements which they were unable to control.

But the numerous reports by these very officials, even after the Foreign Office approval of Moyne's advice, suggest that the Arab regimes were not united behind the idea of an Arab Conference. Therefore, the possibility of postponing the Conference was far more real than it seemed to Moyne and his team of Oriental advisers. Thus, for example, Ibn-Sa'ud's opposition to the Conference was so strong that at first he rejected British advice to take part in it.[100] Moreover, contrary to Moyne's anticipation that the Arab States would be reluctant to delay the Conference, Nahhas decided to postpone the Preliminary Conference until after Ramadan (25th September) on the grounds that replies had not yet been received from all Arab States to whom invitations were sent. Lampson suspected that Nahhas postponed the Conference for fear that Iraq and the Levant States were formulating a common policy against him.[101] Nahhas was evidently concerned by the possibility of a future Syro-Iraqi bloc in the Conference. In the beginning of August, when Shaykh Yusuf Yasin arrived in Cairo to ask for a postponement of the Conference, Nahhas perhaps feared he might face such a bloc alone, and at first agreed to postpone it, at least until after the American elections.[102] Although he soon afterwards changed his mind, and readopted his original plan, he persisted in his attempts to neutralise the so-called bloc. He communicated with 'Abdullah and promised him his complete friendship, co-operation, and support in the forthcoming Conference.[103]   He further sent Sabri Abu 'Alam to the Levant,[104] in an apparent attempt to win local sympathy.   In addition, Nahhas made a "personal" request that Nuri should be excluded from the Iraqi delegation to the Conference.[105]

All these moves only emphasised how unstable the whole future of the Conference was even at that late stage. But British officials in Cairo appeared to be convinced that a Conference was inevitable. Moyne, whose previous prediction that the Conference could not be postponed was so decisively refuted by Nahhas's postponement of it, remained adamant that no further delay was possible. Yasin's requests to advise other Arab states to adhere to the Saudi view were rejected. Moyne's rejection gave a fatal blow to Churchill's desire to establish Ibn-Sa'ud as "the Lord of the Middle East-- the Boss of the [other Arab] bosses".[106]   Although Ibn-Sa'ud was acclaimed as the biggest and most important Arab figure in the Arab world,[107] no British official could suggest how to persuade other Arab leaders to acknowledge Ibn-Sa'ud's supremacy. Moyne evidently believed that such a possibility did not even exist. He argued that even if Saudi-Arabia and Egypt withdrew from the Conference, the other Arab states might still go ahead with this project.[108]

This fantastic assumption, the natural conclusion of the illusive belief in the energetic force that Middle Eastern movements commanded, was to dictate future British politics. Moyne's opinions were shared by, probably even developed with, other personalities such as Clayton[109] and Lampson.[110] The British officialdom in Cairo was adamant that the only remaining possibility was to try and moderate the agenda of the Conference. Aside from repeated appeals to Nahhas[111] and other Arab leaders[112] not to embarrass Britain with the Palestine question, British officials now sought the participation of Saudi-Arabia as the main moderating force.[113] The Foriegn Office, once again, agreed with the recommendation of the senior officials on the spot.[114]

British officials were now pressing the biggest figure in the Arab world to take part in a Conference which was bound to reduce Britain's political options in the Middle East. Since the convocation of the Confernce was taken as an irreversible development, Cairo, where British influence was strong and dominant, became Moyne's preferred site for such a Conference. Riad, especially after the Americans began to establish their relations with Ibn-Sa'ud, was a far less attractive alternative. The surrender of Ibn-Sa'ud to British pressure already reduced one political option. Cairo rather than Riad became the recognised centre of the Arab world, and Ibn-Sa'ud's superiority in this world, so desired by British officials, was never to be acknowledged by the other Arab parties.

Years after the convocation of the Alexandria Conference, Walter Smart told Christopher Sykes that "the Conference was only indirectly British inspired and was not at all British directed".[115] This Statement is true, of course, inasmuch as it describes Britain's non-intervention in the inter-Arab consultations. The Statement ignored, however, the vital role British officials played in keeping the consultations going. It also ignored the crucial role that British officials had in persuading Ibn-Sa'ud to take part in the Conference. These moves, far from being indirectly inspired, were carefully planned acts. Nahhas's success in assembling the Arab leaders must be assessed in light of British indirect assistance which removed first 'Abdullah's and then Ibn-Sa'ud's opposition to the Conference. Smart's admission that the Conference was in no way British-directed was a clear acknowledgement of British failure to persuade the Arab leaders to omit the Palestine issue from the agenda of the Conference. Had British officials played a more active role in the inter-Arab consultations, they would not have been placed in the position of an observer at the Conference.

D.   Britain and the Palestinian Arab participation in the Conference

Although British officials repeatedly rejected the requests to release the interned Palestinian Arab leaders, they did not express any objection to the presence of Palestinian Arab delegates at the Conference. About a week before the Conference, Nahhas reminded British officials that although Palestine would not be represented at the Conference, he expected certain Palestinian Arabs to attend.[116] Nahhas could not give any particular names because, even then, the Palestinian Arab politicians could not decide who would go to Egypt. These politicians chose their representatives only on the eve of the conference. The chosen nominee was the lawyer, Musa al-'Alami.[117]

'Alami attributed his non-participation in the first meetings of the Conference to British pressure.[118] This seems to be only partially true. While Nahhas certainly bore in mind his numerous promises to British officials concerning Palestine, there were other important considerations that prevented the early participation of 'Alami. 'Alami's presence at the Conference raised a serious legal problem. Since only independent Governments had been invited, his participation might have aroused other North African delegates to ask for their inclusion as well. Moreover, Faruq's intervention on behalf of 'Alami might have further complicated 'Alami's position. The King, who took offence at hardly being informed by Nahhas about the Conference,[119] attempted to promote his own prestige by closer relations with the delegates. Thus, for example, he arbitrated between the rival Syrian and Lebanese delegations,[120] and was further said to have caused, 'Alami to be sent a series of invitations to functions held in connection with the Conference, some addressed to 'the Prime Minister of Palestine', other to 'the Chief Palestinian delegate'.[121]

'Alami's position was finally settled on 30th September during discussions between Amin 'Uthaman, Clayton, and Terence Shone (Lampson did not find the occasion important enough, and left earlier for his annual vacation, leaving Shone in charge of the Embassy). Clayton, whose advice was accepted by both Shone and Moyne, raised no objection to 'Alami's presence at the Conference, provided that it was clear that he would not be representing Palestine or the Palestine Government. It was Amin who promised, in the name of Nahhas, that 'Alami would not take part in any decision or sign any resolutions.[122] A day after this agreement, the Secretariat of the Committee of the Alexandria

Conference declared 'Alami as "representative of the Palestinian Arabs".[123]

By and large Amin's agreement was honoured, to the growing annoyance of 'Alami. Perhaps bearing in mind their own promises to British officials concerning the Palestinian issue, the Arab delegates placed the Palestine issue last on the agenda of the Conference. It was dealt with in detail only during the seventh meeting of the Conference (5th October). Nahhas, who presided over this meeting, presented to the Conference an Iraqi proposal to open Propaganda Bureaux in London and Washington. The Arab delegates unanimously approved the project in principle, but decided to leave the details to later exmination by a special Committee which had been created for this purpose.

After the delegats had taken this decision, Nahhas invited 'Alami to deliver his speech on the Palestine problem. 'Alami gave an emotional account of the disasters that had befallen the Palestinian Arabs during the British mandate. Aside from describing the economic and social plight of the Palestinian Arabs, he also made some proposals on how the Arab countries could help the Palestinian Arabs. He called for the creation of an Arab National Fund which would be responsible for the preservation of the Arab land in Palestine. He further called for an economic boycott of the Zionists, and urged the Arab Governments to prevent the illegal smuggling of Jews to Palestine through Arab territories. 'Alami also thought that the best way to demonstrate Arab solidarity concerning Palestine was by organising a delegation from the various Arab countries which would visit the main capitals of the world (Moscow, London, and Washington), advocating the Arab cause in

Palestine.[124]

Although his speech was generally described as "forceful" and
"moving",[125] 'Alami's proposals were not entirely accepted by the
Conference. The Egyptian delegates, Hilali and Nahhas, dismissed his
last proposal as "impracticable". In fact, only one of 'Alami's
proposals -- the creation of a special Arab Fund to preserve the Arab
lands in Palestine -- was incorporated by Nahhas in his proposed draft
of Resolution on Palestine which he read to the Conference. Nahhas
proposed to state that Palestine was "an important part" of the Arab
countries. An infringement of the right of the Palestinian Arabs
endangered the peace and stability of the Arab world. The statement
expressed sympathy with the plight of the European Jews but
distinguished between the problem they presented and Zionism. Britain
was called upon to stop Jewish immigration, to preserve the Arab lands,
and to grant independence to Palestine. The economic and financial
sub-committee was to be asked to examine a proposal that the Arab
governments and peoples should contribute to an Arab National Fund for
securing Arab land in Palestine.[126]

This draft, which was described as a compromise between the Iraqi
and Egyptian views,[127] appeared to appease all the Arab parties
in the Conference. Nahhas's proposed Resolution was unanimously
approved by all the delegates.

The special resolution concerning Palestine was the last of five
resolutions which the Conference adopted on 7th October 1944, at the
end of its eighth session. These Resolutions, which became known as the
"Alexandria Protocol",[128] signalled the creation of the Arab

League. The first of these Resolutions called for the formation of a League of Arab States, in accordance with plans to be drawn up by an interim sub-Committee. Other sub-Committees were to be set up to promote co-operation on economic matters, communications, cultural matters, questions of nationality and passports, social affairs, and public health. A further special Resolution affirmed the independence of Lebanon.

The resolutions were not signed by the Saudi and Yemenite delegation, but were signed by 'Alami, in spite of a Syrian objection.[129] Although 'Alami's signature breached the Anglo-Egyptian agreement on this matter, and though neither the secrecy nor the a-political nature of the Conference was maintained, British officials by and large expressed optimism concerning the Resolutions.[130] Being unable to decide how to control the Middle East, British officials were inclined to regard the idea of an Arab League as a positive move for Britain. Affected perhaps by the creation of the United Nations, these officials viewed the Arab League as a necessary regional body with which Britain had to co-operate.

CHAPTER FOUR

EGYPT AND THE ARAB LEAGUE

A.   Egypt and the Arab World During Ahmad Mahir's regime 1944-1945

Nahhas did not celebrate the successful conclusion of the Arab Conference in Alexandira for long. On 8th Octboer 1944, only one day after he had signed the 'Alexandira Protocol', Nahhas was dismissed from office by Faruq. The King invited Ahmad Mahir, head of the Sa'dist Party, to form the new Government.[1]

The new Egyptian Cabinet lost no time in emphasising its loyalty to the Arab cause. Ahmad Mahir, upon accepting his new post, stated that he regarded Arab Unity as a national cause and promised to do his best to promote it.[2] During his short period in office -- he was assassinated by an Egyptian fanatic on 24th February 1945 -- Mahir advocated, on various occasions, the idea that Arab Unity was a national cause standing above and beyond partisan ocnflicts.[3] Other Ministers in the Cabinet also expressed support for Arab Unity.[4] This issue was further adumbrated in the platforms of the various coalition parties.[5]

The need to respond to the obvious concern of many Arab delegates who were still in Egypt while the governmental changes took place might have encouraged this spate of pan-Arab pledges. It soon became clear that Egypt's new leaders did not intend to keep all their promises regarding the Arab issue. Thus, for example, Mahir, who began his mandate with a statement that Arab Unity was a non-partisan issue, never acknowledged the Wafdist contribution to this Unity. None of the

Wafdist politicans, whose role was so vital to the success of the Arab
Conference, had been invited to the special reception that the new
Premier gave for the Arab delegates.[6] Moreover, in spite of his
repeated promises to further unity, Mahir, uhlike Nahhas, had never
been directly involved in inter-Arab discussions. Although quick to
install himself as head of the new Egyptian delegation to the
Preparatory Talks for Unity,[7] Mahir had never actually taken part in
them. He had to spend most of his time appeasing the rival coalition
parties,[8] whose conflicts posed a constant threat to the stability of
the Government. The conduct of Arab affairs was left to the Minister
for Foreign Affairs, Mahmud Fahmi al-Nuqrashi.

Nuqrashi began his period in office with the disadvantage of
knowing "almost nothing" on Arab affairs.[9] He might have been quite
embarrassed, therefore, by the outcome of the Alexandria Conference.
Had he refused to proceed with the talks on Arab Unity, he might have
faced sharp criticism even within the Government. Had he proceeded with
the Arab talks without proper adivce, he might have brought shame on
himself.

Therefore, the first step Nuqrashi took, an unusual one in
Egyptian politics, was to ask Muhammad Salah al-Din, Nahhas's chief
henchman in the inter-Arab talks,[10] to remain in office in the
Ministry of Foreign Affairs. Next, Nuqrashi formed a new Department of
Arab Affairs in his Ministry. 'Abd al-Rahman 'Azzam was appointed to
head it.[11]

While taking these steps, which were interpreted as proof of the
Government's devotion to Arabism, Nuqrashi also promised Clayton that

he would react "very cautiously" to the talks on Unity.[12] Nuqrashi's attitude towards these talks proves that his promise to Clayton was a sincere one. The changes in the Syrian and the Trans-Jordanian Governments shortly after the change in Egypt might have encouraged Nuqrashi to proceed cautiously with the discussions. Although Moyne predicted that these changes would have no great effect on the promotion of Arab Unity,[13] the Egyptian Press, not long afterwards, announced that the Arab talks had been postponed "owing to internal political events in some of the Arab countries".[14] Aside from postponing the Arab talks, Nuqrashi also shelved the issue of Egypt's contribution to the Propaganda Bureaux. He did not seem to like the idea that the Egyptian Government should grant 'Alami, a non-Egyptian, huge sums of money to run Propaganda Bureaux in London and Washington. 'Alami complained that Nuqrashi's attitude towards this issue was "very unhelpful". Although 'Alami explained the urgent need for these Offices, Nuqrashi insisted that they should operate first on a modest scale and develope gradually.[15]

The Government's attitude towards Arab affiars was watched carefuly by the Wafdist Opposition. This Opposition, bitter because of its 'betrayal' by the other Arab delegates who ignored Nahhas after his downfall,[16] was looking for an opportunity to attack Government mismanagement of Arab affairs. During October, 1944, an opportunity presented itself when news reached Cairo of fresh pro-Zionist statements by both Franklin Roosevelt and Thomas Dewey, the two contestants in the American Presidential election. Mahir brushed aside these statements as election slogans which did not reflect the opinion of the U.S. Government.[17] The Wafdist media hurried to criticise the Premier's mistaken attitude and initiated a new crusade for the Palestinian Arab cause.[18]

The crusade gained the support of the pan-Islamic and pan-Arab Soceities in Egypt. Although these Societies -- in significant contrast to their neighbouring Arab and Islamic Societies -- had not demonstrated on Balfour Declaration Day (2nd November), they renewed their anti-Zionist campaign after the murder of Lord Moyne by Jewish extremists on 6th Novembert, 1944. Although the leadership of both the Jewish Agency in Palestine[19] and the Jewish community in Egypt[20] condemned the murder in no uncertain terms, Zionism was, once again, denounced as a terrorist movement. The participation of Tawfiq Doss, an ardent advocate of Arabism, in the assassins' team of legal advisers, did not change the negative attitude to the Zionist cause. Societies, such as the Arab Union and the Muslim Brethren, protested against statements concerning Palestine made by lawyers of Moyne's assassins.[21]

These Societies attracted further headlines after Roosevelt won the election. Together with other pan-Arab and pan-Islamic organisations in Egypt, they sent a joint petition to the American President calling for a change in the pro-Zionist policy of the U.S.[22] During the Arab Feminist Congress, held in Cairo in December 1944, the Press gave additional publicity to pan-Arab and anti-Zionist speeches.[23] The Congress, which received the blessing of the Ministry of Education,[24] adopted resolutions calling for both the independence of Arab Palestine and an immediate halt to Jewish immigration.[25]

The anti-Zionist campain waged by the Wafd and the pro-Arab and Islamic organisations took place during a period of growing tension between the French and the Arabs in the Levant. The combination of news reports on the Levant crisis and anti-Zionist activities probably promoted an atmosphere of expectation for a joint Arab reaction to both issues. These expectations were further encouraged by numerous Press interviews given by various delegates during their frequent visits to Egypt. However, public expectations were evidently insufficient to press the Government into action. As late as the beginning of January, 1945, Nuri al-Sa'id returned frustrated to Iraq complaining that the Egyptian Government was "too occupied with domestic issues to take any further steps concerning the projected Conference on Arab Unity".[26]

Had Nuri been more aware of 'Azzam's activities, he would surely have changed his opinion. Nuri, who held talks with Nuqrashi, failed, perhaps, to realise that much of the direction of Arab affairs had moved from the hands of either Nuqrashi or Salah al-Din to those of 'Azzam.[27] 'Azzam, regarded by Lampson as "a fanatic" advocate of Arabism,[28] had no intention of slowing down the pace of future Arab talks. Having been supported by the Palace,[29] 'Azzam must have found it comparatively easy to promote his plans. He believed that if he succeeded in persuading Ibn-Sa'ud to join the Arab talks, the political Committee which had been commissioned to draft the Pact of the Arab League could begin its work. Both the Palace and the Government accepted this view and, consequently, 'Azzam was appointed Amir al-Hajj.[30] As head of the Egyptian pilgrims' caravan to Mecca,

'Azzam had good reason to believe that he would meet the Saudi King.

Ibn-Sa'ud, who rightly suspected that 'Azzam had arrived to discuss Arab Unity, refused at first to see him. The King rejected the proposal for an Arab League on the grounds that such a project was unsuitable and inapplicable to his country. Ibn-Sa'ud further suspected that there were "interests at play behind the scenes, working secretly for their own ends. In order to frustrate this conspiracy, which he attributed to the Hashemites, the King proposed substituting the projected League with a network of mutual alliances similar to the one already existing between himself and Iraq and Yemen.[31]

However, British officials, whose guidance and advice the King has sought, refused to support his proposal. The Eastern Department feared that Ibn-Sa'ud's boycott of the League would alienate him from the other Arab parties. The Department did not like this, because Ibn-Sa'ud was regarded as a great moderating force whose influence on other Arab parties was expected to prevent them from taking decisions which might conflict with British interests in the Middle East. The King, therefore, was advised to meet 'Azzam to discuss a satisfactory solution to the difficulties he had found in the Alexandria Protocol.[32]

Following this advice, Ibn-Sa'ud met 'Azzam and found him most co-operative. 'Azzam immediately accepted the King's offer to enter into a close alliance with Egypt in order to neutralise the Hashemite bloc of Iraq and Trans-Jordan. 'Azam also readily endorsed a further proposal of Ibn-Sa'ud that Egypt would represent his Kingdom in a new campaign for Arab Palestine in London and Washington.[33]

With these issues settled, and having been flattered by three
personal letters from Faruq, Mahir, and Nuqrashi,[34] Ibn-Sa'ud found
no difficulties in signing the Alexandira Protocol.[35] His sanction
was interpreted in Egypt as a great achievement for Egyptian diplomacy.
Mahir issued a statement to the Press praising 'Azzam's success,
applauding Ibn-Sa'ud's decision, and announcing that the way to Arab
Unity had been opened.[36]

Mahir, nonetheless, must have been less pleased with 'Azzam when
he found out that this civil servant had also been engaged in promoting
King Faruq's visit to Saudi-Arabia. Mahir, who had not been consulted
by the King about the visit, opposed it.[37] Faruq dismissed this
opposition on the grounds that his visit was a private tour, intended
to make personal acquaintance with the Saudi King.[38] A British
request to the King to take a Cabinet Minister with him was also turned
down. The King's advisers argued that it was too late to change the
private nature of the visit, and that the King was quite content with
the company of 'Azzam.[39]

Faruq's meeting with Ibn-Sa'ud strengthened the fresh Egypto-Saudi
entente. Although no substantial issues had been discussed, the two
rulers were greatly impressed by each other and agreed to proceed with
'frank and free' discussions on "all questions relating to the welfare
of the Arabs".[40]

The success of this meeting boosted the talks for Arab Unity.
Faruq, who was evidently delighted by the opportunity to champion a
cause previously denied him by Nahhas, took great pains to emphasise
the importance of this private encounter. In front of the whole

Cabinet and the various Arab diplomats who were waiting to welcome him upon his return, the king announced that his meeting with Ibn-Sa'ud had done more for Arab Unity than any Conference.[41]

Such statements obviously increased expectations of immediate advances towards Unity. This time, these expectations received a due response from a Government which had been pressed into immediate action by Faruq's personal intervention in the issue. Soon after the King's return to Egypt, the public was informed by the Press that the Government had issued invitations to the signatories of the Protocol to come to Egypt for further consultations.[42]

Following the invitations, delegates from Saudi-Arabia, Trans-Jordan, Syria, and Lebanon arrived in Cairo. On 14th February 1945, these delegates began discussing a draft Pact of the Arab League. A few days later, the delegates decided to invite 'Alami as the representative of the Palestinian Arabs to the discussions.[43]

Nuqrashi, who headed the Egyptian delegation to these talks, presided over the discussions. However, his interest was soon distracted from the talks. Not long after Ahmad Mahir's assassination, Nuqrashi was nominated as the new Premier. He at first retained his post as Minister of Foreign Affairs, but soon became entangled in the struggles within the Cabinet, and had to leave the actual conduct of Arab affairs to 'Azzam.

"'Azzam", a British report asserted, "was the main surprise of the Cairo discussions. His reputation in the Arab world as an Arab nationalist and statesman was as great at the beginning of the meetings as was the disillusion he occasioned at the end. He proved to be out of touch with the main currents of thought in the Asiatic Arab world, in Baghdad, Damascus, Beirut, and Palestine. Neither as draftsman did he show the ability of [Muhammad] Salah al-Din, nor as a statesman the realism of Nahhas". A man of uncontrolled "impulses", 'Azzam refused "to face facts" and was a "stranger to all compromises".[44] These characteristics not only produced conflict between 'Azzam and other Arab delegates, but also aroused British concern for the direction of the talks.

B. Britain and the Arab League, 1944-1945

The various changes of Arab Governments soon after the conclusion of the Alexandria Conference did not convince British officials in the Middle East of a possible delay in the Arab talks. The constant visits of Arab politicians to Cairo and the numerous conversations they held with British officials there[45] might have fostered the belief in the inevitability of Arab Unity.

This belief evidently dictated the Foreign Office's objection to Ibn-Sa'ud's wish to leave the 'united' Arab camp. When Ibn-Sa'ud refused to see 'Azzam, the Foreign Office, supported by the Minister in Jedda, hurried to advise the King to change his mind. The Eastern Department agreed that Ibn-Sa'ud's only choice was to participate in future discussions under the Alexandria Protocol, or to see them taking place without him. London, of course, preferred Ibn-Sa'ud's participation in these discussions, so that he could guide them "on the right line".[46] No official in the Department suggested that in light of the absence of a Middle Eastern policy it might be better to suggest Ibn-Sa'ud's walking aloof from union projects.

One possible explanation for this phenomenon is that those British officials who were to determine the Foreign Office reply to Ibn-Sa'ud had already been convinced that Arab Unity was not only inevitable but also desirable. The Dumbarton Oaks proposals, two days after the end of the Alexandria Conference, encouraged the impression that the future world organisation would be based on regional arrangements. The Arab League had been considered by British officials as one of these regional arrangements.

The expected League was further taken as the best means to block possible Russian penetration into the Middle East. Having been greatly concerned by a Communist uprising in Greece (December 1944 - October 1945), British officials believed that a united Arab world, guided by Britain, would secure the Empire and her communication routes from Russian penetration into the Middle East. A disunited Arab world, as a contemporary observer described the new British outlook, "might be easily picked off piece by piece by the Soviets". The traditional maxim of 'divide and rule' had to give way to a new one: 'unite and rule'.[47]

Arab leaders were quick to take advantage of British apprehensions of a Communist takeover in the Middle East. King Faruq, in his first audience with Sir Edward Grigg, Lord Moyne's successor, pointed out the danger to his country and the whole region from the anticipated collaboration between Russia and a future Jewish State.[48] Similarly, Nuri assured Lampson that most of the Arabs sought closer relations with Britain, as well as Union among themselves, because of their fear of Russian occupation. Nuri could see only two problems obstructing a friendlier and closer Anglo-Arab alliance: the French presence in the Levant and the Zionist activity in Palestine.[49] Nuri ignored, of course, the fact that the Arabs were also opposed to British presence in the Middle East. Nuri preferred to ignore this fact in order to attract Lampson's support for his plans on the Levant and Palestine.

Nuri's views could not have found a greater sympathiser than Lampson. For several years now, Lampson had been making repeated calls for the expulsion of the French from the Levant and the suppression of the Zionists in Palestine. He believed that if London followed his advice, Britain could retain both Arab friendship and her prominent position in the Middle East. All these years, Lampson, supported by his team of Oriental advisers, was collating suitable evidence intended to prove that British policy in the Levant and Palestine was the main obstacle, in fact the only one, to an Anglo-Arab alliance. In December, 1944, shortly after the Foreign Office had instructed the Minister in Jedda to advise Ibn-Sa'ud to enter into discussions with 'Azzam, Lampson sent a long despatch to London reiterating his views on British policy in the Middle East. Britain, Lampson warned, seemed to have been pursuing "two diametrically opposing policies" at the same time. "On the one hand", he argued, "we have been encouraging the Arab Union, and on the other, we have been promoting Zionism in Palestine, and French predominance in Syria". An inevitable clash between these two conflicting policies, which would not be late in coming, would certainly damage Britain's position in the Middle East. "If we allow the French to impose a treaty on the Lebanon by force", he warned, "we shall become involved in a conflict with ninety per cent of the Arab world and sooner or later we shall end by losing the Middle East unless we are prepared to keep very large forces scattered throughout the Middle East to hold the population down."[50] Lampson estimated that when such a revolt erupted, at least nine divisons would be needed to pacify the area. Britain, of course, could not afford to raise such a huge force because of her further commitments in liberated areas such as Greece.[51]

Lampson did not explain how the Arabs in Syria and Lebanon could rise against the British while they were still under French supervision. He did not elaborate how clients, such as Nuri al-Sa'id or 'Abdullah, could revolt against their British master or why Ibn-Sa'ud should join forces with the Hashemites, his fiercest enemies, against Britain, his best ally. Similarly, Lampson made no effort to explain why the Egyptians, who avoided militant action against British presence in Egypt and the Sudan, would resort to fighting British policy in Palestine and the Levant. While ignoring such queries, Lampson was quick to point to other 'facts' which were supposed to substantiate his gloomy predicion. He suggested looking at de Gaulle's visit to Moscow as a fore-warning of future French treachery.

Lampson's views were supported by the Commander in Chief, Middle East, the Ambassador in Baghdad, and the Minister in Jedda.[52] While none of them made serious reservations about Lampson's fantastic scenario, all of them emphasised the conflicting nature of British policies in the Middle East. Britain's support for Arab Unity inevitably contradicted her support for French or Zionist claims in the Levant and Palestine. Any British support for either French or Zionist interests in the Levant or Palestine helped to alienate Britain from the supporters of Arab Unity.

The sudden 'discovery' of contradiction in British policy, so dramatically portrayed by Lampson, led British officials in London to review their general policy in the Middle East. It was perhaps then that the real implications of British support for Arab Unity became clear to British policy-makers. Churchill marked Lampson's telegram to Eden 'Important', and the Eastern Department also valued it highly.

Although the Department thought that Lampson misunderstood British policy in the Levant, it, nevertheless, agreed strongly with his claim that Britain was practising two conflicting policies. No one in either the Department or the Office could suggest how to solve this contradiction, without giving up support for either the Arabs or the French and the Zionists. Although British officials acknowledged that both Zionist and French presence in the Middle East aroused Arab opposition, London still refused to depart from its "general sympathy" with Arab Unity (a cause which was built up largely on Arab opposition to the French and the Zionist presence in the Levant and Palestine). This was because Arab Unity was believed to have been a very popular issue, and opposition to it was expected to lead to condemnation from "the whole Arab world" and, consequently, to arouse "all the latent xenophobia of the Arabs". In view of the popularity of Arab Unity on the one hand, and British interests on the other, British officials believed that they were left with no option but to support Unity, and to try to guide it to British advantage. Since Arab Unity covered the whole Middle East, London found additional justification in reviewing the Middle East "as a whole" during the expected formulation of British policy.[53] Ibn-Sa'ud's opposition to the projected League and the growing Lebanese reluctance to join it[54] did nothing to shatter the British belief that this scheme had the support of the whole Arab world.

Had Ibn-Sa'ud really been the moderating force that British officials expected him to be, there might have been a case for British insistence on his participation in the League. But Ibn-Sa'ud's views on French presence in the Levant did not differ from those of other Arab leaders. His devotion to the Arab cause in Palestine was even greater than that of his Arab neighbours. The King hardly missed an opportunity to discuss this issue with any interested party. Thus, for example, he raised the Palestine problem during his conversation with 'Azzam in December, 1944. The King proposed sending special envoys equiped with personal letters to the leaders of Britain and the U.S. calling for justice for the Arabs in Palestine.[55]

This proposal took London by surprise. British officials, who earlier had pressed the King to discuss Arab affairs with 'Azzam, were now proposing to dissuade Ibn-Sa'ud from his plan.[56] However, both Lampson and Grigg disagreed with London's proposal. Both feared that the King might take offence at British objection to his plan, and strongly recommended not to object to it.[57]

Since Ibn-Sa'ud did not persist in the plan, the Foreign Office decided to shelve the directive,[58] but the King soon revived his project. He was now thinking of drafting a letter which would present the Arab stand on Palestine and be approved by all the Arab rulers. Ibn-Sa'ud intended to present the joint Arab letter during his forthcoming meetings with Roosevelt and Churchill.[59] Once again, both Lampson and Grigg advised London "to allow matters to take their course",[60] and once again the Eastern Department agreed that "the most important thing" was "not to give offence" to the King.[61]

The safeguarding of Arab pride rather than British interests badly affected these interests during Ibn-Sa'ud's meeting with Roosevelt in February, 1945. Although the Foreign Office had been informed in advance of the King's intention to raise the Palestine and the Levant problems in these talks,[62] no action had been taken to warn the King that discussions on such issues might embarrass HMG. The Foreign Office also took no steps to co-ordinate the American and British point of view on these issues.

The result of this neglect was that Roosevelt, acting upon the advice of his Middle Eastern experts, gave Ibn-Sa'ud the impression that the U.S. supported his stand on Arab Palestine and the repatriation of the Palestinian Jews.[63] When Churchill met Ibn-Su'ud, three days later, the King, having been assured of Roosevelt's support, did not respond to Churchill's request to promote a definite and lasting Jewish-Arab settlement which should take into account a National Home for the Jews in Palestine.[64]

The outcome of these talks seemed to have a great effect on the Arab rulers as well as on the joint Arab stand on Palestine. After his audience with Roosevelt, Ibn-Sa'ud met both Faruq and Shukri al-Quwatli, the Syrian President.[65] It is likely that the King disclosed to them the content of his discussions with Roosevelt. The Arab leaders probably learnt that the U.S. strongly approved of their stand and that, consequently, they could ignore British representations to moderate it. This lesson might have been further conveyed to the various Arab delegates discussing the League's future stand concerning Palestine at the Political Committee in Cairo.

It should not be surprising that the Arab talks at the Political Committee took such a bad turn, from the British point of view, concerning Palestine. Out of all of Britain's Arab 'friends' and 'allies' in the meetings, only Henri Pharaon, the Lebanese Minister of Foreign Affairs, objected to a proposal to invite 'Alami to the discussions of the Committee.[66] Pharaon, whose country belonged to the French zone of influence, was also the only member of the Committee who was opposed to its recommendations to "recognise the right of Palestine to participate in the League of independent Arab States on an equal footing with the founding states".[67]

Lampson, for his part, hardly pressed the other Arab delegates to adopt Pharaon's stand. The various conversations that he held with Arab delegates during the meetings of the Political Committee might have even given additional impetus to the hard-liners in the Committee. Thus, for example, he told Samir al-Rifa'i, the Trans-Jordanian Premier who took part in these talks, how good it was that the Arab world could speak with one voice and be able, in contrast with the past, to expound their united views in the future. Lampson reported that he had great sympathy with the Premier's "true thesis" that the French were "really out of place in the Middle East". Although he claimed not to have disclosed his support for this particular thesis, Lampson revealed to Rifa'i his private opinion that Ahmad Mahir's murder "might never have happened if the assassins of Lord Moyne had been more expeditiously dealt with". Rifa'i, quite obviously, "fully shared" Lampson's extraordinary views on this issue.[68]

With such views in mind, it is not surprising that Lampson did not interfere in the discussions of the Political Committee on Palestine. He hurried to see Nuqrashi only after the Committee had decided to invite 'Alami to the League as a member with full voting rights. Lampson told Nuqrashi, the self-proclaimed author of this decision,[69] that this resolution contradicted the Pact of the Arab League. Palestine, a non-independent country, should not share equal voting rights at a Council of Independent Arab States. He suggested that 'Alami should attend the council's meeting but should not sign any resolutions.[70] However, Nuqrashi was not convinced. He further rejected the Foreign Office advice that 'Alami would attend the meetings of the League as an 'observer'.[71] Nuqrashi insisted that 'Alami should sign the Pact and suggested leaving the issue "to the astute legal mind of Badawi", the new Egyptian Minister for Foreign Affairs, to decide in what capacity 'Alami would sign.[72]

A day before the conclusion of the Arab Conference, Badawi met Lampson and discussed with him at some length the problem of Palestine. Badawi asked for information on British policy in Palestine so that "the Egyptian Government might then be able to assist with co-signatories of the Arab Pact". However, Badawi made it clear that he, as well as the rest of the Arab Governments, would not acquiesce to the "common danger of an aggressive Jewish State implanted in the heart of the Middle East". Lampson reported that he "carefully" confined himself to "generalities and the pious hope" that Palestine would be allowed to sleep as long as possible, though "every one"-- including his superiors in London--had to realise that it could not do so forever.[73]

C. The Pact of the League of the Arab States and its Palestinian
    Annex-- Some Contemporary Appreciations

When Badawi held his talk with Lampson, the draft of the Pact of the Arab League had already been initialled. Therefore, Badawi's conversation with Lampson had no effect on the drafting of the Palestinian Annex to this Pact. The Pact was approved by the general Arab Conference on 22nd March 1945. It contained 20 Articles and three Annexes, one of which was devoted to Palestine.[74]

The Annex on Palestine was shorter than the one agreed to by the Alexandria Conference. It also differed from the one recommended by the Political sub-Committee in which 'Alami had a rather influential say. One of the suggestions made by 'Alami in that Committee-- a use of Article 22 of the Covenant of the League of Nations to substantiate Palestinian claims for independence-- was dropped from the final Pact. Minor changes were further made in the language of the Annex.

Nevertheless, the Annex still emphasised the claim that Palestine was an Arab country and that she had to be integrated into the Arab world. The Annex opened with a statement that "since the termination of the last great war the rule of the Ottoman Empire over the Arab countries, among them Palestine, which had become detached from the Empire, had come to an end. She has come to be autonomous, not subordinate to any other state". The Annex went on to support the undeniable right of Palestine to independence and ended by stating that owing to the special circumstances of Palestine, and until her independence, the Council of the League would take charge of the selection of an Arab representative from Palestine.

The Annex on Palestine was to become the only criticised clause in the generally praised Pact. Lampson, who was pleased with the deletion of Article 22 of the Covenant of the League of Nations from the Annex, was nonetheless disturbed by the "imprudent phraseology" which opened it.[75] Smart remarked that Grigg was also greatly upset by the Palestinian Resolution, particularly the opening phraseology. Smart attempted to appease Grigg by pointing out that this had been the Arab attitude towards Palestine ever since the beginning of the Palestinian mandate. But Grigg was not appeased. He still thought that the resolution would dispose many people, "maybe Churchill", to be against the Arabs.[76]

The reaction of British officials in London was similar; although Hankey, of the Eastern Department, attempted first to defend the Arabs by attributing "the rather unfortunate reference to Palestine" to "the pressure of Zionist agitation",[77] he changed his emphasis when the full text of the Annex had become known. The mounting protests against the language of the Annex from pro-Zionist circles compelled British officials to re-examine the Annex. After this review even Hankey admitted that the Annex on Palestine was "a deplorable production".[78]

The Palestinian Annex was also criticised by Palestinian Arabs and Egyptians, though for entirely different reasons. 'Alami, for example, was upset by the fact that he had failed to achieve official recognition as a member with full voting rights in the Council of the League. As a result of this failure 'Alami was greatly disgruntled about the League. He claimed that the League had been reduced to a status of "a debating society", and 'threatened' to retire from public activity.[79]

'Alami's criticism of the Annex was shared by other Palestinian Arabs[80] and various Egyptian circles, notably the Wafd Part. During the Parliamentary debate before the ratification of the Pact, various Egyptian Deputies qeustioned whether the Annex safeguarded the Palestinian Arab cause. Both Fikri Abaza, now a prominent coalition member, and Nuqrashi had to assure the Chamber of Deputies that Palestine was one of the main pillars (da'ama) of the League, and that Egypt would do her best to help the Palestinians.[81]

A day later, the Government had to face further criticism over the Palestinian Annex. This time the critic was Sabri Abu 'Alam, now head of the Wafdist Opposition in the Senate. Condemning the Annex, Abu 'Alam argued that the Palestinian Arabs were "shocked and surprised" to see the achievements obtained in the Alexandria Protocol transformed in the Annex to the Pact into a historical survey of their situation. He regretted that the Censor had prevented the newspapers from publishing any comment on the differences between the two texts.[82]

Abu 'Alam might not have expressed such a criticism had not the

Wafd been relegated to the Opposition. But this does not mean that the criticism was unjustified. The Annex not only deprived the Palestinian Arabs of their right to choose their representatives to the League, but also offered them no remedy for their plight. Aside from repeating existing Arab claims concerning Palestine, no precise assistance had been offered to the Palestinian Arabs. No mention of the previous promise to form a National Arab Fund had been made.

Moreover, the substance of the Palestinian Annex suggests that it was serving inter-Arab politics rather than the ostensible cause it championed. Since the Arab leaders repeatedly told their public that the deliverance of Palestine was one of the main motives for Arab Unity, they had to demonstrate this in the Pact. Hence, the strong language of the Palestinian Annex. The strong moral support for the Palestinian Arabs also distracted attention from the fact that no material assistance to Arab needs in Palestine had been promised. The language of the Palestinian Annex was perhaps an ateempt to make up for the loss of the original conception of Unity by the League. By showing that they and not weakened their position on Palestine, the Arab delegates might have attempted to cover up the fact that much of "the spirit of Alexandria" had vanished from the final Pact of the League.[83]

Since all those Arab leaders who were reluctant to realise Arab Unity advertised the Pact as a positive, and even a vital, stage towards greater Unity, none of the Arab politicians who criticised the Pact voted against it. The Egyptian Parliament, like the Iraqi and Syrian ones, ratified the Pact unanimously (bi al-ijma'). By and large the Arabic Press also acclaimed the Pact as a great achievement for the Arab Nation. In Egypt, even personalities such as Taha Husayn, who had previously doubted the desirability of a political Arab Union, applauded the Pact. The Pact fostered hopes for better economic and cultural ties between the Arab States. Schemes for an Arab Economic Coummunity had been drawn up,[84] new pro-Arab Societies were created,[85] and a general feeling of euphoria surrounded the conclusion of the Pact.

A similar euphoria privailed among British officials who examined the Pact. Although they failed in their attempts to persuade the Arab delegates to declare the League a regional organisation,[86] and in spite of their criticism of the Palestinian Annex, British officials still thought that the Pact as a whole was an immense achievement for the Arab world and a positive development in the area. Hankey of the Eastern Department was pleasantly 'surprised' that the Arab States could have drafted such a Pact. "A collection of European States", he appreciated, "would hardly have produced anything more impressive".[87] Eastwood, of the Colonial Office, was no less impressed. The Pact, he remarked, was "a document of some statesmanship", "a considerable achievement", and the outcome of "a remarkable readiness among all to sink differences with the object of achieving the major aim of establishing the League". Eastwood did not think that the text of the Palestinian Annex was nearly as bad as the Jewish Agency feared it would be. "A good deal of foolish talk in the first half of it", but nothing more. He maintained that it would be very unfortunate if Palestine remained altogether outside practical

activities of the League on such matters as agriculture and so
on.[88]

The satisfaction of British officials with the Pact was well
relfected by the British Press. Public opinion in Britain learnt that
the "swiftness" which marked the completion of the Pact was a good
promise for the future. The Pact facilitated "the political and
economic healing and rebuilding of the Middle East". It was "an
essential step" in the security arrangements of this area. Moreover,
certain outstanding issues, such as that of Palestine, could only reach
"satisfactory determination" if they could be approached as matters
which jointly concerned on the one side the U.N., and on the other the
entire Middle East. Furthermore, Britain, with her long-standing record
of friendship with these countries, would benefit more than any other
Power from this Pact.[89]

Significantly, British officials in Cairo, where the Pact had been
concluded, were more cautious in their appreciation. They preferred to
express their optimism about future rather than present developments in
the League. An intelligence report, which sharply criticised the manner
in which the Arab talks were conducted, pinned some hopes on the
persons who would participate in the League, and in particular the
Secretary General of the Council. The report concluded that unless the
League was "hopelessly wrecked" at the very beginning, it would
"certainly" become "a powerful moral factor in the Middle East".[90]

The nomination of 'Azzam, a supposed fanatic, as Secretary-General
of the new League,[91] was only one of the factors that worried
British officials in Cairo. They were equally concerned by the creation

during the talks of two rival blocs in the Arab world. Lampson, who had
been "a good deal surprised" at the "solid and serious shape" of the
Pact,[92] could not, however, ignore some disturbing developments
which had occurred during the drafting of this Pact. A day after the
Arab members approved the Pact, Lampson sent a detailed report to
London describing what in fact had taken place in the meetings.
"Ibn-Sa'ud", the report said, "alligned himself with Egypt against his
old enemies, the Hashemites and Nuri. The Lebanon, which was fearful of
domination by a still uneuropeanised Moslem hinterland, naturally
followed suit, regarding Egypt as more modernised and less fanatical
than Syria and Iraq.... Syria, which at the beginning was not
enthusiastically pro-Egyptian, has gradually evolved towards Egypt
owing to the desire of the present governing elements in Syria to
preserve the republican regime and their apprehensions of Hashemite
designs on Syria. King Faruq has always treated the Emir Abdullah very
superciliously and there is no love lost between them. Moreover,
inevitably a Hashemite Emir, with his dreams of a Syrian throne, would
find himself in the opposing camp to that of the present Syrian rulers.
It was equally inevitale that, in spite of rivalries between Abdullah
and the Iraqi Royal family over Syria, the two Hashemite Powers should
find themselves standing together against the Egyptian bloc". This
"unhappy" state of affairs aroused Lampson's concern. He thought that
Britain ought to prevent the Hashemites' isolation in the new League,
not only because Britain was obliged to help the Hashemites for their
loyalty and assistance during the War, but also because Britain had a
vital interest in the operation of the League. Lampson believed that

Britain could not afford the disintegration of the League. Such a disintegration would divide the Arab world. This, in turn, would 'invite' Russian penetration and would de-stabilise a large area lying across British lines of communication and containing Britain's vital oil supplies. In case London might see certain advantages in the disintegration of the Arab world, Lampson re-emphasised that whatever discords might weaken the Arab League, it was still united on two issues: "getting rid of the French from Syria, and of preventing the Zionist domination of Palestine".[93]

Lampson's report was carefully studied in London. The Foreign Office agreed "entirely" with Lampson that is was in Britain's interest that the Arab world should not be divided. Rival Arab groups were an invitation to outside Powers. Political stability was the key to maintaining both British interests and friendly relations with the various Arab states. While it was true that the Arab League might play an embarrassing role over Palestine or the Levant or even Britain's treaty rights in Egypt or Iraq, it was equally true, so it was believed, that "the whole Arab world" would in any case be united on topics such as the Palestine and the Levant problems. Having to choose between the two risks, the Department preferred that presented by the Arab League, because Arab Unity during the pre-League period lacked "any representative Arab body competent to handle the Arab case". The League would concentrate on its internal affairs rather than on "showy and dangerous agitation on behalf of the non-independent Arab countries". Economic and cultural relations, and abolition of internal frictions between the member states, seemed to the Deapartment to be the most popular issues for future discussions in the League. Such expectations encouraged the Eastern Department to believe in Britain's ability to guide the League, and in particular 'Azzam, away from "showy agitation" towards "internal affairs". Following Lampson's advice, the Department instructed British representatives in the Middle East to reconcile the rival Arab blocs.[94]

D. The League's Activities During 1945 - A Critical Review

The record of the League in its first year of activity did not seem to justify the many hopes and expectations that had been pinned on this body. The frictions and divisions between the Arab members of the League continued to dominate inter-Arab politics. Towards the end of 1945, these divisions reached a new climax when both Hashemite rulers refused an invitation by Faruq to attend a meeting with Ibn-Sa'ud[95] and were even considering the idea of leaving the League altogether.[96]

The activity of 'Azzam during this period did not help heal suspicions between the rival Arab parties. The Secretary-General of the Arab League did not take the trouble to resign his other positions in the Egyptian Senate and the Ministry of Foreign Affairs. The Arab impression that the League was merely a means for Egypt's Arab policy might have been encouraged by the offices of the League being in the buildings of the Egyptian Ministry of Foreign Affairs.

The affiliation of the League to Egypt must have been so clear that none of the Arab members of the League paid his proportional share to the budget of the League. Badawi, who was faced with the unpleasant surprise of playing the debts of the League, refused to allocate substantial sums for its operation. The major part of the budget of his Ministry for Foreign Affairs was spent on other expenditures, especially the U.N. Conferences in the U.S. Years later, 'Azzam recalled that he had received a mere 10,000 Egyptian Pounds for the operation of the League during 1945.[97]

The combination of internal divisions and a small budget dictated the nature of the League's activities during 1945. Having been either reluctant or unable to abolish their internal divisions, the members of the League were content with joint opposition to the French and Zionist presence in the Middle East. During May, 1945, the Secretariat of the League, as well as the Arab countries, sent memoranda to London and Washington, emphasising their objection to Jewish immigration into Palestine.[98] In June, the League devoted its activity to condemning French aggression in the Levant.[99] During July and August, the Economic and Agricultural Committees were convened to discuss financial, commercial, industrial, and agricultural questions of interest to the states of the League. They were further expected to consider the safe-guarding of Arab lands in Palestine against Jewish encroachment.[100] However, aside from advertising the meetings,[101] no definite recommendations or decisions were taken. Sub-Committees were appointed to continue discussions on all those issues.[102] From the end of August until the middle of October, the Secretariat of the League was once again engaged in initiating new protests against Truman's fresh declarations in favour of Jewish immigration into Palestine.[103]

In November, 1945, the Council of the League was reconvened for its annual meeting. The Secretariat had planned to discuss the development of Arab co-operation in the various cultural, economic, and political fields. Instead, the meeting was dominated by a long debate on the League's response to the new British initiative on Palestine. This initiative had been disclosed in a Parliamentary speech which was delivered by Ernest Bevin, the new Secretary of State for Foreign Affairs, on 13th November 1945.[104] The British initiative included the setting up of an Anglo-American Commission of Enquiry to examine conditions in Palestine. Jewish immigration was expected to continue at the existing rate (of 1500 per month) which had been determined by the previous 1939 White Paper Policy on Palestine.

After rather long deliberations, the Council of the League decided to reject the British initiative.[105] Internal conflicts in the Council led to the replacement of a moderate and positive reply with a negative one.[106] Explaining why the negative reply had been favoured by the members of the Council, the Trans-Jordanian Premier told Smart that "each delegate taken apart might be reasonable, but when two or more gathered together nobody dared to agree to future immigration".[107] Since the Arab stand on Palestine became the index of Arab Unity, a compromise over this stand meant a compromise on Arab Unity. No Arab leader wished to be attacked by either his Arab neighbours or his political rivals for neglecting this cause. While Nuri or 'Abdullah could develop, outside the League, their Greater Syria projects which made some concessions to the Jewish community in Palestine, during the League's discussions, they restricted themselves to joint Arab statements which denied any political rights to this community. Thus, the League, far from developing the possibility of an Arab-Zionist dialogue, became the main obstacle to such an option. Positive thinking gave way to negative decisions. Total opposition to any political aspiration of the Jewish community in Palestine and unquestionable support for the Palestinian Arab stand, soon became the main characteristic of the League.

Although British officials in the Middle East were evidently aware of the possibility of such a negative development, they remained adamant that the League could not endanger British interests. All attempts to dissuade them from this belief failed. In June, 1945, Prince Muhammad 'Ali made yet another attempt to attract Foreign Office attention to the potential dangers of the League. The Prince warned Lampson that the Arab League, especially under Egyptian domination, was a "menace". Britain, the Prince thought, should be on guard against pan-Arab intrigues. At present, Arab efforts were directed against French presence in the Levant, but in future Britain would become the target.[108] A few days after meeting Lampson, the Prince repeated his warnings during a conversation with Hamilton, of the Office of the Minister of State in Cairo. Muhammad 'Ali asserted that it was "a calamity" that Egypt had been allowed to join the League, and even more to lead it. The League, he said, was now busy getting the French out of Syria and Lebanon, but in due course it would be Britain's turn. 'Azzam, the Prince complained, was "quite unreliable, and fanatical, and lacking in any statesmanship".

Hamilton disagreed. He thought that the League was not so dangerous in spite of its "considerable nuisance value". Egypt's domination of the League would prove a source of weakness rather than of strength because Egypt "really did not belong to the Arab world", and her position in the League was, therefore, "somewhat of an anomaly". Hamilton further thought that even 'Azzam would prove a source of weakness rather than of danger.[109]

Hamilton's conversation with Prince Muhammad 'Ali may illustrate the anomaly of Britain's attitude towards the League. British officials in the Middle East were taking great pains to point out how important to British interests in the Middle East a united Arab world was. However, when the dangerous potentialities of such a union were pointed out to them, they belittled the danger by claiming that the League was a thin cover for the constant intrigues and deep conflicts dominating Arab politics. Not surprisingly, the Foreign Office agreed entirely with Hamilton's analysis. Prince Muhammad 'Ali was belittled as an old man, whose unrealistic warnings did not warrant particular consideration.[110] No official appeared to be aware of the immanent contradiction between Hamilton's analysis and the Foreign Office stand that Britain should encourage co-operation and unity among the members of the League.

Owing to this paradox, these officials also agreed with entirely different analyses that were sent by Walter Smart. In September, 1945, the Embassy issued a Note on the Arab League, Smart's particular field of responsibility. Britain, the Note said, had more to gain than to lose by a united Egypto-Arab world because divisions in this world were believed to have exposed the area more easily to political penetration by other foreign Powers.[111]

In November, 1945, Smart prepared a further report on the Egyptian
Treaty revision and the British position in the Middle East.   The
report opened with a statement that Britain could not maintain her
strategic and economic position in the Middle East except on a regional
basis.   Therefore, Smart assumed that since separate and isolated
negotiations with Egypt would not guarantee British presence there, the
question of Egypt's Treaty revision should be brought into any general
discussion with the Ministers for Foreign Affairs of the States of the
Arab League.   Smart believed that if these ministers were satisfied
with British policy in Palestine and the Levant, they would be ready to
consider   mutual   co-operation   for   the   defence   of   the   Middle
East.[112]

Smart was very confident that his analyses were correct. In March,
1945, after having differences with Grigg over the possibility of
growing anti-Semitism in Egypt, Smart minuted: "We [the officials of
the Embassy] are the only people who can see the whole picture....
We have always had to barge in on Arab affairs because we saw many
sides of the picture through our contacts with frequent visitors from
all over the Arab world, while our missions in other Arab States must
inevitably have a one-sided vision of Arab matters".[113]   Lampson
"quite agreed" with Samrt,[114] his "principal adviser".[115]

Smart was right, of course, in assuming that British officials in
Cairo could have seen "the whole picture".   Smart, as well as other
Arab experts in Cairo and London, repeatedly reported on the endless
conflicts and wide divisions among the Arab countries.   Therefore, the
fact that a deceptive picture had been drawn should not be attributed

to lack of information on the Arab world. Rather, to the misuse of this information by the officials in Cairo, and notably Smart. Having developed a certain conception of Anglo-Arab relations, Smart preferred to adjust the observations to the conception rather than to change the conception. Thus, for example, London was informed that a potential Russian threat would be enough to unite a divided Arab world, and that a sacrifice of both the French and the Zionists would win Arab friendship and preserve Britain's interests and position in the Middle East.

Both Smart and Lampson, affected, perhaps, by the personal good relations that they had developed with Arab politicians during their long period of service, were inclined to ignore, or maybe forget, the ambivalent Arab attitude towards Britain. Having been the strongest Power in the area, Britain obviously aroused considerable Arab resentment. British domination, rather than the Russian or Zionist threat, remained the dominant concern of Egyptian, Trans-Jordanian and Iraqi politicians during this period. It was quite obvious that the various Arab countries would use every means, the Arab League being one, to rid themselves of foreign influence. No British concession could have saved Britain, as well as France, from Arab opposition.

Smart's and Lampson's illusive reliance on the deceptive picture they had drawn prompted both to express optimism that Bevin's new initiative would be readily accepted by the League. After meeting Faruq, Lampson reported optimistically that the King agreed "entirely" with Bevin's Parliamentary statement. Lampson further interpreted Nuqrashi's non-committal response as a favourable reception of this statement.[116]

This assumption was completely mistaken. In spite of their personal agreement or indifference to Bevin's statement, none of the Arab or Egyptian politicians was prepared to endorse it publicly without the League's approval. Once the British initiative had been discussed in the League, "nobody", as the Trans-Jordanian Premier had declared, dared to agree to Jewish immigration. Once again, the Palestinian Arab stand was endorsed by all the other members of the League. British officials, who had sought to use the influence of the League to moderate the Palestinian Arab stand, were now facing joint Arab pressure to concede to the Palestinian Arab demands.

Against the strong advice of both Smart and Clayton, the Council of the League decided to declare an economic boycott against Zionist industry.[117] Worse was still to come. British pressure on the Arab delegates to accept Bevin's initiative[118] proved futile. In spite of Britain's 'friends' and 'allies' in the Council of the League, the British initiative was rejected. Typical of this new development was the reaction of Ibn-Sa'ud, Britain's believed-to-be most loyal ally, to the initiative. The King, on whose moderate influence the British had pinned so many hopes, asserted that the League's response to Bevin's statement was "moderate and reasonable".[119] He even took the unprecedented step of assembling the whole diplomatic corps, telling them that the League's decision resembled his own views.[120]

This development was not to remain the only surprise with which British officials were faced. During the final session of the Council of the League, Jamil Mardam, President of the current meeting, after expressing the League's support for the Palestinian Arab cause, also declared in the name of all members, the solidarity of the League with the Egyptian question.[121] Prince Muhammad Ali's prediction began materialising.

E. Egypt, The League and The Palestine Question in 1945

While expressing in public their enthusiastic support for Arab Palestine, Arab and Egyptian politicians showed in camera a marked reluctance to bear the financial burden of the various aid projects for the Palestinian Arabs. 'Alami, who had been entrusted by the Council of the League with organising the Propaganda Bureaux, found that the Arab Governments, which had promised two million Pounds, were not prepared to fulfil this undertaking. Nuqrashi, for example, told 'Alami that he did not believe in propaganda, and refused to contribute an annual sum which, he said, amounted to as much as the whole budget of the Egyptian Foreign Office. 'Azzam, for his part, thought that the Propaganda Offices should be run by the League.[122]

'Alami was greatly offended by the Egyptian refusal to finance the propaganda. He blamed 'Azzam for the propaganda 'flop', and returned frustrated to Palestine, where he issued a statement implying that he was going to resign his post.[123] This 'threat' helped. Arab delegates went to Palestine and asked 'Alami to continue the organisation of the Bureaux. As a result of these conversations, 'Alami renewed his efforts to obtain Arab funds, but met with little success. Both the Egyptian and Iraqi regimes tied their financial assistance for this project to their supervision of the propaganda and the inclusion of their nominees in these Bureaux.[124] Consequently, the Propaganda Offices were badly financed and conducted, and failed to realise the great expectations pinned on them.

Financial difficulties and political rivalries also frustrated the project of safeguarding the Arab lands in Palestine. In July, 1945, the Economic and Agricultural Committees of the League discussed for the first time how to safeguard the Arab lands in Palestine. The members of these Committees decided to send an observer to Palestine "to get certain practical and technical information to enable the Committees to decide between the claims of different projects".[125]

The observer, Taqi al-Din al-Sulh, Counsellor in the Lebanese Legation in Cairo, found that the Arab politicians were still at "sixes and sevens" over the rescue of the Arab lands.[126] The Palestinian Arab Party, the Husaynis' organ, mistrusted the Nation's Fund (Sunduq al-Umma), which had been founded by the Independence Party (Hizb al-Istiqlal). Consequently, the Husaynis formed a new organisation to deal with land problems. The organisation, a company for the rescue and development of the Palestinian Arab land, was expected to collect one million Pounds through the stock market. 'Alami was nominated to head the new company. This company, which received the name, the Constructive Project (al-Mashru' al-Inshai), was tangled from its inception in bitter conflicts with the rival company.[127]

When Taqi al-Din arrived in Palestine, the conflict between these two companies was brewing. Consequently, the observer made a pessimistic report, which, in turn, provided the Committee with a good excuse to withhold contributions from both companies. Although the Committee adopted in principle 'Alami's plan to form a society for the safeguarding of the Arab land in Palestine, it made a few changes. 'Alami's scheme was based on a contribution of one million pounds a year for five years to a land development company, the organisation of which would be subject to the approval of the Council of the Arab League. The capital was to be used to assist the fallahin to pay off their debts, to carry out various improvements in agricultural methods and in village constructions, to promote village industries and cultural and social activities, and to assist in the marketing of village products. Any financial asisstance was to be subject to an essential condition that the fallahin who received it should convert their lands into Family Endowment (Waqf Dhurri), or in the case of land held in common (musha') into village endowment. This condition was intended to ensure that the land would never be sold to non-Muslims.[128]

The Economic Committee decided, however, that a total capital of one million pounds would be quite sufficient to cover all necessary expenditures. Moreover, even this sum was not to be released immediately. The Committee decided to form a special sub-Committee to examine the best way to spend the money.[129]

In November, 1945, when the Council of the League reconvened, the issue was again discussed. A further mission consisting of Taqi al-Din al-Sulh and Khayr al-Din al-Zirikly, Counsellor in the Saudi Legation in Cairo, was sent to examine the situation in Palestine. The mission failed in its attempts to reconcile the rival Palestinian Arab

companies.[130]   Far from deciding how to break the deadlock, the
Council appointed a new Technical Committee to examine the question of
the utilisation of funds for the purchase of Palestinian land and for
improving the conditions of the villagers, with a view to preventing
Zionist purchase of lands.   The Technical Committee included two
Egyptians, two Palestinian Arabs, and one Lebanese. Hafiz 'Afifi, the
Director General of Bank Misr, headed the Committee.[131]

   The new Committee could not agree on the best way to spend the
money. It prepared two different schemes. The first scheme, which
had been proposed by the two Egyptian experts, Hafiz 'Afifi and Ahmad
Mamduh Mursi, suggested investing the capital in an Arab agricultural
Bank which would assist the Palestinian fallahin with special
allowances. The second scheme was drafted by two other members of the
Committee, Rijai al-Husayni from Palestine, and Sa'id Himda from
Lebanon. They thought that 'Alami's company should unite with the
Nation's Fund and operate as one company with the same
purpose.[132]

   It was as late as April, 1946, that the League determined in
favour of the first project.[133] However, by this time the Arab
Governments felt no urgency to contribute any funds to their scheme
because 'Alami, disappointed by the long delay in the receipt of
contributions, had begun operating his own project without the League's
assistance.   In December, 1945, 'Alami registered his company, the
Constructive Project, as a company in Palestine, and through a moderate
contribution of 150,000 pounds from the Iraqi Government, began working
on his scheme. However, owing to lack of funds, the Project collapsed

and soon ceased its activities.[134]

In contrast to the poor practical assistance to the Palestinian Arabs, Egyptian and Arab politicians expressed great concern for this people during conversations with British officials. Soon after the conclusion of the Pact, Nuqrashi renewed his appeal for the release of Jamal al-Husayni from his internment in Rhodesia.[135] He further disclosed his sympathy for the Mufti and requested British officials to change their attitude towards him.[136] Other Egyptian Ministers and officials, such as Makram 'Ubayd and 'Azzam, also expressed sympathy with the Palestinian Arab cause and even warned the public of the danger to Egypt from the Zionist economy.[137]

The Government, in addition, sent several representations to the U.S. Government to adopt the Arab stand on Palestine. The representations demanded a complete and immediate halt to Jewish immigration into Palestine, and warned that the Arabs would resist "at all costs" the Zionist aspirations for a Jewish State in Palestine.[138]

King Faruq supported the Government's anti-Zionist campaign. The King was "sure" that the Russians stood behind the Zionist movement, encouraging Jewish extremists to cause havoc in the Arab world in order to prepare the ground for a Communist takeover. Faruq further believed that the Russians financed no less than 300,000 people in Egypt for this purpose.[139]

With such suspicions in mind, it should not be surprising that the regime permitted, and perhaps even encouraged, the new crusade against the Zionist Jews conducted by the pan-Arab and pan-Islamic associations in Egypt. After the completion of the Pact of the Arab League, various pan-Arab and Islamic organisations sent special missions to the Arab countries to examine ways to promote co-operation among the Arab countries. Palestine attracted the special interest of these missions.[140] Although some of the members were greatly disasppointed with the divisions between the political parties in Palestine,[141] they all published upon their return emotional accounts of the plight of the Arab population there.[142]

From the middle of August onwards, the campaign for the Palestinian Arabs intensified as a result of Truman's statement favouring the opening of Palestine's gates to Jewish immigration. 'Azzam issued a sharp warning comparing Jewish immigration to the Crusaders' invasion.[143] Attempts had been made to organise youth and other associations for collective action in defence of the Palestinian Arabs.[144] Nahhas urged Britain and the U.N. to move forward to a speedy resolution of the Palestine problem, and asked for an extraordinary meeting of the League to discuss Truman's statement.[145]

The King attempted to use Nahhas's call to his advantage. Faruq proposed an urgent meeting of the Arab rulers in order to draw up a joint anti-Zionist declaration.[146] The plan fell through owing to inter-Arab rivalries rather than British representations,[147] and the King restricted himself to another meeting with Ibn-Sa'ud. Nevertheless, the atmosphere that led to Faruq's initiative did not change. In fact, during the very days that Faruq met Ibn-Sa'ud, the Press and political circles in Egypt were again stirred by a further statement from Truman calling for the immediate immigration of 100,000 Jews into Palestine.[148] Nuqrashi told the American Minister in Cairo that the Egyptians were "shocked and mystified" by the American reaction towards the Palestine problem, not only because of the internal political implications involved, but also because of the Americans' "amazing indifference to, and ignorance of, the Arab side of the problem".[149]

It is partly because of this reason that Nuqrashi did nothing to defuse the growing tension in the streets during October. Although he met al-Banna (who was believed to have mustered about 1.5 million adherents[150]), and warned him not to hold street demostrations,[151] Nuqrashi did not take preventive measures when the leader of the Ikhwan defied this order. During October, al-Banna was making consistent public appearances calling for the return of the Mufti, and urging the use of force to solve the Palestine question.[152]

Al-Banna did not remain the only popular leader who incited the public to action. Misr al-Fatat also issued warnings to the Egyptian Jews to condemn Zionism or face public wrath.[153] Egyptian notables, such as the proprietor of al-Misri, Muhammad Abu al-Fath, now a Wafdist Senator, put their weight behind the Palestinian Arabs. They described Zionist activities in Palestine as the main source of violence in the East and the greatest threat to world peace.[154]

On 31st October, Jamil Mardam, President of the meeting of the League, opened the session of the Council of the League with a speech warning that any harm done to a part of the Arab world would touch the

whole of the Arab League.[155]   The atmosphere became so tense that
Amin 'Uthman believed that the Palestine question was a most disturbing
issue, a problem even more dangerous than that of the Treaty
Revision.[156]   The police reported that feelings in Cairo ran so
high that any violence against Palestinian Arabs would lead to a
violent reaction in Egypt.[157]

As it turned out, no violence in Palestine was needed to incite
the already agitated streets to action. From the middle of October,
students' committees and the newly created Front (Jabha) of pan-Arab and
Islamic organisations in Egypt began calling for a strike and
demonstrations on 2nd November-- Balfour Declaration Day.[158]   On
that day, after a meeting in al-Azhar, Banna led a demonstration
estimated at 10,000 to 20,000 people to Abdin Square, where he and
other personalities delivered emotional speeches calling for the
liberation of Palestine. During the demonstration and afterwards a mob
broke into the Jewish quarter, attacked Jewish shops, and desecrated
synagogues.   The riots, which spread also to Alexandria and to the
European community there, lasted two days. When they ended, police and
Press reports counted six dead, five of them Jews, and 670 injured, 500
of them in Alexandria.[159]

The riots were condemned by all the political circles in Egypt
except Misr al-Fatat. Nuqrashi personally visited some of the scenes
of violence and promised a firm hand against the rioters.[160]
Faruq invited the Chief Rabbi of Egypt to an audience and expressed his
sorrow for the damage.[161]   'Azzam, who had stressed before that
the Egyptian Jews had, as citizens, equal rights,[162] also

condemned any Arab or Jewish violence. The Palestine problem, he declared, could only be resolved by a "mutual entente".[163]

The problem was that while none of these personalities probably anticipated that the demonstrations could degenerate into riots, all of them evaded any call for an Arab-Jewish dialogue. In fact, they even encouraged the already high tension of the public. Nuqrashi, for example, was reported to have endeavoured to enlist Labour unions for the demonstrations in order to create a strong pro-Arab atmosphere for the meeting of the League.[164]

The Government's efforts to promote such an atmosphere might explain why no steps were taken before and after the riots to curb the anti-Jewish propaganda that inflamed the streets. Typical of this propaganda was a new play entitled the New Shylock (Shyluk al-Jadid) which had been written by 'Ali Ahmad Bakathir[165], and circulated by the Students' Publishing Committee. The play, which was introduced by personalities such as Huda Sha'rawi and the journalist, 'Abd al-Qadir al-Mazini, contained sharp anti-Zionist and anti-Jewish themes. Its hero, Shylock, a greedy Jew who directed the Zionist activity in Palestine, conspired to turn Palestine into a Jewish base from which he intended to rule the Arab world. Through the other Arab characters in the play, the audience could learn that Judaism was the source of religious fanaticism in the world and a threat to humanity. Among the suggestions made by the playwright to solve the Palestine conflict was a demand for the repatriation of the Jewish immigrants, the transfer of Jewish villages to Arab hands and the destruction of Tel-Aviv. The play ends with a contemporary 'happy ending': Shylock, the symbol of the Zionist movement, commits suicide.[166]

The fact that a play like this, far from being censored, was allowed to be published and circulated, illustrates the atmosphere that prevailed in Egypt. The critics of the riots did nothing to prevent the distribution of anti-Jewish propaganda in Egypt. The Egyptian Jews continued to be harassed by pan-Arab and Islamic societies, as well as by Government officials, and pressed to make anti-Zionist declarations.[167] Calls for the boycott of all Jewish goods from Palestine attracted growing support. Thus, for example, the Seventh Arab Medical Congress held in Cairo in November, 1945, resolved to boycott all Zionist pharmaceutical products from Palestine.[168] A month later, the League decided to boycott all Zionist products from Palestine as long as Jewish immigration into Palestine continued.[169]

Egypt's leaders, eager to lead the Arab world, were inclined to head the more radical and militant views rather than to fight for the adoption of moderate views which would take into account the political aspirations of the Jewish community in Palestine. No Egyptian politician ever attempted to suggest in public the possibility of involving the Palestinian Jews in the negotiations on Palestine. The idea that the Palestinian Jews also deserved a hearing, if not consultations, on the future solution of the Palestine question had been abandoned. Prominence was given to the Palestinian Arab stand which denied any political rights to the Jewish community in Palestine. This was also determined as the official Egyptian stand.

CONCLUSION

At the height of the political campaign supporting the Palestinian Arabs in September - October 1945, the Arabic press in Egypt gave great publicity to views that the Zionist Jews in Palestine posed a threat to Egypt's economic independence as well as to her social and even territorial integrity. The conflict, therefore, was not only portrayed as an Arab and Islamic cause, but also as a national Egyptian issue affecting Egypt's very basic interests.

These arguments were not new. Since the beginning of the 1930s, Egyptian advocates of Arabism, such as 'Alluba, had been warning the public against the mighty economic power of the Zionist Jews, whose activity endangered Egypt's potential markets in the Arab East. Such arguments, no doubt, made some headway and might even have affected the thinking of Egypt's national leaders. Between 1937 and 1945, various Egyptian leaders, such as Nahhas, 'Ubayd, and even King Faruq, warned British officials that a Jewish State in Palestine would endanger the territorial integrity of Egypt. These leaders expressed further fears that a Zionist - Jewish State would not only pose a formidable economic threat to Egyptian markets, but would also be a centre of Russian-backed Communist propaganda devised to spread socialist views among neighbouring societies in order to destabilise them, and, thus, to ease or prepare the ground for Russian occupation.

While it is possible that such apprehensions affected Egypt's opposition to the Zionists, it is clear that these fears never dominated the thinking of Egyptian politicians. In spite of expressing such fears, Egypt's policy makers never initiated a practical policy to fight or resist the Zionist enemy. Far from mobilising all the national resources to fight the Zionists, Egypt's leaders even permitted pro-Zionist activity in Egypt .

Moreover, in spite of the general Egyptian solidarity with the Palestinian Arabs, actual official support for them was limited and always conditional. Pro-Palestinian Arab activity in Egypt was suppressed when it appeared to endanger friendly relations with Britain, or when it degenerated into anti-Jewish agitation. Money raised for the Palestinian Arabs sometimes remained in local party accounts. During the whole period, neither economic nor commercial concessions had been made to the Palestinian Arab people.

Furthermore, most of the circumstances in which Egypt's politicians intervened in the conflict were a reaction to external developments rather than an outcome of particular Egyptian initiatives. Egypt's politicians reacted to appeals for help by Palestinian Arabs; to the mediation efforts of other Arab leaders in the conflict; to the various pan-Arab projects initiated by Arab leaders; and to the changing British policy towards the conflict. In contrast to Nuri or 'Abdullah, Egyptian leaders never initiated an original scheme to solve the conflict. The ideas they expressed regarding the conflict had always been voiced before by other Arab or British parties, and their policy, far from being imaginative and creative, was simply a response to initiatives taken by other protagonists.

In spite of the occasionally expressed fear of Zionist domination, Egypt's policy makers never treated the Palestine conflict as a leading national issue warranting particular and continuous attention like the issue of Anglo-Egyptian relations. Rather, it was dealt with as a part, admittedly an important one, of Egypt's regional policy. During the 1920s, when Egyptian leaders rejected any involvement in Arab affairs, they showed little interest in the Palestine conflict. Even the 1929 disturbances in Palestine failed to bring about political intervention, because the Egyptian Government still refused to meddle in Arab affairs. However, during the 1930s and 1940s, when they did voice their views and further expressed sympathy for the Palestinian Arab cause, Egypt's politicians usually placed their attitude to the conflict within a larger Arab or Islamic frame.

It is, therefore, within the broader context of Egypt's regional policy that an attitude towards the conflict had been determined and practised. This policy was a new phenomenon starting as late as 1936.

The reason for the growing Egyptian interest in Arab and Eastern affairs should not be attributed solely to the internal political struggle in Egypt. There is, indeed, considerable circumstantial evidence that the Opposition's stand concerning Arab and Palestinian affairs was influenced by the internal political struggle (the Wafd in 1931, 1938; the Liberal Constitutionalists in 1937, 1943). However, there is no conclusive evidence that the regional policy of the various Egyptian Governments was dictated by this struggle. Since 1936, all of Egypt's leaders (with, perhaps, the exception of Hasan Sabri in 1940) aspired to play a leading role in the politics of the region. The Palace bid for either the Caliphate (1938-1939) or the leadership of the Arab world (1945-1946), and the Opposition's statements on Arab affairs, probably encouraged the various regimes (Mahmud's 1938-1939, Nahhas's 1943-1944) to persist in their own bids for leadership. Moreover, the internal rivalry between Egyptian leaders influenced, indeed dictated, personal nominations which, in turn, affected Egypt's Arab policy ('Ali Mahir, 1939; 'Azzam, 1944). However, the desire to play a leading role in regional politics was common to all Egyptian parties.

Since 1936, Egypt's national leaders, in public speeches and conversations with British officials, emphasised their Islamic and Arab relations as motivating their intervention in Arab affairs, and particularly the Palestinian conflict. However, the attitude of Egypt's leaders towards their co-religionists in Palestine raises doubts whether these motives can satisfactorily explain Egyptian intervention in regional and Palestinian affairs. It is true that Egypt's leaders, as members of an Islamic society, probably felt a genuine sympathy with the plight of Muslims in neighbouring countries. The support of the pan-Islamic Societies for the Palestinian Arabs surely helped to remind people, and especially the various Governments, of their religious Islamic duty to assist their co-religionists in Palestine. Nevertheless, the failure of these societies to obtain Government assistance for the Palestinian Arabs during the 1929 and 1933 disturbances in Palestine, and during the Arab revolt there (1936-1939), raises doubts as to whether the politicians were greatly affected by the religious sense of duty. Their marked reluctance to make economic and commercial concessions to the Palestinian Arabs further suggests that Egypt's national leaders, as numerous other national leaders, placed the welfare of their own society, rather than the Arab or Islamic ones, foremost amongst their considerations.

The impact of pan-Arab ideology on Egypt's leaders seems even fainter. Egypt's national leaders were rather proud of their Egyptian society and quite contemptuous towards their Arab co-religionists. They regarded Egyptian society as the most advanced in the region, far more competent than the Arab one. Indeed, the small number of members of pan-Arab Societies in Egypt illustrates both the marginal attraction and the limited influence of Arabism in Egypt.

Thus, regarding their society as the most competent in the region, Egypt's national leaders could not allow other Arab leaders to play the dominant role in the region. Those leaders, particularly Nuri al-Sa'id and the Hashemites, attempted to acquire such a role through mediation in the Palestine conflict and by initiating various pan-Arab projects. Since the Arab leaders presented their Islamic and Arab ties as the reason for their intervention in the conflict, these ties also became the main Egyptian excuse for intervention in Palestinian and Arab affairs.

Because Egyptian intervention in the Palestine conflict was motivated more by political calculation than by ideological beliefs or principles, the attitude towards the Palestinian Arabs could still remain ambivalent. While praising their Arab relations, the politicians did not hesitate to suppress the Palestinian Arab advocates in Egypt when they appeared to be endangering friendly relations with Britain. While paying tribute to the Arab cause, the politicians still flirted with Zionist officials and allowed pro-Zionist activity in

Egypt.

This ambiguity was intended to persuade British officials that Egypt was the most moderate and reasonable force in the region. Since Britain was not only deeply involved in this conflict, but was also the greatest Power in the area, the choice of the regional leader became very much a British choice. The Palestine conflict became one of the main means through which Egyptian and Arab leaders expected to promote their regional influence. By mediating in the conflict, Egyptian, like other Arab leaders hoped to impress British officials that they were the only leaders who deserved British support.

Owing to British permission, Cairo became the centre of Arab talks on the Palestine question (1938-1939). The talks, however, failed to induce greater Egypto-Arab co-operation. Until as late as 1941, in spite of making repeated statements asserting their Arab and Islamic ties, Egyptian leaders rejected the various Arab projects for economic and political alliance. Their rejection was largely owing to an Egyptian belief that the issue of regional leadership of the area should be determined by mutual discussions with Britain rather than through negotiations with the Arabs.

This attitude changed during the War for several reasons. Following Eden's Parliamentary Statement (1943), Egyptians, as well as Arab politicians, became convinced that Britain had begun supporting Arab Unity. This belief induced Nahhas to respond favourably to Nuri's initiative for fear that he and Egypt might be left out of the new British plan for the Middle East.

Nahhas's response, which initiated the talks for the Arab League, was probably also affected by the growing belief, shared by British and Arab officials alike, that regional arrangements were bound to become the dominant factor in the future world order. The Arab League was an outcome of such thinking.

The League was not so much a realisation of Arab aspirations for unity as a compromise between the unionist ideas of Nuri and 'Abdullah and the separatist views of Lebanon and Egypt. Egyptian leaders took pains to form a body, the Arab League, which preserved existing separate loyalties. They did so in accordance with their particular policy, which viewed a territorial union of Arab countries as a threat to an Egyptian political hegemony in the Middle East.

British officials believed that the League was the result of the inevitable tendency among Arabs to unite. They thought themselves powerless to oppose this alleged tendency, but hoped to turn the League into a regional body which would deter possible Russian penetration into the Middle East.

For Egypt and the other Arab countries, the League was a further means to fight the Zionist, British, and French presence in the Middle East. Having been reluctant to promote closer unity between themselves, Egyptian and Arab politicians described the Zionist, French, and British presence in the Middle East as the main obstacle, in fact the only one, preventing unity. Defining the Zionists as obstructive to Arab unity, the members of the League, under Egyptian leadership, far from developing the possibility of an Arab-Zionist dialogue, supported the Palestinian Arab stand which denied any political aspirations to the Jewish community in Palestine. The

Palestinian Arab solution for the conflict became the joint Arab solution of the conflict. It became the demonstration of Arab Unity. The publicity given to the various meetings of the League further amplified this stand, and, in turn, diminished the prospects for compromise.

FOOTNOTES

INTRODUCTION - pp. 6-40

1. For a detailed examination of this belief, consult: Fritz Steppat, "Nationalismus und Islam bei Mustafa Kamil", Die Welt des Islams (1956), Vol. IV, pp. 274-277, 281-294; Israel Gershoni, Mitzrayim, bein Yihud le-Ahdut (Tel-Aviv, 1980), pp. 38-39.

2. On Egyptian support for, and participation in, the Ottoman campaigns in Libya and the Balkans consult: Muhammad Husayn Haykal, Mudhakkirat fi al-Siyasa al-Misriyya (Cairo, 1951, 2nd ed. 1977), Vol. I, pp. 43-44, 62-64; Jamal Zakariya Qasim, "Mawqif Misr min al-harb al-Tarablusiyya, 1911-1914", al-Majalla al-Ta'rikhiya al-Misriyya 1967, Vol. 13. pp. 306-340; Jamil 'Arif, Safhat min al-mudhakkirat al-Sirriyya li Awal Amin 'Amm li-l-Jami'a al-'Arabiyya (Cairo, 1977) Vol. I, pp. 78-83, 188.

3. As'ad Daghir, Mudhakkirati 'ala hamish al-Qadiyya al-'Arabiyya (Cairo, 1959), p. 10; Ahmad Husayn, Nisf Qurn ma'a al-'Uruba wa Qadiyat Filastin (Beirut, 1971), p. 11; For the Palace opposition to Arab nationalism, consult: John Presland [pseud. Gladys Skelton], Deedes Bey, a study of Sir Windham Deedes, 1883-1923 (London, 1942), pp. 247-249; John Hamilton's Record of conversation with Prince Muhammad 'Ali, 4th July, 1945, Public Record Office, Foreign Office 371/45239/E5427.

4. For 'Aziz ambivalent attitude towards the Revolt, consult: Eli Kedourie, In the Anglo-Arab Labyrinth (Cambridge, 1976), pp. 26, 96, 106-107, 154; Majid Khadduri, "'Aziz 'Ali al-Misri and the Arab Nationalist Movement", in A. Hourani (ed.), St. Antony's Papers, No. 17 Middle East Affaris, No. 4, (Oxford, 1965), pp. 140-155; Ahmad 'Abd al-Mu'ti, 'Urubat Misr (Beirut, 1979), pp. 205-208.

5. For a detailed account of Lutfi's views, consult: Charles Wendell, The Evolution of the Egyptian National Image (California, 1972) p.p.215, 225-238, 260-271; Haykal, Vol. I, pp. 90-151.

6. Ahmad Lutfi al-Sayyid, Qissat hayati (Kitab al-Hilal, No. 131, Feb. 1962), pp. 137-139.

7. Al-Jarida, 30th September, 1911, quated by Ahmad Lutfi al-Sayyid al-Muntakhabat (Cairo, 1937), Vol. I, pp. 250-251.

8. An account of the interview between the Wafd and Wingate on 13th November, 1918, appears in Wingate's papers, SAD/170/3/2, Sudan Archives, Durham. The official version of this account was sent by Wingate to Lord Harding (London) on 14th November,1918, FO 848/2 (Copy: FO 141/773/7819/3). Another version with slight differences, appeared in 'Abd al-'Aziz Fahmi, Hadhihi Hayati (Kitab al-Hilal, No. 145, 1963), pp. 76-81.

9. Cited by Anwar G. Chejne, "Egyptian attitudes toward Pan-Arabism",
    Middle East Journal, Vol. 11 (1957) p. 253; Anis Sa'igh, al-Fikra
    al-'Arabiyya fi Misr (Beirut, 1959), p. 142.

10. Al-Muqattam, 13-14, 16th June, 1920; ha-Aretz, 15th, 16th, June, 1920.

11. 'Azzam to John Hamilton (Sudan Agency, Cairo), 10th October, 1933,
    FO 141/744/834/2/33; al-Usbu'u al-'Arabi, 17th January, 1972,
    p. 43, interviewing 'Azzam.

12. Cf. Marius Deeb, Party Politics in Egypt: the Wafd and its Rivals,
    1919-1939 (Oxford, 1979), pp. 70-150 who could not find any trace of
    pan-Islamic or pan-Arab ideology in any of the platforms of the major
    political parties in Egypt.

13. Y. Burla, "Biqur ha-morim be-Mitzrayim", ha-Aretz, 12th, 13th April,
    1926; R. Mosseiri, "ha-Ahdut ha-'Arvit", ha-Aretz, 4th December, 1927.
    Mosseiri was an Egyptian Jew.

14. An article by the Dutch-American reporter, Pierre van Paassen, as
    published in ha-Aretz, 25th October, 1929.

15. Ziwar Pasha, Egyptian Prime Minister and Minister for Foreign
    Affairs, to Lord Lloyd, High Commissioner (Cairo), 4th February,
    1926, FO 371/11605/J397; Ahmad Shafiq, Hawliyat Misr al-Siyasiyya
    (Cairo, 1929), Vol. 3 - 1926, pp. 38-39. The British approval of
    this reservation was sent on 25th June, 1926 after consultations
    between the Colonial and Foreign Offices (FO 141/585/12840/86).

16. Cf. the debate in the Chamber of Deputies on the Egyptian-Palestinian
    border, 19th May, 1927 in Journal Official, No. 69, 15th August,
    1927, Supplement, the Chamber debate, pp. 841-842.

17. Muhammad 'Ali al-Tahir, Mu'taqal Hakstab (Cairo, n.d.), p. 600,
    quated in Khayriyya Qasimiyya, "Muhammad 'Ali al-Tahir - Qalam
    Filastini fi Misr", Shu'un Filastiniyya (Nov. 1974), No. 39, p. 151.

18. Al-Muqattam, 26th March, 1925.

19. Invitations to these parties sent to Zionist leaders are in S25/7516,
    Central Zionist Archives, Jerusalem. For further details on parties
    and invitations during 1928-1938, see: File 00693, Division 65,
    Israel State Archives, Jerusalem.

20. William Yale, American Diplomatic Agency (Cairo) to Leland Harrison,
    Department of State (Washington D.C.), 26th November, 1917 (Report
    No. 5), Yale Papers, MEC, (Oxford).

21. A copy of the letter dated 2nd August, 1922, is in S30/2493d, CZA;
    ha-Aretz, 5th September, 1922, published parts of this letter.

22. Frederick H. Kisch, Palestine Diary (London, 1938), pp. 109-110.

23. Ha-Aretz, 8th March, 1925, Siham Nasar, Al-Yahud al-Misriyun bayna
    al-Misriyya wal-Sahyuniyya (Cairo, 1980), p. 38.

24. Ben-Zion Taragan, Le-korot ha-Kehila ha-Yehudit be-Alexandria
    be-arba'im shanim ha-ahronot, 1906-1946 (Alexandria, 1947), pp. 83-84;
    Bat-Yeor, (pseud.), Yehudei Mitzrayim (Tel-Aviv, 1974), pp. 83-85,
    97-99; David Tidhar, be-Madim u-be-lo Madim (Tel-Aviv, 1938),
    pp. 159-161; Ahmad Muhammad Ghanim and Ahmad Abu Kaf, al-Yahud wa
    al-haraka al-Sahyuniyya fi Misr, 1897-1947 (Kitab al-Hilal,No. 219, June
    1969), pp. 27-50, 82-87, 101-104, Nasar, pp. 47-67.

25. J.M. Landau, Jews in Nineteenth Century Egypt (New York, 1969),
    pp. 115-125, 327-329; Haim Y. Cohen, ha-Pe'ilut ha-tzionit be-artzot
    ha-Mizrah ha-Tichon (Tel-Aviv, 1973), pp. 8-10; Taragan, pp. 87-88,
    110, 129-130.

26. See, for example, Taragan, pp. 116-125 for the pro-Zionist activity
    of the Jewish Senator, Joseph de Piccioto

27. Nasar, pp. 20, 34-35, 54-55. Early in 1925, the newspaper was sold to
    the Unionist Party (Hizb al-Ittihad), and its editor replaced.

28. Tidhar, p. 193; David Tidhar, be-Sherut ha-Umma (Tel-Aviv, 1960/61),
    p. 215. According to Tidhar, the meeting was cancelled because the
    British were opposed to such an idea.

29. Taragan, pp. 143-144.

30. Department of Public Security, Ministry of the Interior, (Cairo) to
    Chancery (Cairo), 29th March, 1921; same to same, 7th April, 1922,
    FO 141/585/13089/4,6. For the participation of a Palestinian Arab
    delegation in Zaghlul's funeral in 1927, consult: Emil al-Ghuri,
    Filastin 'ibra sittin 'amman (Beirut, 1972), Vol. I, pp. 97-98.

31. Ahmad Shafiq, Mudhakkirati fi Nisf Qurn (Cairo, 1938), Vol. III,
    pp. 334-339; A. Shafiq, A'mali ba'da Mudhakkirati (Cairo, 1941)
    pp. 53-54, 158-159, 443-444.

32. On the Society and its platform, see: Director-General, Department
    of Public Security (Cairo) to High Commissioner, Palestine, 25th
    June, 1922; same to High Commissioner, Egypt, 30th June, 1922.
    FO 141/585, pp. 41-42; Note on al-Rabita al-Sharqiyya, FO 141/795/
    18375/1; al-Rabita al-Sharqiyya, Vol. I. No. 1, 15th October, 1928,
    pp. 3-11.

33. Cf. RSh., Vol. I, 15th October, 1928, pp. 59-61; No. 3, 15th February,
    1929, pp. 32-33.

34. RSh., Vol. I. No. 1, 15th October, 1928, p. 53.

35. For the formation of this society and its aims, consult:
    Daghir, pp. 152-155; Fish (Cairo) to the Secretary of State
    (Washington DC), 12th July, 1939, RG 59, 867N.01/1621.

36. On the formation of this organisation and its aims, consult:
    Department of Public Security (Cairo) to the Chancery (Cairo), 18th,
    30th May, 4th December, 1921; 19th November, 1922, FO 141/585/13089/6-24.

37. Ha-Aretz, 27th May, 1921; 17th March, 1922; 19th June, 1922; 5th July; 28th August, 1922; 31st October; 11th November, 1923; 4th November, 1924; 25th October, 1929; al-Muqattam, 25th October, 1924.

38. E. Rubinstein, "ah-Protocolim shel Ziknei Tzion ba-Sikhsuck ha-Yehudi-'Arvi be-Eretz Israel bi-shnot ah-esrim", Ha-Mizrah he-Hadash, Vol. 26, 1976, No. 1-2, pp. 39-41.

39. Taragan, pp. 159-160.

40. Al-Jadid, quoted by ha-Aretz, 31st March, 1926.

41. Muhammad 'Ali al-Tahir, Nazrat al-Shura (Cairo, 1932), p. 118, Khayriyya Qasimiyya, Tahir, p. 151. Also File 3192, Div. 65, IS A, for a Palestinian Arab protest to the Egyptian Government dated 3 Jan. 1926, against the closure of al-Shura.

42. 'Abd al-Qadir Yasin, "Suhuf al-Yasar al-Misri wa-Qadiyat Filastin", Shu'un Filastiniyya (September, 1972), No. 13, p. 118; Rif'at al-Sa'id, al-Yasar al-Misri wa-Qadiyat Filastin (Beirut, 1974), pp. 27-28, regards the small Marxist magazine al-Hisab, which appeared from October, 1924 until May, 1925, as the leading Egyptian supporter for the Palestinian Arabs during this period. Such a statement only emphasises the insignificance of the political circle interested in the Palestine conflict. Deeb, pp. 82-82, 188-189, points at the Watani Party as the only political party with a vision which went beyond the boundries of Egypt to other Muslim countries of the Near East. However, he adds, after the First World War the party "ceased to have any of the features of a mass party as it was transformed into a cadre party".

43. Muhammad Bey Ahmad 'Abadin, Consul (Jerusalem) to Acting Minister for Foreign Affairs, Muhammad Mahmud (Cairo), 11th May, 1929, File 01573, Div. 65, ISA. The Consul described the activities of the former Consul, and asked for specific details on the financial transactions.

44. For this emergence consult: J. Heyworth-Dunne, Religious and Political trends in modern Egypt (Washington, 1950), 1-21; M. Colombe, L'Evolution de l'Egypte, 1924-1950 (Paris, 1951), pp. 121-154.

45. For details on this Society, consult: G. Kampffmeyer, "Egypt and Western Asia", in H.A.R. Gibb (ed.), Whither Islam (London, 1932), pp. 101-165; "The origins of the YMMA, and their nature", Yalkut ha-Mizrah ha-Tikhon, Vol. 1, 1936/7, No. 11, pp. 40-46.

46. For the activities of this society, consult: Gershoni, pp. 104, 339-340.

47. Al-Muqattam, 1-3 September, 1929; Majallat al-Shubban al-Muslimin, Vol. 1, No. 1, 1st October, 1929, pp. 73-79; No. 2, November, 1929, pp. 211-213, 224.

48. Al-Muqattam, 1st September, 1929, an appeal dated 14th October, 1929, "to the governments and the peoples", in Shafiq, Mudhakkirati, III, p. 329. Further activities of the Society are detailed in RSh. Vol. 2, No. 2, 1st December, 1929, pp. 46-47.

49. Zaki's appeal was published in Filastin, 17th December, 1929. Tidhar, be-madim, pp. 173-175; be-sherut, pp. 193-195, asserts that Zaki's call was rejected by many in Egypt. As a result Zaki retracted his original statement, and contemplated forming a Jewish-Arab Peace Committee. However, when his new proposal met no sponsors, Zaki reverted to his radical anti-Zionist attitude.

50. A call by Jam'iyat al-Azhar al-'ilmiyya in al-Muqattam, 29th August, 1929; al-Muqattam, 3rd September, 1929; Report on Egyptian Press reaction to the disturbances by R.H. Hoare, High Commissioner (Cairo) to Arthur Henderson (London), 31st August, 1929, FO 371/13753/E4575; extracts from various Egyptian newspapers appeared in Filastin, 13th 14th March, 1930; ha-Aretz, 13th September, 1929.

51. Tidhar, be-madim, p. 172; Tidhar, be-sherut, p. 191.

52. R.H. Hoare, Acting High Commissioner (Cairo) to Henderson (London), 31st August, 1929, FO 371/13753/E4575.

53. Filastin, 4th January, 1930; Tidhar, be-sherut, p. 201, Tusun's letter urging Premier MacDonald to recognise the Arabs' rights in Palestine was published in al-Muqattam, 17th December, 1929, and obtained favourable reactions (al-Muqattam, 18th, 19th December, 1929). The Prince's name also appears in the contributors' list for the Palestinian Arabs, in MShM, Vol. I, No. 2, November, 1929, p 150.

54. Muhammad 'Ali to High Commissioner (Jerusalem), 29th August, 1929, FO 371/13746/E4557.

55. Al-Muqattam, 3rd September, 1929.

56. For this phenomenon, consult: Gershoni, pp. 105, 341; Deeb, p. 189.

57. RSh, Vol. 2, No. 2, 1st December, 1929, 46-47.

58. Al-Sirat al-Mustaqim, 13th January, 1930.

59. Hoare (Cairo) to Henderson (London) 31st August, 1929. FO 371/13753/E4575.

60. Report on leading personalities in Egypt, FO 371/23362/J2876/478/16.

61. His memorandum dated 3rd September, 1929, appears in FO 371/13753/E4860.

62. Percy Loraine, High Commissioner (Cairo) to Henderson (London), 14 September, 1929; FO minute, 24th September, 1929, FO 371/13753/E4860.

63. The Rabbi's letter of 30th October, 1929, and the Consul's subsequent report are in File 01506, Division 65, ISA.

64. Al-Siyasa, as quoted by Khairiyya Qasimiyya, Tahir, pp. 151-152. For the neutral attitude of the Government, see also: al-Siyasa, 1st September, 1929. Further extracts from this newspaper showing similar themes were quoted by ha-Aretz, 3, 6, 11th September, 1929.

65. Al-Sirat al-Mustaqim, 13th January, 1930; Filastin, 14th October, 1936.

66. Tidhar, be-madim, p. 176; Tidhar, be-sherut, pp. 195-196.

67. The exchange of communications over this issue between the Mufti and 'Ali Shamsi of the Wafd was published by Filsatin, 3rd May, 1935.

68. Al-Sirat al-Mustaqim, quoted by ha-Aretz, 27th March, 1930.

69. Miraat al-Sharq, 12th September, 1931, in an article titled: "let us not forget". For the same incident, see also: Filastin, 14th October, 1936.

70. Russel, Cairo City Police, to Keown-Boyd, Residency (Cairo), 10th September, 1930; Ralph Stevenson's report, 30th October, 1930, FO 141/625/808/5/30.

71. Misr, 20th October, 1929, quoted with other Egyptian newspapers concerning this issue in File 01506, Division 65, ISA.

72. Muhammad 'Ali 'Alluba, Filastin wa Jaratiha, asbab wa nata'ij (Cairo, 1954), p. 5; and his later Filastin wa al-damir al-Insani Kitab al-Hilal, No. 156, March 1964), p. 37.

73. For this split, which began probably in June 1932, see: Extracts from Egyptian Press, 2-9th July, 1932; FO 371/16116/J1721. However, according to a short biography on 'Alluba (FO 371/19091/ J725/16), the rift between him and his party came about only in January, 1934.

74. Among these associates one could find members of the al-Rabita al-Sharqiyya, such as Ahmad Zaki, Shaykh Muhammad al-Ghanimi al-Taftazani and Mansur Fahmi. Other companions included 'Abd al-Hamid Sa'id and Huda Hanum Sha'rawi. Further details on these guests and their activities in Palestine are in Filastin, 25-29th June, 1930.

75. Filastin, 20th July, 1930.

76. Al-Muqattam, 19th August, 1930; 30th December, 1930; al-Siyasa, 5th October, 1930, Filastin, 5th, 21st August, 1930.

77. Husayn Mahmud, "Misr wa al-Duwal al-'Arabiyya", al-Muqattam, 9th August, 1930.

78. Al-Muqattam, 13-16th August, 1930, for the responses of Nisim Sib'a, Fahmi Najib and Sami al-Saraj to Mahmud's article.

79. Police Report on activities of 'Alluba, 18th October, 1933, FO 141/698/596/1/33.

80. Loraine (Cairo) to London, 27th February, 1931, FO 371/15282/E1205.

81. Al-Muqattam, 25th December, 1930; al-Fath, 12 Sha'ban 1349, p. 5(501).

82. Kisch, p. 386.

83. For the goals of the delegation, see: extracts from the Iraqi media, FO 371/15285/E1117/2/25; Nuri's letter from Haifa to Naji Shawkat, 27th March, 1931, in Dr. Muhammad Anis and Dr. Muhammad Husayn al-Zubaydi, Awraq Naji Shawkat (Baghdad, 1977) p. 142.

84. See, for example, Taha al-Hashimi's sharp criticism of what he saw in Egypt during the visit of the delegation in Sati' al-Husri (ed.), Mudhakkirat Taha al-Hashimi (Beirut, April 1967) pp. 103-106.

85. Filastin, 26th April, 1931; Do'ar ha-Yom, 11th February, 1932; Loraine (Cairo) to London, 24th April, 1931, FO 371/15404/J1420.

86. The Agreement was signed on 2nd May, 1931, by Nuri al-Sa'id and 'Abd al-Fatah Yahya, FO 141/771/394/13/31; FO 141/769/458/4-8/31.

87. For their branches in Palestine and activities there, see: Al-Fath, 12 Sha'ban 1349 (1930), pp. 1-2; Kampffmeyer, p. 108; Ylakut, p. 42; Miraat al-Sharq, 24th January, 1931; al-Jam'ia al-'Arabiyya, 25, 28th January, 1931; al-Fath, 10 Ramadan 1349, pp. 8-9 (568-569); Mu'tamar Majalis al-Idara li-Jam'iyat al-Shubban al-Muslimin (Cairo, 1930/1349).

88. For Tal'at's beliefs and activities in the Arab East, consult: R.L. Tignor, "Bank Misr and Foreign Capitalism", IJMES, Vol. 8, April 1977, pp. 161-165; Fathi Radwan, Tal'at Harb, bahth fi al-'azama (Cairo, 1970), 82-89; Tawfiq Ahmad al-Bakri, "Tal'at Harb wal-duwal al-'Arabiyya wal-Sudan", al-Thaqafa, 26th August, 1941, pp. 1126-1128; Memorandum on the subject of the History and activities of Banque Misr by Larkin, Commercial Secreteriat (Cairo), 6th September, 1930, FO 141/560/1094.

89. For the creation of associations such as Jam'iyat al-Wahda al-'Arabiyya, and their platforms, see: al-Jami'a al-'Arabiyya, 12th March, 1931; Filastin, 12th May, 1931; Department of Public Security to Oriental Secretary (Cairo), 17, 19th March, 1931, FO 141/763/495/5/31.

90. Loraine (Cairo) to London, 12th June, 1931, FO 371/15282/E3355.

91. The whole text of the speech appears in Qasim Jawda, Al-Makramiyyat (Cairo, n.d.), pp. 151-154.

92. Loraine to London, 2nd April, 1931, FO 371/15404/J1112.

93. Filastin, 24, 27th March, 1931.

94. Consult, for example, Kisch's conversation with Barakat as was noted in his entry for 1st May, 1931, in Kisch, pp. 408-409.

95. Ha-Aretz, 19th August, 1931.

96. Ha-Aretz, 19th August, 1931; al-Jami'a al-'Arabiyya, Filastin, 8-12th September, 1931.

97. The New York Times, 12th September, 1931; Davar, 14th September 1931.

98. Extracts from a speech delivered in the Wafdist National Congress in 1935, as quoted by Jawda, pp. 126-127.

99. JA and Filastin, during September, 1931.

100. Arlozorov (Jerusalem) to Prof. Brodezki (London), 17th November, 1931, Z4/3848/II, CZA.

101. Al-Sha'b (Cairo), quoted by Egyptian Gazette, 9th September, 1931.

102. Le Liberté, quoted by ha-Aretz, 25th August, 1931.

103. For 'Ubayd's growing influence in the Wafd and on Nahhas, consult: Haykal, Mudhakkirat, Vol. II, pp. 223-224; Muhammad al-Tab'i, Misr ma qabla al-Thawra, min Asrar al-Siyasa wa al-Siyasiyun (Cairo, 1978), pp. 52, 148, 234, 238; Dr. Yunan Labib Kizq, al-Wafd wa al-Kitab al-Aswad (Cairo, 1978), pp. 35-38; Report on leading personalities in Egypt (1939), FO 371/23362/J2876; Lampson (Cairo) to London, 24th December, 1943, Annual Report for 1942, FO 371/41326/J79.

104. Misr, quoted by Filastin, 23rd August, 1931; JA, 26th August, 1931; EG, 14-15th September, 1931; 'Ubayd's interview with the Wafdist Kawkab al-Sharq, as quoted by Filastin, 18th September, 1931.

105. This was the fate of JA and Filastin at that time for adopting a pro-Wafdist attitude during and after 'Ubayd's visit.

106. James Paul Jankowski, Egypt's Young Rebels: "Young Egypt", 1933-1952 (Stanford, 1975), pp. 10-11.

107. For details consult my "Egypt and the General Islamic Conference at Jerusalem in 1931" in Middle Eastern Studies, Vol. 18, 1982, pp. 311-322.

108. 'Alluba, Filastin, pp. 5-6; 'Alluba, al-damir, pp. 37-38.

109. Minutes of the 15th session during which 'Azzam delivered this speech are given by Filastin, 17th December, JA, 18th December, 1931.

110. Al-Balagh quoted by Davar, 17th December, 1931; Filastin, 20th January, 1932. In an interview in Filastin, 13th January, 1932, Muhammad Sa'id al-Jaza'iri stated that when he had met King Fu'ad, the latter had expressed his sympathy for the resolutions.

111. Tahir, Nazrat, p. 240.

112. A detailed description of this journey and its failure is to be found in 'Alluba, Filastin, pp. 113-115; Muhammad Amin al-Husayni, Haqa'iq 'an Qadiyat Filastin (Cairo, 1954), pp. 142-143; al-Jami'a al-Islamiyya, 5th May, 3, 4th June, 1933; al-Balagh, 15th June, 1935, published 'Alluba's own account of the journey.

113. Police Report on activities of 'Alluba, 18th October, 1933, FO 141/698/566/1/33.

114. Wauchope (Jerusalem) to London, 13th February, 1932, on a conversation with Sidqi who discussed with him the "real business" -- 'Abbas Hilmi's intentions in this area, FO 141/722/352/6/32.

115. In an interview with al-Sha'b, quoted by Filastin, 16th February,
     1932; Filastin, 11th February, 1932, 12th February, 1932.

116. In an interview with al-Sha'b, quoted by Filastin, 12th February,
     1932. For Sidqi's meetings with Zionist leaders see Do'ar ha-Yom,
     10th February, 1932.

117. Do'ar ha-Yom, 9, 10th February, 1932; Filastin, 11th February, 1932.

118. Z. Avramovitz and Y. Gelfet, ha-Meshek ha-'Aravi (Tel-Aviv, 1944),
     p. 321; M. Nemirovski and Dr. Preuss, Survey of Recent Economic
     Developments in Palestine (Tel-Aviv, 1932), p. 11.

119. Filastin, 11th February; Do'ar ha-Yom, 9, 10th February, 1932.

120. For these talks and their results, see ha-Aretz, 26th-31st May,
     1935; Draft of the Economic Agreement dated 29th May, 1935,
     in FO 371/19093/J9715 (copy: FO 141/539/612/19/35).

121. Memorandum on the proposed Arab Congress, 30th December, 1932
     (apparently prepared by Keown-Boyd) in Loraine to London, 20th
     January, 1933, FO 371/16854/E955 (copy: FO 141/768/1190/2/32).
     Director-General, European Department, to Smart, 18th December,
     1932, FO 141/768/1171/1/32.

122. Details of the internal disputes appear in the various reports by
     the CID on the Congress between March 1933 - June 1933, in
     FO 371/16926. For British objection, see Loraine's report, ibid.;
     Rendel's report, 27th March, 1933, FO 371/16854/E1732.

123. 'Abd al-Rahman 'Azzam to John Hamilton, Sudan Agency (Cairo),
     10th October, 1933, FO 141/744/834/2/33.

124. Loraine (Cairo) to High Commissioner (Jerusalem), 9th November,
     1933, FO 371/17010/J2717; Filastin, 11th, 14th November, 1933,
     on the Shaykh of al-Azhar' refusal to issue a statement denouncing
     British policy; Filastin, 6th, 11th, 14th, 17th November, 1933;
     Yencken, Acting High Commissioner (Cairo) to London, 23rd December,
     1933, FO 371/17875/E18; same to same, 1st February, 1934,
     FO 371/17875/E1033.

125. Ha-Aretz, 7th November, 1933.

126. Filastin; al-Muqattam, 5th August, 1930.

127. Al-Balagh, 19th June, 1935; ha-Aretz, 28th June, 1935.

128. Yalkut, Vol. 1, No. 2, February, 1935, p. 41; ha-Aretz, 17th, 22nd
     January, 1935.

129. One of 'Ubayd's pro-Arab speeches at the Congress appears in Jawda,
     pp. 126-127.

130. Nahhas Pasha to Lampson, High Commissioner (Cairo), 19th January,
     1935, enclosing the Four Resolutions of the Wafdist Congress,
     FO 371/19068/J431.

- 318 -

131. Eliyahu (Elias) Sasson's report, 16th September, 1935, quoted in
     Eliyahu Sasson, <u>Ba-Derech el ha-Shalom</u> (Tel-Aviv, 1978), p. 23,
     Sasson was one of the officials commissioned to promote Arab-
     Jewish relations.

132. Haykal, <u>Mudhakkirat</u>, Vol. 1, pp. 353-354; Similar and even sharper
     views on Egyptian isolation appear in <u>Yalkut</u>, Vol. 1, No. 1,
     January, 1935, p. 34; Kelly to Hoare (London), 16th September,
     1935, FO 141/568/1009/1/35.

PART ONE

CHAPTER ONE - pp. 41-82

1. The appointment was signed by the King on 2nd April, 1936 (FO 141/
    596/81/6/36). However, 'Azzam submitted his letter of Credence to
    the Iraqi King only on 3rd August, 1936. See: Bateman (Baghdad)
    to London, 4th August, 1936, FO 141/596/81/14/36.

2. The absence of any Arab approach is particularly noticeable in
    a book by Mahmud 'Azmi, himself a pan-Arab advocate, who wrote a
    detailed account on Mahir's regime, al-Ayam al-Mi'a (Cairo, 1937).

3. The report dated 28th March, 1936, was enclosed in Lampson (Cairo)
    to Eden (London), 2nd April, 1936, FO 371/19980/E1886. For the
    various visits to Egypt also: Bateman (Baghdad) to London, 3rd
    April, FO 371/19980/E23 E2306; Lampson to London, 8th April, 1936,
    FO 371/19980/E2120.

4. For its content, cunsult: 'Azmi, pp. 102-106.

5. Yehoshua Porath, The Palestinian Arab National Movement 1929 -
    1939 (London, 1977), p. 199.

6. Lampson to London, 28th May, 1936, FO 371/19980/E3153; Hasan
    al-Banna, Mudhakkirat al-Da'wa wa al-Da'iyya (Cairo, n.d.),
    pp. 223-225; Jaridat al-Ikhwan al-Muslimin, 26th May, 1936,
    pp. 14-15 (147-148); Filastin, 27th May, 1936; Huda Hanum
    Sha'rawi, al-Mar'a al-Arabiyya wa Qadiyat Filastin (Cairo, 1939),
    pp. 13-15.

7. For the Committee, its aims and list of members, see: JIM, 2nd
    June, 1936, p. 17 (183); Al-Fath, 14 Rabi'a al al-Awal, 1355,
    pp. 5-6 (1193-1194).

8. Special Section Ministry of Interior (Cairo) to the Director
    of the European Department (Ministry of the Interior), and the
    Oriental Secretary (Cairo), 17th May, 1936, FO 141/536/403/12/36;
    JIM, 19th May, 1936, pp. 19-20 (129-130).

9. Lampson to Wauchope (Jerusalem), 3rd July, 1936, FO 371/20035/E4415.

10. Al-Jihad, 18th, 21st, May, 1936; Al-Ahram, 2nd June, 1936
    al-Balagh, 12th June, 1936; Kelly (Cairo) to London, 4th June,
    1936, FO 371/20035/E3483; same to same, 5th June, 1936,
    FO 371/20110/J5245.

11. Both his letter to Wauchope and the High Commissioner's reply
    were published in, Filastin 13th June; al-Balagh, 11th June, 1936.

12. Al-Balagh, 3rd, 10th June, 1936; Kelly to London, 4th June, 1936,
    FO 371/20035/E3507 (original: FO 141/536/403/1/19/36).

13. The content of about twelve different petitions sent by Muslim
    believers from various mosques on 12th June, 1936, appears in
    FO 141/536/403/34/36.

14. FO 141/536/403/67/36. Kelly himself was, however, convinced that there was "no real anti-Jewish feeling" in Egypt. Kelly to London, 22nd June, 1936, FO 371/20035/E3753.

15. Lampson to London, 12th August, 1936. FO 371/20023/E5207.

16. Porath, pp. 199-200; al-Ahram, al-Balagh, 8th June, 1936; Kelly to London, 11th June, 1936, FO 371/20035/E3452.

17. Kelly to London, 10th June, 1936, FO 141/536.403/29-13/36; same to same, 11th June, 1936, FO 371/20035/E3453-E3454.

18. Same to same, 4th, 5th, 22nd, 11th June, 1936, FO 371/20035/E3452, E3483, E3753.

19. Same to same, 4th, 16th, 22nd June, 1936, FO 371/20035/E3483, E3598, E3753.

20. Lampson to Wauchope (Jerusalem), 21st July, 1936, FO 371/20116/J6832.

21. A note, ibid, referred to Mahmud's statement saying "yes, he is an Arab, but with a lot of black blood".

22. Kelly to London, 16th June, 1936, FO 371/20035/E3598.

23. Same to London, 22nd June, 1936, FO 371/20035/E3753.

24. Lampson to London, 12th August, 1936, FO 371/20023/E3527.

25. Majallat al-Rabita al-'Arabiyya, No. 1, 27th May, 1936.

26. For a further pursuit of this matter, consult: Nabiha Bayumi 'Abd alla,Tatawwur fikrat al-qawmiyya al-'Arabiyya fi Misr (Cairo, 1975), pp. 149-153.

27. Al-Rabita al-'Arabiyya, 23rd June, 22nd July, 1936.

28. Daghir, p. 242.

29. This will be discussed later in this Chapter.

30. Kelly to London, 4th September, 1936; same to Rendel, Eastern Dept. (London), 12th October, 1936, FO 371/19980/E5831.

31. Keown-Boyd, Director-General, European Dept. (Cairo) to Smart (Cairo), 7th June, 1936, FO 371/20110/J5575.

32. Kelly to London, 21st June, 1936, FO 371/20035/E3704.

33. Bert Fish, American Legation (Cairo) to Secretary of State (Washington DC) 15th June, 1936, RG 59,867N.00/320.

34. Filastin, 14th October, 1936; al-Difa', 14th September, 1936; Qasimiyya, Tahir, pp. 153-154, ignores the Wafd's responsibility for these restrictions.

35. Vilenski (Cairo) to Shertok (Jerusalem), 22nd May, 1936, S/25/3242, CZA; Filastin, 14th October, 1936.

36. Kelly to London, 4th, 16th, 22nd June, 1936, FO 371/20035/E3483, E3598, E3753.

37. Lampson to London, 4th August, 1936, FO 371/20022/E5061.

38. Kelly to London, 4th June, 1936, FO 371/20035/E3483; Lampson to London, 8th July, 1936, FO 371/20021/E4327.

39. Lampson to Wauchope, 21st, 24th July, 1936, FO 371/20116/J6833; same to same, 24th July, 1936, FO 371/20035/E4745; same to London, 3rd August, 1936, FO 371/20035/E4940. The content of the resolution of the Chamber of Deputies, suggested by Hamad al-Basil and adopted unanimously on 20th July, 1936, in Lampson to London, 22nd July, 1936, FO 371/20035/E4667; For the Senate's resolution, suggested by 'Abbas al-Jamil and adopted unanimously on 27th July, see: Lampson to London, 3rd August, 1936, FO 371/20035/E4940; al-Ahram, 28th July, 1936.

40. Same to London, 12th August, 1936, FO 371/20035/E5160.

41. Same to London, 24th February, 1936, FO 371/19980/E1826.

42. Same to same, 8th July, 1936, FO 371/20021/E4257.

43. Same to Wauchope (Jerusalem), 21st July, 1936, FO 371/20116/J6832.

44. Wauchope to Kelly (Cairo), 9th June, FO 371/20110/J6832; London to Cairo, 29th June, 1936, FO 371/20035/E3875.

45. Kelly to London, 31st October, 1936, FO 371/20035/E6824.

46. Lampson to London, 12th August, 1936, FO 371/20023/E5207.

47. Kelly to London, 4th September, 12th October, FO 371/19980/E5831.

48. Lampson to London, 12th August, 1936, FO 371/20023/E5207.

49. Cf. G. Sheffer, "The involvement of Arab States in the Palestine conflict and British-Arab relationship before World War II", Asian and African Studies, VO. 10, No. 1, 1974/75, p. 72; Elie Kedourie, Islam in the Modern World, (London, 1980), pp. 93-170.

50. Campbell's memorandum, 28th August, 1936, FO 371/20024/E5492; Oliphant's memorandum, 28th August, 1936, FO 371/20023/E5462; Ormsby-Gore to Shuckburgh, 10th September, 1936, FO 371/20025/E5785; Rendel's memorandum, 8th September, 1936, FO 371/20024/E5691; same's memorandum, 10th September, 1936, FO 371/20025/E5749; Phipps (Berlin) to London, 29th September, 1st, 2nd October, 1936, FO 371/20026/E6131, E6164, E6240.

51. Rendel's report, 8th September, 1936, FO 371/20024/E5691.

52. Phipps (Berlin) to London, 1st October, 1936, FO 371/20026/E6164.

53. Same to same, 2nd October, 1936, FO 371/20026/E6240.

54. For its content see: Kelly (Alexandria) to London, 13th October, 1936, FO 371/20027/E6476. Kelly believed that Ghali, being "a Copt" and "well-read in French literature", was quite detached from the conflict (Kelly to London, 9th October, 1936, FO 371/20027/E6476.

55. Filastin, 14th October, 1936.

56. Lampson to London, 10th November, 1936, FO 371/20028/E7038; same to same, 10th November, 1936, FO 371/20029/E7554.

57. London to Lampson, 16th November, 1936, FO 371/20028/E3708.

58. Journal Officiel, 24th August, 1936, No. 95, Rescrit Royal No. 56, Journal Officiel, 7th Sept., 1936, No. 99, Rescrit Royal, No. 64, p. 1.

59. Lampson to London, 29th December, 1936, FO 371/19980/E8028.

60. Ahmad M. Gomaa, The Foundation of the League of Arab States (London, 1977), p. 36.

61. A note of Samuel Bey 'Atiyah (Sudan Agency, Cairo), 30th December, 1936, FO 141/675/52/1/37.

62. Ibid.

63. For the various rumours: ibid.; Lampson to London, 17th December, 1936, FO 371/19980/E8028; EG, 15th December, 1936.

64. Lampson to London, 9th January, 1937, FO 141/675/52/5/37.

65. 'Atiyah's Note, 30th December, 1936, FO 141/675/52/1/37.

66. Ibid.; al-Rabita al-'Arabiyya, 2nd January, 1937; al-Risala, 11th January. 1937; Filastin, 15th April, 1937.

67. The first Arab Cultural Congress was held in Bayt Mary (Lebanon), 2-10th September, 1947, under the auspices of the Arab League.

68. A. Clark Kerr (Baghdad) to London, 18th January, 1937, FO 371/20801/E698.

69. Kelly to London, 4th September, 1936, FO 371/19980/E5831.

70. Same to Rendel, Eastern Department (London), 12th October, 1936, FO 371/19980/E6696.

71. Clark Kerr (Baghdad) to London, 18th January, 1937, FO 371/20801/E698.

72. Williams' note, Egyptian Dept. (London), 6th February, 1937, FO 371/20801/E698; Lampson to London, 1st February, 1937, FO 371/20801/E987.

73. London to Lampson (Cairo), 11th March, 1937, FO 371/20801/E1361.

74. Kelly to London, 26th March, 1937, FO 371/20801/E1870.

75. Filastin, 7th April, 1937.

76. See, for example, reports from Egypt on a projected union between Egypt, Iraq and Saudi Arabia in al-Jami'a al-Islamiyya, 8th March, 1937.

77. Lampson to London, 28th May, 1937, FO 371/20801/E3080.

78. Jawda, Makramiyat, pp. 151-154.

79. Filastin, 24th March, 1937.

80. Al-Liwa, 8th, 28th February, 1937.

81. Al-Liwa, 19th March, 1937.

82. Ministry of foreign Affairs, Egypt to Embassy (Cairo), 10th June, 1937, FO 141/644/138/11/37; High Commissioner of Palestine to Ormsby-Gore (London), 16th December, FO 141/644/138/14/37.

83. Dr. Yusuf Haykal, Nahwa al-Wahda al-'Arabiyya (Cairo, 1943), p. 28.

84. Sati's al-Husri, Abhath Muhtara fi al-Qawmiyya al-'Arabiyya, 1923-1963 (Cairo, 1964), pp. 124-126; and his Muhadarat fi nushu'u al-fikra al-qawmiyya (Beirut, 1959), 4th ed., pp. 255-257.

85. Vilenski (Cairo) to Shertok (Jerusalem), 30th May, 1936, S25/3242, CZA; Vilenski's report, S25/9166, CZA; D. Ben-Gurion, Sihot 'im manhigim 'arviyim (Tel-Aviv, 1967), p. 101; Lampson to Wauchope (Jerusalem), 30th June, 1936, FO 371/20035/E4414.

86. For details of these talks, consult: M. Sharet, Yoman Medini, 1936 (Tel-Aviv, n.d.), pp. 208, 210, 215; A. Sela', "Sihot wu-maga'im bein manhigim tzionim ve-'aravim", Part One, ha-Mizrah he-Hadash Vol. 22, 1972, pp. 422-423.

87. Vilenski to Shertok, 30th May, 1936, S25/3242, CZA

88. For details of these talks, see: S25/9166.

89. Vilenski to Shertok, 9th June, 1936, S25/3242, CZA

90. For the various Zionist efforts to recruit 'Azmi, consult: A. Cohen, Israel ve ha-'olam ha-'aravi (Tel-Aviv, 1964), pp. 279-281; Susan Lee Hatis, The bi-National idea in Palestine during mandatory times (Haifa, 1970), pp. 138-144.

91. For the Zionist propaganda campaign in Egypt, consult: Sharet, Vol. II - 1937, pp. 146-147, 190; Haykal, Mudhakkirat, III (1978), p. 13; Husayn, pp. 61-64, Nasar, pp. 41-44.

92. Memorandum of reaction of the Egyptian Press to the Palestine report, 7-26th July, 1937, p. 1, FO 371/20811/E4746.

93. Muhammad 'Ali to Wauchope, 11th May, 1937, FO 141/676/52/48/37.

94. Lampson to Vansittart (London), 17th June, 1937, FO 141/676/52/44/37.

95. Cited by Filastin, 30th June, 1937.

96. Mackereth (Damascus) to London, 7th August, 1937, FO 371/20786/E4719.

97. Lampson to London, 8th May, FO 141/675/52/26/37.

98. For British preparations, see: FO 141/675/52/23,27,30/37.

99. Memorandum of reaction of the Egyptian Press, p. 2, FO 371/20811/E4746.

100. Op. cit., p. 3.

101. Op. cit., pp. 3-4

102. Ibid.: Vilenski to Shertok, 11th, 15th July, 1937 S25/5171, CZA

103. Lampson to Wauchope, 12th July, 1937, FO 371/20809/E4077.

104. J. Hamilton, Acting Oriental Secretary (Cairo), 22nd July, 1937, FO 141/678/52/98/37.

105. For the activities of the Revisionists in Egypt, see: FO 141/676/52/69, 79, 94/37.

106. Lampson to Wauchope, 12th July, 1937, FO 371/20809/E4077; Amin Sa'id, al-Dawla al-'Arabiyya al-muttahida (Cairo, 1938), III, pp. 589-590.

107. Memorandum of reaction of the Egyptian Press, p. 3, FO 371/20811/E4746.

108. Op. cit., pp. 4, 6.

109. Ibid., Amin Sa'id, III, p. 587.

110. Lampson to London, 21st July, 1937, FO/20809/E4194.

111. Same to same, 15th July, 1937, FO 371/20808/E4051.

112. EG, 21st July, 1937; Filastin, 23rd July, 1937, Sa'id, III, pp. 587-588.

113. Lampson to London, 17th, 22nd July, 1937, FO 371/20809/E4077.

114. Vilenski to Shertok, 22nd July, 1936, S25/5151, CZA.

115. Filastin, 24th July, 1937.

116. Kelly to London, 21st August, 1937, FO 371/20812/E5054; same to same, (Sep., 1937, FO 371/20814/E5497).

117. The Parliamentary Debates, Fifth Series - Vol. CVI, House of Lords, 22nd Oct., 1937, cols. 628-645. For the debate in the Commons, see: Parliamentary Debates, 326 H.C.Deb, 5⁵, cols. 1997-1998, 2179-2180, 2235-2367. See also C. Sykes, Crossroads to Israel (London 1965), pp. 207-210.

118. Lampson to London, 26th July, 1937, FO 371/20810/E4320.

119. Kelly to London, 6th September, 1937, FO 371/20813/E5246.

120. Lampson to London, 26th July, 1937, FO 371/20810/E4320. Copy: Trevor E. Evans (ed.) The Killearn Diaries, 1934-1946 (London, 1972), pp. 83-84.

121. Phipps (Berlin) to London, 18th November, 1936, FO 371/20122/J8602; The Times, 6th October, 1936.

122. Kelly to London, 19th August, 1937, FO 371/20812/E4957; Alexandria City Police, Special Branch, Intelligence Note, 25th August, 1937, FO 141/678/52/140/37; Al-Rabita al-'Arabiyya, 2nd, 23rd June, 1937; Muhammad 'Ali al-Tahir, al-Yahud wa al-Islam, (al-lajna al-'Arabiyya al-Filastiniyya fi Misr, 1937).

123. See, for example, Husayn Haykal's introduction to Yusuf Haykal's book on Arab Unity.

124. Lampson to London, 26th July, 1937, FO 371/20810/E4320.

125. A. Napier (Cairo) to Tweedy (London), 24th July, 1937, FO 371/20811/E4746; Ibid.

126. London to Kelly, 20th August, 1937, FO 371/20811/E4668.

127. Kelly to London, 19th August, 1937, FO 371/20812/E4858; same to same, 25th August, 1937, FO 371/20813/E4985.

128. Kelly to London, 6th September, 1937, FO 371/20813/E5246.

129. Views of Presidence du Conseil des Ministres, [Nahhas] FO 371/20813/E5337.

130. Kelly to London, 6th September, 1937, FO 371/20813/E5246; same to same, 14th September, 1937, FO 371/20814/E5403.

131. Text of the speeches in Sa'id, III, pp. 620-623, 626-627; FALCOR's report, 21st September, 1937, Z4/17011, CZA.

132. Sharet, II, 1937, pp. 320-321; Filastin, al-Difa', 22-24th Sept. 1937

133. Kelly to London, 28th September, 1937, FO 371/20816/E5903.

134. Al-Ahram, 2nd, 3rd, 19th-20th September, 1937.

135. Kelly to London, 27th October, 1937, FO 371/20819/E6568.

136. Fish to the Secretary of State (Washington DC), 30th August, 1937, RG 59, 867N.01/910; George Allen, Charge d'affaires, to the Secretary of State (Washington DC), 11th October, 1937, 867N.01/960; Lukasz Hirszowicz, The Third Reich and the Arab East (London, 1966), pp. 36-37; Tawfiq al-Suwaydi, Mudhakkirati, (Beirut, 1969), pp. 292-293; other Egyptian, Arab and Zionist sources have already been mentioned.

137. Kelly to London, 27th October, 1937, FO 371/20819/E6568.

138. Lampson to Wauchope, 9th December, 1937, FO 371/20823/E7571; Khayriyya Qasimiyya (ed.), 'Awni 'Abd al-Hadi, Awraq Khassa (Beirut, 1974), pp. 89, 96-97. Fish to the Secretary of State, 3rd February, 1938, RG 59 867N.01/1027.

139. JIM, 5th November, 1937; Kelly to London, 27th October, 1937, FO 371/20819/E6568.

140. Al-Muqattam, 8th October; 14th December, 1937; al-Difa', 16th December, 1937, al-Jami'a al-Islamiyya, 15th December, 1937.

141. Kelly to London, 16th October, 1937, FO 141/678/52/202, 219/37.

142. The manifesto dated 21st November, 1937 reached the Embassy only of 6th January, 1938, see: Lampson to London, 9th January, 1938, FO 371/21872/E443.

143. Al-Jihad, 7th November, 1937.

CHAPTER TWO - pp. 83 - 137

1. Vilenski (Cairo) to Weizmann (London), 13th March, 1938, Z4/17397,
    CZA. For the Islamic and anti-Coptic campaign consult: Deeb,
    pp. 399, n.147.

2. Lampson to London, 17th May, 1938, FO 371/21877/E3172; same to
    MacMichael (Jerusalem), 22nd June, 1938, FO 371/21878/E3907; same to
    London, 20th July, 1938, FO 371/21879/E4559; al-Rabita al-'Arabiyya,
    17th May, 1938.

3. Filastin, 14th April, 1938.

4. Lampson to London, 28th April, 1938, FO 371/21875/E2462; Vilenski to
    Shertok, 29-30th April, 1938, S25/5171, CZA; Fish to the Secretary
    of State (Washington DC) 4th May, 1938, RG59, 86N.01/1082.

5. Lampson to London, 30th April, 1938, FO 371/21876/E2482; same to
    same, 3-4th May, 1938, FO 371/21876/E2575, E2576.

6. Special Department, Ministry of the Interior (Cairo), in Lampson
    to London, 7th May, 1938, FO 371/21876/E2652.

7. Lampson to London, 3rd May, 1938, FO 371/21876/E2575.

8. Same to same, 9th May, 1938, FO 371/21876/E2983; al-Ahram, 8th May,
    1938; Khayriyya Qasimiyya (ed.) 'Awni, pp. 99-100.

9. Lampson to London, 17th May, 1938, FO 371/21877/E3172;
    al-Rabita al-'Arabiyya, 18th May, 1938.

10. Lampson to London, 7th May, 1938, FO 371/21876/E2652; same to same
    16th June, 1938, FO 371/21877/E3677, E3678.

11. Same to same, 8th June, 1938, FO 371/21877/E3389.

12. Same to same, 17th May, 1938, FO 371/21877/E3172.

13. Same to same, 10th June, 1938, FO 371/21877/E3570.

14. See, for example, his interview with Shakir al-Khardaji, al-'Arab fi
    Tariq al-Ittihad (Damascus, 1947), Vol. I, pp. 78-80.

15. Al-Khradaji's book is an account of interviews with 177 Egyptian
    personalities, who, with the exception of Maraghi, expressed
    sympathy with closer co-operation with the Arab countries.

16. Cavendish Bentinck, Egyptian Department (London), 22nd March, 1938,
    FO 371/21875/E1670.

17. Khayriyya Qasimiyya, 'Awni, pp. 99-100.

18. Op.cit., p. 99; Vilenski to Shertok, 30th May, 1938, S25/3156, CZA

19. Egyptian Gazette; al-Ahram, 30th May, 1938.

20. Text of the debate in al-Ahram, 20th May, 1938.

21. Text in Bayumi, pp. 132-133.

22.   'Alluba to Embassy, 25th June, 1938, FO 371/21878/E4257; Fish to
      Washington DC, 3rd August, 1938, RG 59, 867N.01/1141, speaks
      already about 200 signatories,

23.   Bateman (Alexandria) to London, 26th September, 1938, FO 371/21881/
      E5898.

24.   Ibid.; al-Difa' 31st, July, 1938.

25.   Al-Wafd al-Misri, 17th, 27th, 31st July, 1938.

26.   Filastin, 10th July, 1938; al-Difa', 31st July, 1938, 21st July, 1938;
      Khayriyya Qasimiyya, 'Awni, pp. 100-101.

27.   Bateman to London, 26th August, 1938, CO 733/368/75156/16.

28.   Lampson to London, 9th July, 1938, FO 371/21878/E4212.

29.   Same to same, 20th July, 1938, FO 371/21879/E4558.

30.   Ruz al-Yusuf, 25th July, 1938; al-Balagh, 30th July, 1938;
      al-Dustur, 28th July, 1938.

31.   Lampson to London, 9th July, 1938, FO 371/21878/E4212.

32.   London to Lampson, 23rd July, 1938, FO 371/21878/E4415.

33.   MacDonald's Note of interview with Mahmud, 29th July, 1938,
      FO 371/21879/E4618.

34.   B. Locker's Note of the conversation, 30th July, 1938, S25/7516,
      CZA; Antonius maintained that Mahmud was asked to mediate by the
      Zionists. See: Childs' Memorandum of conversation with Antonius,
      10th January, 1939, RG 59, 867N.01/1391.

35.   Text of his speech in al-Dustur, 11th September, 1938.

36.   Minutes of the League's meeting in Z4/17011, CZA.

37.   Bateman to London, 7th September, 1938, FO 371/21880/E5238.

38.   Cadogan to Shuckburgh, 16th September, 1938, FO 371/21880/E5238.

39.   Shuckburgh to Cadogan, 22nd September, 1938, FO 371/21880/E5556.

40.   London to Bateman,   29th September, 1938, FO 371/21880/E5330.

41.   London to Lampson,   30th September, 1938, FO 371/21881/E5651.

42.   Lampson to London,   3rd October,   1938, FO 371/21881/E5785.

43.   Same to London,   5th October,   1938, FO 371/21881/E5816, E5831.

44.   Same to London,   6th October,   1938, FO 371/21881/E5844.

45.   London to Phipps (Paris), 21st September, 1938, FO 371/21880/E5551;
      Downie (CO) to Baxter (FO), 28th September, 1938, FO 371/21881/E5651.

46.   Legation (Jedda) to London, 26th September, 4th October, 1938,
      FO 371/21881/E5655, E5791.

47.   Eliahu Sasson, Baderech el ha-Shalom, (Tel-Aviv, 1978), pp. 127-131,
      140-141.

- 328 -

48. Filastin, 3rd July, 1938.

49. Chapman Andrews' report on a conversation with Nahhas, 18th August, 1938, CO 733/368/75156/16; al-Difa', 4th, 25th July; 18th September, 1938; Ruz al-Yusuf, 25th July, 1938.

50. Gordon Merriam to Washington DC, 21st October, 1938, RG 59, 867N.01/1250; Yalqut ha-Mizrah ha-Tichon, No. 29, September-October, 1938, pp. 22-24.

51. Lampson to London, 5th October, 1938, FO 371/21881/E5816.

52. Same to same, 6th October, 1938, FO 371/21881/E5844.

53. Same to same, 6th October, 1938, FO 371/21881/E5849.

54. Same to same, 9th October, 1938, FO 371/21881/E5895, E5907.

55. Lampson to London, 10th October, 1938, FO 371/21881/E5925.

56. Details of the various controversies, in: Periodical Appreciation Summary, No. 4/38, Deputy Inspector-General, CID (Jerusalem) to Chief Secretary (Jerusalem), 1st November, 1938, CO 733/359/7502.

57. Lampson to London, 8th October, 1938, FO 371/21881/E5931; Filastin; al-Ahram, 9th October, 1938.

58. Al-Ahram, 12th October, 1938.

59. Text of the Resolution in 'Alluba to American Minister, 21st October, 1938, RG 69, 867N.01/1251.

60. Lampson to London, 8th October, 1938, 371/21881/E5931.

61. Ibid.

62. Lampson to London, 12th October, 1938, FO 371/21881/E5964.

63. Same to same, 14th October, 1938, FO 371/21881/E6179.

64. Filastin; al-Difa', 12th October, 1938; Lampson to London, 24th October, 1938, FO 371/21883/E6508.

65. Lampson to London, 20th October, 1938, FO 371/21882/E6209.

66. Same to Same, 17th October, 1938, FO 371/21864/E6048.

67. London to Lampson, 22nd October, 1938, FO 371/21882/E6150.

68. Downie to Baxter, 16th November, 1938, FO 371/21866/E6848; MacDonald's Note on the conversation, 21st December, 1938, FO 371/21866/E6986.

69. 'Alluba, Filastin, pp. 117-118.

70. Khayriyya Qasimiyya, 'Awni, p. 99.

71. For the congratulations of the Congress by personalities such as 'Ali Mahir, consult: al-Mar'a al-'Arabiyya wa Qadiyat Filastin, al-Mu'tamar al-Nisa'; al-Sharqi, 15-18 October, 1938 lil-difa' 'an Filastin (Cairo, 1939), pp. 32-33, 146-147.

72. Op.cit., pp. 170-173; Munira Thabit, Mudhakkirati fi 'ishrin 'amman 'an huquq al-mar'a al-siyasiyya (Cairo 1946), pp. 98-101; Gordon Merriam to Washington DC 24th October, 1938, RG 59. 867N.01/1283.

73. Lampson to London, 10th November, 1938, CO 733/368/75156/16.

74. See, for example, Merriam's reports on petitions by students, Palestinian Arabs, Dar al-'Ulum, and al-Hidaya al-Islamiyya, dated 25th October, 1st, 4th November, 1938, RG 59, 867N.01/1252, 1278, 1281, 1929.

75. Lampson to London, 19th October, 1938, FO 371/21882/E6211.

76. For the various activities of the Wafd, consult: al-Misri, 14th November, 1938; Filastin, 17th November, 1938; Lampson to London, 27th October, 1938, FO 371/21883/E6327.

77. Lampson to London, 24th October, 1938, FO 371/21883/E6508.

78. The joint appreciation of a Foreign and Colonial Office team, 10th November, 1938, FO 371/21883/E6508.

79. Kelly's note, 11th November, 1938, FO 371/21883/E6508.

80. Lampson to London, 5th November, 1938, FO 371/21883/E6489.

81. Lampson to Mahmud, 31st October, 1938, FO 371/21883/E6494.

82. Lampson to London, 5th November, 1938, FO 371/21883/E6489; Same to same, 10th November, 1938, CO 733/368/75156/16.

83. Same to same, 2nd November, 1938, FO 371/21884/E6729; same to same, 31st October, 1938, FO 371/21883/E6429.

84. Ibid.; Haykal, Mudhakkirat, III, p. 18.

85. Lampson to London, 30th October, 1938, FO 371/21883/E6353.

86. Chamberlain to Mahmud, 26th October, 1938, FO 371/21882/E6304.

87. Baggallay's note, 3rd November, 1938, FO 371/21883/E6429.

88. Content of the Speech, in al-Ahram, 18th November, 1938.

89. London to Middle East representatives, 9th, 14th November, 1938, FO 371/21865/E6672, E6775; same to same, 16th November, 1938, FO 371/21884/E6827.

90. Bateman to London, 18th November, 1938, FO 371/21866/E6871.

91. Same to same, 15th November, 1938, FO 371/21884, E6812.

92. Bateman to London, 18th November, 1938, FO 371/21866/E6871.

93. London to Bateman, 24th November, 1938, FO 371/21867/E7049.

94. Bateman to London, 26th November, 1938, FO 371/21867/E7093.

95. Lampson to London, 28th November, 1938, FO 371/21867/E7140.

96. Same to same, 24th October, 1938, FO 371/21883/E6508; same to same, 6th December, 1938, FO 371/21868/E7543.

97. MacDonald to Halifax, 14th December, 1938, FO 800/321, H/XXVI/6, pp. 187-190.

98. Halifax to MacDonald, 16th December, 1938, FO 800/321, H/XXVI/7, pp. 191-192.

99. London to Lampson, 2nd December, 1938, FO 371/21867/E7169.

100. Porath, p. 281; Lampson to London, 16th January, 1939, Fo 371/23304/J377.

101. Lampson to London, 14th December, 1938, FO 371/21868/E7595.

102. Same to same, 15th December, 1938, FO 371/21868/E7577.

103. London to Lampson, 16th December, 1938, FO 371/21868/E7577.

104. Bullard (Jedda) to London, 20th December, 1938, FO 371/21868.E7677

105. Eliav (Cairo) to Shertok (Jerusalem), 6th January, 1939, S25/7644, CZA; Lampson to London, 16th January, 1939, FO 371/23304/J377; Sasson, p. 149.

106. Lampson to London, 4th January, 1939, FO 371/23219/E115.

107. Same to same, 21st December, 1938, FO 371/23219/E14.

108. Same to same, 18th December, 1938, FO 371/21868/E7597; same to same, 16th January, 1938, FO 371/23220/E435.

109. Same to same, 4th December, 1938, FO 371/21868/E7440; MacMichael to Lampson, 6th December, 1938, FO 371/21868/E7444.

110. Lampson to London, 2nd January, 1939, FO 371/23219/E244.

111. Same to same, 4th, 6th, 7th January, 1939, FO 371/23219/E116, E186, E234.

112. Same to same, 9th January, 1939, FO 371/23220/E603.

113. London to Lampson, 6th January, 1939, FO 371/23219/E115.

114. Lampson to London, 18th January, 1939, 371/23220/E482.

115. Same to same, 2nd Jan. 1939, FO 371/23219/E244; Tab'i, pp. 148-149.

116. Same to same, 10th January, 1939, FO 371/23219/E304.

117. Same to same, 11th, 17th January, 1939, FO 371/23220/E417, E459.

118. Same to same, 18th January, 1939, FO 371/23220/E482.

119. Same to same, 16th January, 1939, FO 371/23304/J377.

120. Lampson to London, 10th January, 1939, FO 371/23219/E304.

121. Same to same, 18th January, 1939; Bentinck's note, 20th January, 1939, FO 371/23220/E482.

122. Same to same, 18th January, 1939, FO 371/23304/J236.

123. Bentinck's note, 20th January, 1938, FO 371/23220/E482. This evidence contradicts Haykal's argument in Mudhakkirat, II, pp. 132-3 that Mahir aspired to go to London.

124. Lampson to London, 19th January, 1939, FO 371/23220/E543; Khayriyya Qasimiyya, 'Awni, p. 111.

125. Lampson to London, 21st January, 1939, FO 371/23220/E558.

126. Same to same, 21st January, 1939, FO 371/23220/E557.

127. Same to same, 14th February, 1939, FO 371/23224/E1371; Baggallay's note on a conversation with Alexander, 19th January, 1939, FO 371/23220/E579.

128. Kamil Mahmud Khilla, Filastin wa al-intidab al-Baritani, 1922 - 1939 (Beirut, 1974), pp. 471-472; Ahmad Tarbin, Filastin fi khitat al-Sahyuniyya wa al-isti'mar, 1922-1939 (Cairo, 1971), pp. 234-236.

129. Lampson to London, 18th January, 1939, FO 371/23220/E510.

130. London to Cairo, 21st January, 1939, FO 371/23220/E546.

131. Lampson to London, 6th February, 1939, FO 371/23222/E978; Darwaza, al-Qadiyya al-Filastiniyya, pp. 240-241; Tarbin, pp. 235-236.

132. Lampson to London, 21st, 23rd January, 1939, FO 371/23220/E559, E560, E631; Cab. 2(39), 25th January, 1939, CO 733/398/75156[1].

133. Darwaza, ibid.; Abdul Wahab Kayyali, Palestine, A Modern History (London, 1978), p. 219; Fish (Cairo) to Washington DC, 9th February, 1939, RG 59, 867N.01/1446; minutes of these talks are in S25/7644, CZA.

134. Lampson to London, 18th January, 1939, FO 371/23220/E510.

135. Same to same, 20th January, 1939, FO 371/23221/E754.

136. Same to same, 24th January, 1939, FO 371/23304/J358; same to same, 3rd February, 1939, FO 371/23361/J564; Kedourie, Chatham, p. 240.

137. Lampson to London, 14th February, 1939, FO 371/23224/E1371.

138. Nash'at to FO, 25th January, 1939, FO 371/23221/E664.

139. Lampson to London, 6th February, 1939, FO 371/23222/E925; Khayriyya Qasimiyya, 'Awni, p. 111.

140. Hindle James's note, 7th February, 1939, in Lampson to London, 9th February, 1939, CO 733/406/75872/11.

141. Meeting of 9th February, 1939, FO 371/23223/E1059.

142. London to Lampson, 25th February, 1939, FO 371/23224/E1372.

143. Bentinck's note, 31st January, 1939, FO 371/23304/J417.

144. Bentinck's note, 9th March, 1939, FO 371/23304/J1039.

145. Cab.7(39), 15th February, 1939, CO 733/406/75872/11.

146. Cab.8(39), 22nd February, 1939, CO 733/406/75872/11.

147. Minutes of Seventh meeting, 16th February, 1939, FO 371/23224/E1248.

148. Minutes of Eighth meeting, 18th February, 1939, FO 371/23224/E1271.

149. Minutes of Ninth meeting, 20th February, 1939, FO 371/23224/E1342.

150. Minutes of Tenth meeting, 22nd February, 1939, FO 371/23225/E1431.

151. Minutes of informal meeting, 23rd February, 1939, FO 371/23225/E1448; copies: S25/7662 and Sharet, IV, pp. 78-83.

152. Eleventh meeting, 27th February, 1939, FO 371/23226/E1551.

153. London to Cairo, 3rd March, 1939, FO 371/23227/E1684.

154. Minutes of the Four meetings, 2, 4, 6, 7th March, 1939, in
     FO 371/23227. Copies in S25/7638, <u>CZA</u>.

155. Sharet, IV, p. 78.

156. Chaim Weizmann, <u>Trial and Error</u> (London, 1949), p. 502.

157. Third informal meeting, 7th March, 1939, FO 371/23228/E1875.

158. Minutes of these sessions, 10, 13, 14th March, 1939, in
     FO 371/23229/E1915, E1956; FO 371/23230/E2036; file 00570,
     G. Antonius' Papers, <u>ISA</u>.

159. Cab.10(39), 8th March, 1939, CO 733/406/75872/11.

160. Cab.11(39), 15th March, 1939, Ibid.

161. Informal meeting with Arab delegates, 14th March, 1939, FO 371/23230/E2306.

162: Cab.11(39), 15th March, 1939, CO 733/406/75872/11.

163. Thirteenth and Fourteenth meetings, 15th, 17th March, S25/7637, <u>CZA</u>

164. Cab.14(39), 22nd March, 1939, CO 733/406/75872/11.

165. Fourteenth session, 17th March, 1939, S25/7637, <u>CZA</u>.

166. Cab.14(39), 22nd March, 1939, CO 733/406/75872/11.

167. <u>Al-Ahram</u>, 4th March, 1939; <u>Filastin</u>, 7th March, 1939; <u>al-Fath</u>,
     18 Muharam 1358 (9th March, 1939).

168. Lampson to London, 18th March, 1939, FO 371/23230/E2051.

169. Note on Egyptian personalities, 24th July, 1939, FO 371/23362/J2876;
     'Abd al-'Azim Muhammad Ramadan, <u>Tatawwur al-haraka al wataniyya fi
     Misr 1937-1945</u> (Beirut, 1970), Vol. I, pp. 262-265; Haykal,
     <u>Mudhakkirat</u>, II, pp. 134-136.

170. Lampson to London, 20th March, 1939, FO 371/23232/E2237.

171. Same to same, 18th March, 1939, FO 371/23230/E2051.

172. London to Lampson, 21st March, 1939, FO 371/23230/E2051.

173. Memorandum communicated to MacDonald by Egyptian Ambassador,
     23rd March, 1939, FO 371/23232/E2289.

174. For the minutes of the meetings on 23rd, 24th March, 1939, see:
     FO 371/23232/E2414, E2306.

175. MacDonald's minute, 23rd March, 1939, CO 733/406/75872/11/26a.

176. Butler's Note on a conversation with the Egyptian Ambassador,
     31st March, 1939, FO 371/23233/E2541.

177. Memorandum for the Egyptian Ambassador, FO 371/23233/E2621.

178. Lampson to London, 11-13th April, 1939, FO 371/23233/E2691, E2702, E2724; same to same, 21st April, 1939, FO 371/23234/E2956.

179. Same to same, 18th March, 1939, FO 371/23304/J1105; same to same, 1st April, 1939, FO 371/23232/E2444.

180. Same to same, 24th April. 1939, FO 371/23234/E3029.

181. For example, the directive of 27th March, 1939, FO 371/23232/E2289, or the earlier one of 21st March, 1939, FO 371/23231/E2051.

182. London to Lampson, 26th April, 1939, FO 371/23234/E3029.

183. Lampson to Oliphant (London), 28th April, 1939, FO 371/23234/E3241. Lampson blamed the CO for this mistaken dicision.

184. Same to London, 26th, 28th April, 1939, FO 371/23234/E3084, E3158.

185. Proces-Verbal of the meeting on 29th April, 1939, FO 371/23236/E3945.

186. Lampson to London, 29th April, 1939, FO 371/23234/E3159.

187. Same to same, 30th April, 1939, FO 371/23234/E3161.

188. Same to same, 30th April, 1939, FO 371/23234/E3160.

189. Ibid.; Lampson thought that Britain should accept all the Arab demands for a timetable for Palestinian independence. See: Lampson to London, 18th April, 1939, FO 371/23233/E2899.

190. Baxter's note, 4th May, 1939, 371/23234/E3161.

191. London to Lampson, 4th May, 1939, FO 371/23234/E3161.

192. Same to same, 15th, 17th May, 1939, FO 371/23235.E3560, E3618.

193. Same to London, 21st July, 1939, FO 371/23238/E5276; Havard, Consul-General (Beirut) to London, 25th May, 1939, CO 733/75872/30 Part I; On the other hand Tawfiq al-Suwaydi, pp. 327-329 complains that Muhammad Mahmud, because of his hatred to Mahir, vehemently supported Palestinian Arab opposition to the White Paper policy in spite of Iraqi attempts to support the Paper.

194. Ibid.; Havard to London, 19th May, 1939, CO 733/75872/30, pt.I.

195. Lampson to London, 18th May, 1939, FO 371/23235/E3673; al-Muqattam, 19th May, 1939.

196. See, for example, the Ikhwan's protests in Filastin, 28th, 31st May, 2nd June, 1939; Lampson to London, 22nd May, 1939, FO 371/23236/E3743, E3746.

197. A.W. Robertson, Consul-General (Cairo) to Smart, 30th July; Sterndale-Bennet, Embassy (Cairo) to London, 26th July; Lampson to London, 5th July, 1939, CO 733/408/75872/28.

198. Consul-General (Damascus) to London, 3rd June, 1939, FO 371/23237/E4272.

199. Same to same, 12th July, 1939, FO 371/23238/E5174; Fish to Washington Dc, 18th July, 1939, RG 58, 867N.01/1646.

200. Lampson to London, 15th June, 1939, FO 371/23237/E4357; same to same, 15th June, 1939, FO 371/23238/E4644.

201. Same to London, 4th July, 1939, FO 371/23238/E5102.

202. Newton (Baghdad) to London, 28th June, 1939, CO 733/408/75872/20.

203. Lampson to London, 16th January, 1939, FO 371/23304/J377.

204. Daghir, Mudhakkirati, p. 235.

205. Weizmann, p. 502.

206. Eliahu Epstein Eilat to Dr. B. Joseph (Jerusalem), 13th April, 1939, S25/7516, CZA.

207. Weizmann, p. 503. Fish was far less optimistic. In his report to Washington Dc, 20th April, 1939, RG 59,867N.01/1562, he anticipated their failure following Weizmann's refusal to agree to halt Jewish immigration during a projected six months truce in Palestine.

208. All citations are in Eliav (Cairo) to Shertok, 6th January, 1939. S25/7644, CZA.

PART TWO

CHAPTER ONE - pp.138 - 163

1. Bateman (Alexandria) to London, 31st August, 1939, FO 371/23239/E6186.

2. Butler's report (London) on a conversation with Nash'at, 6th Sept., 1939, FO 371/23239/E6365.

3. Filastin, 30th August, 1939.

4. Lampson (Alexandria) to London, 10th September, 1939, FO 371/23240/E6529.

5. A. Cadogan's note (London, 10th October, 1939, on a conversation with the Egyptian Ambassador, FO 371/23240/E6885; Lampson (Cairo) to London, 20th November, 1939, FO 371/23242/E7726; same to same, 14th April, 1940, FO 371/24566/E1684; same to same, 24th April, 1940, FO 371/24566/E1829; Nash'at to Butler (London), 2nd March, 1940, FO 371/24565/E1010; same to same, 2nd May, 1940, FO 371/24566/E1952.

6. 'Ali Mahir (Alexandria) to Lampson (Alexandria), 24th September, 1939, FO 371/23240/E6719; Lampson (Cairo) to London, 1st November, 1939, FO 371/23241/E7318.

7. Muhammad 'Ali al-Tahir, Zalam al-Sijn, Mudhakkirat wa Mufakkirat (Cairo, 1951), p. 66.

8. Op.cit., pp. 15, 18, 51-52.

9. 'Alluba was Minister for Parliamentary Affairs; Salih Harb, the Minister of National Defence. He became President of the YMMA after 'Abd al-Hamid Sa'id's death in July 1940.

10. Al-Difa', 22nd October, 29th December, 1939, for pro-Arab statements by Egyptian Consuls in Palestine and Iraq.

11. Mahir told the Chamber that Egyptian representations succeeded in mitigating court penalties of Palestinian Arabs. He further promised Egyptian help for Syria. See: Lampson to London, 25th April, 1940, FO 371/24625/J1322; Note to Weizmann (London), 3rd May, 1940, Z4/14651, CZA.

12. Lampson (Cairo) to London, 21st March, 1940, FO 371/24623/J929, same to same, 4th April, 1940, FO 371/24623/J1054; same to same, 9th, 15th May, 11th June, 1940, FO 371/24625/J1424, J1466.

13. Lampson (Alexandria) to Halifax (London), 16th October, 1939, FO 371/23240/E7141.

14. 'Ali Mahir (Alexandria) to H. MacMichael (Jerusalem), 24th Sept., 1939, FO 371/23372/J4028.

15. Lampson (Cairo) to MacMichael (Jerusalem), 1st November, 1939, FO 371/23241/E7412; Mahir (Cairo) to MacMichael (Jerusalem), 2nd December, 1939, FO 371/23372/J5001.

16. Al-Balagh, 19th December, 1939, Filastin, 27th December, 1939.

17. See, for example, Filastin, 18th March, 1940; al-Sirat al-Mustaqim, 13th, 17th April, 1940.

18. Stonehewer-Bird (Jedda) to London, 8th April, 1940, FO 371/24566/E1527.

19. Al-Difa', 2-5th May, 1940; al-Sirat al-Mustaqim, 3, 10th May, 1940.

20. Al-Ahram, Filastin, 2nd November, 1939.

21. Lampson (Cairo) to London, 8th November, 1939, FO 371/23141/E7399.

22. Al-Misri, 3rd November, 1939; al-Ahram, 3-4th, 10-18th, 22nd November, 6th December, 1939, al-Muqattam, 6th, 14th, 17th Nov. 1939.

23. Eliyahu Epstein (Eilat) to M. Shertok, 17th July, 1939; same to Dr. B. Joseph (Jerusalem), 8th November, 1939, S25/7516, CZA; same to A. Kaplan, "Sikumei Peulot" (Summaries of activities), No. 2 (14th-21st November, 1939), 5 (10-17th December, 1939), 9 (13-31st Jan. 1940), 10 (1st April - 1st May, 1940), 11 (1st May - 1st June, 1940), S25/436, CZA.

24. E. Epstein to M. Shertok (Jerusalem), 17th July, 1939, S25/7516, CZA.

25. Same to A. Bahjat (Jedda), 18th October, 1939, Z4/14651, CZA; Bahjat (Jedda) to Epstein (Jerusalem), 20th September, 1939, Z4/14651, CZA.

26. A Note on the meeting which was held on 28th September, 1939, is to be found in Z4/14651, CZA.

27. Bateman (Alexandria) to London, 31st August, 1939, FO 371/23239/E6186.

28. Lampson (Alexandria) to London, 10th Sept., 1939, FO 371/23240/E6529.

29. Lampson (Cairo) to London, 1st November, 1939, FO 371/23241/E7318.

30. 'Ali Mahir to Lampson (Alexandria), 24th September, 1939, FO 371/23240/E6719.

31. Newton (Baghdad) to London, 28th October, 1939, FO 371/23240/E7234.

32. Lampson (Cairo) to London, 1st November, 1939, FO 371/23241/E7318; R. Bullard (Jedda) to London, 21st November, 1939, FO 371/23241/E7622.

33. See, for example, Lampson's account, 20th November, 1939, on a conversation with both leaders, FO 371/23242/E7726.

34. Bullard (Jedda) to London, 30th November, 1939, FO 371/23242/E7768.

35. Fish, American Minister (Cairo) to the Secretary of State (Washington DC), November 21st, 1939, FRUS, 1939, Vol. VI, pp. 809-810; Same to same, December 4th, 1939, RG 59, 867N.01/1679.

36. Newton (Baghdad) to London, 8th December, 1939, FO 371/23242/E7886; Bullard (Jedda) to London, 11th December, 1939, FO 371/23242/E7932.

37. Note on 'Egypt's Youth' by Middle East Intelligence Service, 26th March, 1940, FO 371/24625/J1424.

38. Ahmad Husayn to Lampson, 15th April, 1940, FO 371/24625/J1424. In this letter Husayn, however, continued to preach for the Union of Palestine with Syria as a solution of the conflict.

39. Lampson (Cairo) to London, 14th April, 1940, FO 371/24566/E1684; same to same, 18th April, 1940, FO 371/24566/E1742.

40. Newton (Baghdad) to London, 29th April, 1940, FO 371/24566/E1901.

41. Lampson (Cairo) to London, 24th April, 1940, FO 371/24566/E1829; Nash'at to Butler (London) 2nd May, 1940, FO 371/24566/E1952.

42. See, for example, Egyptian Dept.'s minute, 4th May, 1940, FO 371/24566/ E1952; Baggallay's Minute, 17th July, 1940, FO 371/24549/E2283.

43. For a detailed account of these beliefs, see: M. Cohen, pp. 88-94.

44. For these accusations, consult: Weizmann to Ormsby-Gore (CO), 25th February, 1938, S25/5151, CZA; Same to Halifax (FO), 14th March, 1938, FO 371/21875/E1670; N.A. Rose (ed.), Baffy, the Diaries of Blanch Dudgale, 1936-1947 (London, 1973), p. 78.

45. Lampson (Cairo) to London, 13th July, 1940, FO 371/24549/E2283,

46. Lampson to London, 22nd December, 1939, FO 371/24565/E36; same to same, 20th January, 1940, FO 371/24565/E455; same to same, 30th August, 1940, FO 371/24565/E2789.

47. Lampson to London, 12th January, 1940, FO 371/24565/E80.

48. Lampson (Cairo) to London, 20th November, 1939, FO 371/23242/E7726; same to same, 25th November, 1939, FO 371/23307/J4740.

49. Lampson to London, 19th August, 1940, FO 371/24549/E2474.

50. Lampson to London, 13th July, 1940, FO 371/24549/E2283.

51. Lampson to London, 2nd February, 1940, FO 371/24563/E578; same to same, 17th February, 1940, CO 733/426, 75872/28; same to same, 13th July, 19th, 23rd August, 1940, CO 733/426, 75872/85.

52. Baggallay's Note, 17th July, 1940, FO 371/24549/E2283.

53. Baggallay's Note, 30th April, 1940, FO 371/24625/J1335; in the same spirit he wrote three months later that "so long as we have to maintain our position in Egypt, Iraq, Palestine and to support the Jewish National Home, then we are against Arab aspirations" (Baggallay's Note, 17th July, 1940, FO 371/24549/E2283).

54. M. Cohen, Palestine: Retreat from the mandate (London, 1978) pp. 93-94.

55. Baggallay's Note, 30th April, 1940, FO 371/24625/J1335.

56. Butler's Note, 11th May, 1940, FO 371/24566/E1952.

57. Butler to Nash'at, 14th June, 1940, FO 371/24566/E2096.

58. Lampson to London, 29th January, 1940, FO 371/24623/J454.

59. For the quick deterioration of Mahir - Lampson relations, see: FO 371/24625.

60. B. Newton (Baghdad) to London, 25th July, 1940, CO 733/426, 75872/85.

61. Newton (Baghdad) to London, 1st August, 1940, FO 371/24548/E2027; Stonehewer-Bird (Jedda) to London, 16th August, 1940, FO 371/24548/E2432.

62. Newton (Baghdad) to London, 31st August, 1940, FO 371/24548/E2572.

63. Lampson (Cairo) to London, 25th August, 1940, FO 371/24548/E2511.

64. For the falling trade, consult: Egypt, Ministry of Finance, Statistical Department, Annual Statement of the Foreign Trade, 1939-1946, part I, Summary tables, especially tables VI-VIII; Charles Issawi, Egypt at Mid-Century (London, 1954), p. 201.

65. Lampson (Cairo) to London, 29th April, 1941, FO 371/27431/J1509.

66. Same to same, 7th June, 1941, FO 371/27431/J1806.

67. Jankowski, pp. 82-85; Anwar al-Sadat, Safhat majhula (Cairo, 1954), pp. 86-87; Lampson to London on Political Developments in 1941, 12th February, 1942, FO 371/31569/J1111.

68. For the communications between the two ldeaders, see: Lampson (Cairo) to London, 17th January, 1941, FO 371/27061/E223; also, Hirszowicz, p. 105.

69. Lampson (Cairo) to London, 14th May, 1941, FO 371/27070/E2333; Lampson (Cairo) to London, Weekly Appreciation, 7th April. 1941, FO 371/27429/J899.

70. Sir Kinahan Cornwallis (Baghdad) to London, 3rd April, 1941, FO 371/27062/E1254; Lampson (Cairo) to London, 8th April. 1941, FO 371/27063/E1375; Cornwallis (Baghdad) to London, 9th April, 1941, FO 371/27064/E1448.

71. for this damage, see: S. Perwone, Public Relations Section, (Baghdad), 2nd September, 1941, on a conversation with Egyptian Charge d'affaires (Baghdad), FO 371/27101/E6205.

72. Lampson (Cairo) to London, 21st April, 1941, FO 371/27066/E1643.

73. Lampson (Cairo) to London, 7th June, 1941, FO 371/27431/J1773; same to same, 17th, 24th June, 1941, FO 371/27431/J2157, J2418; same to same, Report on Political Developments in Egypt in the year 1941, 12th February, 1942, FO 371/31569/J1111; Tahir, Zalam al-Sijn, pp. 3, 150, 155-162, 173, 186-187, 210-213; Jankowski, pp. 84-85.

74. Lampson (Cairo) to London, 10th June, 1941, FO 371/27431/J1802; same to same, Weekly Appreciation, 15th June, 1941, FO 371/27431/J1886.

75. Lampson (Cairo) to London, 3rd June, 1941, FO 371/27043/E2797; same to same, 3rd June, 1941, FO 371/27431/J1972.

76. A. Kirk (Cairo) to the Secretary of State (Washington DC), 28th June, 1941, F.R.U.S., 1941, Vol. III, pp. 612-614.

77. See, for example, the Secretary of State (Washington DC) to Winant, Ambassador in the United Kingdom (London), 5th August, 1941, F.R.U.S., 1941, Vol. III, pp. 616-617.

78. Kirk (Cairo) to the Secretary of State (Washington DC), 8th August, 1941, F.R.U.S., 1941, Vol. III, pp. 619-620.

79. Egypt, Ministry of Finance, Statistical Department, Monthly Summary of the Foreign Trade, December 1940 - December 1941 (Cairo, 1941-42), Table IV.

80. Al-Difa', 23rd July, 1940, 9th September, 1940, 16-17th March, 1941, 24th, 28th April, 1941, 25th June, 1941, 20th January, 1942, 2nd March, 1942; Filastin, 28th August, 1940, 1-2nd October, 1940, 13th March, 1941, 15th, 29th May, 1941; al-Sirat al-Mustaqim, 6th September, 1940, 6th July, 1941, 1st May, 1942.

81. Dr. M. Simon to M. Shertok (Jerusalem), 26th August, 1941, Z4/14651, CZA, on a visit of Egyptian Deputy Ministers to Palestine; N. Vilenski's report, 15th September, 1941, S25/460, CZA; E. Eilat, "Sikumei Peulot" (Summaries of activities) No. 10 (1st April - 1st May, 1940), S25/436, CZA; N. Vilenski to Dr. B. Joseph, 22nd December, 1943, S25/7516, CZA.

82. Vilenski to Shertok (Jerusalem), 15th September, 1941, S25/460, CZA.

83. For the increase in Egyptian trade with these countries, consult: Monthly Summary of the Foreign Trade, December 1942 (Ministry of Finance, Statistical Department, Cairo, 1943), Table IV.

84. "Review of Economic Conditions in the Middle East", Supplement to World Economic Report, 1949 - 1950 (U.N. Department of Economic Affairs, N.Y., March, 1951), E/1910/Add.2, Table 41, pp. 120-121.

85. A short biography on Ahmad Amin is to be found in Nadav Saffan, Egypt, in search of Political Community (Cambridge, Mass., 1961), pp. 138-139; Ahmad Amin wrote an autobiography, Hayati (Cairo, 1950) in which he mentioned with affection his trips to Arab countries (pp. 248-260), and also his service as editor of al-Thaqafa (pp. 294-295).

86. Ahmad Amin, "al-Hilf al-'Arabi", al-Thaqafa (Cairo), 5th August, 1941, pp. 1001-1003.

87. Al-Thaqafa, 16th August, 1941, pp. 1037-1040; 19th August, 1941, p. 1092; 2nd September, 1941, pp. 1135-1137; 16th September, 1941, pp. 1219-1220.

88. Fu'ad Abaza, "al-Wahda al-'Arabiyya", al-Muqattam, 16th September, 1941.

89. Lampson to London, 10th June, 1941, FO 371/27075/E3008.

90. S. Perowne, Public Relations Section (Baghdad), 2nd September, 1941, on a conversation with 'Abd al-Mun'im, FO 371/27101/6205.

91. Outline of Noteworthy Portions of Report by an Egyptian Diplomat [Mustafa 'Abd al-Mun'im] on Egypt's future Foreign Policy, sent by the Embassy (Baghdad) to Eastern Department (London), 28th December, 1941, FO 371/31568/J492.

92. Lampson to London, 2nd October, 1941, FO 371/27045/E6864.

93. By March 1945, 'Abd al-Mun'im still was only a Consul in Jerusalem, after serving some time as Charge de la Section de la Societe des Nations et des Traites in Cairo. He took part in the Egypto-Iraqi talks in August 1943 and the Pact talks in March 1945 (al-Ahram, 18th March, 1945).

94. See, for example, his articles on Egypt and the Eastern countries in al-Muqattam, 30th September, 29th October, 11th November, 1941.

95. Al-Muqattam, 1st November, 1941; Lampson to London, 1st December, 1941, FO 371/27045/E8275; same to MacMichael, 18th December, 1941, FO 371/31337/E255.

96. Al-Muqattam, 6-9th October, 1941; Lampson to London, 19th December, 1941, FO 371/27434/J4013.

97. Lampson to London, Review of Political Developments in Egypt in 1941, 12th February, 1942, FO 371/31569/J1111.

98. Lampson to London, 14th November, 1941, FO 371/27434/J3601.

99. Same to London, 23rd November, 1941, FO 371/27434/J3692; same to same, 8th January, 1942, FO 371/31576/J322.

CHAPTER TWO - pp. 164 - 215

1. For the various versions of the crisis, consult: Tab'i, pp. 201-231; Evans, pp. 197-216; Haykal, Mudhakkirat, II, pp. 191-209; Ramadan, pp. 192-218.

2. For an account of these activities, see: Lampson to London, 28th September, 1942, FO 371/31574/J4332; same to same, Annual Report for 1942, 22nd December, 1943, FO 371/41326/J79.

3. Al-Muqattam, 16th February, 1942.

4. Text of the Speech, in al-Muqattam, 30th March, 1942; FO 371/31571/J1946.

5. Al-Muqattam, 15th November, 1941. Karim Thabit's enthusiastic reception of the speech, in al-Muqattam, 16th November, 1941.

6. Tahir, Zalam al-Sijn, pp. 495-515.

7. Lampson to MacMichael (Jerusalem), 19th April, 1942, FO 371/31570/J2107.

8. Lampson to London, 10th March, 1942, FO 371/31469/E1619.

9. Same to same, 10th May, 1942, FO 371/31337/E2986.

10. Spears (Beirut) to London, 4th June, 1942, FO 371/31473/E3465.

11. For various accounts of these talks; see: Lampson to London, 21st June, 1942, FO 371/31473/E3998; Spears to Minister of State (Cairo), 24, 26th June, FO 371/31473/E3812, E3863.

12. Clayton (G.H.Q., Cairo) to Smart, 22nd April, 1942, FO 141/840/356/2/42G.

13. Smart's Memorandum on Egypt and the Arab world, 10th June, 1942, FO 141/840/356/13/42G.

14. Gomaa, p. 154.

15. Smart,s Note, 10th June, 1942, FO 141/840/356/11/42G.

16. Ibid.; Lampson to London, 10th May, 1942, FO 371/31337/E2986.

17. Samrt's Memorandum, 10th June, 1942, FO 141/840/356/13/42G.

18. For Ahmad Ramzi's affection for the Arabs, consult his, Min Wahi Filastin (Cairo, 1949).

19. Spears to London, 4th June, 1942, FO 371/31473/E3465.

20. Note of an interview by the Chief Secretary (Jerusalem) with the Egyptian Consul-General (Jerusalem), 20th June, 1942, FO 371/31338/E4624.

21. Lampson to London, 16th December, 1942, FO 371/35528/J125.

22. Text of the speech in al-Ahram, 14th November, 1942.

23. Al-Ahram, 20th November, 1942.

24. Al-Muqattam, 23-24th, 26th, 28th, 30th December, 1942.

25. Nuri to Casey (Cairo), 14th January, 1943, FO 371/34955/E196; for further pursuit of this matter, consult: Lord Birdwood, Nuri as-Said (London, 1959), pp. 202-209.

26. Lampson to London, 6th January, 1943, FO 371/34990/E446.

27. Wikeley (Jedda) to London, 14th February, 1943, FO 371/34955/E1234.

28. Lampson's minute, 30th January, 1943, FO 141/865/140/1/43.

29. Lampson to London, 21st January, 1943, FO 371/35528/J398; same to same, 5th February, 1943, FO 371/35031/E937.

30. Summary of Telegrams relating to activity in Iraq, Egypt, and Saudi Arabia in the cause of the Arabs, FO 921/113/90(2)43/25.

31. Lampson to London, 3rd February, 1943, FO 371/35175/E966; Nahhas to Lampson, 6th February, 1943, FO 371/35175/E1160.

32. Filastin, 29th January, 1943, Lampson to London, 8th June, 1943, FO 371/35534/J2530.

33. Lampson to London, 22nd January, 1943, PER 15-22nd January, 1943, FO 371/35529/J784; same to same, 1st Fabruary, 1943, PER 22-28th, January, 1943, FO 371/35529/J810; al-Ahram, 18th, 19th, 24-26th, January, 1943; EG, 17th January, 1943, Filastin, al-Difa', 27th January - 1st Fabruary, 1943.

34. Text of Nahhas's reply in the Senate, in al-Balagh, 10th August, 1944.

35. Egyptian Aide Memoire, 30th January, 1942, F.R.U.S., 1943, vol. IV, pp. 751-754.

36. Cordell Hull's memorandum, 3rd February, 1943, F.R.U.S., 1943 Vol. IV, pp. 754-755.

37. Kirk to Washington D.C., 5th February, 1943, F.R.U.S., 1943, Vol. IV, pp. 755-756; Philip Baram, The Department of State in the Middle East, 1919-1945 (Philadelphia, 1978), pp. 73-96.

38. Al-Balagh, 10th August, 1944.

39. Content of the Memorandum in F.R.U.S., 1943, Vol. IV, p. 766.

40. Alling's memorandum, 30th March; Summer-Well's memorandum, 30th March, 1943, F.R.U.S., 1943, Vol. IV, pp. 765-767.

41. Text of the Resolutions, in ESCO Foundation for Palestine, Palestine, a study of Jewish Arab and British Policies (Yale University, 1947), Vol. II, pp. 1014-1016, 1080-1088.

42. See, for example, Alling's and Summer-Well's memorandums in F.R.U.S., 1943, Vol. IV, pp. 765-767.

43. Summer-Well's memorandum, 30th March, 1943, F.R.U.S., 1943, Vol. IV, p. 767.

44. H.C.Deb., 5^S, Vol. 387, Col. 139.

45. Abaza's manifesto, 31st March, 1943, FO 921/114/90(2)43/135; al-Ittihad al-'Arabi wa qanunuhu al-'amm, Nadi al-Qahira wa laihatuhu al-dakhiliya (Cairo, n.d.); Jalal al'Urfali, al-Diplomasiya al-'Iraqiyya wa al-Ittihad al-'Arabi (Baghdad, n.d.[1944] pp. 298-301, 306-311.)

46. Lampson to London, 10th February, 1943, FO 371/35175/E1161; Shone to London, 20th February, 1943, FO 371/35052/E1510; same to same, 10th March 1943, FO 371/34956/E1749.

47. Shone to London, 19th March, 1943, PER 11-17th March 1943, FO 371/35530/J1445; same to Cornwallis (Baghdad), 20th March, 1943, FO 816/42, p. 68a.

48. Muhammad 'Ali 'Alluba, Mabadi fi al-Siyasa al-Misriyya (Cairo, 1942).

49. See, for example, 'Alluba's article in al-Musawwar, 6th, 27th November, 18th December, 1942.

50. Wikeley (Jedda) to London, 14th February, 1943, FO 371/34955/E1234.

51. Al-Ahram, 28th February, 1943.

52. Al-Ahram, 1st March, 1943.

53. Vilenski to B. Joseph, 8th April, 1943, on a conversation with Tawfiq Hanna, Assistant Consul General after his arrival from Egypt, S25/7516, CZA; Political Section, Cairo City Police, on the Opposition's view regarding Arab Unity, 19th August, 1943, FO 141/866/149/104/43; Sasson's report of Mahmud 'Azmi's conversation with Sharet and Ben-Gurion, on 22nd August, 12th September, 1943, Sasson's Papers; Monthly Intelligence Summary, Nos. 6-7 for March-April 1943 appreciating the Wafd's and Nuqrashi's reactions to Arab Unity, WO 169/9012.

54. Overseas Planning Committee, Ministry of Information, Appreciation of Propaganda to Egypt, p. 10, June 1942, FO 371/31579/J3599.

55. A. Hourani, Report on Great Britain and Arab Nationalism (June, 1943), FO 371/34958/E2459. First draft of the report was written in Cairo, March 1943.

56. Killearn to London, 13th March, 1943, PER 4-10th March, 1943 FO 371/35530/J1366.

57. For details, consult: Gomaa, pp. 155-157.

58. Nuri to Nahhas, 17th March, 1943, FO 921/114/90(2)43/74.

59. Urfali, pp. 291-306; Cornwallis (Baghdad) to London, 13th March, FO 371/34955/E1494.

60. Urfali, pp. 302-306, 311-313; Cornwallis (Baghdad) to London, 31st March, 1943, FO 371/34956/E1920.

61. For Rashid al-Hajj Ibrahim and the Commercial Committee, see: The Shay Archives (Sherut Yedi'ot), Set B; Y.Sim'oni, 'Arviyei Eretz Israel (Tel-Aviv, 1947), pp. 239, 313, 318.

62. Cornwallis to London, 8th March, 1943, FO 371/34955/E1398.

63. Yoseph Nevo, The Political Development of the Palestinian Arab National Movement, 1936-1945 (Unpublished Ph.D. dissertation, Tel-Aviv University, May 1977) pp. 277-286.

64. Urfali, pp. 314-315. In May 1945 Abaza told smart that he wanted to open a branch of his Society in Palestine. Abaza to Smart, 9th May, 1945, FO 371/45238/E3472.

65. Killearn[Lampson]to London, 13th March, 1943, FO 371/35530/J1203;

same to same, 31st March, 1943, FO 371/34956/E1919; Habib Jamati's report, 9th April, 1943, FO 141/866/149/46/43G.

66. Jamati's report, 9th April, 1943, FO 141/866/149/46/43G; Killearn to London, 16th June, 1943, Review of Political situation in Egypt in the last four and a half months, FO 371/35536/J2855.

67. Killearn to London, PER 11-17th March, 1943, FO 371/35530/J1445.

68. same to same, 10th April, PER 1-7th April, 1943, FO 371/35532/J1755; Smart's minute on "Arab Unity Society", 9th June, 1943, FO 141/866/149/59/43; Killearn to London, 2nd July, PER 24-30th June, 1943, FO 371/35536/J3040.

69. Killearn to London, 31st March, 1943, FO 371/34956/E1917. Monthly Intelligence Summary, No. 6 for March, 1943, WO 169/9102.

70. Same to London, 16th June, 1943, FO 371/35536/J2855.

71. For the Press coverage of this issue: Killearn to London, 4th March, PER 25-3 March, 1943, FO 371/35530/J1322; Publicity Section to Middle East Section, Ministry of State (Cairo), 4th March, 1943, FO 921/113/90(2)/43/33.

72. Killearn to London, 1st April, 1943, FO 371/34956/E1910; same to same, 2nd April, PER 23-31st March, 1943, FO 371/35531/J1615.

73. See, for example, the Parliamentary debate on 29th November, 1943, Annales de la Chambre des Deputés, November, 1943, No. 1, pp. 10-13.

74. For general accounts of this debate, consult: 'Asim Ahmad al-Dasuqi, Misr fi al-harb al-'alamiya al-thanjyya, 1939-1945 (Cairo, 1976), pp. 271-336; Bayumi, pp. 54-65, 148-155; Ramadan, Vol. II, pp. 356-376. Among the participants in this debate were Husayn Haykal, 'Alluba, 'Azzam, 'Abbas Mahmud al-'Aqad, Mahmud 'Azmi, Karim Thabit, Fu'ad and Fikri Abaza and Mustafa Amin.

75. Al-Ahram, al-Balagh, 31st March, 1943.

76. Ibid. Also Abd al-Sattar al-Basil participated in this debate.

77. For a detailed discussion of the Book, Labib Rizq, pp. 69-138; Mostafa Muhamed Moustafa el-Feki, Makram Ebeid, A Coptic Leader in the Egyptian National Movement (Unpublished Ph.D. dissertation, S.O.A.S., July 1977), pp. 149-195.

78. Killearn to London, 16th June, 1943, FO 371/35536/J2855; Evans, pp. 248-250.

79. Killearn to London, 25th February, 1944, General Political Review - 1943, FO 371/41327/J828; FO to Rowan, 9th May, 1943, PREM 4, 19/2, pp. 330-332.

80. Killearn to London, 22nd April, 1943, PER 15-21 April, 1943, FO 371/35533/J1951; Al-Musawwar, 23rd April, 1943, interview with Wafdist President of the Chamber of Deputies, 'Abd al-Salam Fahmi Jum'a.

81. Killearn to London, 16th June, 1943, FO 371/35536/J2855; Sasson, pp. 285-286.

81. Text of the manifesto which was published on 8th April, 1943, in al-'Athar al-Kamila lil-Malik 'Abdullah ibn al-Husayn, (Beirut n.d.) Vol. II, al-Mudhakkirat, pp. 212-214.

83. Wikeley (Jedda) to London, 27th May, 1943, FO 371/34958/E3117; same to same, 10th June, 1943, FO 371/34959/E3388.

84. For the Iraqi moves, consult, Gomaa, pp. 162-165.

85. Y. Haykal, Wahda, pp. 26-36.

86. For the growth of the Ikhwan, see: H.A.R.Gibb, "The political forces in Egypt", 25th February, 1943, FO 371/35530/J1407; Dr. J. Heyworth-Dunne's Report, 18th November, 1943, FO 371/35539/J4741.

87. Heyworth-Dunne's report, op.cit.; According to the author's published version, Religious and Political trends in Modern Egypt, pp. 30, 89-91, by 1947 he already counted 135 Societies.

88. Killearn to London, 12th March, 1942, FO 371/31569/J1190; same to same, 28th March, 1942, FO 371/31570/J1477; same to same, 28th September, 1942, FO 371/31574/J4332; same to same, 28th May, 1943, 371/35534/J2519; same to same, 3rd March, 1944, PER 24th February - 1st March, 1944, FO 371/41326/J79.

89. This issue is being dealt with in my, "The Military Force of Islam: the Society of the Muslim Brethren and the Palestine question, 1945-1948", in Kedourie, Haim (eds.), Zionism and Arabism in Palestine and Israel (London, 1982), pp. 109-117.

90. For the debate between the Embassy and Political Intelligence about the importance of the Ikhwan see, WO 208/1578. This debate was summed up by Major General Davidson of the War Office on 2nd November 1943, He concluded that both sides agreed about the growing importance of this Society, FO 371/35539/J4441 (Copy : WO208/1578).

91. Kellar, M.I.5 (London) to P.M. Loxley, Foreign Office, 19th July, 1943, FO 371/35536/J3177.

92. Jordan (Jedda) to London, 1st April, 1944, FO 371/39987/E2323.

93. Al-Ikhwan al-Muslimun, 12th June, 1943; Sasson, pp. 288-289. Security Summary, M.E., No. 135 (SIME), 3rd June, 1943, WO 208/1561.

94. Heyworth-Dunne's report, FO 371/35539/J4741.

95. Security Sammary, Middle East, No. 103, The Muslim Brethren, reconsidered, 10th December, 1942, FO 371/35578/J245.

96. Killearn to London, 13th August, 1943, PER 5-11th August, 1943, FO 371/35537/J3628.

97. Cited from a letter sent by 'Abd al-Rahman Kadash, Mayt Selsil Branch, Daqhaliya province to American Legation, Cairo, RG 59, 883.43/3.

98. Y. Bohem, "Agudat ha-Ahim ha-Muslemim be-Mitzrayim", ha-Mizrah he-Hadash, 1952, No. 4, p. 349. For similar expressions, see also: Anwar al-Jundi al-Banna, Kifah al-Dhabihayn: Filastin wa al-Maghrib (Cairo, 1946).

99. Sasson, pp. 333-334.

100. Samrt's memorandum on "Egypt on the Arab world", 3rd May, 1943, FO 141/866/149/2/43G.

101. Thompson (Baghdad) to London, 1st August, 1943, Report on Heads of
     Foreign Missions at Baghdad, FO 371/35027/E4953. For the small
     Egyptian interest in Arabs consult also: Dr. Salah al-'Aqad,
     al-'Arab wa al-harb al-'alamiyya al-thaniyya (Cairo, 1966), p. 179;
     al-Shahid Salah Labib, Dhikriyati fi 'Ahdayn (Cairo, 1976), p. 176.

102. Sasson's report, 5th March, 1946, Sasson's Papers; Sharet's minute,
     on Vilenski's report, 5th January, 1944, S25/7516, CZA; B. Joseph's
     minute, 8th February, 1944, S25/7516, CZA

103. Killearn to London, 8th June, 1943, FO 371/35534/J2530; The tour
     was in connection with the efforts to appease Nazli, the Queen
     Mother, to go back to Egypt. See: Labib, p. 53.

104. Samrt's minute, 9th June, 1943, FO 141/866/149/58/43.

105. Al-Musawwar, 18th June, 1943; Filastin, 9-14th June, 1943; Killearn
     to London, 19th June, PER 10-16th June, 1943, FO 371/35535/J2786;
     MacMichael to Killearn, 25th June, 1943, FO 371/35536/J3115.

106. Throughout his stay in Palestine, Nahhas refused to taste any of
     the food offered to him by his Palestinian Arab hosts, and insisted
     on eating food prepared only by his own cook.

107. MacMichael to Killearn, 25th June, 1943, FO 371/35536/J3115;
     Jamati's report, 16th June; Killearn's note, 17th June, FO 141/866/
     149/66,67/43.

108. George Kirk, The Middle East in the War (London, 1952), p. 337

109. Jamati's report, 16th June, 1943, FO 371/35536/J2893.

110. Killearn to London, 2nd July, PER 24-30th June, 1943, FO 371/35536/J3040;
     same to same, 9th July, PER 1-7 July, 1943, FO 371/35536/J3118.

111. Killearn to London, 25th February, 1944, General Political Review -
     1943, FO 371/41327/J828; al-Ithnayn wa al-Dunya, 21st, 28th June,
     12th July, 2nd August, 1943.

112. Samrt's minute, 9th June, 1943, FO 141/866/149/59/43; al-Ithnayn
     wa al-Dunya, 21st June, 1943.

113. Killearn to London, 2nd July, 1943, PER 24-30th June, 1943, FO 371/
     35536/J3040; same to same 9th July, PER 1-7th July, 1943, FO 371/
     35536/J3118.

114. R. Giles, Assistant Inspector General, CID to Chief Secretary
     (Jerusalem), 6th July, 1943, FO 816/43, pp. 50-50a.

115. Information received from Cairo on the Opposition, 13th July,
     1943, FO 816/43, p. 86b.

116. Gomaa, pp. 163-165; Moyne to London, 27th July, 1943, FO 371/
     34960/E4394.

117. Nuri's request to Cornwallis, 30th March, 1943, FO 371/34956/E1894 to permit sending a copy of his Note to Nahhas appears superficial since he probably had sent it to Nahhas even earlier. In any case the Iraqi Government published their version of Arab Unity in May 1943 (See: PIC paper No. 30, on Arab Unity, PICME, 18th November, 1943, p. 21, FO 141/866/149/163/43).

118. Al-Musawwar, 30th July, 1943; Killearn to London, 30th July, PER 22-28th July, 1943, FO 371/35537/J3408.

119. Wikeley (Jedda) to London, 29th July, 1943, FO 371/34960/E4631.

120. Same to same, 27th July, 1943, FO 371/34960/E4543.

121. Same to same, 5th August, 1943, FO 371/34960/E4630.

122. Proces Verbal of the talks in FO 371/34961/E5376. It is noteworthy that on the eve of the Nahhas - Nuri talks on Arab Unity, Amin 'Uthman, Nahhas's confidant, rediculed "the chase of Arab Federation" as "considerable nonsense". See Killearn's minute, 28th July, 1943, FO 141/866/149/81/43/

123. Al-Ahram, 7th August, 1943.

124. Minister of State to London, 7th August, 1943, FO 371/34960/E4719; Clayton's report, 7th August, 1943, FO 141/866/149/90/43/

125. Al-Muqattam, 13th August, 1943; Killearn to London, 19th August, 1943, FO 371/35537/J3761.

126. Killearn to London, 8th August, 1943, FO 371/34960/E4688.

127. Same to same, 13th August, PER 5-11th August, 1943, FO 371/35537/J3628; same to same, 31st August, 1943, FO 371/34961/J3849.

128. Al-Ithnayn wa al-Dunya, 2nd, 16th August, 1943, on Nuri's talks with 'Azzam on the creation of an Eastern League of Nations. At the same time, the magazine (2nd August) also published Lutfi al-Sayyid's opposition to a political unity.

129. Killearn to MacMichael, 23rd August, 1943, FO 816/43. p. 86a.

130. Note of the Political Section of the Cairo City Police, 19th August, 1943, FO 141/866/149/104/43; Killearn to London, 30th August, 1943, FO 371/35537/J3744.

131. Al-Musawwar, 13th August, 1943; al-Ithnayn wa al-Dunya, 16th Aug. 1943,

132. Killearn to London, 30th August, 1943, FO 371/35537/J3744.

133. Same to same, 13th August, 1943, PER 5-11th August, FO 371/35537/J3628.

134. Minister of State to London, 7th August, 1943, FO 371/34960/E4719; Wikeley (Jedda) to London, 9th August, 1943, FO 371/34960/E4690; MacMichael to London, 17th August, 1943, FO 371/34961/E4940.

135. Wikeley (Jedda) to London, 30th August, 1943, FO 371/34961/E5171.

136. Kirkbride (Amman)to MacMichael, 8th September, 1943, FO 816/43, p. 90.
Even Newcombe found Nahhas as late as 4th October, 1943, to know
"very little" of Arab affairs, and was "struck by the simplicity or
crudeness of some of the questions he asked", FO 141/866/149/138/43.
For similar impression, consult also: 'Abdullah, Vol. III al-Takmila
p. 237.

137. Shone (Cairo) to London, 6th October, 1943, FO 371/34962/E6291;
Sasson, pp. 293-294; Al-Ahram, 3rd September, 1943; Killearn to
London, 11th September, 1943, PER 2-8th Spetember, FO 371/35538/
J3955.

138. Kirkbride to MacMichael, 8th September, 1943, FO 816/43, p. 90.

139. Jordan (Jedda) to London, 12th September, 1943, FO 371/34961/E5483.

140. Al-Musawwar, 24th September, 1943; al-Ithnayn wa al-Dunya, 27th
September, 1943.

141. Killearn to London, 11th September, 1943, FO 371/35538/J3903; same
to same, 1st October, 1943, PER 23-29th September, 1943, FO 371/
35538/J4295.

142. Samrt's memorandum on Arab Unity, 12th October, 1943, FO 141/866/
149/140/43; PIC paper, No. 30 on Arab Unity by PICME, 18th Nov.,
1943, FO 141/866/149/163/43/

143. Jordan to London, 12th September, 1943, FO 371/34961/E5483;
al-Ithnayn wa al-Dunya, 13th September, 1943.

144. Shone to London. 5th September, 1943, FO 371/34961/E5352.

145. Same to same, 12th September, 1943, FO 371/34961/E5466; Jordan to
London, 2nd October, 1943, FO 371/34962/E6264; PIC paper on
Arab Unity, 18th November, 1943, FO 141/866/149/163/43/

146. Proces-Verbal of these talks, FO 371/34963/E6706, E8115.

147. Shone to London, 26th October, 1943, FO 371/34963/E6706; al-Musawwar,
29th October, 1943; al-Ithnayn wa al-Dunya, 25th October, 1st
November, 1943.

148. Shone to London, 7th November, 1943, FO 371/35539/J4604; same to
same, 9th November, 1943, FO 371/34963/E7349.

149. Same to same, 9th November, 1943, op.cit.; Hafiz Wahba to Baxter,
8th December, 1943, FO 371/34963/E7797.

150. Shone to London, 7th November, 1943, FO 371/34963/E7350.

151. Al-Ahram, 1st August, 1943, al-Ithnayn wa al-Dunya, 9th August, 1943.

152. Gomaa, pp. 172-173.

153. Killearn to London, 16th March, 1944, FO 371/39987/E1876.

154. Proces Verval of the talks with the Lebanese delegation in
FO 371/39987/E1349.

155. Sasson's memorandum on 'Azmi's conversations with Sharet and
Ben-Gurion on 22nd August, 12th September, 1943, 5th March, 1946,
Sasson's Papers.

156. Nevo, pp. 285-286.

157. 'Abd al-Rahman 'Azzam, "al-Wahda al-'Arabiyya", al-Hilal, 1st October, 1943, pp. 462-466.

158. Al-Ahram, 12th November, 1943; Shone to London, 16th November, 1943, FO 371/35185/E6960; same to same, 16th November, 1943, FO 371/35540/J4819.

159. Al-Ahram, 15th November, 1943; Shone to London, 16th November, 1943, FO 371/35540/J4719; al-Musawwar, 19th November, 1943; Killearn to London, 25th November, 1943, FO 371/35541/J5045.

160. Complete text in FO 371/35541/J5024.

161. Al-Ahram, 12th December, 1943; al-Musawwar, 17th December, 1943; Killearn to London, 24th December, 1943, PER 16-22nd December, 1943, FO 371/41316/H14.

162. Al-Ithnayn wa al-Dunya, 11th October, 1943; Jacobs to Washington DC, 31st December, 1943, FRUS, 1943, Vol. IV. pp. 851-852.

163. Al-Ahram, 6th December, 1943.

164. Nahhas to Killearn, 27th December, 1943, FO 141/866/149/170/43;
Killearn to London, 16th March, 1944, FO 371/39987/E1731;
Nahhas to Killearn, 22nd March, 1944, FO 371/40143/E2163;
Killearn to London, 24th March, 1944, FO 371/40143/E2933.

165. G. Furlonge (Beirut) to Spears, 21st January, 1944, FO 371/39987/E871.

166. Killearn to London, PER 6-12th January; 13-19th January; 10-18th February, 1944, FO 371/41316/J328, J399, J737.

167. See, for example, the Parliamentary debate on 13th March, 1944 in Annales de la Chambre des Deputés No. 5, March, 1944, p. 195; Nahhas to de Gaulle, 16th April, 1944, FO 371/42170/Z2996.

168. Killearn to London, 18th February, 1944, FO 371/40143/E1151.

169. Filsatin, 15th, 22nd February, 1944; al-Difa', 28th February 1944; Killearn to London, PER 17-23rd February, 24th Feb-1st March 1943, FO 371/41316/J827, J906.

170. Test of the Aide Memoire, 24th February, 1944, in FRUS, 1944, Vol. V, pp. 571-573.

171. Moyne to London, 24th March, 1944, FO 371/39987/E1924; Killearn to London, 26th March, 1944, FO 371/39987/E1947.

172. E. Epstein to Shertok, 28th January, 1944; Joseph;s minute 8th February, 1944, S25/7516, CZA; Note regarding Palestine which appeared to Lampson to be composed for Nahhas in the Office of the Presidency of the Council or in the Foreign Ministry, in Killearn to London, 24th March, 1944, FO 371/40135/E2123; Vilenski to Cohen, 27th July, 1944, S25/7516, CZA.

173. FRUS, 1944, Vol. V. pp. 589, 598, 608-9; Moyne to London, 28th
     March, 1944, FO 371/40135/E2041; Killearn to London, PER 13-19th
     April, 1944, FO 371/41317/J1630; Nahhas to Attlee, 10th May, 1944,
     FO 371/40136/E3117; Summary of Press reactions to American pro-
     Zionist declarations, 7th August, 1944, FO 371/40137/E5081;
     Abaza's protest, 1st August, 1944; al-Banna's protest, 5th August,
     1944, FO 141/981/727/22/44.

174. MacMichael to the Secretary of State (Cairo), 31st January, 1944,
     FO 816/44, p. 3; Cornwallis to London, 8th February, 1944,
     FO 371/39987/E915.

175. Cornwallis to London, 22nd March, 1944, FO 371/39987/E1891.

176. Nahhas to Killearn 24th March, 1944, FO 371/40143/E1933. For the
     anger of other Palestinian Arab leaders at Nahhas's attitude
     towards them, consult file 8/5, T/D No. 2086, 18th July, 1944,
     Hagana Archives (Tel-Aviv).

CHAPTER THREE - pp. 216 - 257

1. Memorandum respecting Arab Federation, Eastern Department, 28th September, 1939, 371/23239/E6357 (Copy: Cab.95/1, ME(0)(41) Memorandum 5).

2. London to Basil Newton (Baghdad), 4th August, 1940, FO 371/24548/E2027.

3. George Antonius (Jerusalem) to Harold MacMichael (Jerusalem), 3rd October, 1940, Memorandum on Arab Affairs, FO 371/27043/E53.

4. Parliamentary Debates, House of Commons, Fifth Series, Vol. 365, col. 680, 16th October, 1940.

5. Eastern Departments minute, 14th Oct., 1940, FO 371/24542/E2811.

6. Winston Churchill (London) to Sir Kinahan Cornwallis (Baghdad), 11th March, 1941, FO 371/27061/E694.

7. Lampson (Cairo) to Sir Horace Seymour, Assistant Secretary of State for Foreign Affairs (London), 26th April, 1941, FO 371/27043/E2191.

8. F.O. Minute, 20th May, 1941, FO 371/27043/E2191.

9. Churchill to Eden (London) on Syrian Policy, 19th May, 1941, PREM 4, 32/5, pp. 120-121 (Copy: FO 371/27043/E2685).

10. WP (41) 116; FO 371/27043/E2716/53/65.

11. The Times (London), 30th May, 1941.

12. The Earl of Avon, The Eden Memoirs, Vol. II - The Reckoning, (London, 1965), pp. 247-248.

13. Op.cit., p. 250; This principle was publicly emphasised by Churchill in the House of Commons in a Speech on the War Situation, 9th September, 1941, Parliamentary Debates, 374, H.C. Deb. 5s., col. 75-76. This policy was wholly shared also by Eden's Under-Secretary in charge of Eastern Department, Sir Maurice Peterson. In his memoirs, Both sides of the Curtain (London, 1950), p. 237, Peterson recalls his belief that "there was no place, in Foreign Office policy at least, for the ambitions of those who wished to set Britain in the place of France".

14. Avon, Eden Memoirs, Vol. II, p. 249; Churchill's Speech, ibid.

15. For the scope of British intervention, see, for example: Charles De Gaulle, War Memoirs, Vol. I - The Call to Honour 1940-1942 (translated by Jonathan Griffin), (London, 1955) pp. 188-210; Vol. II - Unity, 1942-1944 (translated by Joyce Murchie and Hamish Erskine), (London, 1959), pp. 37-59; General Catroux, Dans la Bataille de Mediteranee: Egypte - Levant - Afrique du Nord, 1940-1944 (Paris, 1949), pp. 199-216, 255-267; Lord Wilson, Eight Years Overseas, 1939-1947 (London, 1950), pp. 110-127, emphasises in his account how difficult it was for the military to avoid local politics.

16. De Gaulle (Cairo) to Rene Pleven and Maurice Dejean (London), 9th August, 1942, de Gaulle, Unity, pp. 33-35.

17. For a detailed account of some of these projects, consult: Gomaa, pp. 104-114; Gavriel Cohen, Churchill ve She'elat Eretz-Israel, 1939-1942, (Jerusalem, 1976), pp. 39-47; Nathaniel Katzburg, Mediniut be-Mavoch, 1940-1945 (Jerusalem, 1977), pp. 38-41.

18. Cab. 95/8, MSC (41) 14, War Cabinet, Conference with the Minister of State, 26th September, 1941.

19. For details, consult: Gomaa, pp. 108-110; G. Cohen, pp. 47-48.

20. Cab. 95/1, ME(O)(42) 4, 1st meeting, 9th January, 1942.

21. CO's Directive to High Commissioner of Palestine, 6th November, 1941, CO 732/87 part I/79238/41, piece 41.

22. Cab. 95/1, ME(O)(41) 5th meeting, 8th October, 1941; ME(O)(41) 6th meeting, 8th December, 1941; ME(O)(42) 4, 1st meeting, 9th January, 1942.

23. Lampson to London, 2nd October, 1941, FO 371/27045/E6864 (Copy: Cab. 9511, ME(O)(41)10).

24. De Gaulle, Memoirs, Vol. I. pp. 193-4, 199, 202, Edward Spears, head of the British mission in the Levant, recalled in his memoirs, Fulfillment of a Mission (London, 1977), pp. 115-116, his warnings against the potential activities of "Lawrences", in Syria. General Wilson, however, who also recalls some of the incidents mentioned by de Gaulle, blames in his Eight Years Overseas, pp. 122-125, either French officers or local Francophobia for them.

25. For example, consult: De Gaulle, Unity, pp. 37-59; Sir Llewellyn Woodward, British Foreign Policy in the Second World War (London, 1975), Vol. III, pp. 211-254.

26. J.P. Domvile to K.C. Buss, Air Commodore (G.H.Q., Cairo), 3rd April, 1942, FO 141/840/356/2/42G.

27. I. Clayton to Domvile (G.H.Q. Cairo), 13th April, 1942; same to W. Smart (British Embassy, Cairo), 22nd April, 1942, FO 141/840/356/2/420.

28. Tahsin al-'Askari (Cairo) to Nuri al-Sa'id (Baghdad), 5th April, 1942, FO 141/840/356/1/42.

29. Lampson (Cairo) to London, 10th May, 1942, FO 371/31337/E2986.

30. Ibid.; MacMichael (Jerusalem) to London, 15th May, 1942, FO 141/840/356/9/42.

31. Eden (London) to Lampson (Cairo), 17th, 28th May, 1942, FO 141/840/356/10,11/42.

32. Lampson (Cairo) to London, 24th June, 1942, FO 371/31473/E3990.

33. Spears (Beirut) to London, 24th June, 1942, FO 371/31473/E3812; same to Minister of State (Cairo), 26th June, 1942, FO 371/31473/E3863.

34. Minister of State (Cairo) to London, 30th June, 1942, FO 371/31473/ E3920.

35. Lampson (Cairo) to London, 21st June, 1942, FO 371/31473/E3998.

36. Same to London, 31st January, 1943, FO 371/35529/ J812.

37. Same to same, 5th February, 1943, FO 371/35031/E937.

38. Smart's Memorandum on "Egypt and the Arab World", 3rd May, 1943, FO 141/866/149/2/43G.

39. For a detailed account of these despatches, see our previous Chapter.

40. For the inter-departmental discussions between the Foreign and Colonial Office in which both Peterson and Baxter took part on behalf of the Foriegn Office, and Cranborne replies of 19th August and 23rd October, see: CO 732/87 part I/79238/41, pieces 41, 42, 50.

41. Casey (Cairo) to London, 28th November, 1942, FO 371/31338/E7305; Cab.95/1, ME(O) 43, 1st meeting of the Middle East Official Committee, 19th January, 1943; Gomaa, pp. 117-118.

42. Foreign Office to Cornwallis, 27th January, 5th, 9th February, 1943, FO 371/34955/E538, E636.

43. Parliamentary Debates, 23rd February, 1943, 387, H.C.Deb. 5[S], Col. 139.

44. For Nuri's initiative and advertisement of his scheme, consult: Chapter II of this part.

45. Cornwallis (Baghdad) to London, 8th March, 1943, FO 371/34955/E1893.

46. Lampson (Cairo) to London, 18th March, 1943, FO 371/34956/E1640; Minister of State (Cairo) to London, 25th March, 1943, FO 371/ 34956/E1838.

47. Terence Shone, British Minister (Cairo) to R. Casey, Minister of State (Cairo), 12th March, 1943, FO 921/114; Cornwallis (Baghdad) to London, 18th March, 1943, FO 371/34956/E1894.

48. Foreign Office to Middle East representatives, 26th March, 1943, FO 371/34956/E1640.

49. Cornwallis (Baghdad) to London, 8th March, 1943, FO 371/34955/E1893.

50. Lampson (Cairo) to London, 31st March, 1943, FO 371/34956/E1919.

51. Kirkbride (Amman) to MacMichael (Jerusalem), 14th April, 1943, FO 816/43, p. 3.

52. Charge d'affaires (Jedda) to London, 27th May, 1943, FO 816/43, p. 29.

53. Cab. 95/1, Middle East War Council (43) 25, 19th May, 1943.

54. Casey presented his proposal to the Cabinet on 17th June, 1943, Cab. 66/39 WP (43) 247 (copy: FO 371/34975/E3234); For the Cabinet's discussions, consult: Gomaa, pp. 122-123.

55. Cab. 95/1, MEWC (43) 3, Annex II, Memorandum, 2nd April, 1943; Gomaa, pp. 119-123.

56. For the Middle East representatives' requests to contemplate such a policy, see: Lampson (Cairo) to London, 16th June, 1943, FO 371/ 35536/J2855; For the various complaints of the British Minister in Saudi-Arabia about American penetration, see: FO 371/34975; and Cab. 66/39 WP (43) 301 when Eden presented to the Cabinet on 12th July, 1943, a first general Memorandum on British Policy in the Middle East (copy: FO 371/34975/E4079).

57. Halifax, British Ambassador (Washington) to the Secretary of State, 2nd November, 1943, Memorandum (dated 30th October), FRUS 1943, Vol. IV, pp. 6-7.

58. For detailed accounts of the Anglo-American dialogue concerning the Middle East, consult: FRUS, 1943, Vol. IV, pp. 6-18; FRUS, 1944, Vol. V, pp. 6-7; Amitzur Ilan, America, Britanya ve Eretz-Israel (Jerusalem 1979), pp. 148-9; Peterson, pp. 238-239; Baram, pp. 155-170; For a record of the conversations held in London, see: FO 371/39985/ E2736 (copy: CO 732/88 part 4/79303); Woodward, Vol. IV, pp. 359-365, 383-411.

59. For detailed accounts of these discussions, consult: Katzburg, 1940-1945, pp. 70-147; M. Cohen, Palestine, pp. 151-182; Gomaa, pp. 131-150; Woodward, Vol. IV, pp. 366-383.

60. Foreign Office's Aide Memoire to Washington, 30th October, 1943, FRUS, 1943, Vol. IV, pp. 6-7.

61. Anglo-American's Agreed Minute, 28th April, 1944, FO 371/39985/ E2736 (copy: CO 732/88 part 4/79303). It is, however, noteworthy that although British officials agreed in theory to include Egypt in Middle Eastern projects, Egyptian Department in the Office still maintained its independent activity, and Egypt was still excluded from Departmental discussions on Arab affairs.

62. Lord Casey, Personal Experience, 1939-1946 (London, 1962), p. 139.

63. Lord Moyne (Cairo) to Eden (London), 9th May, 1944, FO 371/40135/E2987.

64. Lampson's Report on his talks with Amin 'Uthman, 31st March, 1943, FO 371/34956/E1919; Nuqrashi's assessment on Arab Unity, in Montyly Intelligence Summary, No. 6, for March 1943, giving an account of the Wafd's reaction to Eden's Speech, ibid.

65. Kirkbride (Amman) to MacMichael (Jerusalem), 14th April, 1943, FO 816/43, p. 3; MacMichael (Jerusalem) to Killearn (Cairo), 29th June, 1943, FO 921/115/90(2)/43/161.

66. Killearn (Cairo) to London, 25th July, 1943, FO 371/34960/E4335.

67. Wikeley (Jedda) to London, 9th August, 1943, FO 371/34960/E4690.

68. Jordan (Jedda) to Eden (London) 2nd October, 1943, FO 371/34962/E6264.

69. Evidence of this belief can be found in almost every Arabic book about this period. See, for example, 'Arif, 'Azzam, p. 263, al-'Aqad, pp. 179-180; Haykal, III (1978), pp. 19-20; Husayn, pp. 68, 79.

70. See for example, Smart's Minutes in 11, 13th October, 1943, FO 141/866/149/137/43.

71. Foreign Office to Middle East representatives, 8th October, 1943, FO 371/34962/E5994.

72. Smart's Minutes, 11, 13th October, 1943, FO 141/866/149/143/137/43; Smart's Memorandum on Arab Unity, 12th October, 1943, FO 141/866/149/140/43.

73. Samrt's Memorandum, 20th October, 1943, FO 141/866/149/144/43.

74. Shone (Cairo) to London, 26th October, 1943, FO 371/34963/E6706.

75. Ibid.

76. Shone (Cairo) to London, 9th November, 1943, FO 371/34963/E7349.

77. Same to same, 9th November, 1943, FO 371/34963/E7350.

78. Killearn (Cairo) to London, 24th February, 1944, FO 371/39987/E1264.

79. R.M. Hankey, Eastern Department (London), 28th February, 1944, FO 371/39987/E1264; Foreign Office to Killearn (Cairo), 2nd March, 1944, FO 371/39987/E1330.

80. Killearn (Cairo) to London, 11th, 16th March, 1944, FO 371/39987/E1627, E1743; same to same, 24th March, 1944, FO 371/40143/E1933.

81. Foreign Office to Killearn (Cairo), 6th April, 1944, FO 371/40143/E1933.

82. Memorandum by Minister Resident in the Middle East, summarising views expressed at the Conference on Palestine held in Cairo on 6-7th April, 1944, in Moyne (Cairo) to Eden (London), FO 371/40135/E2987.

83. Killearn (Cairo) to London, 11, 12th April, 1944, FO 371/40143/E2229, E2265; same to same, 20th April, 1944, FO 371/39988/E2456.

84. Killearn (Cairo) to London, 11, 22nd May, 1943, FO 371/40143/E2935, E3165.

85. Lampson's recommendation was coldly received by Spears. Spears argued that with so many Arab factors operating in the form Britain "desired" it would be "most inadvisable" to come out too openly against the Conference. Spears (Beirut) to Cairo, 22nd April, 1944, FO 371/39988/E2500. As a result of this refusal neither Riad al-Sulh nor Jamil Mardam were advised to slow down their activities concerning the Conference.

86. Killearn (Cairo) to London, 22nd May, 1944, FO 371/40143/E3165.

87. Same to same, 5th June, 1944, FO 371/39988/E3374.

88. Same to same, 14th June, 1944, FO 371/39988/E3516; Nahhas's draft letter is to found in FO 371/39988/E3627.

89. Foreign Office to Killearn (Cairo), 19th June, 1944, FO 371/39988/E3516.

90. Killearn (Cairo) to London, 22nd June, 1943, FO 371/39988/E3675.

91. Same to same, 23rd June, 1944, FO 371/39988/E3686.

92. Foreign Office to Killearn (Cairo), 3rd July, 1944, FO 371/39988/E3686.

93. Summary of Telegrams relating to Arab Unity 31st January - 12th August, 1944, FO 921/220/48(2)(44)/109.

94. Killearn (Cairo) to London, 26th June, 1st July, 1944, FO 371/39988/E3777, E3873 reporting on conversations with 'Abd al-Illa, the Iraqi Prince Regent; Cornwallis (Baghdad) to London, 5th July, 1944 on a conversation with the Iraqi Premier, FO 371/39988/E3990.

95. Ellison (Jedda) to London, 5-6th July, 1944, FO 371/39988/E4006, E4008.

96. Spears (Beirut) to Cairo, 11th July, 1944, FO 371/39988/E4155.

97. Killearn (Cairo) to London, 10th July, 1944, FO 371/39988/E4075.

98. Moyne (Cairo) to London, 11th July, 1944, FO 371/39988/E4076.

99. Foriegn Office to Ellison (Jedda), 13th July, 1944, FO 371/39988/E4015.

100. Ellison (Jedda) to London, 14, 16th July, 1944, FO 371/39988/E4191, E4203; same to same, 20th July, 1944, FO 371/39989/E4335; Jordan (Jedda) to London, 27th July, 1944, FO 371/39989/E4512, E4525.

101. Killearn (Cairo) to London, 26th July, 1944, FO 371/39989/E4478.

102. Moyne (Cairo) to London, 11th August, 1944, FO 371/39989/E4826; Jordan (Jedda) to London 12th August, 1933, FO 371/39989/E4854/

103. MacMichael (Jerusalem) to London, 12th August, 1944, FO 816/44, p. 86.

104. Abu 'Alam was officially sent to represent Egypt in the Arab Lawyers' Conference in Damascus. However, he extended his stay in this area after the Conference ended. See: Killearn (Cairo) to London, 1st September, 1944, PER 24-30th August, 1944, FO 371/41318/J3198.

105. Thompson (Baghdad) to London, 10th August, 1944, FO 371/39989/E4816; Same to same, 13th September, 1944, FO 371/39990/E5617.

106. Cited by Weizmann, Trial and Error, pp. 417-418.

107. For the high regard in which Ibn-Sa'ud was held, see: Note on the Palestine question, circulated for the Committee on Palestine, 1st November, 1943, P(M)(43) 16; Evans, p. 327; David Dilks (ed.), The Diaries of Sir Alexander Cadogan, 1938-1945 (London, 1971), p. 714.

108. Moyne to London, 11, 31st August, 1944, FO 371/39989/E4826, E5378; Summary to Telegrams, FO 921/220/48(2)(44)/109.

109. Calyton's Report on results of a journey to Arab countries, 24th August, 1944, FO 921/220/48(2)(44)/108. A further result was a long report on the solution of the Palestine question through the internationalisation of this country. For details, see: I. Calyton's Papers, Box II, MEC (Oxford).

110. Killearn (Cairo) to London, 3rd September, 1944, FO 371/39990/E5567.

111. Killearn (Cairo) to London, 31st July, 1944, FO 371/39989/E4617;
same to same, 8th September, 1944, FO 371/39990/E5595.

112. Thompson (Baghdad) to London, 5th August, 1944, FO 371/39989/E4714;
it is noteworthy that the Legation in Beirut was instructed by the
Foreign Office to tell Nuri that "if there was any reason to
suppose that the Conference intended to discuss Palestine, HMG
would advise all concerned against it". See: Foreign Office to
Mackereth (Beirut), 12th August, 1944, FO 371/39989/E4776.

113. Moyne (Cairo) to London, 31st August, 1944, FO 371/39989/E5378;
same to same, 7th September, 1944, FO 371/39990/E5488.

114. Foreign Office to Jordan (Jedda) 11th Sept. 1944, FO 371/39990/E5387.

115. Sykes, Crossroads, p. 304.

116. Nahhas expressed such views during an interview for The Times.
See Killearn (Cairo) to London, 22nd September, 1944, PER 14th-
20th September, 1944, FO 371/41318/J3444.

117. On 1st April, 1945, 'Alami, in a Statement to the High Commissioner
on Palestine (copy: FO 921/324/48(1)45/85), produced a copy of a
letter by the heads of the local Palestinian Arab parties nomin-
ating him on the 23rd September, 1944, to represent them in the
Conference. See also: 'Abd al-Latif Salah (President of the
National Bloc) to 'Alami, 24th September, 1944, File 02948,
Division 65, ISA; Nevo, pp. 290-293; Geoffrey Furlonge, Palestine
is my Country, the Story of Musa Alami (London, 1969), pp. 132-133.

118. Furlonge, p. 133.

119. Shone (Cairo) to London, 30th September, 1944, Weekly Appreciation,
FO 371/41318/J3399.

120. Shone (Cairo) to London, 6th October, 1944, Weekly Appreciation,
FO 371/41318/J3514; same to same, 6th October, 1944, PER 28th
September - 4th October, 1944, FO 371/41319/J3638.

121. Furlonge, p. 133.

122. Shone (Cairo) to London, 6th October, 1944, FO 371/39990/E6328;
Clayton's Report, 30th September, 1944, ibid. 'Alami's own account
of the talks in Furlonge, pp. 133-135, contradicts these reports.

123. The decision was unanimously approved by the Conference during
the third meeting on 1st October, 1943. See Proces Verbal of the
Preparatory Committee, FO 371/45235/E455.

124. Proces Verbal of the Preparatory Committee, Seventh Meeting, 5th
October, 1944, FO 371/45235/E455.

125. Clayton (Cairo) to Smart (Cairo) on a conversation with Yasin,
7th October, 1944, FO 921/221/48(2)44/159; Notes on the meeting
of the Preparatory Committee of the Arab Unity Conference
25th September— 6th October, 1944, made by an unofficial observer.
PIC/71, FO 371/39991/E6800.

126. Proces Verbal of the Preparatory Committee, Seventh Meeting,
5th October, 1944, FO 371/45235/E455.

127. MacMichael's Report (Jerusalem) on a conversation with Tawfiq
     Abu al-Huda, 13th October, 1944, FO 816/44, p. 113.

128. English text in Gomaa, pp. 272-274 App. I; Arabic text in
     al-Ahram, 8th October, 1944.

129. Clayton's Report, 29th October, 1944, FO 921/221/48(2)44/164;
     Notes on the meetings, PIC/71, FO 371/39991/E6800.

130. For detailed accounts of these feelings, consult: M. Cohen,
     Palestine, pp. 148-149; Gomaa, pp. 229-231.

CHAPTER FOUR - pp. 258 - 300

1. Haykal, Mudhakkirat, II, pp. 244-245, recalled that he had been informed of this development as early as the afternoon of 7th October.   Shone to London, 15th October, 1944, FO 371/41319/J3469 argued that Nahhas, following his long dispute with Faruq, decided to resign on 8th Oct., and it was only then that Hasanayn, the King's Chamberlain, foiled the plan by dismissing him first.

2. Al-Ahram, 10th October, 1944.

3. Al-Ahram, 9th, 10th, 25th October, 1944;   19th January, 1945 (Speech from the Throne); Shone to London, 13th October, 1944, PER 5-11th October, 1944, FO 371/41319/J3749; al-Muqattam, 25th January, 1945.

4. See, for example, al-Ahram, 9th-11th October, 1944, for interviews with Nuqrashi and 'Ubayd.

5. For the platform of the Nationalist Party, see Fikri Abaza's article in al-Ahram, 30th October, 1944. For the platform of the Wafdist Bloc, see: Killearn to London, 17th February, 1945, Weekly Appreciation, FO 371/45930/J670.

6. For the list of the participants, see: al-Ahram, 11th October 1944.

7. Shone to London, PER 21-27th October, 1944, FO 371/41319/J3964.

8. Political Intelligence Centre, Middle East (PICME), PIC/71, 11th March, 1945, Appriciation on Arab discussions since the Alexandria Conference, FO 141/100 1/32/77/45.

9. Ibid.

10. This was Tahir's appreciations, Zalam al-Sijn, p. 573. Salah al-Din was Nahhas's Private Secretary during the 1930s.

11. Shone to London, 24th October, 1944, FO 371/41362/J3755; al-Muqattam, 2nd November, al-Ahram, 3-4th November, 1944.

12. Clayton to Smart (Cairo), 15th November, 1944, FO 141/983/769/2/44.

13. Moyne (Cairo) to London, 19th October, 1944, FO 371/39991/E6697.

14. Al-Ahram, 10th November, 1944; Killearn to London, 17th November, 1944, PER 9-15th November, 1944, FO 371/41319/J4366.

15. Killearn (Cairo) to London, 26th November, 1944, FO 371/39991/E7560.

16. For Nahhas's disappointment with the reaction of the other Arab delegates to his dismissal, see: Outlines of Political Situation in the Middle East, PICME, PIC 190/30, FO 141/998/1485/2/44.

17. Al-Ahram, 20th October, 1944; Shone (Cairo) to London, 22nd October, 1944, FO 371/40132/E6806.

18. Shone (Cairo) to London, 27th October, 1944, PER 21-27th October, 1944, FO 371/41319/J3964; same to same, 3rd November, 1944, PER 26th October-1st November, 1944, FO 371/41319/J4031; same to same, 10th November, 1944, PER 2-8th November, 1944, FO 371/41319/J4108.

19. Ben-Gurion and Shertok, Executive of the Jewish Agency (Jerusalem) to Ahmad Mahir (Cairo), 8th November, 1944, S25/7516, CZA; al-Ahram, 10th November, 1944.

20. Grand Rabbi of Egypt to British Embassy (Cairo), 7th November, 1944, FO 141/1001/1546/10/44.

21. Tuck, American Legation (Cairo) to the Secretary of State (Washington DC), January 16th, 1945, RG59, 883.00/1 - 1645, NA .

22. Al-Ahram, 19th November, 1944; Tuck (Cairo) to the Secretary of State (Washington DC), 21st November, 1944, FRUS, 1944, Vol. V, pp. 638-640. Copy of this petition was also sent to the British Embassy. See: Killearn (Cairo) to London, 1st December, 1944, FO 371/40148/E7793.

23. Al-Ahram, 10-23, 25th December, 1944; Killearn (Cairo) to London, 17th December, 1944, Weekly Appreciation, FO 371/41319/J4645; same to same, 15th December, 1944, PER 3-15th December, FO 371/45930/J70; same to same, 22nd December, PER 14-20th December, 1944, FO 371/45930/ J98; same to same, 29th December, PER 21-27th Dec., FO 371/45930/J161.

24. Killearn to London, 15th December, 1944, PER 3-15th December, 1944, FO 371/45930/J70.

25. Al-Ahram, 24th, 25th December, 1944; Killearn to London, 29th December, 1944, FO 371/45931/E133.

26. Gort (Jerusalem) to London, 13th January, 1945, FO 371/45235/E383 on a conversation held on 3rd January, between the Iraqi Minister for Foreign Affairs and the Trans-Jordanian Premier.

27. Salah al-Din did not stay in his office for long. In December 1945, he was appointed adviser for the Syrian Ministry for Foreign Affairs for a trial period of three months. See: Killearn to London, 12th December, 1945, PER 5-11 December, 1945, FO 371/ 45932/J4332.

28. Killearn (Cairo) to Spears (Beirut), 23rd June, 1944, FO 371/ 41362/J2420.

29. 'Azzam was the Palace choice to replace Ahmad Ramzi in Beirut. See: Killearn (Cairo) to Spears (Beirut), ibid; Shone (Cairo) to London, 20th October, 1944, FO 371/41362/J3739; a Royal Decree on the nomination of 'Azzam to his new post was issued on 2nd November, and published in al-Ahram, 3-4th November, 1944.

30. For 'Azzam's nomination as Amir al-Hajj, see: al-Ahram, 12th November, 1944; 'Arif, 'Azzam, pp. 265-6. This appointment stresses 'Azzam's relations with the Palace, since the King had to approve it.

31. Jordan (Jedda) to London, 14th November, 1944, FO 371/39991/E7003; Ibn-Sa'ud to Shaykh 'Abdallah Sulayman, Acting Minister for Foreign Affairs, for communication to HM Minister (Jedda), annexed in Jordan (Jedda) to London, 30th November, 1944, FO 921/222/48(2)44/186.

32. Foreign Office to Jedda, 28th November, 1944, FO 371/39991/E7003.

33. Jordan (Jedda) to London, 3rd, 5th January, 1945, FO 371/45235/E63, E144.

34. For these letters, see: al-Ahram, 26th November, 1944, 8th Jan. 1945.

35. 'Azzam's telegram of 3rd January, 1945, was published by al-Ahram 4th January, 1945. Also Ellison (Jedda) to London, 3rd January, 1945, FO 371/45235/E88; 'Arif, 'Azzam, pp. 265-266.

36. Al-Ahram, 8th January, 1945; Killearn (Cairo) to London, 12th Jan. 1945, PER 4-10th January, 1945, FO 371/45930/J273.

37. Killearn (Cairo) to London, 25th January, 1945, FO 371/45542/E739.

38. Same to same, 22nd January, 1945, FO 371/45542/E738.

39. Same to same, 2nd February, 1945, Weekly Appreciation, FO 371/45930/J503.

40. For Ibn-Sa'ud's account of the meeting, see: Jordan (Jedda) to London, 2nd February, 1945, FO 371/45542/E790; For Faruq's account: Killearn (Cairo) to London, 7th February, 1945, FO 371/45542/E950. For 'Azzam's account: al-Ahram, 1st February, 1945; 'Arif, 'Azzam p. 266.

41. Al-Ahram, 1-2nd February, 1945; al-Muqattam, 31st January, 1945.

42. Al-Ahram, 2nd February, 1945; Killearn (Cairo) to London, 2nd February, 1945, Weekly Appreciation, FO 371/45930/J503.

43. Killearn (Cairo) to London, 16th February, 1945, FO 371/45236/ E1158; same to same, 15th February, 1945, PER 8-14th February, FO 371/45930/J755; al-Ahram, 18th February, 1945.

44. PICME, PIC/71, 11th March, 1945, FO 141/1010/32/77/45.

45. See, for example, Nuri's conversations with British officials: Shone (Cairo) to London, 8th November, 1945, FO 371/39991/E7004; same to same 1st November, 1945, FO 371/39991/E6875; Edward Grigg's Press Conference with Arab Journalists: al-Ahram, 4th January, 1945.

46. Foriegn Office to Jedda, 28th November, 1944, FO 371/39991/E7003.

47. Hal Lehrman, The Nation, 14th April, 1945, pp. 413-414, cited by Kirk, p. 344. The various affects of this belief are discussed later in this Chapter.

48. Killearn (Cairo) to London, 21st December, 1944, FO 371/41335/J4672.

49. Same to same, 24th January, 1945, FO 371/45235/E715.

50. The version in the copy of the Minister's Residence in Cairo even says: "if we allow the French to impose a treaty on the Lebanese by force, we shall become involved in a conflict with the whole Egypto-Arab world, and sooner or later we shall end by losing the Middle East" etc. Killearn (Cairo) to London, 25th December, 1944, FO 921/222/48(2)44/197.

51. Killearn (Cairo) to London, 25th December, 1944, FO 371/40307/E7876.

52. Copies of all three reports are in WO 208/1580.

53. Foriegn Office to Cairo, 5th January, 1945, FO 371/40307/E7876.

54. See, for example, British Legation (Beirut) to London, Weekly Political Summary, 21st February, 1945, for the Maronite opposition to the Arab League, FO 371/45543/E1647.

55. Jordan (Jedda) to London, 3rd January, 1945, FO 371/45235/E63.

56. Foreign Office to Jedda, 24th January, 1945, FO 371/45235/E63.

57. Killearn (Cairo) to London, 29th January, 1945, Grigg to same, 29th January, FO 371/45235/E688, E694.

58. Foreign Office to British Representatives, Middle East, 6th Feb., 1945, FO 371/45235/E744.

59. Jordan (Jedda) to London, 3rd February, 1945, FO 371/45235/E809; same to same, 8th February, 1945, FO 371/45235/E946.

60. Killearn (Cairo) to London, 11th February 1945; Grigg to same, 11th February, 1945, FO 371/45235/E1004, E1005.

61. Foreign Office to Cairo, 14th February, 1945, FO 371/45236/E1005.

62. Jordan (Jedda) to London, 4th February, 1945, FO 371/45236/E976.

63. Memorandum of coversation between Ibn-Sa'ud - Roosevelt, 14th February, 1945, aboard the U.S.S. "Quincy" (written by William Eddy), FRUS, 1945, Vol. VIII, pp. 2-3. Eddy was the official interpreter in the rulers' talks, and his version, signed by the two rulers became the official account of this talk.

64. Record of Conversation with Ibn-Sa'ud in Fayum, 17th February, 1945, FO 171/1047/828/2/45G. The King's version of the conver- sation (FRUS, 1945, Vo. VIII, pp. 689-690), emphasises the King's growing confidence following his conversation with Roosevelt. Ibn- Sa'ud maintained that he did not yield to Churchil's "big stick" to compromise with the Jews.

65. Al-Ahram, 21st February, 1945. Quwatli arrived on 13th February, from Saudi Arabia and left on 18th February, after meeting the Arab rulers and Churchill.

66. Killearn (Cairo) to London, 21st February, 1945, FO 371/45236/E1275.

67. Same to same, 3rd March, 1945, FO 371/45236/E1483; The content of the proposed text of the League was sent by 'Azzam to Smart on 5th March, FO 371/45237/E1930.

68. Killearn (Cairo) to London, 28th February, 1945, FO 371/45415/E1582.

69. Same to same, 17th March, 1945, FO 371/45237/E1859.

70. Killearn (Cairo) to London, 5th March, 1945, FO 371/45236/E1583.

71. Foreign Office to Killearn (Cairo), 10th March, 1945, FO 371/ 45237/E1639.

72. Killearn (Cairo) to London, 17th March, 1945, FO 371/45237/E1859.

73. Same to same, 21st March, 1945, FO 371/45392/E1961.

74. Arab text of the Pact was published in every Egyptian newspaper on 23rd March, 1945, (see, for exampls, al-Ahram). English text of the Pact is in Gomaa, pp. 295-301.

75. Killearn (Cairo) to London, 24th March, 1945, FO 371/45930/J1143.

76. Smart's minute, 23rd March, 1945, FO 141/1011/32/107/45.

77. Hankey's minute, 27th March, 1945, FO 371/45237/E2010.

78. Hankey's minute, 27th April, 1945, FO 371/45238/E2594. R. Campbell, 23rd May, 1945, and Beckett, 30th April, ibid., shared Hankey's appreciation.

79. Smart's Report, 20th March, 1945 on a conversation with 'Aalami FO 371/45238/E2184.

80. Killearn (Cairo) to London, 6th April, PER 29th March - 4th April, 1945 FO 371/45930/J1345, on Nasir al-Din al-Nashashibi's criticism of the Palestinian Annex in al-Misri. For further Palestinian Arab criticism, consult: Tahir, Zalam al-Sijn, p. 583.

81. Text of the debate in the Chamber of Deputies, in al-Ahram, 3rd April, 1945.

82. Text of the debate, in al-Ahram, 4th April, 1945. For further criticism of the Pact by the Ikhwan and Huda al-Sha'rawi, see: Killearn to London, PER 5-11th April, 1945, FO 371/45930; al-Muqattam, 25th March, 1945.

83. For the great differences between the "Alexandria Protocol" and the pact of the Arab League, consult: Cecil Hourani, "The Arab League in Perspective", The Middle East Journal, Vol. I, No. 2, April 1947, pp. 125-136; Gomaa, pp. 217-231, 239-271.

84. For Arabic Press cover of the Pact, see: al-Ahram, 23-30th March, 1945; Killearn (Cairo) to London, 9th February, 30th March, 6th April, 13th April, PER 17th February - 11 April, FO 371/45930.

85. For example, the Society for the Strengthening of Arab Relations, the President of which was a certain, Muhammad Mahmud al-Ghandur, a Government employee. The honorary President was 'Abd al-Hamid al-Haq, a former Minister in the Wafdist Ministry. For details on this Society, see: FO 141/1011/32/149/45; T.W.Fitzpatrick's Report, Cairo city Police, 1st June, 1945, FO 141/1011/32/153/45.

86. For the failure of various British appeals to include in the Pact an article referring to the regional character of the League, consult: Smart's minutes, 22nd January, 10th February, 1945. FO 141/1010/32/6/45; Lampson to London, 27th February, 1945, FO 371/45236/E1417.

87. Hankey's minute, 27th March, 1945, FO 371/45237/E2010.

88. C.G. Eastwood's minute, (No. 57), 26th March, 1945, CO 732/88 Part IV/ 79238 Part I.

89. The Times, 24th March, 1945.

90. PICME, 11th March, 1945, PIC/71, FO 141/101/32/77/45.

91. Al-Ahram, 23rd March, 1945. James Bowker (Alexandria) to London, 15tn March, 1946, General Political Review - 1945, reported that 'Azzam was nominated after strong pressure by Nuqrashi on the non-Egyptian delegates (FO 371/53289/J1330).

92. Killearn (Cairo) to London, 28th February, 1945, FO 371/45415/E1582.

93. Same to same, 23rd March, 1945, FO 371/45237/E2091.

94. Foreign Office to British representatives, Middle East, 4th April, 1945, ibid.

95. Harold Farquhar, Assistant Oriental Secretary (Cairo) to London, 27th September, 1945, FO 371/45393/E7284; Bowker (Cairo) to London, 2nd October, 1945, FO 371/45393/E7409.

96. Hugh Stonehewer Bird (Baghdad) to London, 5th December, 1945, FO 371/45241/E9518 on Nuri's suggestion to his Premier to leave the League.

97. 'Arif, 'Azzam, p. 268.

98. See, for example, al-Ahram, 9th May, 1945.

99. Al-Ahram, 1-8th June, 1945, for the special session of the League.

100. Al-Ahram, 16th July, 1945; Farquhar (Cairo) to London, 24th July, 1945, FO 371/45239/E5658.

101. The Committee was also named: the Committee for the rescue of the Arab Land in Palestine in al-Ahram, 16th, 20th July, 1945.

102. Al-Ahram, 8th, 10th August, 1945.

103. Al-Ahram, 25th September, 1945; 11-12th November, 1945; Killearn (Cairo) to London, 23rd August, 1945, Weekly Appreciation, FO 371/45932/J2816; Bowker (Cairo) to London, 29th September, 1945, FO 371/45932/J3226; The Director of the Office of Near Eastern and African Affairs (Loy Henderson) to the Acting Secretary of State (Acheson), 1st October, 1945, 867N.01/10-145, FRUS, 1945, Vol. VIII, pp. 751-753.

104. Parliamentary Debates, House of Commons, 13th November, 1945 Vol. 515, Cols. 1931-1934.

105. Killearn (Cairo) to London, 5th December, 1945, FO 371/45396/E9852; al-Ahram, 6th December, 1945.

106. Nuri told Smart that 'Azzam, together with Haykal, replaced his moderate reply with an uncompromising one: Killearn (Cairo) to London, 4th, 5th December, 1945, FO 371/45396/E9431, E9499. However, Jamil Mardam told Smart that 'Azzam was the moderate one, and it was Nuri's pressure that determined the radical reply (Killearn to London, 15th December, 1945, Weekly Appreciation, FO 371/45932/J4234).

107. Killearn (Cairo) to London, 3rd December, 1945, FO 371/45396/E9419.

108. Killearn (Cairo) to London, 25 June, 1945, FO371/45922/J2163.

109. J.R. Hamilton's report, 4th July, 1945, FO 371/45239/E5427.

110. Foreign Office to the Chancery, 7th July, 1945, Ibid.

111. Note on the Arab League, prepared by the Embassy, Cairo, 1st September, 1945, FO 371/45239/E6937.

112. Smart's report, 5th November, 1945, FO 371/45928/J3947.

113. Smart's minute, 31st March, 1945, FO 141/1010/32/5/45.

114. Killearn's minute, 1st April, 1945, ibid.

115. Killearn's minute, 6th April, 1945, FO 141/1010/32/7/45. Leo Ameri, in his obituary of Smart, in Walter Smart by some of his friends (Middle East Centre, St. Antony's College), p. 1, declared that "Smart was the mainstay of British power in both Egypt and through the Middle East for thirty years and more". Similar appriciations were given by John Hamilton (op.cit., p. 7), and Grafftey-Smith in his Bright Levant (London, 1970), pp. 15, 134-135.

116. Killearn to London, 15th November, 1945, FO 371/45395/E8907; Lyon, Charge d'affaires (Cairo) to the Secretary of State (Washington DC), 19th November, 1945, 867N.01/11-1945, FRUS 1945, Vol. VIII, pp. 826-827.

117. Killearn to London, 20th November, 1945, FO 371/45295/E8974.

118. Same to same, 17th November, 1945, FO 371/45295/E8795; same to same, 20th November, 1945, FO 371/45395/E8974; Bevin to Killearn (Cairo), 16th November, 1945, FO 371/45395/E9014; Killearn to London, 26th, 27th, 28th November, 1945, FO 371/45395/E9191, E9196, E9261; London to Killearn, 1st December, 1945, FO 371/45396/E9306.

119. Grafftey-Smith (Jedda) to London, 15th December, 1945, FO 371/45396/E9833.

120. FO 371/45396/E9494; Sands, Charge d'affaires (Jedda) to the Secretary of State (Washington DC), 7th December, 1945, 867N.01/12-745, FRUS, 1945, Vol. VIII, p. 838

121. Al-Ahram, 15th December, 1945.

122. Killearn (Cairo) to London, 7th April, 1945, FO 371/45238/E2475; Furlonge, pp. 137-138.

123. Statement by Musa 'Alami, 1st April, 1945, FO 921/324/48(1)45/85; al-Ahram, 2nd April, 1945 published part of the statement, omitting the sentence implying 'Alami was going to resign his mission.

124. Stonehewer-Bird (Baghdad) to London, 10th, 14th May, 1945, FO 371/45238/E3027; Killearn (Cairo) to London, 1st July, 1945, PER 21-27th June, 1945, FO 371/45931/J2216; Ravensdale's report, 29th June, 1945, FO 371/45239/E5080.

125. Clayton's report on a conversation with Shaykh Yusuf Yasin, 31st July, 1945, FO 921/325/48(1)45/138.

126. Killearn (Cairo) to London, 2nd August, 1945, FO 371/45239/E5771;
     Ravensdale's report, 10th August, on a conversation with Habib
     Jamati, FO 141/1011, Part II/32/202/45.

127. Nevo, pp. 373-378; 'Alami even attempted to involve the British in
     this conflict. See: Ravensdale's report, 29th June, 1945, FO 371/
     45239/E5080.

128. Al-Mashru' al Inshai al-'Arabi (Jerusalem, n.d.), pp. 19-31;
     Furlonge, pp. 135-6; Gort (Jerusalem) to Killearn (Cairo), 26th July,
     1945, FO 371/45239; Iltyd Clayton's Papers, Box II, file I, Middle
     East Centre, St. Antony's College, Oxford.

129. Al-Ahram, 8th, 10th. August, 1945.

130. Sasson, Baderech, p. 351; Proces Verbal of the League's session,
     24th November, 1945, File 00909, Division 65, ISA.

131. Bowker (Cairo) to London, 12th November, 1945, FO 371/45394/E8717.

132. Al-Mashru' al-Inshai, pp. 42-81; al-Wahda, 10th February, 1946,
     Filastin, 21st December, 1945.

133. Nevo, p. 379.

134. Nevo, pp. 379-380; Furlonge, pp. 137-138.

135. Killearn to London, 27th March, Smart's minute, 22nd May,
     27th June; Killearn's minute 28th June, 1945, FO 141/1011/32/
     103, 146, 180/45.

136. Killearn to London, 21st May, 1945, FO 141/1062/1171/1/45;
     Smart's minute, 25th August, 1945, FO 141/1062/1171/8/45.

137. Al-Ahram, 15th May; 16th July, 1945; Killearn to London,
     23rd August, 1945, PER 16-22nd August, 1945, FO 371/45932.J2882.

138. Memorandum by the Acting Secretary of State to President Truman
     on an Egyptian memorandum, 2nd June, 1945, 867N.01/5-2545,
     FRUS, 1945, Vol. VIII. pp. 708-709; the Arab Ministers (Washington)
     to the Secretary of State, 12th October, 1945, 867N.01/10-1245,
     FRUS, 1945, Vol. VIII, pp. 766-769; Memorandum by the Director
     of the Office of the Near Eastern and African Affairs (Loy
     Henderson) on conversation with Arab representatives in Washington
     13th November, 1945, 867N.01/11-1345, FRUS, 1945, Vol. III, pp. 820-821.

139. E. Grigg's Record of farewell conversation with Faruq, 23rd May,
     1945, FO 141/1008/22/36/45.

140. For Fu'ad Abaza's mission, see: Abaza to Smart, 9th May, 1945,
     FO 371/45238/E3472; Muhammad Mahmud al-Ghandur, President of the
     Society for the strengthening of Arab Relations, to the High
     Commissioner of Palestine, 12th May, 1945, FO 141/1011/32/149/45;
     For the Ikhqan activity in Palestine, consult my The Military
     Force of Islam; For Huda Sha'rawi's visit to Palestine, see:
     al-Difa', Filastin, 1-7th September, 1945; For Ahmad Husayn's
     visit; Filastin, al-Difa' 16-21 November, 1945.

141. For Abaza's disillusionment over the political situation in Palestine; Killearn (Cairo) to London, 22nd June, 1945, PER 14-20 June, 1945, FO 371/45931/J2191; Secretariate (Jerusalem) to Chancery (Cairo), 15th June, 1945, FO 141/1011/32/174/45.

142. See, for example, the various manifestos of the Arab Union, FO 141/1011/32/252/45; The Ikhwan's; 5th November, 1945, FO 371/ 45395/E8978; YMMA: FO 371/45395/E9003; Killearn to London, 13th November, 1945, FO 371/45395/E9072, attached a pamphlet by the "Front of the anti-Zionist and Islamic Societies.

143. Al-Ahram, 20th August, 1945; Killearn (Cairo) to London, Weekly Appreciation, 23rd August, 1945, FO 371/45932/J2816; Farquhar to London, 23rd August, 1945, FO 371/45379/E6615.

144. Killearn (Cairo) to London, 31st August, 1945, Weekly Appreciation, FO 371/45392/J2905.

145. Al-Ahram, 19-20th August, 1945.

146. Adams (Jedda) to London, 17th September, 1945, FO 371/45393/E6947.

147. For British representations, see: Bevin to Jedda, 25th September, 1945, FO 371/45393/E7195; Grafftey-Smith (Jedda) to London, 27th September, 1945, FO 371/45393/E7258. For the Hashemites' reluctance to join the Conference: Farquhar (Cairo) to London, 27th September, 1945, FO 371/45393/E7284; Thompson (Baghdad) to London, 30th September, 1945, FO 371/45393/E7314; Bowker to London, 2nd October, 1945, FO 371/45393/E7409.

148. The Director of the Office of Near Eastern and African Affairs (Loy Henderson) to the Acting Secretary of State (Acheson), 1st October, 1945, 867N.01/10-145, FRUS, 1945, pp. 751-753; Bowker (Cairo) to London, Weekly Appreciation, 29th September, 1945, FO 371/45932/J3226; Same to same, 6th October, 1945, FO 371/45932/ J3313. Al-Ahram, 24th, 26-30th September, 1945.

149. Memorandum by the Minister to Egypt (Tuck), temporarily in the United States, to the Director of the Office of Near Eastern and African Affairs (Henderson), 26th October, 1945, 867N.01/10-2645, FRUS, 1945, Vol. VIII, pp. 793-794.

150. Cairo City Police Report, 23rd September, 1945, FO 141/1005/1/ 212/45; al-Ahram, 10th September, 1945 mentioned an Ikhwan's claim for 2500 branches in Egypt.

151. Smart's minute, 1st October, 1945, FO 141/1005/1/212/45.

152. Bowker (Cairo) to London, Weekly Appreciation, 13th October, 1945, FO 371/45932/J3226; Bowker to London, 13th October, 1945, PER 4-9th October, 1945, FO 371/45932/J3550.

153. Al-Difa', 9th October, 1945, Eshnav, No. 104, 21st October, 1945, p. 3.

154. Filastin, 25th October, 1945; For other dennounciations of Zionism by Fu'ad Abaza and even Taha Husayn, see: al-Difa' 14-15th, 23-25th October, 1945.

155. Al-Ahram, 1st November, 1945.

156. Bowker (Cairo) to London, Weekly Appreciation, 20 Oct., 1945, FO 371/45932/J3484; The Pres cover on news from Palestine may indicate the extent of the propaganda campaign. Thus, for example, al-Ahram, the biggest Arabic newspaper in Egypt, issued daily reports from Palestine including commentary during the period between 26 Sep. - 8 Nov., 1945.

157. Bowker (Cairo) to London, 27 Oc., 1945, FO 173/45932/J3585. A Zionist Report (The Egyptian Jews on the eve of Great Decision, letter no. 1, 24 Oct., 1945, Z4/14620, CZA) stated that from 22 Oct., the Police began to send special patrols to the Jewish quarter in Cairo, and place Jewish institutions in Cairo under Police protection.

158. Al-Difa', 19 Oct., 1945; Bowker to London, 19 Oct., 1945, PER 10 - 16 Oct., 1945, FO 371/45932/J3610; al-Ahram, 28, 31 Oct., 1-2 Nov., 1945.

159. Bowker to London, 7 Nov., 1945, PER 31 Oct. - 6 Nov., 1945, FO 371/ 45932/J3923. Doolittle to Wash., DC, 3 Nov., 1945, RG59, 883.00/11-345, speaks about 10 dead and 300 injured in Alexandria alone.

160. Lyon, Charge d'Affaires (Cairo) to the Secretary of State (Wash., DC), 3 Nov., 1945, FRUS, 1945, Vol. VIII, p. 807; al-Ahram, 3-4 Nov., 1945; Bowker (Cairo) to London, 3 Nov., 1945, FO 371/45394/E8418.

161. Bowker (Cairo) to London, 7 Nov., 1945, FO 371/45394/E8535; al-Ahram, 7 Nov., 1945.

162. See, for example, his interview with the Jewish journalist Avraham Farhi in Hed ha-Mizrah, No. 39, 16 Feb., 1945; for similar expressions by 'Ubayd: al-Ahram, 9 May, 1945.

163. Bowker (Cairo) to London, 10 Nov., 1945, FO 371/45394/E8650.

164. Lyon (Cairo) to the Secretary of State (Wash., DC), 3 Nov., 1945, 883.00/11-345, FRUS, 1945, Vol. VIII, p. 807.

165. 'Ali Ahmad Bakathir wrote and translated more than 30 plays. Among his writings are plays such as "Ibrahim son of Muhammad 'Ali - the Emmissary of Arab Unity". and "The God of Israel". Among his translations is Romeo and Juliet by Shakespeare.

166. 'Ali Ahmad Bakathir, Shayluk al-Jadid (Cairo, 1945).

167. See, for example, al-Ahram, 4, 6, 9 Nov,, 1945; M. to Shertok, 11 Nov., 1945, Z4/14620; CZA; Hed ha-Mizrah, no. 30, 7 Dec., 1945; no. 37, 25 Jan., 1946; no. 40, 15 Feb., 1946.

168. For the Congress, and its resolutions, see: al-Ahram, 15, 22 Nov., 1945; Killearn to London, 24 Nov., 1945, FO 371/45241/E9484.

169. Al-Ahram, 4 Dec., 1945.

BIBLIOGRAPHY

UNPUBLISHED SOURCES:

(I) Official:

1. Great Britain, Public Record Office, London:

    a. Cabinet Papers: Cab. 66 - War Cabinet, 1939-1945
                                    WP series.

                           Cab. 95 - Cabinet Committee on Palestine.

    b. Colonial Office: CO 732 - Middle East Original Correspondence.

                           CO 733 - Palestine Correspondence.

    c. Foreign Office: FO 141 - Embassy and Consular Archives, Egypt, Correspondence.

                           FO 371 - Political.

                           FO 800 - Private Papers (Lord Halifax).

                           FO 816 - Embassy and Consular Archives, Jordan, Correspondence.

                           FO 848 - The Milner Mission.

                           FO 921 - Minister of State, Cairo.

    d. Prime Minister's Office: Prem. 4 - Confidential Papers, 1940-1945.

    e. War Office: WO 169 - War Diaries, 1939-1945, Middle East Forces.

                           WO 208 - Directorate of Military Intelligence.

2. Israel:

    a. Central Zionist Archives, Jerusalem:

        S/25 - Political Department.

        S/30 - Secretariat of the Zionist Directorate.

        Z/4 - the London Office.

    b. Israel State Archives, Jerusalem:

        Division 65.

3. The United States, National Archives, Washington, DC;

    Record Group 59 - Diplomatic.

(II) Unofficial:

   1. Archives:

      a) The Hagana Archive, Tel-Aviv

      b) The Shay Archives, the Harry S. Truman
         Institute, Jerusalem

   2. Private Papers:

      a) Iltyd Clayton Papers, in the Middle East Centre,
         St. Antony's College, Oxford, England.

      b) Walter Smart by some of his friends, in the
         Middle East Centre, St. Antony's College,
         Oxford, England.

      c) Eliahu Sasson's Papers, in private hands, Tel-Aviv.

      d) Reginald Wingate Papers, in the Sudan Archives,
         Durham, England.

      e) William Yale Papers, photocopies in the Middle
         East Centre, St. Antony's College, Oxford, England.

   3. Unpublished dissertations:

      a) el-Feki, Moustafa Mohamed Moustafa, Makram Ebeid,
         A Coptic leader in the Egyptian National Movement
         (Unpublished Ph.D. dissertation, S.O.A.S., July
         1977).

      b) Nevo Joseph, The Political Development of the
         Palestinian Arab National Movement, 1939-1945
         (Unpublished Ph.D. dissertation, Tel-Aviv
         University, May 1977).

(III) Official Publications:

   1. Egypt:

      a) Annales de la Chambre des Deputés

      b) Journal Official

      c) Ministry of Finance, Statistical Department,
         Annual Statement of Foreign Trade, 1939-1946.

      d) Ministry of Finance, Statistical Department,
         Monthly Summary of Foriegn Trade, 1941-1944

2. Great Britain:

    a) Hansard, 5th Series, <u>Parliamentary Debates,</u>
       Lords and Commons

3. The United Nations:

    a) Department of Economic Affairs, <u>World</u>
       <u>Economic Report, 1949-1950</u> (New York, March 1951)

(IV) <u>Newspapers and Periodicals:</u>

       <u>Al-Ahram</u>, daily (Cairo)

       <u>Ha-Aretz</u>, daily (Tel-Aviv)

       <u>Al-Balagh</u>, daily (Cairo)

       <u>Davar</u>, daily (Tel-Aviv)

       <u>Al-Difa'</u>, daily (Jaffa)

       <u>Doar ha-Yom</u>, daily (Jerusalem)

       <u>Al-Dustur</u>, daily (Cairo)

       <u>The Egyptian Gazette</u>, daily (Alexandria)

       <u>Eshnav</u>, Fortnightly (Tel Aviv)

       <u>Filastin</u>, daily (Jaffa)

       <u>Hed ha-Mizrah</u>, monthly (Jerusalem)

       <u>Al-Hilal</u>, monthly (Cairo)

       <u>Al-Ithnayn wal-Dunya</u>, weekly (Cairo)

       <u>Al-Jami'a al-'Arabiyya</u>, daily (Jerusalem)

       <u>Al-Jami'a al-Islamiyya</u>, daily (Jaffa)

       <u>Jaridat al-Ikhwan al-Muslimin</u>, weekly (Cairo)

       <u>Al-Jihad</u>, daily (Cairo)

       <u>Al-Liwa</u>, daily (Jerusalem)

       <u>Majallat al-Rabita al-'Arabiyya</u>, weekly (Cairo)

       <u>Majallat al-Shubban al-Muslimin</u>, monthly (Cairo)

       <u>Al-Manar</u>, monthly (Cairo)

       <u>Miraat al-Sharq</u>, twice weekly (Jerusalem)

Newspapers and Periodicals (continued):

Al-Muqattam, daily (Cairo)

Al-Musawwar, weekly (Cairo)

The New York Times, Daily (New York)

Al-Rabita al-Sharqiyya, monthly (Cairo)

Al-Risala, weekly (Cairo)

Ruz al-Yusuf, weekly (Cairo)

Al-Sirat al-Mustaqim, twice weekly (Jaffa)

Al-Siyasa, daily (Cairo)

Al-Thaqafa, weekly (Cairo)

The Times, daily (London)

Al-'Usbu' al-'Arabi, weekly (Beirut)

Al-Wafd al-Misri, daily (Cairo)

Al-Wahda, daily (Jerusalem)

Yalkut ha-Mizrah ha-Tichon, monthly (Jerusalem)

(V) Books, articles and other publications:

'Abdulla, al-Malik, Hiqba min ta'rikh al-Urdun, al-'Athar al-Kamila lil Malik 'Abd alla ibn al-Husayn (A period of the History of Jordan, the complete works of King 'Abdullah, son of Husayn) (Beirut, n.d.), 4 Vols.

'Abdalla, Nabiha Bayumi, Tatawwur fikrat al-qawmiyya al-'arabiyya fi Misr (the development of the Arab Nationalist thought in Egypt) (Cairo, 1975).

'Alluba, Muhammad 'Ali, Mabadi fi al-siyasa al-Misriyya (Principles of Egyptian politics) (Cairo, 1942); Filastin wa Jaratiha, asbab wa nata'ij (Palestine and her neighbours,reasons and results) (Cairo, 1954); Filastin wal-damir al-insani (Palestine and the human conscience) (Kitab al-Hilal, March 1964), No. 156.

Amin, Ahmad, Hayati (My life) (Cairo, 1950)

Anis Muhammad, and al-Zubaydi, Muhammad Husayn, Awraq Naji Shwkat's (Naji Shwkat's Papers) (Baghdad 1977).

Al-'Aqad, Salah, Al-'Arab wal-harb al-'alamiyya al-thaniyya (The Arabs and the Second World War) (Cairo, 1966).

'Ariff, Jamil, Safhat min al-mudhakkirat al-sirriya li awal Amin 'Amm lil-Jami'a al-'Arabiyya (Pages from the secret memoirs of the first Secreatry General of the Arab League) (Cairo, 1977), Vol. I.

Avramovitz, Z., and Gelfet Y., ha-Meshek ha-'aravi (The Arab market) (Tel-Aviv, 1944)

'Azmi Mahmud, al-Ayyam al-mi'a (The one hundred days) (Cairo, 1937)

Bakathir, 'Ali Ahmad, Shyluk al-jadid (The new Shylock) (Cairo, 1945)

Al-Banna, Anwar al-Jundi, Kifah al-Dhabihayn, Filastin wal-Maghrib (The struggle of the two slaughtered ones, Palestine and Morroco) (Cairo, 1946).

Al-Banna, Hasan, Mudhakkirat al-da'wa wal-da'iyya (Memoirs of the cause and its advocates) (Cairo, n.d.).

Al-Bishri, Tariq, al-Haraka al-siyasiyya fi Misr, 1945-1952 (The political movement in Egypt, 1945-1952) (Cairo, 1972).

Baram, Philip, The Department of State in the Middle East, 1919-1945 (Philadelphia, 1978).

Bat-Yeor (pseud.), Yehudei Mitzrayim (The Jews of Egypt) (Tel-Aviv, 1974).

Ben-Gurion, David, Shihot 'im manhigim 'arviyim (Talks with Arab Leaders) (Tel-Aviv, 1967).

Birdwood, Lord, Nuri al-Said (London, 1959)

Bohem, Y., "Agudat ha-Ahim ha-Muslemim be-Mitzrayim" (The Society of the Muslim Brethren in Egypt), ha-Mizrah he-Hadash, 1952, Vol. 3, pp. 333-352.

Casey, Lord, Personal Experience, 1939-1946 (London, 1962)

Catroux, General, Dans la Bataille de Mediteranee: Egypt-Levant-Afrique du Nord, 1940-1944 (Paris, 1949).

Chejne, Anwar G., "Egyptian attitudes toward pan-Arabism", Middle East Journal, 1957, Vol. 11, pp. 253-268.

Cohen A., *Israel ve-ha-'olam ha-'arvi* (Israel and the Arab World) (Tel-Aviv, 1964).

Cohen, Gavriel, *Churchill ve-sheelat Eretz Israel, 1939-1942* (Churchill and the Palestine question, 1939-1942) (Jerusalem, 1976).

Cohen, Haim, Y., *ha-Pe'ilut ha-tzionit be artzot ha-Mizrah ha-Tichon* (The Zionist activity in the Middle Eastern countries) (Tel-Aviv, 1973).

Cohen, Michael, J., *Palestine: Retreat from the Mandate* (London, 1978).

Colombe, Marcal, *L'Evolution de L'Egypte, 1924-1950* (Paris, 1951).

Daghir, As'ad, *Mudhakkirati 'ala hamish al-qadiyya al-'arabiyya* (My memoirs on the margin of the Arab question) (Cairo, 1959).

Darwaza, 'Izzat Muhammad, *Hawla al-haraka al-'Arabiyya al-haditha* (About the modern Arab movement) (Sidon, 1950), 3 Vols.
   al-Qadiyya al-Filastiniyya fi mukhtalif marahiliha (The Palestine problem during its various stages) (Beirut, 1959/1960), 2 Vols.

al-Dasuqi, 'Asim Ahmad, *Misr fi al-harb al-'alamiyya al-thaniyya 1939-1945* (Egypt during the Second World War) (Cairo, 1976)

Deeb, Marius, *Party Politics in Egypt: the Wafd and its rivals, 1919-1939* (Oxford, 1979).

De Gaulle, Charles, *War Memoirs* (translated by Jonathan Griffin and others) (London, 1955-1960), 3 Vols.

Dilks, David (ed.), *The diaries of Sir Alexander Cadogan, 1938-1945* (London, 1971).

Eden, R. Anthony (Earl of Avon), *The Eden Memoirs* (London, 1960-1965), 3. Vols.

ESCO Foundation for Palestine, *Palestine, a study of Jewish, Arab and British policies* (Yale, 1974), 2 Vols.

Evans, Trevor E., (ed.), *The Killearn diaries, 1934-1946* (London, 1972).

Fahmi, 'Abd al-'Aziz, *Hadhihi hayati* (This is my life) (Kitab al-Hilal, 1963)

Furlonge, Geoffrey, *Palestine is my country, the story of Musa 'Alami* (London, 1969).

Gershoni, Israel, Mitzrayim bein yihud le-ahdut (Egypt between distinctiveness and unity) (Tel-Aviv, 1980).

Ghanim, Ahmad Muhammad, and Kaf, Ahmad Abu, al-Yahud wal-haraka al-Sahyuniyya fi Misr, 1897-1947 (The Jews and the Zionist movement in Egypt) (Kitab al-Hilal, June 1969) No. 219.

Al-Ghuri, Emil, Filastin 'ibra sittin 'amman (Palestine over sixty years) (Beirut, 1972), Vol. I.

Gomaa, Ahmad M., The Foundation of the League of Arab States (London, 1977).

Hamza, 'Abd al-Latif, Adab al-maqala al-suhufiyya fi Misr, Vol. 8 - 'Abd al-Qadir al-Hamza fi Jaridatay al-Ahali wal-Balagh (The Literature of Press articles in Egypt, Abd al-Qadir al-Hamza in the two newspapers: al-Ahali and al-Balagh) (Cairo, 1963).

Hattis, Suzan Lee, The bi-national idea in Palestine during mandatory times (Haifa, 1970).

Haykal, Muhammad Husayn, Mudhakkirat fi al-Siyasa al-Misriyya (Memoirs of Egyptian politics) (Cairo, 1951-1954 ed. 1977), 3 Vol.
Haykal, Yusuf, Nahwa al-Wahda al-'Arabiyya (Towards Arab Unity) (Cairo, 1943).

Heyworth-Dunne, J. Religious and Political Trends in Modern Egypt (Washington D.C., 1950)

Hirszowitz, Lukasz, The Third Reich and the Arab East (London, 1966).

Hourani, Cecil, "The Arab League in Perspective", The Middle East Journal, 1947, Vol. I, pp. 125-136.

Husayn, Ahmad, Nisf qurn ma'a al-'uruba wa qadiyat Filastin (Half a century with Arabism and the Palestine problem) (Beirut, 1971).

Al-Husayni, Muhammad Amin, Haqa'iq 'an qadiyat Filastin (Facts about the Palestine problem) (Cairo, 1954).

Al-Husri, Sati', Abhath mukhtara fi al-qawmiyya al 'arabiyya, 1923-1963 (Selected studies on arab Nationalism) (Cairo, 1964);
    Muhadarat fi nushu'u al-fikra al-qawmiyya (Lectures on the emergence of the nationalist idea) (Beirut, 1959, 4th ed.).

Al-Husri, Sati' Khaldun, (ed.), Mudhakkirat Taha al-Hashimi (Taha al-Hashimi's memoirs) (Beirut, April 1967).

Ilan, Amitzur, America, Britanya ve-Eretz-Israel, 1938-1947 (America, Britain and Palestine) (Jerusalem, 1979).

Al-Ittihad al-'Arabi wa qanunuhu al-'amm, Nadi al-Qahira wa la-ihatuhu al-dakhiliyya (The Arab Union, and its general statutes, The Cairo Club and its internal regulations) (Cairo, n.d.).

Issawi, Charles, Egypt at mid-Century (London, 1954).

Jankowski, James, P., Egypt's Young Rebels: "Young Egypt", 1933-1952, (Stanford, 1975).

Jawda, Qasim Ahmad, al-Makramiyat (Cairo, n.d.)

Kampffmeyer, G., "Egypt and Western Asia", in H.A.R. Gibb, Whither Islam(London, 1932), pp. 101-165.

Katzburg, Nathaniel, Mediniyut be-mavoch, 1940-1945 (The Palestine problem in British policy) (Jerusalem, 1977).

Kayyali, 'Abdul Wahab, Palestine, a modern history (London, 1978).

Kedourie, Elie, In the Anglo-Arab Labyrinth (Cambridge, 1976).
        The Chatham House Version (London, 1970).
        Islam in the Modern World (London, 1980).

Khadouri, Majid, "Aziz 'Ali al-Misri and the Arab Nationalist Movement in Egypt", in A. Hourani (ed.), St. Antony's Papers, No. 17, Middle East Affairs, No. 4 (Oxford, 1965), pp. 140-163.

Al-Khardaji, Shakir, al-'Arab fi tariq al-ittihad (The Arabs on the way to Union) (Damascus, 1947).

Khilla, Mahmud Kamil, Filastin wal-intidab al-Baritani, 1922-1939 (Palestine and the British mandate, 1922-1939)(Beirut, 1974).

Kirk, George E., The Middle East in the War (Survey of International Affairs, 1939-1946, London, 1952).

Kisch, Frederick H., Palestine Diary (London, 1938)

Labib, Salah al-Shadid, Dhikriyati fi 'ahdayn (My memoirs during two eras) (Cairo, 1976).

Landau, Jacob, M., Jews in Nineteeth Century Egypt (New York, 1969).

Al-Mashru'u al-Inshai al-'Arabi (The Constructive Arab project) (Jerusalem, n.d.; Baghdad, 1946).

Mayer, Thomas, "The military force of Islam: the Society of the Muslim Brethren and the Palestine question, 1945-1948", in Kedourie, E., and Haim, S. (eds.), Zionism and Arabism in Palestine and Israel (London, 1982), pp. 100-117.

"Egypt and the General Islamic Congress at Jerusalem in 1931" in Middle Eastern Studies, Vol. 18, July 1982, pp. 311-322.

Mu'tamar majalis al-idara li-jam'iyat al-Shubban al-Muslimin (Conference of the administrative boards of the Young Men's Muslim Association) (Cairo, 1349/1930).

Al-Mu'ti, Ahmad 'Abd, 'Urubat Misr (Egypt's Arabism) (Beirut, 1979).

Nasar, Siham, al-Yahud al-Misriyyin bayna al-Misriyya wal-Yahudiyya (Beirut, 1980).

Nemirovski, H., and Preuss, W., Survey of Recent Economic Developments in Palestine (Tel-Aviv, 1932).

Peterson, Maurice, Both Sides of the Curtain (London, 1950).

Porath, Yehushua, The Palestinian Arab National Movement, 1929-1939 (London, 1977).

Presland, John, (pseud., Gladys Skelton), Deedes Bey, a study of Sir Windham Deedes, 1883-1923 (London, 1942).

Qasim, Zakariya, Jamal, "Mawqif Misr min al-harb al-Tarablusiyya 1911-1914" (Egypt's attitude towards the Tripolitanian War), al-Majalla al-Ta'rikhiyya al-Misriyya, 1967, Vol. 13, pp. 306-340.

Qasimiyya, Khayriyya (ed.), 'Awni 'Abd al-Hadi, Awraq khassa (Awni 'Abd al-Hadi, Private papers) (Beirut, 1974).
Qasimiyya, Khayriyya, "Muhammad 'Ali al-Tahir - Qalam Filastini fi Misr" (Muhammad 'Ali al-Tahir - a Palestinian writer in Egypt), Shu'un Filastiniyya, November, 1974, No. 39, pp. 150-163.

Radwan, Fathi, Tal'at Harb, Bahth fi al-'azama (Tal'at Harb, a study of a firm will) (Cairo, 1970).

Ramadam, 'Abd al-'Azim Muhammad, Tatawwur al-haraka al-wataniyya fi Misr, 1937-1945 (The development of the national movement in Egypt) (Beirut, 1970), 2 Vols.

Ramzi, Ahmad, Min wahi Filastin (from the inspiration of Palestine) (Cairo, 1949).

Rizq, Yunan Labib, al-Wafd wal-Kitab al-Aswad (The Wafd and the Black Book) (Cairo, 1978).

Rose, N.A. (ed.), Baffy, the diaries of Blanch Dudgale, 1936-1947 (London, 1973).

Rubinstein, E., "ha-Protocolim shel Ziknei Tzion ba-sichsuch ha-Yehudi - Arvi be-Eretz Israel be shnot ha-'esrim" (The Protocols of the Elders of Zion in the Arab-Jewish conflict in Palestine during the 1920s), ha-Mizrah he-Hadash, 1976, Vol. 26, pp. 37-42.

Al-Sadat, Anwar, Safhat majhula (Unknown pages) (Cairo, 1956).

Safran, Nadav, Egypt, in search of political community (Cambridge,Mass., 1961).

Sa'id, Amin, al-Dawla al-'Arabiyya al-muttahida (The united Arab state) (Cairo, 1938), 3 Vols.

Sa'id, Rif'at, al-Yasar al-Misri wa qadiyat Filastin (The Egyptian left and the Palestine problem) (Beirut, 1974).

Sa'igh, Amins, al-Fikra al-'arabiyya fi Misr (The Arab thought in Egypt) (Beirut, 1959).

Sasson, Eliahu, Baderech el ha-Shalom (On the road to Peace) (Tel-Aviv, 1978).

Al-Sayyid, Ahmad Lutfi, Qissat hayati (The story of my life) (Kitab al-Hilal, February, 1962), No. 131.
        al-Muntakhabat (Selected passages) (Cairo, 1938), Vol. I.

Sela', A., "Sihot u-maga'im bein manhigim tzionim ve-'aravim" (Talks and contacts between Zionist and Arab leaders) ha-Mizrah he-Hadash, 1972, Vol. 22, No. 4, Part I.

Shafiq, Ahmad, Hawliyat Misr al-Siyasiyya (Annales of Egyptian politics), Vol. III (Cairo, 1928).
        Mudhakkirati fi nisf qurn (My memoirs during half a century), Vol. III (Cairo, 1938)
        A'mali ba'da Mudhakkirati (my activities after my memoirs) (Cairo 1941).

Sha'rawi, Huda, (ed.), al-Mar'a al-'arabiyya wa qadiyat Filastin, al-mu'tamar al-nisa'i al-sharqi, 15-18 Oct., 1938, lil-difa' 'an Filastin (The Arab woman and the Palestine problem, the Eastern Women's Congress, 15-18 Oct., 1938, for the defence of Palestine) (Cairo, 1938).

Sharet, Moshe, Yoman Medini (Political Diary) (Tel-Aviv, 1968-1970) 4 Vols.

Sheffer, Gavriel, "The involvement of Arab States in the Palestine conflict and British-Arab relationships before World War II", Asian and African Studies,1974/5, Vol. 10.

Shim'oni, Ya'akov, 'Arviyei Eretz-Israel (The Arabs of Palestine) (Tel-Aviv, 1947).

Smith, Laurence, Grafftei, Bright Levant (London, 1970).

Spears, Edward, Fulfillment of a mission (London, 1977).

Steppat, Fritz, "Nationalismus und Islam bei Mustafa Kamil", Die Welt des Islams, 1956, Vol. IV.

Al-Suwaydi, Tawfiq, Mudhakkirati (Beirut, 1969).

Sykes, Christopher, Crossroads to Israel (London, 1965).

Al-Tab'i, Muhammad, Misr ma qable al-Thawra, min Asrar al-Siyasa wa al-Siyasiyun (Egypt before the revolution, secrets of politics and politicians) (Cairo, 1978).

Al-Tahir, Muhammad 'Ali, Nazrat al-Shura (The views of al-Shura) (Cairo, 1932).
    al-Yahud wal-Islam (The Jews and Islam) (Cairo, 1937).
    Zalam al-sijn, mudhakkirat wa mufakkirat (The gloom of prison, memoirs and diaries) (Cairo, 1951).

Taragan, Ben Zion, le-korot ha-kehila ha-yehudit be-Alexandria be-arba'im shana ha-ahronot, 1906-1946 (For the history of the Jewish Community in Alexandria in the past 40 years) (Alexandria, 1947).

Tarbin, Ahmad, Filastin fi khitat al-Sahyuniyya wal-isti'mar, 1922-1939 (Palestine in the Zionist and the Imperialist plans) (Cairo, 1971)

Thabit, Munira, Mudhakkirati fi 'ishrin 'amman 'an hukuk al-mar'a al-Siyasiyya (My memoirs during twenty years concerning the political rights of the woman) (Cairo, 1946).

Tidhar, David, be-madim u-be-lo madim (With and without uniforms) (Tel-Aviv, 1938).
    be-sherut ha-umma (In the service of the nation) (Tel-Aviv, 1960/61)

Tignor, R.L., "Bank Misr and Foreign Capitalism", International Journal of Middle East Studies, 1977, Vol. 8, pp. 161-181.

Al-Urfali, Jalal, al-Diplomasiyya al-'Iraqiyya wal-ittihad al-'arabi (The Iraqi diplomacy and the Arab Union) (Baghdad, n.d.).

Weizmann, Chaim, Trial and Error (London, 1949).

Wendell, Charles, The Evolution of the Egyptian National Image (California, 1972).

Woodward, Sir Llewelyn, British Foreign Policy in the Second World War (London, 1975), 5 Vols.

Wilson, Lord, Eight years overseas, 1939-1947 (London, 1950).

Yasin, 'Abd al-Qadir, "Suhuf al-Yasar al-Misri wa qadiyat Filastin" (Egypt's leftist Press and the Palestine problem), Shu'um Filastiniyya, September 1972, No. 13, pp. 117-136.

I N D E X

Bei Fragen zur Produktsicherheit wenden Sie sich bitte an:
If you have any questions regarding product safety,
please contact:

Walter de Gruyter GmbH
Genthiner Straße 13
10785 Berlin
productsafety@degruyterbrill.com